The Semiotics of Consensus

SPRACHE UND DIGITALKULTUR
LANGUAGE AND DIGITAL CULTURE

Herausgegeben von / Edited by

Gerd Antos, Matthias Ballod, Henning Lobin,
Pablo Pirnay-Dummer & Karola Pitsch

VOL. 2

PETER LANG
Lausanne - Berlin - Bruxelles - Chennai - New York - Oxford

Tobias Gretenkort

The Semiotics of Consensus

Impact of Network Topology on Communication Strategies in Spanish Language Interaction Networks

PETER LANG
Lausanne - Berlin - Bruxelles - Chennai - New York - Oxford

Bibliographic information published by the Deutsche Nationalbibliothek
The Deutsche Nationalbibliothek lists this publication in the Deutsche Nationalbibliografie; detailed bibliographic data is available in the internet at http://dnb.dnb.de.

Zugl.: RWTH Aachen University, Diss., 2021

Library of Congress Cataloging-in-Publication Data
A CIP catalog record for this book has been applied for at the Library of Congress.

Cover design by Dirk Kuntze, Halle (Saale) / Germany.

D 82
ISSN 2626-3394
ISBN 978-3-631-90207-3 (Print)
E-ISBN 978-3-631-90208-0 (E-Book)
E-ISBN 978-3-631-90209-7 (E-PUB)
DOI 10.3726/b21018

Published by: Peter Lang GmbH, Berlin, Deutschland

info@peterlang.com - www.peterlang.com

Für Mama und Papa,
Hannah, Benni, Jakob, Marlene und Ella,
Stephan, Susanne und Maike,
Robin, Gwen und Elias,
Corinna.

Für Regina und Olivia

Table of Contents

List of Abbreviations

AI	Artificial Intelligence
ANN	Artificial Neural Networks
ANT	Actor-Network Theory
AR	Argentina
BO	Bolivia
BOLD	Blood Oxygenation Level-Dependent
BoW	Bag-of-Words
BS4	BeautifulSoup 4
C	Controller, Centrality
CAS	Complex Adaptive System
CC	Centroamérica y Caribe
CL	Chile
CO	Colombia
Coef	Coefficient
CORDE	Corpus Diacrónico del Español
CREA	Corpus de Referencia del Español Actual
CSV	Comma-separated Values
D	Destination, Density
DD	Double Directors
DLT	Distributed Ledger Technology
DNA	Deoxyribonucleic Acid
e	Edge
E	Set of Edges
E*	Edge Space
EC	Ecuador
ES	España
F	Feedback
fa	finite automaton
fMRI	Functional Magnetic Resonance Imaging
G	Graph
GAN	Generative Adversarial Networks
GDPR	General Data Protection Regulation
glm	Generalized Linear Model
html	Hypertext Markup Language
HU	Humanidades
IBM	International Business Machines Corporation

ID	Identifier
ILM	Iterated Learning Model
IP	Internet Protocol
IQR	Inter Quartile Range
K	Economía
Kkk	Ku Klux Klan
L	Ledger Object
LAN	Local Area Network
LDA	Latent Dirichlet Allocation
lm	Linear Model
lme	Linear Mixed-Effects
log	Logarithm
lol	Laughing out loud
LR	Likelihood Ratio
LSP	Linguistic String Parser
m	Number of Traitors
M	Meta
MMORPG	Massive Multiplayer Online Role-Playing Game
MRI	Magnetic Resonance Imaging
MX	México
n	Node
N	Set of Nodes
NLP	Natural Language Processing
NLTK	Natural Language Toolkit
O	Object
OM	Oral Messages
OP	Original Post
P	Path
PC	Personal Computer
PE	Perú
PET	Personal Electronic Transactor
POL	Política, politically incorrect
PoS	Parts of Speech, Proof-of-Stake
PoW	Proof-of-Work
Q	LGBT+
r	Record
RAE	Real Academia Española
RNA	Ribonucleic Acid
RT	Reaction Time

S	Information Source, Sequence, Subject
SD	Single Director
SFG	Systemic Functional Grammar
SM	Signed Messages
SPSS	Statistical Package for the Social Sciences
T	Tecnología
TOR	The Onion Router
URL	Uniform Resource Locator
UY	Uruguay
V	Verb
VE	Venezuela
VL	Validated Ledger Object
VPN	Virtual Private Network
δ	Diameter

0. Introduction

Sie erweisen mir die Ehre, mich aufzufordern,
der Akademie einen Bericht über mein
äffisches Vorleben einzureichen.
Ein Bericht für eine Akademie – Franz Kafka (1917)

Language and technology have a longstanding cultural relationship, which is now more relevant than ever. While technological innovations such as scripture, printing, telegraphing, and the telephone have continuously sped up communicative processes, the Internet supposes a more fundamental change in communicative practices in the 21st century. This is also abundantly accounted for in linguistics, most notably by the description of linguistic innovations in both English (e.g., Crystal 2004; McCulloch 2019) and Spanish (e.g., Yus 2001, 2008; Tascón 2012). This doctoral dissertation aims to investigate more specific mechanisms which lead to this linguistic variation. As the Internet has led to globalised practises in communication and the creation of a dense network of communicative pathways, it is the aim of this study to investigate the role of linguistic and social network dynamics in the usage and variation of language. Changes in network properties of communication as a result of the expansion of the Internet are best illustrated by one of the most striking contradictions in modern media. Human beings in the industrialised regions of the world now have considerably more opportunities to interact with one another and have arguably gone from being mere receivers of information to being more powerful promoters of information. At the same time, much communicative power is concentrated in the hands of relatively few famous individuals and companies, as is reflected in their huge numbers of followers on online social media. Compared to this, most users have close to no following at all. It would thus appear that communication on the Internet has become at the same time more centralised and more decentralised. This paradox lies at the heart of all the following considerations.

The main goal of this doctoral dissertation is to investigate the consequences of this contradiction for the use of language and communication itself. Approaching this dynamic entails a variety of deliberations and methods. Methodologically, this work is based on three observational experiments (Chapters 6, 7 and 8) on data from a self-compiled corpus of comments on an anonymous online social media platform (Chapter 5). But to produce meaningful hypotheses for such a study, the consideration of exclusively linguistic literature is insufficient. To account for the effects of network properties, some mathematical resources from graph theory will be introduced (Chapter 2) as they provide the basis for the formal analysis of networks. The application of such formal resources shows that the linguistic literature, even when explicitly applying the concept of network, lacks a cohesive understanding of what a network is and how it is best applied to the study of language. As a review of the literature (Chapter 3) shows, contributions are either focused on the individual language capacity, on the description of linguistic variation in a dialectological or typological sense, or on the social configuration of interaction. Networks are thus applied to a variety of phenomena and levels of linguistic inquiry. Consequently, a careful exploration of different approaches is in order to identify what is meant by the term *network* in each case. As a baseline for comparison, another social and mathematical theory of networks will be explored and characterised with semiotic means, namely Blockchain technology (Chapter 1). As the chapter shows, lots of literature are available to establish a connection between the Blockchain's graph-theoretic makeup – most notably its "decentralisation" – and the informational and social implications it has for Blockchain-based services. It is argued that informational processes on the Blockchain can, in part, be conceptualised as communicative processes. By identifying commonalities and differences between language and the Blockchain as semiotic systems, in conjunction with the literature reviews of graph theory and linguistics, hypotheses for data analysis can be generated (Chapter 4). After reporting on the findings of three experiments (Chapters 6, 7 and 8), their significance in the context of centralisation and decentralisation is discussed in light of the reviewed literature (Chapter 9).

In this way, the current study aims to contribute to both the consolidation and clarification of the use of networks in the analysis of linguistic and semiotic phenomena and to contribute to the identification and description of some of these phenomena. Before the description of Blockchain technology, however, some remarks on the relationship between linguistics and technology are in order. These serve as justification for the inclusion of a technological description in a linguistic dissertation on the one hand and as a justification of the problem of technology and its impact on communication – and by extension language – on the other hand.

0.1. Linguistics and Technology

While the relationship between language and technology is quite apparent, this is less true of the relationship between linguistics and technology. But the systematic study of technologies from a linguistic standpoint is useful for a variety of reasons. The Blockchain is a technology that, both philosophically and mathematically, provides great insights into the properties and the design of network architectures. It is apparent that graph theory, in turn, has a great deal to offer for the study of linguistic interaction within groups and the emergent properties of these interconnected networks. This ultimately amounts to studying how linguistic systems are affected by the interactions in networks of speakers. For the sake of argument, it will be assumed that networks are the locus of language and that languages exist primarily as an emergent property of communication that takes place in communities which can adequately be described and analysed as networks. Thus, a semiotics of networks, as inspired by the Blockchain will provide predictions for communicative networks of human communities, particularly online communities.

While such an approach is eclectic in nature, preoccupation with a specific technology is nothing unusual in linguistics. This study is not the first to invoke technological descriptions for the analysis of linguistic phenomena, nor is it the first to use networks as a means of linguistic research. In point and fact, such ponderations have a long-standing tradition in linguistics. On a general scale, the question of what (a) language *is* has often spawned comparisons between humans and machines, as well as between humans and animals. Thus, before moving on to the description of the Blockchain, this relationship will be explored to argue why the preoccupation with (communication) technologies is a suitable endeavour for linguists.

To understand this, it is important to point out how fundamental the criterion of language is in the history of human exceptionalism, that is the belief that human beings are fundamentally different from other living things, such as animals. Philosophers and linguists have contributed to this belief by promoting the idea that only humans are capable of using language. The pertinence of this idea can be traced back at least to the book of Genesis, where God tasks Adam with naming the animals and accepting the name that Adam gives each animal. It would appear that, in Abrahamitic tradition, language is not handed down by God but that it exists through and for humans alone. Therein lies ultimately the idea that language is proper to humankind and acts as a clear-cut border between humans and all the other things in the world.

In the more recent history of thought, this idea still finds astonishing resonance. Descartes' *Discours de la Méthode*, first published in 1637, draws the line between automata and human beings on language. Descartes states that no machine, however well-constructed, could ever react to human speech in a satisfactory way (Descartes 1673). Some decades later in 1746, Diderot makes a similar argument stating that human-like intelligence could be attributed to any parrot that responded intelligently to anything a person said to it (Diderot 1746). Here, Diderot defines a criterion for human intelligence and at the same time dismisses the possibility of it being found elsewhere. That is, he doesn't expect any parrot to be found able to sensibly respond to human speech.

Even in the 20th century, much academic activity in humanist departments was devoted to highlighting that humans are special in their use of language. After Chomsky's important reply to uprising behaviourist tendencies in linguistics, mainly represented by B.F. Skinner (Chomsky 1959a), the generative framework took on the most important role for this task in the linguistic landscape. Importantly, one of the core elements of Chomsky's theory, as it is thought of today, is nativism (Chomsky 1965, 1968), which is the idea that language is hardcoded into the human brain. There are several degrees of strength to this claim, with the strongest version advocating that language is a capacity that arose within a fairly short period in human evolution through genetic mutation. The identification of the FOXP2 gene has cemented this idea in popular perception because it was diagnosed to be relevant to the development of human language. Specifically, its variation across different species seems to suggest that its fixation in the human organism is in alignment with the appearance of anatomically modern humans some 200,000 years ago (Enard et al. 2002). On the other hand, it seems to be neither a sufficient nor necessary condition for language as species incapable of language have this gene, while pathological mutations to this gene seem to mainly affect speech production and aspects of motricity (Fisher et al. 1998; Lai et al. 2001) of language, while cognitive abilities seem to be unaffected.

Independently of this neuroscientific debate, linguists and psychologists in some schools of thought still assume that animals do not have language. Titles such as *Why Animals Don't Have Language* (Cheney & Seyfarth 1997) and *The Language Instinct* (Pinker 1994) are reminiscent of this tendency. The question of what distinguishes human language from other kinds of communication in nature appears to be much more prevalent in the scientific community than the question of whether this distinction is relevant at all.

But contrary positions to this stance can be found at least since the 18th century. The first relevant philosophical defiance of this idea can be found in the works of De La Mettrie, who makes a structured attempt at a description of human beings as sophisticated automata in *L'Homme Machine* in 1747 (De La Mettrie 1747), paving the way for materialist philosophy in the 19th century. Here, De La Mettrie argues that animals such as birds already have sophisticated language in their songs and even entertains the possibility to teach human language to an ape. At the same time, he speculates that an automaton could be endowed with language. And although he thinks that this would be achieved in the far future, his idea reduces the difference between humans and machines to an issue of degree rather than an issue of category.

However, human exceptionalism in linguistics has proven to be rather resistant to the argument that universal tendencies in language, such as word order, need not be the consequence of innateness but could be the result of cognitive (Culbertson et al. 2012), functional (Tomasello 1995) or even environmental (Nölle et al. 2020) constraints. Examples of highly advanced communicative systems in animals, such as cephalopods – octopi, cuttlefish, and squid – (Mäthger et al. 2009a, 2009b) and great apes (Bohn et al. 2016), don't seem to compel a broader public or the scientific community to call the uniqueness of human language into question either.

A comparison of the human language with information technology would then appear to be a far-fetched idea since humans are more closely related to animals than to computers in their biological setup. However, modern advances in natural language processing (NLP) would – without further examination – suggest that machines are better suited to learning how to talk than any animal in the world. The universal and free availability of automated translation, the use of chatbots in customer attention, or linguistic voice assistance AI such as Apple's Siri, Microsoft's Cortana, or Amazon's Alexa are indicative of this. Even though they do not exhibit the full-fledged linguistic capabilities of biological human beings, their quality has increased to a level where the line between human language and computer language becomes blurrier. OpenAI's latest advances as showcased by the ChatGPT software only strengthen this impression.

In this context, it becomes clear why linguists should pay close attention to knowledge generated in fields such as animal cognition or computer science. Now, while this study is not concerned with the debate on linguistic differences and commonalities between humans, animals, and machines, this introduction should illustrate why a close examination of 'languages' in other types of beings might be of interest to one's conception of human language. For the remainder of the introduction, the focus will lie on the relationship between language and technology, in so far it has been established in the history of linguistics. In the following, three main reasons will be explored that show why the transfer from one area to the other is not only possible but warranted.

0.2. Enrichment of the Linguists' Toolbox

The most trivial reason for the study of technology is to broaden the scope of linguistic methodology. Consider the technology available to linguists in the past.

In 1974, the year the journal for *Computational Linguistics*[1] was founded, the state-of-the-art parser for syntactic analysis was the *NYU Linguistic String Parser* (*LSP*). The LSP could decompose sentences into more elementary strings and assign grammatical classes (Fitzpatrick & Sager 1974), a task now more commonly referred to as Part-of-Speech (PoS) tagging. In 1974, this was accomplished by a dictionary of 10,000 words, a complex set of classes, and a grammar that specified the possible relations of classes and subclasses in explicit deterministic grammatical rules (Fitzpatrick & Sager 1974). Twenty years later, PoS tagging was done with artificial neural networks (Schmid 1994). These systems are based on statistical models and require less explicitly stated rules, which make them more resilient against researchers' potentially erroneous precepts of grammar. On the other hand, these systems require a huge amount of data and calculating power compared to the first method. More recent approaches include the use of conditional random fields (Lafferty et al. 2001) which integrate classification and co-dependencies between classification outputs. For example, if one verb in a phrase is classified as a finite verb, the neighbouring verb cannot be sorted into the same class. Applications of this (e.g., Gimpel et al. 2010) render parsing and the identification of PoS even more efficient. All of these approaches have steadily increased the performance of PoS tagging and solved ever more issues of this task. In 2009, Bird et al. released the first version of the *Natural Language Toolkit* (*NLTK*) for Python 2. The NLTK library already includes a PoS tagger that can be implemented in a few lines of code and minimal instruction in computer programming. By 2019, an ample selection of blog articles (e.g., Learntek 2019) makes this task solvable for any linguistics student with an average lap or desktop computer and little previous experience in programming, rendering their work easier and being able to focus on more crucial tasks in their investigation. This means that one of the prime tasks in linguistic analysis, which required palpable amounts of time, effort, and training in the past, was virtually automated – if not trivialised – over the past forty years.

How is such a development possible? It is no stretch to claim that technological advancement in the 20th century has been exponential. *Moore's Law* is an adequate example. As soon as 1965, Gordon Moore described and projected that the number of transistors on integrated circuits ('computer chips') had been – and would continue – doubling every year (Moore 1965). A correction in 1975 established that transistor density would continue doubling every two years (Moore 1975). According to Roser and Ritchie (2013), this trend had not

1 https://www.mitpressjournals.org/loi/coli

ceased until as recently as 2018[2]. Similar exponential trends are identified in the growth of computational power as measured by "computations per second" (Koomey et al. 2011; Roser & Ritchie 2013) and price efficiency as measured by "computations per second per $1000" (Roser & Ritchie 2013).

While this tendency is not specific to linguistics and has been lively experienced by anyone born before the year 2000, this goes to show that linguists have a much easier life nowadays as a result of technological advances. Consider the retrieval of word occurrences in documents, that used to be based on searching glossaries on microfilm or microfiche, whereas modern digital corpora (e.g., CREA, CORDE[3]), Internet search engines (e.g., Google Scholar), or document analysis software (e.g., AntConc) trivialise word occurrence queries to a simple *ctrl + F* input on a computer keyboard.

Even though the adoption of new research technologies in linguistics might be somewhat delayed compared to the long-standing development that was pointed out above, the enrichment of the linguists' toolbox seems an obvious but valid reason to justify a scientific interest in technology from a linguistics perspective.

0.3. The Emergence of New Linguistic Fields

But the automation of tasks doesn't only render their execution faster. With faster calculation times and more time to spare, new types of questions become solvable resulting in the emergence of entire new subfields of linguistics. It is not coincidental that the fanning-out of linguistic (sub)disciplines took place mainly during the second half of the 20th century. After all, this development was dependent on technology both in terms of hardware (i.e., calculating power) and methodology (i.e., algorithmic architecture).

The 1960s and 1970s were in a frenzy of computer modernisation, and although computers were far from nowadays' degree of adoption, they started to become quite important for researchers and enterprises. And expectations were high. In 1950, British Mathematician and pioneer Computer Scientist Alan Turing had famously claimed that by "[…] the end of the [20th] century the use of words and general educated opinion will have altered so much that one will be able to speak of machines thinking without expecting to be contradicted" (Turing 1950, p. 442). In 1962, the word *Personal Computer* (PC) was first used in the *New York Times*, when John W. Mauchly anticipated that, one day, 'housewives' would use

2 Initially published in 2013, the article is steadily amended with more current data.

3 These are the Spanish language corpora provided by the *RAE* for contemporary and historical Spanish respectively.

'pocket computers' to tell the store what they want beforehand so that their only business at the store would be paying and picking up the requested merchandise[4] (Maulchy 1962). These were also the years in which Moore's Law held true every year (Moore 1965, 1975). In 1977, commercial personal computers became competitive enough to be adopted in the workplace. This was the year when the *1977 Trinity* hit the market (Byte 1995). That year, competition between Tandy, Commodore, and Apple led to the release of the *TRS-80* (also known as the *Model I*), the *PET 2001*, and the *Apple II* respectively. Until *IBM* entered the market, these were the most commercially successful computers (Chandler 2005).

During this period of technological innovation, most of today's relevant linguistic subdisciplines develop, not out of thin air, but as the result of at least two drivers. The first of these drivers was an academic reaction to the then-prevalent preoccupation with mathematical truth, structural analysis, and formalism in the study of language. This academic reaction resulted in the *linguistics wars* (Harris 1995), in which Noam Chomsky tried to defend his highly formalised linguistic theory of Universal Generative Grammar against a number of his students, who sought to break with the structuralist tradition.

The concept of language hitherto had been shaped by schools of thought such as the logical positivist philosophy of language (e.g., Russell 1905; Wittgenstein 1922), structuralist schools (following De Saussure 1916[5]), and Universal Generative Grammar (Chomsky 1965). These accounts ground their conception of language in the idea that language is the communicative extension of the human logical apparatus and that its main function is the faithful representation of logical truth. At the same time that Universal Generative Grammar was consolidated, new fields of studies arose in opposition to this conception. For instance, Austin (1962) rejected the idea that sentences can ubiquitously be

4 This idea has of course not held true, because it didn't anticipate digital payment schemes and the option of free delivery. However, the article does anticipate which branch of our everyday life would be affected the most by the use of personal computers, namely shopping, and it anticipated the mobile phone as a "pocket computer". Furthermore, the outdated and sexist use of the word 'housewife' is here merely reproduced as a means of giving the reader a sense of the imagery of technology in society at the time.

5 The case of De Saussure is more complex. The structuralist tradition is based on De Saussure's *Cours de Linguistique Générale* (1916) but the volume is heavily edited by its publishers Charles Bally and Albert Sechehaye. The analysis of De Saussure's manuscripts by Johannes Fehr (2003) has revealed striking misrepresentations of de Saussure's work in structuralist semiotics and the *Cours de Linguistique Générale*. This point will be addressed further below in Section 1.3.1.

assigned truth values. He bases his arguments on his descriptions of *performative* sentences, which bring about truth by virtue of having been uttered (cf. Section 1.3.2). Other important linguists such as Searle (1969) and Grice (1975) followed this argument (and others) and paved the way for what is now known as *Speech Act Theory* in pragmatist linguistics.

On a different note, important authors such as Labov (1966) reject – at least implicitly – the idea that language is stratified merely on the level of the linguistic system and the grammatical functions that it has. They foreground the fact that the usage of language is also stratified by social class. Labov's 1966 study about the *Stratification of English in New York City* is one of the first examples of importance in this line of investigation and gave rise to the paradigm of *socio-linguistics.*

Lastly, George Lakoff, along with some fellow doctoral students of Noam Chomsky's, challenged their teacher's belief that grammar is innate as a logical or linguistic module. They instead promote the idea that the immersion of an organism in a perceptual environment and the interaction therewith (i.e., *embodied cognition,* cf. Varela et al. 1991) gives rise to meaningful (linguistic) categories. This ultimately results in an approach to linguistics, in which language is not a clear-cut faculty of the human brain, but a phenomenon that is interwoven with general cognition, perception, and other aspects of human biology. Most importantly, the driver for linguistic behaviour is not an innate grammatical faculty. Rather, language is driven by a need of making sense of the world through cognitive strategies such as *conceptual metaphors* (Lakoff & Johnson 1980a), *image schemas* (Johnson 1987), and others. Linguistics studies that are preoccupied with these questions are nowadays subsumed under the term *cognitive linguistics.*

While this development needn't be linked directly to the development of technology in the same period, it is nevertheless conceivable how the development of computers and cheaper prices for statistical computing would fuel such approaches to language. Take a sociolinguistic study such as Qi et al. (2003), in which the authors assess the premise of whether or not African American children from low-income families represent a high-risk group for language delays. In this study, more than 750 children across different pre-school age groups, income levels, and ethnicities (African American and European American) are compared. To make a valid statistical assessment, the authors compute means, standard deviations and other statistical measures such as p-values for significance. Even though the mathematics of this type of study is rather simple, it is no stretch to argue that few linguists would want to (or know how to) tackle such statistical analysis without a personal computer, let alone without a calculator. So, while the first driver for the development of new linguistic disciplines was an internal theoretical opposition, the development of technology boosted the emancipation of new linguistic lines of investigation from formal linguistics.

Other linguistic disciplines depend very clearly on the development of new technological advances. Two approaches exemplify how the theoretical development of linguistics alone wasn't enough to provoke the fundamental paradigm shifts in the 20th century, namely psycho and neurolinguistics. Both of these disciplines go back to before the Chomskyan era of formal syntactic theory. An account as early as the mid-19th century systematically linked brain damage to the loss of speech (Broca 1861). After various autopsies on patients with speech aphasia, Paul Broca localized what came to be known as Broca's area in the left hemispherical frontal lobe above the lateral sulcus (*fissura lateralis cerebri*). This account is important in that it shows that there is a structural connection between some level of linguistic behaviour as an immaterial phenomenon and a specific portion of brain tissue as its material base. Even though some studies during the first half of the 20th century are preoccupied with language and the human brain (e.g., Hinshelwood 1917; Nielsen 1946), those are typically clinical observations rather than scientific studies in the modern sense. Hence, the term neurolinguistics first appears prominently in Luria's *Basic Problems of Neurolinguistics* (1976), when computation was more readily available. Also, the journal for *Brain & Language*[6] was founded in 1974 by Harry Whitaker (Peng 1985), the same year that the journal for *Computational Linguistics* was founded. What's more, as soon as 1979, famous neuroscientists Michael Arbib and David Caplan reviewed the taxonomy of neurolinguistic studies and split the models created into three categories: faculty models, process models, and representational models. They explicitly argue that neurolinguistics needs modern[7] computational models, based on artificial intelligence, to be able to (a) integrate the different modelling approaches and (b) connect the high-level modelling with the low-level synapse-cell-circuit level of physiological research. The title of this important publication is both concise and frank: *Neurolinguistics must be computational* (Arbib & Caplan 1979). In 1980, electroencephalography (EEG) was powerful enough to help discover the event-related potential N400, a 'brain-wave' that is produced as a result of high processing cost upon the detection of unexpected semantic elements in

6 https://www.journals.elsevier.com/brain-and-language/
7 "modern" in the 1970s.

a given context[8] (Kutas & Hillyard 1980). Forty years later, the N400 is still an important marker used in neurolinguistic experiments. Another technological improvement in the field was the introduction of the oxygen-sensitive BOLD contrast for brain imaging (Ogawa et al. 1990), which converted fMRI into one of the leading techniques in neuroimaging and neurolinguistic research (Huettel et al. 2004).

The case of psycholinguistics is equivalent. Linguists, even at high times of structuralism, were intuitively certain that language as a human faculty had to have a cognitive or psychological component. In Romance Studies, J. Francis Lemon tried to account for the use of the subjunctive mood not through formal or historic arguments like his colleagues at the time, but with a psychological account. For him, the use of the subjunctive is not merely a question of whether or not something that is said is factually true, but whether or not the speaker wishes to present it as such (Lemon 1927). The study is, in other words, preoccupied with speakers' internal states and not language as a grammatical system. Consider also Karl Bühler's *Crisis of Psychology* (1927) in which he attempts to reconcile the then deeply entrenched positions of *Gestalt*, Developmental Psychology, and Behaviourism. He does this by discussing various phenomena of language from all these different standpoints showing that, ultimately, a complete psychological image of language can only be attained if all of the aforementioned positions are integrated. These accounts – even though useful both at the time and nowadays – are more speculative than scientific in a modern sense due to a lack of access to empirical data and processing tools for these data.

Levelt (2012) reviews psycholinguistic studies from as early as the second half of the 18th century up to the 1950s, the moment that most scholars mark as the beginning of the cognitive turn. It is at that time, that Osgood and Sebeok published one of the first books to contain the term psycholinguistics in its title (1954). From that time on, psycholinguistics has been improved on a techno-methodological level with various methods including reaction time (RT) tasks, eye-tracking, and others. RT makes a perfect example for the technological influence on linguistics. While the first RT experiment was performed in 1868 by F. C. Donders, and only some pioneering experiments used this method during the first half of the 20th century, the number of experiments based on RT has been continuously growing ever since the 1950s (Baayen & Milin 2010). Most importantly, Baayen and Milin point out that, even though the method is quite

8 For instance, "I want to drink a glass of car" would produce an N400 as opposed to "I want to drink a glass of water".

old, the possibilities for data analysis have increased in the last couple of years to an important extent. They describe the capacities of regression models, variance analysis, multiple regression and covariance analysis in the framework of mixed-effects modelling (Baayen & Milin 2010). Again, the arithmetic behind this type of analysis isn't ground-breaking from a mathematical standpoint, but the ease in computing has made the mainstream application of these methods possible. Also, it is not only the quality and speed of computers but especially the ease of access to pre-fabricated software (e.g., SPSS) and computing libraries such as the *lme4* package for linear mixed-effects models (Bates et al. 2020) for *R*, that render these tasks very simple to solve, even for the less maths- or tech-savvy scientist.

0.4. Technology Becomes Theory – The Computer Metaphor

Finally, technology is not only important to heighten researchers' ability for data processing and analysis. The technology available to linguists ultimately can and does influence linguistic theory and the underlying concept of language. This also explains the mechanism by which the enrichment of the toolbox and the creation of new linguistic subfields rise to importance. This argument is based upon the Tools-To-Theory Heuristic (Gigerenzer & Goldstein 1996) which posits that the use of new scientific tools, such as the computer, "suggest new theoretical metaphors and concepts" (p. 132) and that "[once] proposed by an individual scientist (or a group), the new theoretical metaphors and concepts are more likely to be accepted by the scientific community if the members of the community are also users of the new tools" (Gigerenzer & Goldstein 1996, p. 132).

But why are metaphors so important for the development of new theories of language? Linguistic evidence from recurrent metaphors led the aforementioned authors Lakoff and Johnson (1980a) to argue that the conceptual basis of the human mind is at its core metaphoric. A metaphor is a cognitive process that involves the detection (or creation[9]) of similarities, and the mapping of the structure of one thing onto another based on these similarities. That is, the human mind can use well-understood, experienceable, concrete things and map their structure onto abstract things to make them conceivable. A famous and cross-culturally stable example of this is TIME IS SPACE (Radden 2011). Since the dimension of time is abstract, in the sense that it cannot be directly

9 Which, given Vico's Axiom (1710) "verum et factum reciprocantur seu convertuntur" do not seem to differ from one another at all.

experienced, people across the world make metaphoric borrowings from spatial concepts to express time. This works because space is experienceable. Hence, for many languages, much time is a "long time", whereas little time is a "short time". Languages borrow structural descriptors from the domain of space to be able to talk about time.

Outside the linguistic community perceptual symbol systems (Barsalou 1999) as opposed to arbitrary symbol systems (de Saussure 1916) have also gained territory, substantiating the importance of metaphoric meaning for the understanding of human language. Neuroscientific data seems to support the idea of perception-based symbolic knowledge (Barsalou 2003). In this context, a specific conceptual metaphor is of interest, namely THE MIND IS A COMPUTER. These examples go to show that the computer metaphor isn't a mere rhetorical device, but that conceiving of the mind as a computer determines the current understanding of a human mind in terms of how machines are constructed. Providing ample textual examples and linguistic evidence for his claim, Lakoff himself states:

> Because of the recent technological innovations in computer science, the mind-as-computer metaphor has taken hold, not only in the popular imagination, but among professional cognitive psychologists as well. (Lakoff 2012, p. 338)

The term 'computer' however, didn't always refer to machines. Gigerenzer and Goldstein (1996) provide a history of the computer metaphor, pointing out that "In the Enlightenment, calculation was not considered a rote, mechanical thought process. In contrast, philosophers of the time held that intelligence and even moral sentiment were in their essence forms of calculation" (Daston 1988, 1992 in Gigerenzer & Goldstein 1996, p. 133). Computers were people tasked with such calculations, comprising a vast array of tasks, from calculations in the modern sense up to pondering moral arguments. This conception notwithstanding, Leibniz had articulated as early as 1685 that it was "unworthy of excellent men to lose hours like slaves in the labour of calculation, which could be safely relegated to anyone else if [a] machine were used" (credited in Marquand 1886, p. 303) when he presented his first binary mechanical calculation machine, something that in modern terms could be called a mechanical digital computer.

In point and fact, the idea of computation, in the sense that Hilbert, and later Turing, conceived of it, can be traced back to the 13th century Franciscan Scholastic Ramon Llull (Raimundus Llullus), native to the Balearian island of Mallorca, from whom Leibniz inherited the idea that the Truth could be calculated based on the logical combination of arguments (Sales 1997). But not only was Llull, who is often overlooked in the presence of his contemporary

Thomas Aquinas, the *spiritus rector* of the idea of calculus (ibid., p. 16), but he also anticipated the idea of generative systems, that is, systems which, on the basis of "a *finite* set of *rules* as well as a finite set of truths [,] can then generate from them a presumably infinite set of *derived* truths" (ibid., p. 18). This is strikingly similar to the Chomskyan definition of grammar, which will be explored in more detail below (Section 0.4.1.2). What's more, even the notion of graphs, quite in the sense that they are explored in this dissertation (cf. Chapter 2), is already defined in Llull's *Ars Magna* and is functionally equivalent to a "decision tree (as in AI) in a decision procedure" (Sales 1997, p. 19), when he proposes to combine his axiomatic truths with lines which can then be followed to derive correct conclusions. Therefore, Llull's *Ars Magna* is arguably the highest expression of sophistication of formalised thinking in Medieval philosophy. Being grounded in the ideas of alchemy, cabbalism, and mysticism, his ideas mainly miss one step of abstraction, namely the reduction of calculation to a binary system, which was later introduced into European[10] Philosophy and Mathematics by Leibniz.

Given the long existence of the idea of computation, and the development of the Computer-as-Brain metaphor to the Computer-as-Mind metaphor (Gigerenzer & Goldstein 1996), it was no long shot for Turing to ask himself whether or not machines could be said to think. As Gigerenzer and Goldstein importantly point out, this is the opposite direction of what is of interest to the current study. Rather than seeing the mind as a machine, Turing saw the machine as a mind. The metaphor THE MIND IS A COMPUTER didn't come about until Allen Newell and Herbert Simon, two of the most important figures in the early development of artificial intelligence, first suggested that computers were more than calculators, but machines for symbol-manipulation. They hypothesized that a physical symbol system is both a necessary and sufficient condition for intelligence (Gigerenzer & Goldstein 1996). Independently of whether this assessment is correct or not, it had a huge influence on the conception of the human mind in both specialists and the broader public:

> The first general statement of Newell and Simon's new vision of mind appeared in their 1972 book, *Human Problem Solving*. Newell and Simon argued for the idea that higher level cognition proceeds much like the behaviour of a production system - a formalism from computer science (and before that symbolic logic) that had never before been used in psychological modelling. [...] Here we do not attempt to probe the depths of how Newell and Simon's idea of information processing changed theories of mind; the

---

10 According to various research publications and news articles, binary systems have been in use in other cultures, such as the Polynesian Mangareva culture (Bender & Beller 2013) or Chinese Mathematics (Ball 2013) for 600 or even 2,800 years respectively.

commonplace usage of computer terminology in the cognitive psychological literature since 1972 is a reflection of this. How natural it seems for present-day psychologists to speak of cognition in terms of *encoding, storage, retrieval, executive processes, algorithms,* and *computational cost.* (Gigerenzer & Goldstein 1996, p. 138)

Evidence for the metaphor THE MIND IS A COMPUTER and their manifold variations is given in various psycholinguistic accounts, which the reader is invited to consult (e.g., Sternberg 1993; Lakoff 2012).

This goes to show that Turing's belief in "thinking machines" (1950, p. 442) still carries weight. His 'prophecy', that by the end of the 20th century people would seamlessly talk about thinking machines, has been fulfilled, in the sense that people nowadays have very little problems talking about computers as if they were intelligent. That having been said, it is worth pointing out that this particular conception of intelligent machines is more of a marketing stunt. Hardly anyone today would on second thought claim that computers are conscious in the way biological life is, although projections into the future of this question differ greatly, and the debate has recently resurged in the context of the presentation of GPT-4. Also, the effort it took to make technology 'smart' in the way it is, was considerably greater than what Turing had anticipated. He thought that calculating power would be the main issue, whereas computers are nowadays not short of calculating power at all. Whether Turing thought that machines by now could think or just would be attributed the capacity in the common use of language is up to speculation. In the latter sense, however, Turing's idea has held true.

0.4.1. The Computer Metaphor in Linguistics

Now, the Tools-to-Theory Heuristic (Gigerenzer & Goldstein 1996) is more of a general trend in the history of ideas. This section will be concerned with two relevant examples from the specifically linguistic realm. It has been shown that the Tools-to-Theory Heuristic is dependent on both the A MIND IS A COMPUTER, and the A COMPUTER IS A MIND metaphors. Hence, examples for both versions of the computer metaphor will be examined. First, it will be shown how knowledge of human neural circuits has led to the development of one of the most important states of the art technologies in artificial intelligence, namely *Artificial Neural Networks* (*ANN*). Then, it will be shown that one of the most influential linguistic theories of the 20th century is highly dependent on automata theory, namely Noam Chomsky's Generative Transformational Grammar. This examination supports the claim that linguistics and technology are highly linked to one another, and that searching to incorporate knowledge about technology into linguistic theory can be beneficial if due account of the differences between the two is given.

0.4.1.1. Artificial Neural Networks

ANN are distinct from but largely based on the architecture of natural neurons (Jain et al. 1996). It could be argued that trying to imitate neurons in computational architecture might not have been conceivable had the computer metaphor not already had a considerable impact on modern thought. Their history dates back to the 1940s, when knowledge of the function of human neurons became more reliable and when the McCulloch-Pitts model of the neuron broke ground in the mathematical description of neural activity. Despite the model's "simplifying assumptions that do not reflect the behaviour of biological neurons" (Jain et al. 1996, p. 34), this model was of vital importance to the popularisation of knowledge about neurons. A further advancement was the layering of artificial neurons, such that the limitations of a single artificial neuron were overcome. This architectural element, even though not exactly homologue to biological processes in the human brain, is an important factor in mirroring the functioning of natural cognition. That is because the power in processing information does not stem from the concatenation of very quickly executed serial calculations but from the connectivity between the information sent to and sent from the artificial neurons. Put differently, the revolution of ANN does not lie in a mere enhancement of calculating power, but in the processability and connection of information. The *connectionist* architecture was a breakthrough in artificial intelligence (Jain et al. 1996) that exhibits at least some degree of similarity to actual brains in the sense that it leverages the power of connectivity. Also, the functions that neural networks execute are precisely those that cannot be automatised by simple serial automation. Jain et al. (1996) enumerate tasks such as pattern recognition, clustering, function approximation, and optimisation. To give an everyday example, the processing of handwriting and its conversion to digital characters can't be approached with classical serial computation, but with the connectionist ANN.

The state-of-the-art of ANN are *Generative Adversarial Networks* (GAN) and are illustrative of more sophisticated tasks of this type. GAN are the most advanced way of implementing neural networks at the time of writing[11]. They consist of a pair of networks that, in a competitive process, train each other,

---

11 This thesis was presented for examination in 2021 almost eighteen months before GPT-3 was released to the public and GPT-4 was presented. Hence, comparisons to their capacities are not systematically included in this publication.

thereby being able to learn deep representation (meaning) from data without the necessity of previously annotating the data (Creswell et al. 2018). That means that they are not only able to recognise previously labelled data but that they can define meaningful classes and tell them apart from one another without previous definitions. The difference is the following: With defined classes, an algorithm knows which labels to give to data, and 'only' has to learn the patterns that correspond to each existing label. With unlabelled data, the algorithm doesn't have a previously established standard of comparison and doesn't 'know' what to look for in classification. Instead, the algorithm has to create classes on its own and assign each object to the classes it defines for itself. This is also known as the difference between supervised and unsupervised learning tasks. In less technical terms, this allows GAN to automatically execute processes such as gradually making a person smile more and more on a photograph (Creswell et al. 2018, p. 62), turning a Monet painting into a photograph (or vice versa), turning a video of a zebra into a video of a horse (or vice versa), or turning a picture of a winter landscape into a summer landscape (Creswell et al. 2018, p. 63). These tasks, while easy to imagine for a human, are notoriously difficult for machines to achieve because they involve a complicated entanglement of many meaningful elements (e.g., snow, shades of light, a 'concept' of what a painting is, 'knowing' that a 'zebra' is a 'horse with stripes', etc.)

Another example, more closely related to language, is analogous thinking, which resembles propositional logic and requires lots of external world knowledge. This is the case of problems such as MADRID IS TO SPAIN WHAT PARIS IS TO …? This type of task can be solved using word embeddings in vector spaces, where the semantic and syntactic meaning of a word is represented as a vector, that expresses the distance from one word to another. In that way, "[binary] *gender* can be expressed as the translation vectors $\overrightarrow{woman} - \overrightarrow{man}$ and $\overrightarrow{queen} - \overrightarrow{king}$ " (Ethayarajh 2019, p. 3503). This analogy comes easily to humans, while the representation of these vectors has to be learned by machines with a high cost for training. This is a task that can (among other strategies) also be solved via neural networks through the prediction of co-occurrences of words in large corpora of text. Neural language models are designed such that

> Having seen the sentence 'The cat is walking in the bedroom' in the training corpus should help us generalise to make the sentence 'A dog was running in a room' almost as likely, simply because 'dog' and 'cat' (resp. 'the' and 'a', 'room' and 'bedroom', etc…) have similar semantic and grammatical roles. (Bengio et al. 2003, p. 1139)

and hence occur in similar contexts. These examples show how the functions that machines are often tasked with, more and more resemble work that is done by humans. The composition of symphonies, elaboration of paintings, and the writing of novels in an automated fashion are all indicative of how ANN are – not only in function but in purpose – greatly inspired by human creativity.

The fact that ANN are called 'neural' is of course no evidence for their employing the same problem-solving strategies as humans. What these examples are illustrative of is the fact that computer scientists are inspired to teach machines those aspects of information processing that are hard to formalise but come very easily to biological minds. Also, but probably to a lesser degree, the way in which machines attempt to solve these problems is inspired by how biological systems solve them. To fully grasp this argument, consider the task carried out by aeroplanes. While the ability to fly may be inspired by birds, the mechanism that flight is based on differs greatly, even though it still involves the usage of wings rather than rotors, as is the case for helicopters. Thus, a similar output is by no means an argument for a similar mechanism. One of the most notable endeavours in this avenue is teaching machines how to use human language in the most convincing way possible.

0.4.1.2. Generative Transformational Grammar and Automata Theory

In the opposite direction of the computer metaphor, the influence of technological advances on the field of linguistics becomes even clearer. It is no stretch to state that the course of linguistic tradition in the 20th century is dependent on some of the work that was previously reported on, specifically the work of Alan Turing. This is especially true for one of the most important linguistic theorists of the 20th century, Noam Chomsky. His theories on Universal Grammar (Chomsky 1965, 1968) and Generative Grammar (Chomsky 1957) are to be regarded as some of the major leaps in terms of the scientific formalisation and popularisation of linguistics. Even though, to the knowledge of the author, no description of a putative Universal Grammar has been produced hitherto, and Generative Grammar is almost irrelevant in most practical applications of linguistics, such as language pedagogy and automated translation, Chomsky's work was ground-breaking for the development of modern linguistics. He introduced a number of considerations about the inner workings and genetic condition of language into the field, and even though most of his arguments have been seriously rebutted, the opposition to his theory has undoubtedly spawned several modern theories, as was pointed out above. Furthermore, one should not throw the baby out with the bathwater in terms of the psychological shortcomings in Chomsky's theory. To date,

Chomsky's method remains the most coherent theory of grammar as such, and the methodological tools allow for very precise predictions about the acceptability of grammatical constructions. Thus, rather than feeding into the work against Generative or Universal Grammar, the following paragraphs will merely describe how Chomsky's theory hinges on Automata Theory, an early mathematical model of computation that Alan Turing crucially contributed to.

Prior to elaborating his *Syntactic Structures* (1957), Chomsky had elaborated *Three Models for the Description of Language* (1956) which are concerned with modelling the grammar of languages. It is important to understand that grammar and language don't mean what they mean in laypeople's terms. When Chomsky talks about grammar at that time, he means an algorithmic process or set of rules, that "generate all of the sentences of English and only these" (Chomsky 1956, p. 113) from a finite corpus of signs (i.e., characters or words). The resulting language is, then, nothing more than the set[12] of all correct sentences of English, and only these. At this stage, grammar is hence already defined as an algorithmic process, which presupposes the calculability of the language in this formal sense. As the next paragraphs will show, the calculability of language is not a trivial assumption.

The three models under investigation in Chomsky's paper are Finite State Markov Processes, Phrase Structure, and Transformational Grammar. Chomsky estimates that the latter is the most promising candidate. The input to this transformational algorithm is a "small, possibly finite kernel of basic sentences with phrase structure [...] along with a set of transformations which can be applied to produce new and more complicated sentences from elementary components" (Chomsky 1956, p. 124). In this model, there is an inventory of axiomatically 'correct' English sentences that, by checking the rules of transformation, let speakers accept or reject new sentences. At this point in Chomsky's work, this conception isn't assumed to be the psychological reality of speakers. He explicitly states that these mathematical models are formal models of language, which is not necessarily how they are handled by human speakers (ibid.).

The degree to which this conception of language is influenced by the knowledge of technology at the time becomes more apparent when inspecting

12 The fact that this set is infinite is irrelevant for Chomsky's argument, because a sufficiently powerful algorithm can generate infinite elements with a finite inventory. Think of a computer, which with a finite physical inventory of transistors representing 0's and 1's ("electricity" vs. "don't electricity") can represent any computable information. This was also intuitively true for Llull in the 14th century (Sales 1997, cf. Section 0.4.).

the Chomsky-Schützenberger-Hierarchy[13] (cf. Chomsky 1959b; Chomsky & Schützenberger 1959). Further developing his models of language (1956), he investigates the different types of grammars or "device[s] that [enumerate] the sentences of a language" (Chomsky 1959b, p. 137) and the respective automata that can emulate them. He defines four classes of grammars which are called[14] Type 0 grammars, or unrestricted rewriting systems, Type 1 grammars, or context-sensitive, Type 2 grammars, or context-free, and Type 3 grammars, or finite-state grammars (Wall 1972, p. 212). They respectively generate Type 0 languages, or recursively enumerable, Type 1 languages, or context-sensitive, Type 2 languages, or context-free, and Type 3 languages, or finite-state languages (Wall 1972, p. 213). Again, when speaking of grammars and languages, this is a metaphoric usage of the word, because they refer to mathematical objects and sets respectively, that can be represented algorithmically. The actual automata that can emulate these grammars respectively are Turing-Machines (Wall 1972, p. 274), Linear Bounded Automata (p. 285), Pushdown Automata (p. 282), and Finite Automata (p. 261) also called finite-state-machines or finite Markovian sources (Chomsky 1959b, p. 138). The basic logic of this hierarchy of languages and respective automata is that, as one runs down the hierarchy from type 0 to type 3, the grammars (i.e., formal rules) that generate each language get ever more restrictive. That means that the machines that can emulate each grammar need to become more complex in their capacities, as one moves up the hierarchy from type 3 to type 0.

The most complex machine is the Turing Machine, which is "an automaton that can carry out any set of operations that could reasonably be called a computation[15]" (Wall 1972, p. 274). In fact, the Turing Machine as a theoretical device defines what can be computed and what cannot (Turing 1937). It can thus emulate the least restricted grammars and generate the least restricted languages, while of course being able to generate all other types as well. On the other end of the spectrum, "a finite automaton (*fa*) is an abstract device that receives a string of symbols as input, computes for a finite number of steps, and halts in some configuration signifying either that the input has been accepted or else that is has been rejected" (Wall 1972, p. 254). While this is what Chomsky envisions

---

13 The hierarchy is depicted in the cited work, the origins of the term "Chomsky-Hierarchy" or "Chomsky-Schützenberger-Hierarchy" are not clear to the author.

14 For ease of reading and to abide by professional conventions, Robert Wall's (1972) terminology will be used.

15 A rather accessible formal description of the Turing Machine – and the necessary mathematics to understand it – are given in Wall 1972 (pp. 276–278).

to describe language, he had already proven the insufficiency of *fa* to describe English (Chomsky 1956). On the other hand, he claims that describing language with Turing Machines

> has no interest. We learn nothing about a natural language from the fact that its sentences can be effectively displayed, i.e., that they constitute a recursively enumerable set. [...] a theory of language must also indicate how, in general, relevant structural information can be obtained for a particular sentence generated by a particular grammar (Chomsky 1959b p. 138).

While this is of course true for the explanatory power of the theory, one has to also entertain the option that a formal description of all the correct sentences of the English language with these criteria ("devices with more generative power than finite automata, and more special structure than Turing machines" Chomsky 1956, p. 139), however desirable may be impossible in principle.

Chomsky's endeavour rests upon the assumption that for any imaginable sentence, it can be decided whether or not the sentence is correct. This is a lot less trivial than it seems, because one may well be able to imagine sentences that would not be judged as correct by all native speakers of English. That means that there is possibly no algorithmic way to determine whether or not there is a solution (i.e., assignment of correctness or incorrectness) for each conceivable English sentence, be it by Turing Machines, *fa*, or any machine between the two. This statement may be covered by Hilbert's *Entscheidungsproblem*, which Turing proved has no solution (Turing 1937, p. 259), and which states that one cannot determine algorithmically whether a given problem can be computed or not. In terms of Chomsky's desired algorithm, this means that it is not possible to determine beforehand whether or not a grammar will eventually be able to identify a given English phrase as correct or incorrect. In more technical terms, The *Halteproblem* "for a particular Turing-Post program [i.e., a formal grammar] is the problem of distinguishing between initial tape configurations [i.e., sentences of the English language] which lead to the program's eventually halting [i.e., deciding whether the sentence is correct] and initial tape configurations which lead the program to compute forever" (Davis 1978, p. 254). According to Davis (1978), it has been proven that the *Halteproblem* has no solution, meaning that it cannot be known beforehand whether or not a formal grammar will ever reach a decision on the grammaticality and/or acceptability of any given phrase. Ironically, the non-solvability of the *Entscheidungsproblem* is what Turing set out to prove with the conception of the Turing Machine, or *a(utomatic)-machine* (Turing 1937, p. 232). Note that the concepts *Entscheidungsproblem* and *Halteproblem* are used interchangeably in the previous considerations because in the consulted literature they are also often conflated (e.g. Davis 1978). This, in unison with the author's insufficient mathematical knowledge, obscures whether Turing's proof is a suitable argument against Chomsky's assumption that sentences in human language are computable problems in this sense. While this is a conceptual argument worthy of exploration there is, at least, an empirical question of whether language can be computed, that is, whether an algorithm can be found that can judge the grammaticality of sentences; especially given the fact that Chomsky requires this to be achieved for a more restricted machine than a Turing machine.

Independently of the inadequacy and incompleteness of the foregoing argument, it is not the goal of this study to prove whether or not formal grammar is capable of executing the task that Chomsky wants it to execute. The point of this description is to show how advances in mathematics and automation theory are intricately linked to Chomsky's conception of language and have greatly influenced the subsequent half-century of linguistic inquiry. Ultimately, this argument – in unison with the first two – should be compelling as to why the interest in a specific technology is inspiring for a linguistic study.

0.5. Approach and Structure

For the above reasons, the current study is interested in how the novel technical aspects of the Blockchain can inform questions about the use of language. In particular, it sets out to identify the role of network properties of communication in the use and development of language. The ample literature on the Blockchain identifies the importance of network topology – centralisation, decentralisation, and distribution – for the stability of information in the network. Analogously, this dissertation seeks to identify the importance of network topology and other properties of networks on both communication (i.e., *what* is talked about) and language (i.e., *how* it is talked about).

This endeavour warrants the following structure. In Chapter 1, Blockchain technology, its network structure and its implications for the stability of information on the Blockchain will be presented. Where possible, initial parallels to linguistic communication systems will be drawn, albeit only for ease of understanding and to provide a conceptual basis for its understanding. Chapter 2 will be devoted to presenting some basic aspects of graph theory, as it provides the mathematical basis for the description and analysis of networks. The chapter attempts to balance conceptual and formal explanations of graph theory. However, a relatively high degree of formalisation cannot be avoided, because the classification of different network topologies in the corpus was used for analysis, and these formal definitions were coded into the programme that analyses the data. Chapter 3, then, is devoted to a review of the linguistic literature containing the concept of networks. Even though different branches of linguistics employ the term, the chapter shows that the use of the concept is subject to the context in which it is used and that big differences in its application exist. These differences range from diverging formal definitions of network typologies to the process that is modelled by the notion of networks. Chapter 4 binds the former bodies of literature together in an attempt at a linguistics of networks. This chapter's main function is to put forth some elements of a network theory of language and to generate testable hypotheses for the empirical sections of this study. The reasons for developing the argument in the fashion of the first four chapters were given in the introduction. It was shown that inspiring linguistic theory with advances from other lines of research is rather common, and will here be done explicitly. Methodologically, such a study, especially the access to such data, wouldn't be possible without the use of computational methods. The data used for the empirical investigation will then be presented in Chapter 5. This chapter will explain how the datasets were created, most notably by collecting posts and comments from an anonymous *online social media* platform entirely devoted to Spanish speakers, namely *Hispachan*. Rather than only reporting on the empirical description of the data, it will also contain caveats on the choice of this social network, the importance and pitfalls of its anonymous nature, and a statistical assessment of some of its main variables. This will be needed to make correct assumptions for the modelling of data in the subsequent experiments. The first experiment will be reported in Chapter 6. This experiment focuses on the similarity of information in threads of posts, correlating this similarity with the properties of different network topologies. In other words, it will be explained which topologies of communication lead to which degree of similarity, or stability of topics. The second experiment laid out in Chapter 7, assesses hypotheses regarding the communicative success of certain topics and forms of communication (in particular the topic of the Corona-Virus, and methods of secret handshakes) on Hispachan. The relevant notions for this experiment will be explained in the introduction of the chapter. Chapter 8 is devoted to the third experiment, in which the measures of communicative success are contrasted with the expressivity of linguistic behaviour in terms of sensorimotor strategy. The implications of these strategies for processes of grammaticalisation and language development are discussed therein. This experiment attempts to assess whether communicative success in a communication network can be predicted by linguistic means, namely the use of specifically emotive concepts. In Chapter 9, a general discussion of the findings is provided, whereas initial discussions for each experiment are going to be located in each corresponding chapter. The argument is concluded in Chapter 10, containing remarks for further research and summarising the success and relevance of the present findings for the scientific community.

1. A Semiotics of the Blockchain?

In this chapter, the functioning of the Blockchain will be explained. Most notably, the chapter will explain which elements of its network structure are highlighted in the discourse around the Blockchain, and the implications this has for the use of this technology, both on a societal and a technological level. The chapter will furthermore give an overview of the terminology as it is used throughout the dissertation and will furthermore bridge two completely separate bodies of academic literature, graph theory and linguistics. More concretely, the chapter explores how the achievement of consensus in distributed networks can be framed as a problem of communication and will furthermore point out semiotic properties of the achievement of consensus; providing a semiotic comparison between language and the Blockchain.

Two reasons justify the focus on the Blockchain as opposed to other (more dedicatedly communicative) technologies. Firstly, the popularity of Blockchain as a novel technology has spawned broad societal interest. One indicator of this circumstance is the wide array of applications that have spawned in the last few years. Healthcare (Agbo et al. 2019), the Internet of Things (Conoscenti et al. 2016), the construction industry (Li et al. 2019), smart cities (Shen & Pena-Mora 2018), cryptocurrencies (Tama et al. 2017), and most recently, decentralised finance (Zetzsche et al. 2020) are some of the areas in which researchers hope to apply Blockchain technologies. On a practical note, the use of Blockchain technology has also been proposed in the context of academic research, for instance, to secure data integrity (Bartling 2018) or to foster efforts of Open Science (Leible et al. 2019). Although neither contribution addresses questions of specifically linguistic sciences, it is evident how both arguments translate to the establishment of coherent data collection and storage methods as well as publication practices in linguistic research.

Secondly and more importantly, the broad technological research on this topic has been accompanied by accounts that link the technology to societal (and sometimes very clearly language-related) issues. For example, the Blockchain's high energy consumption provokes calls for stronger regulation and policy-making toward the decarbonisation of the technology (Truby 2018). Other accounts posit that Blockchain technologies are far from homogenous and that less energy-extensive ways of implementing the Blockchain do exist (Sedlemir et al. 2020). While countless other issues are discussed in light of the advances in Blockchain technology, the following paragraphs will merely present those which are related to language and/or semiotics in one way or another. But it's always the affordance of one of two aspects of Blockchain technology that render this comparison useful, its *decentralisation* and its *ledger setup*.

It is important to understand that many arguments on Blockchain technology are centred around the idea of decentralisation, that is, advocating for the elimination of institutional middlemen in social interactions (Underwood 2016). In much of the literature, the technological decentralisation of social interactions (e.g., payments, notarial procedures, property transfers, etc.) via the Blockchain is regarded as a condition for the political decentralisation of power, placing the technology at the heart of ideological debates around societal questions. It is, for instance, often argued that the use of Blockchain technology for business transactions of any kind would contribute to the liberation of markets because it monetises the integrity of information, thus resulting in more evenly informed business parties (Huckle & White 2016).

It is hence no surprise that the technology as such is often viewed as a vehicle for libertarian and market-radical ideology (Karlstrom 2014). On the other hand, its decentralised nature has also given rise to the argument that Blockchain technologies might be a crucial asset in the implementation of public ownership (Ismaev 2017) and other cooperative market dynamics, ultimately leading to more socialist societies (Huckle & White 2016). It is easily conceivable how such arguments might be extended to fit discussions on linguistic policies or the degree of central control that government entities should or shouldn't have on the codification and fixation of 'correct' language[16]. Another study compares the ideas of decentralisation and its specific application to political institutions, property rights, and democratic governance against social contract theories such as Rousseau's (Reijers et al. 2016). Although the authors do grant that some of the properties of decentralisation might be in tune with social contract theories formulated during the Enlightenment, they claim that the Blockchain, as implemented in a free market regime, doesn't "incorporate Rousseau's idea of the common good" (Reijers et al. 2016, p. 147).

Other researchers are much more optimistic. Philosopher Melanie Swan (2015) sees the *Blueprint for a New Economy* in the Blockchain and points to its

16 While the literature on linguistic policies if of course vast, there are, to the best of the author's knowledge, no academic approaches to linguistic policy from a standpoint that incorporates network structure or graph theory, or a technical interpretation of the term (de)centralisation.

application in fields such as scientific publishing. She argues that the application of Blockchain in this field and the monetisation of scientific contributions could render scientists more independent from publishing monopolies. In the avenue of scientific publishing, the aspect of absolute transparency of Blockchain data is here interpreted as a desirable element, especially with regard to the publication of data prior to analysis (i.e., pre-registered studies). In this way, scientific data and the research process could be made more transparent to the scientific community while eliminating paywalls for access to articles and relevant research information.

These vastly diverging perspectives on the Blockchain are indicative of the circumstance that technological decentralisation cannot simply be equated with the decentralisation of political power. While the contributions quoted above do all work on the concept of decentralisation, it is for the most part, highly conflated with the political pre-conceptions of each author. This becomes evident in reviewing the adequate technological terminology for the description of Blockchain technology, in which decentralisation becomes a much less radical term (cf. Section 1.1).

The second technological property of interest is often referred to in philosophical contributions and is especially useful in the context of linguistics. Blockchains are ledgers, that is, virtual technologies for record-keeping. This means that they are an inherently semiotic technology aimed at representing value. It is hence no surprise that various philosophical studies have focussed on this aspect. Most notably, the Blockchain has been proposed as an instance of notational technologies in the sense of Goodman's *notational system* (Dupont 2017). Dupont argues that by the processes of performance and representation, the Blockchain amounts to a symbolic system by its notational character. This circumstance, in turn, renders it extremely efficient for the management of abstract entities such as money, property (Ismaev 2017), or anything that can be expressed quantitatively.

The representational properties of information on Blockchains are also the topic of another study in which the representation of information on and off the Blockchain is discussed in the context of *Russell's paradox* (Parra-Moyano 2017), a central piece in the 20th century's philosophy of language. Both aforementioned accounts (Dupont 2017; Parra-Moyano 2017) and the notions of *representation* and *performance* are going to be of interest below, albeit from a different standpoint. The application of these notions makes the Blockchain a prime candidate for linguistic inquiry in the study of communication technology.

While the studies on representation and performance are located at the level of propositional linguistic logic, other studies are concerned with a higher-order level of representation and the consequences of the former for the latter. The Blockchain has, for instance, been depicted as a narrative technology (Reijers & Coeckelbergh 2018). This means that, while Blockchains are technically mere devices for notation and bookkeeping, the rigidity that these tools introduce into social processes like financial transactions subsequently renders the affected social processes increasingly rigid. The more rigid the notational system in use to record transactions, the more rigid transactions are expected to be, deeply impacting the cultural relationship with Blockchain-mediated processes. Furthermore, not only does the replacement of human interaction with computer code render the process of financial transactions more abstract from its social environment but it increases the narrative distance between the financial transaction and the human relationship that the former is meant to represent. In other words, the change in the shape of the transaction affects the normative stance taken by humans toward this transaction and its correct execution becomes an objective rather than a means of interaction. This is similar to the impact of the use of language on conceptualization (Section 0.4.1). The previous chapter illustrates the impact that technical wording has on the interaction with the concept as exemplified by the computer metaphor in linguistics. Financial transactions on the Blockchain – much like 'metaphors of transaction' – also change the meaning of the financial transactions themselves (Reijers & Coeckelbergh 2018).

A similar point is made by Wright and De Filippi (2015) who argue that the possibility of having perfectly truthful records of transactions is easily turned into the requirement of perfectly truthful records. This *Lex Cryptographia*, or cryptographical truth, fundamentally challenges the human judgement of the correctness of records, where now only correct transactions – in a technical sense – are also regarded as correct in any other – e.g., moral – sense. This shift from 'being able to' to 'ought to' is not only relevant in philosophy but has been treated from a technical standpoint. Informatic studies have challenged the view that Blockchain records are inherently more truthful than other types of digital records and discuss their potential as well as possible drawbacks. Lemieux (2016) for instance, is sceptical about the supremacy of the Blockchain over other methods of digital records in terms of security.

None of these contributions is concerned with linguistic phenomena, and only three of them are concerned with issues that are easily framed as linguistic at all, namely performance and representation (Dupont 2017), logical representation (Parra-Moyano 2017), and narration (Reijers & Coeckelbergh 2018). But all the aforementioned contributions tap into two main technological features of the Blockchain, record keeping and decentralisation, relating these technical aspects to societal questions. It is hence these two aspects that are going to be of the highest importance for the current study.

Once the terminology is established with a short technical introduction to the Blockchain, this study will attempt to draw a similar analogy between the technical aspects of record keeping and decentralisation and point out some elements of a putative semiotics of the Blockchain. The focus of this technical introduction will be placed on Bitcoin, as it is the earliest implementation of a worldwide public Blockchain, and because it exemplifies the essential elements of decentralisation and record-keeping in its minimalist architecture.

1.1. Terminology – What Is the Blockchain?

As in any scientific inquiry, clear terminology is the basis for a precise description and analysis of the issue at hand. This is especially true in the case of the Blockchain because some authors commit terminological indiscretions in their studies. Especially in the non-technical literature on the topic, there seems to be a rather regular conflation of the terms Bitcoin, Blockchain, and Cryptocurrency (Banach 2019, p. 185). For instance, Swan and De Filippi (e.g., 2017) equate the terms Blockchain and Distributed Ledger Technology. In another contribution, the Blockchain is mixed up with Bitcoin (e.g., dos Santos 2017). Besides, a great deal of attention is placed on the application of Blockchain technology as Cryptocurrency (e.g., Swan 2015), which lets these terms be very easily conflated.

Up to this point, the technology of interest to this dissertation has also been termed the Blockchain, for the sole purpose of confronting the reader with more popular vocabulary, when in fact, Distributed Ledger Technology (DLT) is a more accurate description of the object of study. As stated above, the two aspects of interest to this study are the elements of record-keeping and decentralisation. In the sense in which they have been used, these two elements formally define what a DLT is (Fernández-Anta et al. 2018). But here too, a sharpening of the terminology is in order.

1.1.1. Distributed Ledger Technology – DLT

Firstly, DLT are formally defined as ledger objects (Fernández-Anta et al. 2018), which store historical information for record-keeping. This means that they are not dynamic databases to which information can easily be written, read, and deleted. Instead, DLT are designed to keep track of every event that they are supposed to record in historical order. Such a ledger could represent any information that requires long-term continuous bookkeeping. Bank accounts are a classical example of this. As a mathematical object, a bank account is nothing but an endless list of additions and subtractions starting at a balance of zero. The current amount of money in a bank account is always equal to zero plus all the depositions minus all the withdrawals. Each event of deposit and withdrawal on such a ledger object is a transaction. Each transaction can and usually does contain extra information such as its timestamp and the origin, or destination, respectively, of a given amount of money. Although the information that is recordable on such a ledger object is not limited to financial information, a bank account is a perfect example of how a ledger object functions. Importantly, not only the resulting information but every step on the way is recorded on such a ledger object. This is, of course, not in and of itself a viable basis for its comparison to language, as language isn't recorded along all the steps of linguistic interaction. The basis for this comparison will become apparent further below.

The second defining element of a ledger is distribution, as the term distributed ledger technology implies. The nuance in meaning between decentralisation and distribution is of vital importance. This property of DLT was hitherto referred to as decentralisation because much of the reviewed literature conflates these terms too. However, decentralisation and distribution are fundamentally different properties of ledger implementations, which will be laid out in detail below (Section 2.2). Independently of this terminological pitfall, distributed ledger objects are implemented in such a way that no single entity controls the correctness of the information recorded therein (Fernández-Anta et al. 2018). The absence of a central entity for control (i.e., distribution) also implies that there is no central entity that can deliberately tamper with the information on the ledger. Returning to the example of a bank account, this means that, rather than relying on a bank to be the central authority on correct account balances, accounts can maintain each other through distributed control. Such a procedure renders accounts more secure because no central entity (i.e., the bank itself) can tamper with the balances on the accounts. At the same time, the system becomes more resilient to attacks from the outside. It's no longer enough to illegitimately take control over one central system node to alter information in the accounts because many different agents contribute to the integrity of this information at the same time. Furthermore, it is evident how this property relates to language, as human interactions are not largely coordinated via central agents. People just interact with one another based on local decisions, thereby forming a distributed network.

This goes to show that the technological properties of DLT are connected to the social implications that were cited in the foregoing section. Activists in the Blockchain community often regard banks' central control over financial information as an excess of power because account holders have to place their trust in the good faith of a banking institution. In the Blockchain community, this trust was heavily disturbed by certain events in recent history such as the Lehman Brothers bailout in 2008, which many in the community attribute to reckless business practices of private banks. According to some researchers, DLT can provide a "trust-less" (Klems et al. 2017) solution to record keeping. However, it has been argued that trustlessness is both dependent on the specific conception of trust, and only partly achievable through Blockchain technology (Hawlitschek et al. 2018). Furthermore, trustlessness is sometimes conflated with decentralisation (e.g., Wright & De Filippi 2015). This shows how easily the technical and societal aspects of DLT are confused. Nevertheless, these notions are intuitive and exemplify what it means to "cut out the middle-man" (Underwood 2016, p. 15) in much of the literature. The idea of Blockchain technologies is to design systems that are able to sustain themselves without central governance and to provide security of information that isn't dependent on the benevolence of a powerful 'middle-man'. After all, language does exist without centralised fixation. Even though many countries do have political institutions tasked with the codification of language (e.g., *Real Academia Española* and *Académie Française*), they are by no means necessary to maintain the grammatical system of a given language stable, even across large linguistic communities as is the case in, say, Spanish and English.

To provide clear-cut definitions, the terms distribution and ledger will here be used to denote the two main properties of DLT. These concepts will be introduced more formally in Chapter 2, as they will be relevant to the proper collection and analysis of the empirical data. At this point, a conceptual understanding of these terms is sufficient and merely goes to show where analogies between language and DLT can be drawn. Most notably, it will be argued below (Chapter 4) that language can be conceptualised as some sort of information carrier (i.e., a ledger) that maintains its systematic stability through distributed control (Beckner et al. 2009). That is linguistic information both in terms of the structural setup of a language and the cultural information contained therein maintains itself without a governing entity, as was hinted at throughout this section.

1.1.2. Blockchain

Following DLT, the Blockchain is the next level of specificity. This means every Blockchain is a DLT whereas not every DLT is a Blockchain. The term Blockchain refers to the specific way in which the ledger object is organised. Transactions are grouped into blocks of information, which makes transactions processable. These blocks of transactions are then chained together, such that the entire history of transactions can be revised. In this way, the integrity of the information is secured at any given point in time. The chain is achieved through the use of hashes.

Tab. 1: Example of a fictitious hash function. Note that the random distribution of signs h(x) provokes an enormous change between lines 1 and 2 while the original information is almost the same.

	Information x (arbitrary length)	**Hash function $x \rightarrow h(x)$**		**New information $h(x)$ (length = 9)**
x_1	The dog bites the cat		$h(x)_1$	H429Qrx10
x_2	The dog bit the cat	→	$h(x)_2$	X24Lc91P5
x_3	Alice sends Bob one Bitcoin		$h(x)_3$	L9D1u&vOp

In computer science, a hash is a function h to convert a piece of arbitrarily sized information x into a fixed-length object $h(x)$ (Knuth 1998, p. 513). Furthermore, a good hash function changes the appearance of the information in such a way that it appears random (Tab. 1). The connection of two elements of meaning forming a symbolic relationship of course brings to mind the Saussurean semiotic model of *signifiant* and *signifié* (de Saussure 1916) and will be explored in depth below.

In information systems, these objects are used to quickly identify pieces of information. Even subtle errors in the original information x are easily identifiable when the information is looked up by its hashed value $h(x)$ because a maximum of nine digits has to be compared before the difference is found. If a computer compared instances x_1 and x_2 (Tab. 1), it would take twelve digits before the computer could detect the difference between "the dog bites the cat" and "the dog bit the cat". That is because the evaluation up to "the dog bit" is the same for x_1 and x_2. If, however, the information is compared by the hashes, the computer can determine at the first digit that the information is not equal, because $h(x)_1$ starts with "H" while $h(x)_2$ starts with "X". Furthermore, hash functions ideally produce no coincidental hashes, meaning that for every possible piece of information, a different hash is generated (Knuth 1998, p. 513). This leads to a situation where any possible piece of information can be identified by exactly one hash.

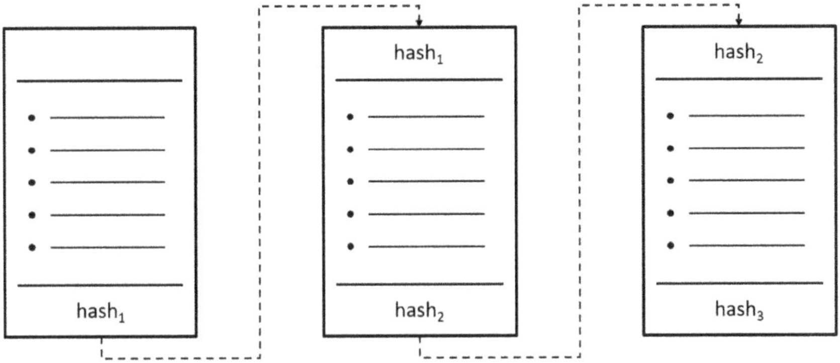

Fig. 1: Schematic representation of the Blockchain. Blocks of transactions are chained together by hashes, making any change made along the chain noticeable in the last hash.

This method is used to chain together blocks of transactions which constitute the literal *block-chain*. The information in each block of transactions is hashed. The hash is then fed into the header of the following block and will be hashed along with the block's transaction information to constitute the next hash. This hash is, in turn, fed into the next block, and so forth *ad infinitum* (Fig. 1). If someone were to change a piece of information in the first block, $hash_1$ would change completely. Since it is fed into the second block and hashed together with the transactions therein, $hash_2$ would now also change its appearance. Even $hash_3$ in the third and most recent block in this example would be affected by any change in the first block. Thus, alterations in the history of transactions would be immediately noticeable.

Blockchains are a specific form of DLT. Hence, all of the claims related to DLT are true for Blockchains as well. This means that this ledger object, the Blockchain, is available not to a central entity, but to an entire network of nodes handling copies of the same ledger object. This means that nodes can detect changes in the transaction history by comparing copies of the same ledger object to one another and agreeing upon which is the correct copy. How this is achieved will be formally addressed below (Section 1.1.4) at which point also a more systematical comparison to language will be introduced.

For now, it suffices to understand the principles of the Blockchain and that it is a specific instance of DLT. This is further evidenced by other renowned DLT projects which are explicitly not Blockchains. For instance, the cryptocurrency *IOTA* calls its network architecture a (Block-) *Tangle* (Popov et al. 2020) in which transactions validate each other rather than being grouped into blocks. The cryptocurrency *Nano* uses a structure called a block lattice in which each account operates on its Blockchain (Pugh & Chung 2017). Another project, *Hedera,* uses a hash graph to secure transactions. In this instance, rather than binding transactions into blocks, they are timestamped and calculated in rounds (Baird et al. 2020). These technologies won't be covered in detail but should illustrate that the technological variety in DLT doesn't allow equating it with the Blockchain.

1.1.3. Cryptocurrency

Cryptocurrencies are another level of specificity. Modern cryptocurrencies are DLT and they can (but needn't) be Blockchains. They are characterised by the type of information that is recorded on them. While DLT can in principle represent any kind of information, cryptocurrencies are built for the specific purpose of being used as digital money. This makes the information to be kept track of simpler. For example, when a DLT is used to keep records of land ownership, proprietaries, changes to the parcel's shape, selling prices, the exact location of the parcel, and more information has to be recorded. For a cryptocurrency, there is only an account and a balance of deposits and withdrawals, making the ledger object less burdened with information.

It is obvious how this specific use case of DLT and Blockchain technologies is more disconnected from the comparison with language than what is tried to achieve in this chapter. But to shed some light on the semiotic properties of cryptocurrencies, one may consider that primitive cryptocurrencies have been used since the Middle Ages or maybe even the Upper Palaeolithic, in the form of tally sticks. A tally stick is a fibrous piece of wood, split in half such that the common origin of both halves can be identified by putting them together. If the split aligns, they stem from the same piece of wood. Now, whenever a transaction of very simple informatic value, such as the liquidation of monthly debt, is accounted for by two parties, the tally is put together and a notch is struck into the surface such that it is visible to both sides of the split. Each party then conserves half of the tally. In principle, this can be regarded as an early form of cryptocurrency. It satisfies the requirement of a DLT in that it is a ledger object without centralised control. It is a ledger because information can be deleted from it; once struck into the wood, notches cannot be taken out of it. And it has simple distributed control because no one person can append information without the other being present and consenting.

The only proper difference between modern cryptocurrencies and the tally technique is that the latter doesn't scale well. It lacks the ability to represent more complex information, such as exact amounts of money. Also, the destination of any payment on the same tally is fixed, in that it refers to two people and those two people only. So, a tally stick can only be used when this contextual information is known. This is semiotically speaking non-trivial because modern transactions require a more sophisticated representation of information. In terms of information technology, this is a mere problem of memory. The mathematically more important difference is that a tally stick can only distribute the information across two parties. Upscaling this technique could be achieved by something like wooden discs cut into 'pizza slices'. Rings of incremental diameter could be cut across the disc for each confirmed transaction. However, this would quickly prove to be impractical, as all the parties would have to be present for each transaction. Also, the slices would have to be arranged in the same order every time, such that the authenticity of each slice can be confirmed at the junction of its two neighbours. Modern digital cryptocurrencies achieve a solution to scale to a degree where hundreds of thousands of users worldwide can make use of the same payment system.

Semiotically, however, there is a subtle but much more fundamental difference than the issue of scalability. Cryptocurrencies are rather interesting because the asset that is recorded on the distributed ledger isn't a good, but the information itself *is* the money. Glaser (2017) distinguishes Type 1 ledgers from Type 2 ledgers. Type 2 ledgers are those in which information from the outside world is recorded onto the ledger. This information can be ownership of land, a security clearance level of access for a government official, or an authenticity certificate for a piece of art. Cryptocurrencies, on the other hand, are Type 1 ledgers, namely those in which the information on the chain only ever refers to information on the chain itself. There is no representation of external, or real-world information. Cryptocurrencies generally do not emulate amounts of money that exist in other currencies, such as Euros or Yens[17]. Rather, the asset of the cryptocurrency is created on the Blockchain itself and only ever refers to information on the Blockchain. In this sense, cryptocurrencies are not representative but self-referential. The transactions *are* the value that they represent. This is going to become evident once Bitcoin's mining algorithm is explained. This is of special interest in that it relates to language, which doesn't exist *a priori* for humans to be

---

17 While some cryptocurrencies such as *Ripple* and *Tether* have attempted to represent or be backed by real-world currencies, such projects are rather scarce.

used, but it comes into existence through usage itself (Tomasello 2003; Beckner et al. 2009)[18] as will be explained in more detail below.

While the self-referential nature of cryptocurrencies has sometimes been used to discredit them, this observation of the semiotics of money is quite old. Since the past century, it has been argued that money doesn't have any representative value whatsoever and only gains its value from its use as a means of exchange (Simmel 1900). It is, so to speak, a non-semiotic object, that only gains value under the notion of credit, which literally means trust (lat.: "crēdere" → "to believe", "to trust that something is true") in the fact that it will be accepted as a means of payment. If the parties in a transaction don't trust the institution of money or each other's intentions for the transaction, the asset becomes meaningless. In this sense, money and cryptocurrencies behave semiotically rather differently from other meaningful objects. This circumstance is one of the reasons why the notion of trust is so central for activists in the space. On the one hand, they seek to eliminate trust in the middle-man (Klems et al. 2017), on the other hand, they trust that a technological system makes the asset inherently more valuable (cf. Wright & De Filippi 2015; Reijers & Coeckelbergh 2018, section 1). This is one specific terminological confusion about trust in the literature that is pointed out by some researchers (Hawlitschek et al. 2018), as was briefly mentioned above. The relevance of this semiotic issue for language will be explored systematically below (Section 1.3.3).

1.1.4. Bitcoin

Bitcoin is designed as a *Peer-to-Peer Electronic Cash System* (Nakamoto 2008)[19]. It is hence a DLT, because it works peer-to-peer, without centralised control. It is furthermore a cryptocurrency since it can only be used for quasi-financial transactions and no other type of information. In the original publication, it is furthermore explicitly stated that Bitcoin is a Blockchain (Fig. 2).

18 Although other conceptions of language exist, this dissertation explicitly subscribes to usage-based accounts of language evolution. The author takes this to be an axiomatic underpinning of this study. Without this presumption, a network-based approach to language would not be feasible.

19 To the knowledge of the author, the identity of Satoshi Nakamoto hasn't been accounted for yet. There is speculation about the person, or group of people, who could have used this pseudonym in order to publish the Bitcoin whitepaper.

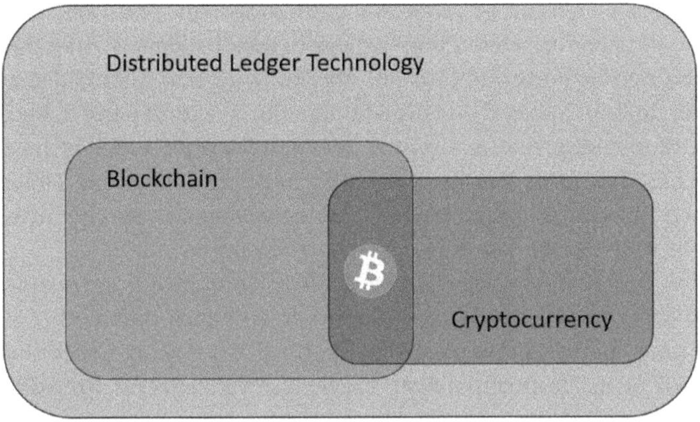

Fig. 2: Venn diagram of the relationship between Bitcoin, Blockchain, Cryptocurrency, and DLT. While every Blockchain and cryptocurrencies are DLT, not all DLT are necessarily either of the latter.

Bitcoin was the first Blockchain to exist in the world, whereas the theoretical conception had been discussed beforehand. But technically, the specificity of Bitcoin as compared to other cryptocurrencies is twofold. Firstly, Bitcoin is the first fully-distributed technology to solve the double-spending problem (Sherman et al. 2019). It, secondly, does so by using Proof-of-Work (PoW), a technique that is not common to all cryptocurrencies or DLT. Understanding these two core concepts is the key to understanding Bitcoin and cohesively discriminating it from other cryptocurrencies. The two concepts are intricately linked to one another. Double spending and PoW as technical terms are of no further interest for the following discussions of language. However, understanding the informatic and semiotic processes behind them on a high level of abstraction is important to understand the subsequent notion of consensus, which will play a key role throughout the linguistic sections of this study.

1.1.4.1. Double Spending

Double spending refers to the possibility that a digital asset such as Bitcoin could be copied, thus spent twice, and inflate the currency available in the system. This can be conceptualised as counterfeit money, which has a similar inflationary effect on traditional assets.

Assume that Alice has one Bitcoin. Alice could send that Bitcoin to Bob and right after that send it to Charlotte because the Bitcoin is not bound to a coin or piece of paper which can be physically given away. Since the coin isn't printed on a piece of paper or pressed onto a piece of metal, counterfeiting this type of money can only be prevented by Charlotte's knowing that Alice had already sent her Bitcoin to Bob. This can be solved by appointing a third party to be the judge of valid transactions, that is a central entity to keep the order of transactions (i.e., the fact that Alice sent her Bitcoin to Bob first) on record. However, the centralised solution is what Bitcoin explicitly attempts to circumvent, thus solving the problem for distributed systems (Nakamoto 2008).

Bitcoin's protocol achieves this by publicly announcing every transaction, such that every node in the network knows 'where' each Bitcoin is at any given point in time. This, however, raises the problem of knowing which transaction has arrived at its destination first. The ledger can become disorderly when transactions are just put into the network without any further authentication. Differing speeds between Internet connections or physical distance between two nodes in the network can lead to conflicting situations. For example, when Alice sends her Bitcoin to Bob and quickly thereafter to Charlotte, Bob and Charlotte might be in disagreement about which transaction was sent first. Hence transactions, when announced, are grouped into blocks which have to be authenticated before being accepted by the Blockchain.

1.1.4.2. Proof-of-Work (PoW)

Since no central entity is granted the constant right to decide on the correct order of transactions in a distributed network, the question of authority on the acceptance or rejection of blocks becomes imminent. If the same node is tasked with the authentication of information for each block, the network stops being distributed, because it centralises decision-making in a single node. Hence, a new node has to be granted the authority of checking the correctness of information for each block. But the network doesn't benefit from randomly granting the authenticator role to a different node each time. Nakamoto (2008) argues that there has to be an incentive to accurately check for the correctness of information in a block, which is an extrinsic motivation that nodes work for.

Bitcoin opts for PoW as a method of providing incentive. PoW was initially created in an effort to make spam emails undesirable (Dwork & Naor 1993). This method proposes attaching a nonce to a piece of information (i.e., an e-mail or a block of transactions). A nonce is a part of a hash that cannot be meaningfully calculated but only 'guessed' by trying out random nonces until the right one is chosen. Trying out random combinations of symbols is called brute forcing. So, the nonce has to be brute-forced before an e-mail can be sent. This random calculation generates a small amount of waste energy, that is electricity spent that doesn't serve to meaningfully calculate anything. In the case of e-mails, this doesn't affect the electricity bill of any normal user of an e-mailing service. However, if e-mails are generated by the millions to be sent out to random people, the amount of energy needed to brute-force nonces skyrockets. This dissuades users from producing millions of emails and sending them out randomly.

Now, with regards to Bitcoin, such a nonce is attached to each block of transactions. Brute-forcing the nonce gives the first node that achieves this the right to verify the block of transactions. This means that any node has to invest big amounts of electric energy in the form of calculating power to get the right to verify a block. If many nodes compete for this right to verification, the amounts of energy needed quickly shoot up, which leads to the ecological concerns about Bitcoin mentioned above (cf. Truby 2018). This raises the question of why nodes would bother to compete and invest such large amounts of calculating power into maintaining a truthful network.

This is where the term mining comes into play. Once the nonce of a block has been brute-forced, and the block has been either accepted or rejected, the node that achieved the verification is rewarded with a fixed amount of Bitcoin. This fixed amount of Bitcoin didn't exist previously in the network, it is created – or mined – in the process of verification. This is why, following Glaser (2017), it was argued above that the status of the representation of information on the Blockchain is entirely self-referential because Bitcoin is created through transactions on the Bitcoin Blockchain.

Nakamoto (2008) argues that this procedure creates incentives because investing calculating power into the maintenance of the network is rewarded with digital currency. At the same time, this reward incentivises nodes to verify blocks responsibly, because the value of the received Bitcoin hinges on the coherence of the network. If a node were to accept an incorrect block of transactions, this would be discovered at soon as the next node verified the chain and detected a discrepancy between the final hashes of the Blockchain. The security of the entire Blockchain would be compromised and the digital currency devalued, meaning that the invested energy would have resulted in being rewarded with a valueless asset.

The functioning of the network is best summarized in Nakamoto's words:

> The steps to run the network are as follows:
>
> 1) New transactions are broadcasted to all nodes.
> 2) Each node collects new transactions into a block.
> 3) Each node works on finding a difficult proof-of-work for its block [the nonce].

4) When a node finds a proof-of-work, it broadcasts the block to all nodes.
5) Nodes accept the block only if all transactions in it are valid and not already spent.
6) Nodes express their acceptance of the block by working on creating the next block in the chain, using the hash of the accepted block as the previous hash.

Nakamoto (2008, p. 3)

A formal description of these networks and the ways that information in these networks can be attacked (i.e., falsified, altered, etc.) will be provided below (Chapter 2). For the high-level conceptual description of the Blockchain, it is sufficient to say that the main goal of Bitcoin and any other distributed network is to achieve consensus. Consensus is defined as a state in which all the nodes in the network agree upon the veracity of the information. In this case, the information to be agreed upon is the record of valid transactions. Since, by architecture, the validity of one transaction depends on the validity of all publicly announced transactions, maintaining consensus between the nodes – in some sense – *is* the Blockchain[20].

To linguists, some elements of this process stand out as very similar to the nature of language. For example, it seems like a good assumption to regard speaker communities as instances of distributed networks, because the usage of language cannot be controlled by a central entity (despite political efforts of that nature in some countries), which is an assumption that is reflected in much of the theoretical, sociolinguistic literature (cf. Labov 1969, 1970, 2001; Milroy & Milroy 1992; Milroy 2002; Trudgill 2009) as well as in the methodological decisions of the experimental literature cited below (cf. Centola & Baronchelli 2015; Raviv et al. 2020). Furthermore, the element of self-reference appears to be cohesive with the classically semiotic literature, especially with Eco's notions of *Hermetic Drift* and *Unlimited Semiosis* (Eco 1990). All of these concepts and their relation to a network theory of language will be explored in more depth below, after introducing the notion of consensus as a mathematical term and its relation to language.

---

20 This is not strictly true from a technical standpoint. Bitcoin, for instance, maintains a Merkle-tree based possibility for nodes to check transactions without having to compute the entire Blockchain. Thus, a single node can be attacked and information can be altered locally, which is a problem for this node. However, it does not compromise the information on the Blockchain itself. For the sake of argument, this will not be of concern. When talking about the *Blockchain*, this refers strictly to the so-called main chain, that is the distributed ledger object containing transaction information.

1.2. Consensus as a Problem of Communication

Consensus describes a specific state in the network, namely one in which all nodes agree upon the correct information shared in the network. It was already stated that Bitcoin achieves consensus by PoW. This is, however, not the only way of achieving consensus in a distributed system. To understand consensus precisely, and to make it useful for a description of language, this section is devoted to conceptualising distributed consensus as a problem in communication.

To characterise consensus in networks properly, the notion needs to be clarified at a simpler level first. Consider communication between only two nodes, *S* and *D*. Communicative processes between an information source *S* and a destination *D* were formalised by American mathematician and cryptographer Claude Elwood Shannon, whose contributions to the aforementioned field put him at the centre of Information Theory. In communication studies and to some degree in linguistics, he is renowned for his *Mathematical Theory of Communication* (1948), republished as a book in 1949 as *The Mathematical Theory of Communication,* co-authored by Warren Weaver (Shannon & Weaver 1949). This theory formalises the process of sending information from *S* to *D* and has been popularised in both informatics and linguistics. It has sometimes been generalised to human communication (e.g., Jakobson 1961b) whereas it was intended to be used for the study of technological systems of information transmission.

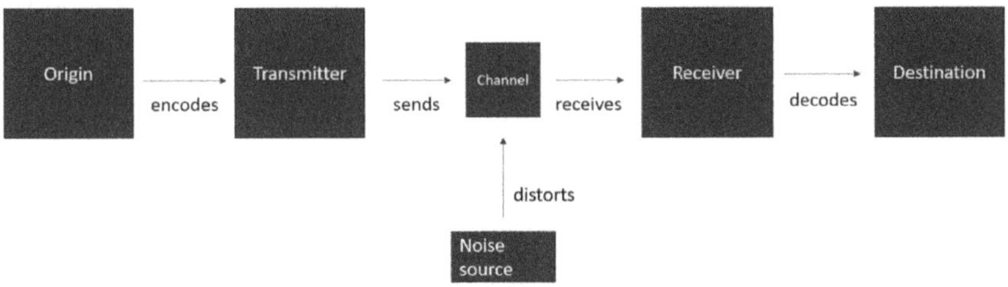

Fig. 3: Visual representation of the communication process. (Adapted from Shannon 1948)

The theory is based on the following conception of communication (Fig. 3). An information source *S* encodes a piece of information. A piece of information such as "Alice sends Bob 1 Bitcoin" for instance is coded into a string of digits by the transmitter. Analogously, a thought is 'coded' into language. This creates a message which is then sent into a channel by the transmitter. An adequate channel for a string of digits is a fibreoptic cable, whereas a linguistic message can travel through the air or be written on paper. The message arrives at a receiver, a device that is similar to the transmitter and decodes the information back into the original format. That is, the string of digits is converted back into "Alice sends Bob 1 Bitcoin", or the sentence is converted back into the original idea. Once the original information is obtained by the receiver it is fed to the destination *D* and communication is achieved. The comparison between technological communication and human language is quite clumsy since thoughts are not simply 'encoded' in language, nor is a thought 'obtained' by 'decoding' a piece of linguistic information. This particular problem will be addressed below (Section 1.3).

Within this conception of communication, consensus is a state where nodes *S* and *D* share the same information. A subtle but non-trivial second condition for consensus is that both nodes not only *share* a piece of information but *know that they share* the same piece of information. This is the core problem that Shannon addresses in his theory. A key obstacle to the communicative process is that one cannot presume to have control over the channel. For instance, if a message is sent over hundreds of kilometres via telegraph, the integrity of the wire cannot be accounted for all the way. The only way to account for the integrity of the received message is to send back a message asking whether the received information was correct or not. This message, in turn, is subject to the same problem. Practically speaking, it could be argued that it is enough to send back and forth an arbitrary number of confirming messages, such that knowledge of the correctness of the information can be assumed in practice. But given the amount of information that is communicated on the Internet, this seems to be a rather poor solution.

Furthermore, this solution is a bad one in principle. Sending messages of confirmation back and forth *ad infinitum* results in an infinite regress or un-breakable loop of messages and confirmations. This is what renders communicative systems inherently fallible (Ungeheuer 1987). To solve this problem, Shannon himself proposed the inclusion of a controller entity *C* . *C* receives both the sent and the received messages from *S* and *D* and compares them to establish *consensus* (Fig. 4).

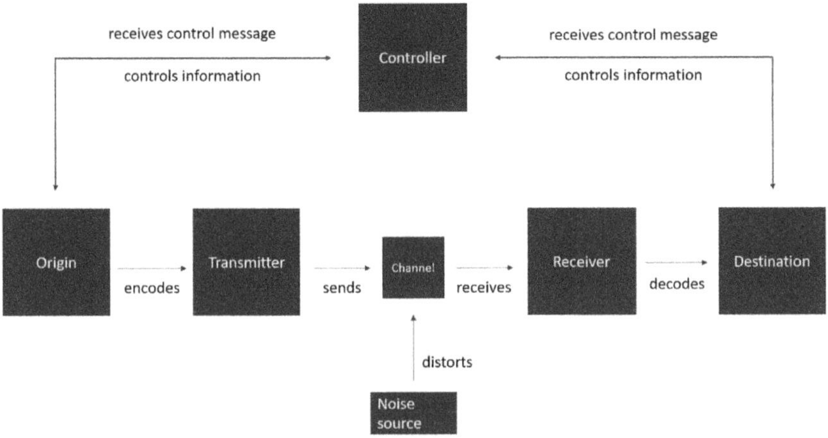

Fig. 4: Communication process with control entity adaptation. (Adapted from Shannon 1948)

With this solution in place, the previously linear communicative process starts to resemble a network structure. If it is assumed that *S*, *D* and *C* have the same technical capabilities and that these labels refer to interchangeable functions rather than distinct devices, they are three interconnected nodes. This is an example of a fully-connected network (cf. Chapter 2), meaning that messages can be sent directly from any given node to any other given node.

The circumstance that nodes are here arranged in a network solves the problem of fallibility. The nodes *S* and *D* no longer have to hope for the correct working of the channel. If something were to interfere in the channel and alter the message that arrives at *D*, either by fault or malicious intent, *C* would immediately pick up the difference between the messages and alert *S* and *D* that the message is incorrect. The judgement of *C* thus establishes consensus between the nodes if no fault is detected in the messages. But this is not a perfect solution. If an external party were to attack both the channel and *C*, they could still make *S* and *D* believe that they share the same piece of information. However, this requires – at the very least – considerably more effort and malicious intent from an external party.

In terms of centralisation and distribution, the question is which node is tasked with the function of *C*. In a centralised network, *C* would always be executed by the same node. For instance, in a centralised banking system, different accounts could take on the function of *S* and *D* and send money back and forth between them. But it would always be the central banking entity that would provide the functions covered by *C*. It was stated above that this centralisation is sometimes regarded as an excess of power concerning central banking entities (Klems et al. 2017). What's more, it is also less secure. If *C* is always executed by the same node in a network, an attacker only needs to control one *C* in order to control all the messages in any potential *S* and *D*. In a distributed network, however, the function of *C* is always executed by a different node. This means that it is unpredictable which node would have to be attacked to control all the information in the system.

The important question to be solved for a distributed system is how to decide on the node to execute the function of *C* for any communication (i.e., transaction). As explained above, Bitcoin uses a PoW algorithm to solve this issue. This means that nodes use their calculating power to compete for their 'worthiness' of executing *C*, thus contributing to maintaining the network and being rewarded with digital currency.

There are, however, a plethora of other ways to achieve consensus. Instead of proving the contribution to upholding the network by work (PoW), other algorithms have been proposed. King and Nadal (2012), for instance, proposed Proof-of-Stake (PoS) as a solution for the high energy consumption of PoW. In PoS, the worthiness to validate transactions is proven by stake, meaning that whoever has the most to lose in the network, has the highest probability of validating a block. Other algorithms include consensus algorithms such as Proof-of-Activity (Bentov et al. 2014) and even Proof-of-Luck (Milutinovic et al. 2016). Witherspoon (2017) distinguishes at least eight different types of consensus algorithms, each with their variations and ways of functioning. Anwar (2018) distinguishes 14 prototypes of consensus algorithms, with each implementation having different properties. These differences between implementations concern mining, for example. Not all cryptocurrencies are mined by validating blocks. For some cryptocurrencies, a fixed amount of currency is in circulation, meaning that establishing consensus doesn't generate new value on the chain and that other incentives have to be found.

In addition, remember that not all DLT are Blockchains. That is, while all DLT face the problem of establishing consensus, not all of them do so by chaining blocks of transactions together (cf. Pugh & Chung 2017; Baird et al. 2020; Popov et al. 2020), further complicating the landscape of different consensus algorithms. This is why, rather than focussing on the specifics of different consensus algorithms, a more general conception of consensus was established. When dealing with semiotic properties of consensus in the next sections, no validity is claimed for all types of consensus algorithms. The focus will either be on the problem of consensus as such or the particular solution being provided for it in each instance.

In light of contemporary theories of language, the description of consensus as a state of shared information between two people appears reductionist. This will be explored in more detail in the following section, drawing upon three distinct axes of comparison: (i) Representation, (ii) perlocution, and (iii) self-containment. But before entering this detailed level, a general description of the disconnect between linguistic and technological theories of consensus and communication is in order.

One of the most integrative theories on language is Halliday's *Systemic Functional Grammar* (SFG) (Halliday & Matthiessen 2014)[21], in that it is based on both the formal analysis of linguistic structures (a legacy of the Prague school's influence on his work) emphasising the concept of system and the description of the eco-social environment in which "language had evolved [...] carrying out certain critical functions" (Halliday 2013, p. 15). This is where Halliday's holistic description of language differs from the technical characterisation of the Mathematical Theory of Communication. In the latter, the achievement of consensus is the end itself, and the means by which this is achieved are mere devices of technical problem-solving. In Halliday's conception, the structures of language are far less straightforwardly goal-oriented, because "the explanations of linguistic phenomena needed to be sought in relationships among systems rather than in relationships among structures" (ibid.). This means that linguistic structures (e.g., subjunctive, conditional, gerund) don't simply evolve to be suited to any one specific objective, such as representing propositional truth or establishing social consensus. Rather, systems of linguistic structure (i.e., mood, as opposed to its structural components: subjunctive, conditional, gerund) interact with other structures (e.g., the lexicon of a language) to suit different *meta-functions* of language that are, in turn, interdependent and modulate each other.

Halliday and Matthiessen (2014) distinguish three metafunctions of language. The (i) ideational metafunction refers to language as an epistemic tool that is, using language to the end of making sense of the world, conceptualising the things that can be observed in the world and planning action. The (ii) interpersonal metafunction of language relates to language as a tool for building relationships with other human beings. Language fulfils this function whenever it adequately reflects (and/or constructs) the relationship with others through the expression

21 For reference in this thesis, the fourth edition from 2014 was used. The first edition of the *Introduction to Functional Grammar* was published by Halliday in 1985.

of appropriate social distance or the negotiation of communicative power. Lastly the (iii) textual metafunction of language calls for its grammatical soundness. That is, language can only adequately fulfil the ideational and interpersonal metafunctions if its systematic properties allow for the creation of cohesion and continuity in discourse.

Importantly, for Halliday, these metafunctions are not hierarchically organized, but are interdependent and support each other. As was briefly mentioned, the interpersonal and ideational metafunctions are dependent on the textual metafunction. But at the same time, the ideational metafunction and the textual metafunctions are dependent on the interpersonal metafunction in that making sense of the world is not merely an individual endeavour. Rather, linguistic meaning and the resulting structures are, to a certain extent, negotiated collectively (Tylén et al. 2013). Lastly, the interpersonal metafunction is dependent on the other two in that the interpersonal relationships that can be constructed through language are restricted by the textual resources that a language puts at speakers' disposition and by how social relations are construed ideationally in a given social context.

Now, it is clear that the notion of consensus becomes, under such a conception of language, more complex. Whereas the previous model of communication reduces consensus to the equality of states of information (including knowledge of the state of equality), consensus in a systemic functional conception of language has to be measured against the function that is foregrounded in a given speech act. If a given speech act is oriented toward the negotiation of a social relationship, (i.e., the interpersonal metafunction of language), consensus may require one type of information to be shared among agents (e.g., using expressions to refer to the other that don't threaten their face; cf. Brown & Levinson 1987), whereas consensus on textual elements of communication might be more oriented toward the most adequate way of phrasing something to make it cohesive. It was argued in the previous paragraph that these levels of meaning are all interdependent, so proper consensus should integrate all three levels of meaning, but one can easily construct situations in which one metafunction takes primacy over the others. Consider the ongoing societal debate on the use of pronouns for different gender identities[22]. Proponents of the usage of novel pronouns might argue that any

22 The author won't cite linguistic literature on this issue, because the example serves to explain how different metafunctions of language relate to the notion of consensus. The example is chosen as a socially relevant issue which readers can relate to, not in order to settle academic questions on the linguistics of gender, for which neither this study nor the author are qualified.

person should have a right to be identified by others in the same way that they identify themselves. This argument appeals to the interpersonal metafunction of language. Supporters of this argument might foreground that adequacy lies in a more appropriate reflection of a respectful relationship between speakers. Opponents of the use of pronouns might argue that the innovation of pronouns may unduly affect the cohesiveness of the grammatical system, that is, the textual metafunction of language because the introduction of new pronouns goes against those speakers' aesthetic intuitions about language. At the same time, opponents might argue that the introduction of new pronouns is inadequate concerning the metafunction of ideation because it introduces linguistic categories that don't reflect the biological categories of human beings. This is not to say that proponents of inclusive language couldn't argue on the ideational or textual level, nor does the author subscribe to the latter two arguments. What the example shows is that consensus between two or three people who would use these arguments in debate are set up to fail in the establishment of consensus from the beginning because they require different things from language. While the former person foregrounds the interpersonal metafunction of language, the latter two insist on the ideational and textual metafunctions respectively, resulting in a situation where consensus is essentially unachievable.

This short example shows that consensus in human communication may well require the integration of much more levels of meaning and communicative choices than what the Mathematical Theory of Communication presumes. The reference to Halliday and Matthiessen (2014) here serves as an introductory consideration about the subtle (or not so subtle) differences between the semiotic properties of consensus in computational vs. human contexts. In the following, the comparison of their semiotic properties in regard to consensus is explored in more detail.

1.3. Semiotic Properties of Consensus

In the previous section, it was argued that the main function of DLT, namely the establishment of consensus in the network, can and has been described as and accounted for as an extension of *The Mathematical Theory of Communication* (Shannon 1948). For the sake of readability, some comparisons between the semiotic aspects of language and distributed computer systems were drawn rather naïvely for ease of reading. The same is true for the reservations expressed above based on Halliday and Matthiessen (2014). The present section now sets out to explore whether and to which degree these simple comparisons are adequate when examined in detail, drawing upon more of the semiotic literature.

The underlying question is whether or not the same model is suitable to describe aspects of both human and computer communication. The attempt is aimed at identifying those aspects of networks which can be used to make meaningful comparisons to communication in human groups and to make educated guesses on human language even when the underlying theory isn't based on human language, to begin with. Three distinct semiotic elements are going to be of interest. The first, *Representation in Language and Distributed Systems* (Section 1.3.1), draws upon the concept of function, in a mathematical sense, to assess the similarities and differences in representational processes between language and computer systems. The second, *Perlocution in Language and Distributed Systems* (cf. Section 1.3.2) integrates notions of speech act theory. Lastly, *Self-Containment of Information in Language and Distributed Systems* (Section 1.3.3) deals with the ontological status of information in either type of system. These sections do, *grosso modo*, correspond to Halliday's metafunctions of language in that representation relates to ideation, speech acts refer to interpersonal relations, and the ontological status of information refers to the cohesiveness of the informational system concerning the information contained therein.

Shannon's (1948) theory was arguably very influential, not only in informatics but in linguistics as well. The tome *Structure of Language and its Mathematical Aspects* (Jakobson 1961a) contains several linguistic contributions which are based on the technological understanding at the time. Chomsky, whose work has earlier been characterised under this perspective (Section 0.4.1.2), is one of the contributors to this volume. But in this context, a contribution by Russian formalist Roman Jakobson himself is of crucial interest. Jakobson (1961b) provides a close examination of Shannon's theory of communication and its applicability to language. This publication reveals that also Jakobson's linguistics in general, and his theory of the poetic function of language in particular, are crucially influenced by the technological precepts of his time.

In *Linguistics and Poetics* (1960), Jakobson distinguishes six functions of linguistic messages. The function of the linguistic message is dependent on which of the six elements of communication the message is directed at. If the message is directed at the addresser it is called "emotive", if it is directed at the addressee it is called "conative", messages directed at the context are "referential", directed at the code "metalingual", at the channel "phatic", and finally, messages directed at themselves are said to be "poetic" (Jakobson 1960, p. 357). These six elements of communication, however, are borrowed from the *Mathematical Theory of Communication*. Even though Jakobson (1960) doesn't cite Shannon's (1948) work in *Linguistics and Poetics*, his comparison between *Linguistics and Communication Theory* (1961b) makes explicit reference to Shannon and Weaver

(1949) and resorts to their theory to inform his own. It would thus be plausible to identify the Jakobsonian theory of linguistic functions as an additional path on which technological knowledge, as shaped by a strong computer metaphor, has found its way into the study of language.

In the following, the adequacy of *the Mathematical Theory of Communication* for the study of language will be examined. Where Jakobson (1961b) restricts his evaluation to simple communicative processes from *sender* to *receiver*, the present evaluation aims to emphasise the aspect of consensus in networks. That is, the comparison is between formal communication in Blockchain (or similar) networks and communication between groups of people, rather than single interactions. Furthermore, there is architectural equivalence between both types of communication networks which motivates our quest for functional comparison. In the terminology employed by Araújo and Banisch (2016), both would be considered level-1 networks, meaning that the constituents of these networks are physically directly linked to each other (i.e., speakers to other speakers via air as their physical medium for interaction and computers to other computers via fibreoptic cable as their physical medium for interaction, Section 3.3.3). In more semiotic terms, these networks exhibit what in Peircean terms would be called *diagrammatic iconicity*. That is, there is a relation of similarity (iconicity) in the organisation of relationships (diagrammaticity) between humans and computers as the nodes of a network and the relationships of interaction among them as edges of such networks (Chapter 2). Both conceptions warrant a further comparison between human and computer network semiotics, in addition to the reasons put forth above (Chapter 0). This will be done in the following three sections comparing Shannon's (1948) and Jakobson's (1961b) conception of communication, focussing on three aspects (i) representation (Section 1.3.1), (ii) perlocution (Section 1.3.2), and (iii) self-containment of information (Section 1.3.3).

1.3.1. Representation in Language and Distributed Systems

The first and most basic level of comparison concerns assumptions about the semiotic processes of representation of information in communication. Shannon was mainly preoccupied with the circumvention of the fallibility of communication. The task for Shannon was to carry messages securely from *S* to *D* ensuring that the correct information be obtained at the destination. The communicative problem that he solves by introducing the controller *C* is that of a noise source, which compromises the channel and hence distorts the message (Fig. 4). The main problem in communication is hence the delivery of a message. Communicative problems at the stage of encoding and decoding the message are not a concern in this model, because codes are not very prone to error, from a mathematical standpoint. This will be problematised in the light of human language further below.

Mathematically speaking, a code is a function, that is a semiotic connection that maps one set of symbols (*X*) onto another (*Y*), resembling the de Saussurean conception of signifiant and signifié creating a bilateral link between ideas and words for these ideas (de Saussure 1916). But the mathematical conception of functions lets us explore this relationship in far greater detail. A function is a rule that determines which elements from a set *X* map onto which elements of a set *Y*. There are different properties that these functions can have with regard to the sets that they connect. It is for instance possible that there is exactly one element in set *X* that is equivalent to exactly one element in set *Y*, in which case mathematicians speak of an injective and surjective, that is a bijective function (Fig. 5a). In other cases, there might be more elements in set *Y* than in set *X*, resulting in a function where not every element in *Y* is assigned an element in *X*, which is an injective but not surjective function (Fig. 5b). Depending on the properties and connections between the two sets of symbols, different classes of function can be determined (Fig. 5).

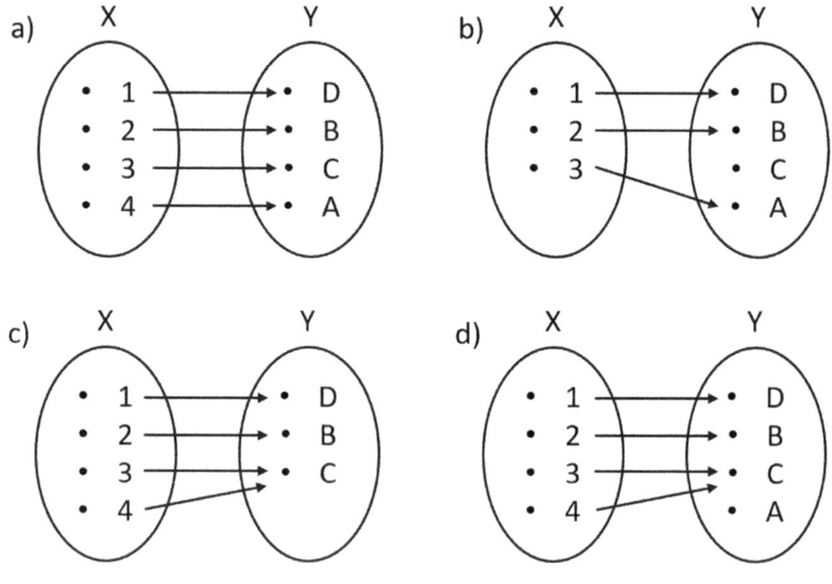

Fig. 5: Different types of function mappings. (a) injection and surjection (bijection), (b) injection and non-surjection, (c) non-injection and surjection, (d) non-injection and non-surjection. (Diagrams adapted from Wall 1972, p. 125)

Compare for example the sets of elements that compose the Morse code to the standard Latin alphabet. If all the symbols in Morse are in *X* and all the letters of the standard Latin alphabet are in *Y*, then there is a function that maps each symbol from *X* onto exactly one character in *Y*; a bijective function. If, however, the Morse symbols are mapped onto the Spanish Latin alphabet that includes the letters <ñ>, <é>, <í>, <á>, …, there are no Morse symbols that map exactly onto these characters – the function is injective but not surjective (Fig. 5b).

There are other cases like the non-injective functions, in which two elements from *X* can map onto the same element in *Y* (Fig. 5c, d). This is the case for instance in the case of the relationship between the Spanish Latin alphabet and the sounds represented by it. For etymological reasons, the two graphemes <v> and <b> both plot onto the same voiced bilabial plosive phoneme /b/ in the onset position and onto its voiced labio-dental fricative allophone /v/ in the intervocalic position. The Spanish Latin alphabet is hence, notwithstanding its high grapheme-phoneme fidelity not a bijective function between writing and phonemic realisation, but an injective and non-surjective function.

An example of a non-injective non-surjective function (Fig. 5d) is the mapping of writing onto pronunciation in those variations of Spanish that have the phoneme /ʃ/. Here, this doesn't refer to the well-described allophone [ʃ] to the Standard Spanish /ʎ/ (<ll>), or /j/ (<y>) like in the Rioplatense varieties (Michnowicz & Planchón 2020), nor to the deaffrication of /ʧ/ to [ʃ] in Panama, Puerto Rico (Lipski 2011, p. 81) and Northern Mexico (Méndez 2017). The example is a proper phoneme which could be argued to exist in Guatemalan Spanish, where the minimal pair /‘ʃeka/, <sheca> (intelligent, m./f.) vs. /‘ʧeka/, <checa> (Czech, f.) occurs. This opposition speaks to the phonemic autonomy of /ʃ/ rather than its being allophone to either /ʧ/ or /ʎ/. In this case, Guatemalans colloquially spell /ʃ/ combining <s> and <h> into <sh>, meaning that no codified spelling exists for /ʃ/. In terms of mappings from spelling onto speech, this means non-surjection because /ʃ/ as an element of *Y* has no correspondent single element in *X*. Furthermore, the convergence of <v> and <b> on /b/ is still given in this Spanish variety, making this mapping a non-injective, non-surjective, function.

Importantly, and this is one of the core elements in the definition of a code as a function, there is no situation (Fig. 5) in which one element of set *X* can map onto various elements of *Y*. A function is never ambiguous with regard to its outcome. If a function such as $f(x) = x + 2$ is applied to $x = 2$, it is inconceivable that $f(x)$ be anything else than 4. On the other hand, there can be the same result for different *x* in certain types of functions. For example, if $f(x) = |x + 2|$, both $x = 2$ and $x = -6$ result in $f(x) = 4$. There is no code in which the same element from *X* maps on various elements in *Y*. In the following, it will be shown that the definition of linguistic signs as code is unsuitable in most cases, precisely because linguistic signs can have more than one meaning at the same time. This is ultimately the result of an attempt at reducing the semiotic capacities of humans (and other animals) to a binary system of a signifying (signifiant) and a signified (signifié) entity, as put forth in the *Cours de Linguistique Générale* (de Saussure 1916), which was edited and published three years after de Saussure had died in 1913 by his students Charles Bally and Albert Sechehaye, who misrepresented de Saussure's authentic triadic semiotics by reducing it to a dyadic model (Fehr 2003; Spielmann 2004).

While the theoretical underpinnings of the semiotic misconceptions of a dyadic model have been sufficiently accounted for, the practical implications of this highly theoretical controversy can be exemplified by evaluating the types of errors that occur in human communication as opposed to computer communication. A definition of representation as dyadic code leads to a mischaracterisation of such errors.

As argued above, Jakobson (1960) was influenced by Shannon and Weaver's *Mathematical Theory of Communication* (1949), but orients his model toward the question of function, leading to different types of communication errors. For a communicative process in the sense of Shannon (1948), the notion of code implies that, as long as the same arbitrary code is selected for encoding and decoding of the message (and as long as the controller *C* protects the message from distortions in the channel), the conditions for successful communication are met. In Jakobson (1960) however, a wrong evaluation of the function of a message results in a different type of communicative error. For instance, if an interlocutor interprets the question "It's so cold in here" as referential rather than conative, chances are that the communication is going to be unsuccessful. In the former case, the interlocutor understands the sentence as a mere description of an extra-communicative circumstance. In the latter case, the interlocutor understands that they are being asked to close the window. Arguably, these interpretations clash and produce unsuccessful situations of communication. In one interpretation, the window is shut by the interlocutor, while it remains open in the other case. If the communicative intention of the speaker was to have it shut, the situation then qualifies as miscommunication. In the behaviourist interpretation of the communicative model (Watzlawick et al. 1967), this leads to the second axiom of communication. According to this axiom, various levels of communication are interwoven with one another, and the referential content of communication is always evaluated against the standard of the relationship between two interlocutors. As for the above example, it could be argued that a conative interpretation of "It's so cold in here" depends on the quality of the relationship between the interlocutors, and the benevolence of the hearer to interpret the sentence as such.

This is precisely why less restrictive theories of human language cannot afford to reduce their theoretical scope to two elements of signification. A popular example of a non-reductionist theory of signification is Karl Bühler's *Sprachtheorie* (1934). The Organon Model produced therein proposes, much as the authentic de Saussure (cf. Fehr 2003), a triadic model, in which the sender *S* and receiver *D* can only engage in communication in reference to a common context *C*[23]. That is, the semiotic relationship mediating the meaning of a linguistic sign has – at the very least – three constituents whose prominence determines the function of language in any given case. If the sign mainly refers to *S*, it is called a symptom; if it refers mainly to *D*, it is called a signal; and if it refers mainly to *C*, it is called a symbol. Now, the above example can be interpreted in this way: If the sentence "It's so cold in here" is interpreted as a symbol, it may not lead to the desired outcome (namely the window being shut by the interlocutor). However, if the sign is correctly interpreted as a signal, the interlocutor may well understand that the sign is meant as an indication to shut the window. Bühler's *Sprachtheorie* is venerable in two regards that can be pointed out in this limited review of his work. Firstly, it is way ahead of its time in terms of the weight it gives to the relationship between interlocutors, a point of view that has been replicated by many scholars in the fields of communication and linguistics (Austin 1962; Watzlawick et al. 1967; Labov 1969, 1970, 2001; Searle 1969; Grice 1975; Latour 1996). Secondly, the Organon Model derives different contextual functions of language from its constituent parts, a formal-logical element that is employed by Jakobson (1960, 1961b) much later and that functionally enables us to characterise different types of miscommunications such as the "It's so cold" example stated above.

This type of miscommunication cannot be reduced to an error in the transmission of information alone, because the same information is transmitted, but with different communicative outcomes. The problem that Shannon (1948) was interested in is hence not a main – or at least not the only – source of error in human communication. That is because a dyadic model of representation, where

23 The shorthands *S*, *D*, and *C* are here maintained to cohere with the previously established terminology resulting from Shannon and Weaver (1949). In Bühler's (1934) original contribution these are referred to as "Sender" (ger.: "Sender" → "sender"), "Empfänger" (ger.: "Empfänger" → "receiver", "addressee", "destination"), and "Gegenstände und Sachverhalte" (ger.: "Gegenstände und Sachverhalte" → "objects and facts", or "context" for short).

reference to information is equalled to meaning, is systematically insufficient for the semiotic behaviour of human beings (Spielmann 2004), for which some examples have been given throughout this section.

In some sense, the presumption of a Classical Saussurean model of representation in Shannon's Theory of Communication (albeit without any reference nor identifiable explicit inspiration thereof) presupposes that information can be unequivocally encoded and decoded into and from a message. In Bally and Sechehaye's interpretation of the Saussurean model of the (linguistic) sign of signifiant and signifié (De Saussure 1916), the word tree refers to the physical object called a tree, which can be observed in nature and, *vice versa* the existence of physical trees calls for the establishment of a name for them by arbitrary social convention (de Saussure 1916).

This model of linguistic representation has been relatively unchallenged in modern introductions to linguistics. But Bally and Sechehaye's interpretation of de Saussure's linguistics has received critique and counterarguments on a variety of levels. On the one hand, the exclusive arbitrariness of the relationship between the signifiant and signifié has been challenged quite quickly after its postulation. Ogden and Richards (1923) argue that a third element lies between the signifier and the signified, which they call symbol and referent respectively. For these authors, the relationship between symbol and referent isn't direct but is mediated by a third element, namely the thought that a referent brings about. Furthermore, the relationship between thought and referent is causal, which implies that signs are not brought about in an entirely arbitrary fashion, but that there is some degree of adequacy in the relationship of meaning between the symbol and the referent. In a more recent, empirical study, it is argued that linguistic sign systems benefit from a mix of differently motivated signs, wherein iconic (e.g., onomatopoetic), systematic (e.g., reduplication of syllables to express higher intensity), and arbitrary signs balance each other out in a language such as to optimise for the cognitive economy of a language (Dingemanse et al. 2015). This ultimately challenges the idea of pure arbitrary linguistic signs that the *Cours de Linguistique Générale* (De Saussure 1916) implies.

Much more important than the nature that governs the relationship between signifiant and signifié (De Saussure 1916) or symbol and referent (Ogden & Richards 1923) is the fact that this relationship is governed by a third entity. The first example of a triadic theory of signs was given under reference to Bühler's Organon Model (1934), which incorporates sender, receiver, and context as a triadic sign relationship. In the case of Ogden and Richards (1923), the triad consists of symbol, referent, and thought. Note that these triads are subtly different in that Orgen and Richards emphasise a single-minded approach to meaning, in which individual thought governs the relationship between symbol and referent, while Bühler's semiotics is already focused on the interaction between various people who interact in context.

The earliest and undoubtedly most relevant example of a triadic sign relation is the semiotics of Charles Sanders Peirce (1903), who wrote extensively about the triadic sign relationship, incorporating an interpretant as the governing relationship between what De Saussure had called signifiant and signifié. The interpretant is the relationship that is established between the two in the process of interpretation. This process of interpretation can be viewed as a communicative one, given that Charles Sanders Peirce occupied an explicit pragmatist (1878) – or later "pragmaticist" – position as also William James (1907) argues. That means that the *use* of signs in a communicative context ultimately determines the concrete meaning of a linguistic sign. Interaction thus assumes a paramount position in the semiotics of Peirce. Importantly, the interpretant is not merely another person or a palpable entity which mediates the meaning between the signifier and the signified. Rather, it is an abstract entity that governs this relationship. For example, interaction, as mentioned above, needn't necessarily refer to interaction with another person. Rather, such interaction can also refer to the interaction of different meanings among each other, for instance when a person tries to identify logical shortcomings in their argument via introspection. Although they aren't in direct interaction with another person, they can simulate objections and get to conclusions on logical fallacies in their thought. Like Jakobson (1960, 1961b) and Bühler (1934), Peirce bases his typology of different interpretants on their system of reference. Where Jakobson derives functions of language on the elements of his (i.e., Shannon's) theory of communication (cf. Jakobson 1961b), and Bühler bases them on the three elements of the *Organon Model*, Peirce (1903) bases his theory of interpretants on his three universal categories, *firstness*, *secondness*, and *thirdness*, which grossly correspond to the semiotic classes of icon, index, and symbol. Icons represent other things based on their similarity, that is by matching the intrinsic characteristics (firstness) of another thing. Indices represent other things through the establishment of a direct connection (secondness) between two things, such as the word "Hello!", pointing at something, or tracks of animals on the ground. Thus, the de Saussurean (1916) two-way-relationship only accounts for a subset of semiotic phenomena. And lastly, symbols derive their meaning from the establishment by a third entity, which can be (but is not reduced to being) a social convention, such as a skull representing "death" or "pirates".

While the metaphysics and logic of the Peircean semiotics are of little interest in this context, the important argument here is that Peirce (1903) discriminates at least ten types of interpretants, depending on the context in which a sign is used and how it is interpreted. This – among other arguments – makes the triadic sign relation much more viable in the context of human language than the dyadic sign model. While dyadic models of sign relations presuppose an unbreakable correspondence between signifiant and signifié *qua* definition, the triadic mediation via the interpretant allows to account for different interpretations of signs in different contexts. This, in turn, allows to explain the above example of communicative failure much more adequately. When a speaker and an interlocutor of the sentence "It is so cold in here" aren't able to converge on the same interpretant given the situation, communication fails. This explanation is much more viable than trying to account for this error by a malfunction in the decoding of an encoded message. If language were to be regarded as code, one would need to resort to arguing that the speaker and the interlocutor aren't applying the same code to the sentence "It is so cold in here". But since the definition of code in a technical sense doesn't allow a sign to refer to more than one object, this doesn't seem to be an adequate metaphor to characterise human linguistic behaviour in semiotic terms.

It is quite useful to keep the definition of code linguistically strict. This permits researchers to discriminate between human languages and programming languages; the latter are code, while the former are not. This distinction appears purely taxonomical at first but becomes relevant when examining the properties of meaning in a distributed network. Information in a distributed network is meaningful when consensus about this information is established. In other words, Alice's having sent Bob one Bitcoin is only 'true' so far as the whole network has acknowledged this fact; that is when consensus about this transaction was established. The establishment of consensus in a distributed network, to a certain degree, resembles the establishment of an interpretant in communication. Just as the interpretant coordinates the mapping of the signifiant onto a meaningful signifié, so does *C* coordinate the convergence of information in *S* and *D* (Fig. 4).

The processes are similar in that the establishment of consensus via *C* makes *S* and *D* aware of their sharing the same information, which makes the information meaningful to the network. In the same way, the interpretant makes the mapping of the signifier onto the signified meaningful, because a word doesn't *mean* anything unless it is being interpreted. At least to the extent where a pragmatic notion of meaning (Peirce 1878; James 1907) is assumed, consensus in distributed networks seems to be subject to a triadic conception of meaning, similar to human signs.

However, some differences shouldn't be put aside too naïvely. The first difference is that distributed networks, ontologically, consist of more than one agent, whereas in the Peircean theory, an individual can form an interpretant. Consensus, on the other hand, requires that various singular agents form a network together. If no transaction is made from an *S* to a *D*, there is no consensus for *C* to establish and no meaningful transmission of information can be done. As a single human being, as was pointed out above, it is possible to deliberate on one's thoughts without having to send information back and forth to another person. Not even one-sided input in the form of a book or movie is necessary to form an interpretant. The process of thinking alone requires the establishment of meaning that is cohesive with other things that are being thought. The triadic process could thus be said to be embedded in the human mind, even a single human mind, whereas nodes in an informatic network are physically dependent on other connected agents to create something like meaning through consensus.

While adult humans are of course equipped with such interpretative capacities, they are – both phylogenetically and ontogenetically – dependent on collaborative meaning-making to ground and fixate linguistic meanings (Tylén et al. 2013). But once established, meanings can be used for further semiotic processes, connecting old meanings to new ones and, in turn, using this connection to create even newer meanings, *ad infinitum*. This is the process that Umberto Eco called Unlimited Semiosis (Eco 1990). This doesn't mean that meaning isn't a collaborative effort. Experimental approaches to language and communication have shown that interaction and mutual coordination shape linguistic meanings and optimise forms for use in effective communication (Fusaroli & Tylén 2012). While computer systems are much more restricted in their semiotic capacities due to the simpler makeup of dyadic code as opposed to triadic language, both systems need interaction with other agents to create more meaningful information. That having been said, the types of meanings that groups of humans can bring forth are much more complex than those of distributed systems, simply because the triadic sign is embedded at the level of the individual, while it only exists on the level of the network in distributed networks, and not on the level of a single agent. In other words, meaning in the interaction of nodes is only triadic when nodes interact, while humans are capable of producing triadic signs on their own, at least once their semiotic capacities are fully developed.

Despite these differences, it should be expected that, if network structure affects shared information (i.e., meaning) in a network of computing agents, it should also affect meaning-making in social groups. While the individual semiotic capacities of nodes in networks are limited compared to humans, the social effects of network properties in human groups should still be detectable. The specific effects of social interaction on language will be discussed below

(Chapter 3). Once a more thorough review of the literature on graph theory (Chapter 2) and networks in linguistics (Chapter 3) has been reported, this idea will be specified such as to provide hypotheses for empirical experiments (Chapter 4).

1.3.2. Perlocution in Language and Distributed Systems

The mere representational status of information in both language and networks is a restricted perspective on the semiotic properties of either system. Much more than just representing information, language is a tool for making information. While this is reflected in Peirce's pragmatist position on semiotics, it wasn't until the 1960s that the idea of language as a tool, with a palpable impact on the real world, gained more territory in linguistics. In his seminal lecture *How to do things with words* (1962), British philosopher John L. Austin proposed an important advance for the description of the relationship between language and human action in the world. He argued that the meaning of language cannot sensibly be reduced to statements of truth and falsehood or logical propositions, as philosophers of language (e.g., Wittgenstein 1922, Russell 1940) often do. Austin evidences his claims by observation of performatives, that is expressions that bring circumstances into being by uttering them, rather than mirroring pre-existing information. For instance, the performative "I apologize" cannot be coded as true or false. Austin explains that

> the truth of the constative utterance 'he is running' depends on his being running. Whereas in [the former] case it is the happiness[24] of the performative 'I apologize' which makes the fact that I am apologizing: and my success in apologizing depends on the happiness of the performative utterance 'I apologize'. This is one way in which we might justify the 'performative-constative' distinction – the distinction between doing and saying. (Austin 1962, p. 47)

This new distinction struck a hole into the classic analytical philosophy of language, and by extension structuralist and generative approaches to language, which are based on the concept of truth for the execution of logical operations. Such operations cannot be executed on performative speech acts because the speech act brings about the reality it represents, rather than reflecting something true before the sentence was uttered.

This distinction was popularised and developed further as *Speech Act Theory* by John Searle (1969) who introduced the notions of illocution and perlocution

24 "Happiness" here means something like "adequacy" or "success in doing what one wants to do".

into linguistic pragmatism. While the illocution is that which the speaker does while uttering a sentence without necessarily saying it – such as making a promise in saying "I'll come to the party" – the perlocution is the consequence of whatever is being said, which may as well be outside the dominion of control of the speaker. For instance, the imperative "Close the window" may or may not result in a shut window. Importantly, these two concepts provide a level of connection between the level of language and the world in which human beings act. What is most important is the circumstance that facts can be brought about in the non-linguistic world via the utterance of linguistic expressions. In the end, a marriage is brought about by the shared belief in the idea that the sentence "I pronounce you wedded people" uttered by a competent authority in the right place and setting brings this marriage about, which is its force of illocution.

In the case of cryptocurrencies, the concept of illocution does appear to apply. In pragmatic terms, payment can be paraphrased as an illocutionary speech act, by which monetary value is transferred from one person to another. The utterance, so to speak, corresponds to the execution of the *send* ( ) function. Any user of a Blockchain who transfers money from their account to another one formulates a request that this transaction is recorded on the Blockchain. This amounts to executing the following function:

$$send(public\ key,\ private\ key,\ receiver's\ key)$$

The request contains the own public key (the account from which money is withdrawn), the receiver's public key (the account to which the money is deposited), and is signed by the sender with their private key to authenticate themself. Analogously, this can be treated as an utterance whose pragmatic value corresponds to an imperative illocutionary act. The user instructs their interface to append information on the Blockchain.

In terms of the limited semiotic properties that programming languages have compared to human language (cf. Section 1.3.1), this could be described as an Austinian performative. The reason for this is that, formally, the above-formulated function statement cannot be evaluated by a computer to be either true or false. This makes it different from informatic statements such as the following:

$$str('I\ have\ a\ dream!') == str("I\ have\ a\ dream!")$$

If this statement was evaluated by an R compiler, the console would just return *TRUE*, because the string '*I have a dream!*' and the string '*I have a dream!*' contain the same characters in the same order, and " " and ' ' are treated as equivalents in the evaluation. Also, consider the following statement:

$$1 + 2$$

An R or Python Console would return 3 because the compilers are constructed to assume that the characters 1 and 2 are to be interpreted as integers, upon which mathematical operations can be executed. In terms of truth statements, this is not fundamentally different from the equal string evaluation. The statement 1 + 2 can be reformulated using truth statements:

$$Return\ x\ such\ that\ "1+2=x"\ evaluates\ to\ true$$

The same reformulation cannot be meaningfully constructed for the above *send* ( ) function. The interface has to communicate an instruction to the Blockchain which then has to append the information to itself. It could of course be argued that the *send* ( ) function becomes true by the Blockchain changing. In Austin's terms, however, the argument is that it is the "happiness" of executing the transaction which makes the statement true. Put differently, the string evaluation statement and the one plus two statement have a true and meaningful answer independently of the changes in the world in which they are embedded. They are dependent on the world in which they are embedded, but it can comfortably be assumed that the symbol "3" hasn't changed its meaning since the inception of the first digital computers. Importantly, the answer to these statements doesn't depend on changes happening in the world that surround these statements – they *are* true.

The happiness of the *send* ( ) function, on the other hand, is highly dependent on the systems' working correctly. The illocution "I, Alice, am sending Bob a Bitcoin" that is implicated (cf. Grice 1975) by executing the above-described *send* ( ) function, will only be true if and when Bob will have received Alice's Bitcoin. Whether this happens or not is something that users have rather limited control over. Indeed, information systems nowadays are usually quite reliable. But problems such as a massive electronic blackout can arise. While this is an extreme example, more typical problems of distributed networks will be explained formally below (Chapter 2). The point of this analogy is that the illocution that follows the *send* ( ) function is different from its perlocution. The fact that Bob has a Bitcoin is not the same as Alice sending the Bitcoin. 1 + 2 = 3 *is* true, $str('I\ have\ a\ dream!') == str("I\ have\ a\ dream!")$ *is* true, but $send(Alice,\ Alice's\ signature,\ Bob)$ *is* not Bob's having a Bitcoin. Rather, the execution of the *send* ( ) function triggers Bob's having a Bitcoin, which is, therefore, the result of the statement's illocutionary force. It is the perlocution of the utterance.

The perlocution of Bitcoin being sent doesn't stop at the level of the ledger. The result of a Bitcoin transaction is of course an appended Blockchain, but not much is gained by paralleling this with linguistic speech acts. What are the consequences of a given 'illocution' on the Blockchain that are not directly linked to the transaction? What happens at the level of the network that is formed by the transactions?

By making a transaction, users strengthen the network as a whole, because the more transactions are made, the more attractive it becomes for miners to compete for the rewards of block validation. This, in turn, leads to a higher supply of security-ensuring resources (i.e., calculating power), at least in PoW-based consensus algorithms. This makes Bitcoin a highly secure digital asset. It can be shown that such Blockchains are in theory almost impossible to hack (Section 2.5.3). However, the security of Blockchains is contingent on certain network properties. Especially networks with fewer nodes are prone to attack, even from relatively few nodes if they have a short enough latency (Shrestha & Nam 2019). This means that the security of the whole network is dependent on the local perlocution of single nodes. Whenever many illocutions are concentrated in very few nodes, this means that the consensus over the whole network becomes fragile. In this sense, single transactions entail the strengthening of the network as a whole, binding the micro- and macro-levels of the network architecture together. A language is arguably only stable in its informational value if it is spoken by enough people to be maintained alive. Also, what happens at a local level, may well affect the global level of meaning. For example, sociolinguistic studies have claimed that highly connected individuals in social networks are responsible for linguistic innovation (Labov 2001). This means that when popular individuals propose highly useful linguistic forms, these spread through the network and stabilise when enough speakers adapt to its use. The specific mechanisms for such propagation will be explored in further detail later on (Chapter 3).

Where this argument appears to be the mere application of vocabulary from one area of investigation in another, it is based on the arguments of ANT or Actor-Network-Theory (Latour 1996). As an extension to post-modern social semiotic theories from the 1960s and 1970s, ANT seeks to consolidate two notions, the actor and the network, in order to "[…] dissolve the micro-macro-distinction that has plagued social theory from its inception" (ibid., p. 371). This means that, while societies are composed of individuals on the micro-level, there are emergent phenomena on the macro-level, which cannot be reduced to explications on the micro-level. The individual, on the other hand, isn't just a passive node in a net, but is explicitly conceived of as an "*actor* that does some *work*; the addition of such an ontological ingredient deeply modifies [the network]" (Latour 1996, p. 371, original emphasis). Therefore, the actor-network isn't just "[…] something that is traced or inscribed […]" (ibid., p. 372), but an "entity that *does* the inscribing […] It was in order to point out this essential feature that the word 'actor' was added to it" (ibid., original emphasis).

While ANT is a dedicatedly social semiotic theory, it extends well to linguistic pragmatism. Actors in linguistic networks create a linguistic network, through interaction at the local level. The network, which is extended through these local interactions carries meaning on both the level of the social reality and the language itself. Both ANT and Speech Act Theory subscribe to the idea that the interaction itself creates social reality. But the linguistic system – that is the system by which actors navigate through their social reality – itself is affected by social interaction and use of the language. Latour himself goes so far as to argue that ANT achieves to overcome the "absolute distinction between representation and things" (Latour 1996, p. 375), meaning that the often-entertained ontological distinction between language and objects in the semiotic analysis doesn't have to be maintained. Rather, language itself – in both its form and content – can be analysed as a result of the actor-network. This point will be of major interest below (Chapter 4), especially with regard to experimental evidence that shows the impact of interaction on the linguistic system. For now, it is sufficient to hint at some empirically-based arguments that language is the result of, rather than the condition for, communication since the latter shapes the former (e.g., Tomasello 2008; Evans 2014).

The analogy to the network capacities of the Blockchain here seems only partly viable. Latour specifically discriminates between actor networks and computer networks, because "nothing is more intensely connected, more distant, more compulsory, and more strategically organised than a computer network" (Latour 1996, p. 369). Linguistic communities are not strategically organised at all because individuals interact with neighbouring individuals due to local preferences of interaction, not because their choice of communication is beneficial to the linguistic system. As was argued above, this is similarly true for public Blockchains like Bitcoin because nodes aren't strategically organised. However, users are locally incentivised to run nodes to compete for the rewards of mining and this incentive is designed so that beneficial connections in terms of the distributed network are formed. In this sense, nodes are not actors to the same extent that human beings are, because their degree of freedom in communicating with one another is rather limited. However, the communication of the nodes to process transactions is what maintains the information. The network and the meaning of the information therein are, like in an actor network, a result of the interaction between the nodes. In the following (Section 1.3.3) this idea will be explored in more detail, in particular the question of where information in both types of networks stems from.

1.3.3. Self-Containment of Information in Language and Distributed Systems

The description of the Blockchain up to this point has, at several stages, entertained the claim that the achievement of consensus, in some sense, *is* the Blockchain. This means that the information on the Blockchain is only meaningful as long as the nodes in the network agree on the transactions (i.e., the information) that are to be regarded as true.

It was argued before that value on the Blockchain is created by distributed representation, which is the result of the interaction between nodes. Furthermore, these interactions mediate the network effects of the illocutive behaviour of nodes at a local level. It was established that signs are fundamentally different in the context of human language and computer systems. However, it was also found that the similarity of the power of both semiotic systems lies in the emergent properties of more complex meanings. The manipulation of singular, primitive meanings is then not the main mechanism in the creation of meaning. Rather, a more complex meaning is brought about as an emergent effect of communication (Beckner et al. 2009; Trasmundi & Steffensen 2016) which in turn hinges on dialogue and communication (Tylén et al. 2013; Fusaroli et al. 2014) similar to the connectivity between nodes.

This can be exemplified through a more detailed description of the mining process. Bitcoin is mined through the authentication of transactions on the Blockchain. Thus, Bitcoin only exists because Bitcoin is circulated in the network. Mining consists of authenticating transactions through PoW and appending these transactions to the ledger. This is also the process by which Bitcoin is created for circulation in the network. The creation of Bitcoin is hence also a perlocution effect of successfully sending Bitcoin. This means that the value that Bitcoin creates is entirely self-contained on the Blockchain and that it is not representative of any type of information outside of the Blockchain. This is where a fundamental difference lies between meaning in human interaction and meaning on the Blockchain.

The creation of meaning from meaning (cf. Eco 1990) is rather insightful when dealing with fully-fledged linguistic systems. This doesn't explain, however, how the first linguistic meaning was created to create all other meanings. When approaching linguistic meaning from a position of total arbitrariness (De Saussure 1916) one ultimately runs into an *infinite regress*. Language can only be explained as long as language already exists. This would be compatible with the concept of mining and self-contained information in a network, but research from the past decades suggests otherwise. The problem has been termed the grounding of linguistic meaning.

Barsalou (1999) argues that symbol systems are by and large perceptually grounded. This means that meaning stems from the interaction of humans with their environment.

> Perceptual states in the sensory-motor system are extracted and stored in long-term memory to function as symbols. As a result, the internal structure of these symbols is modal and they are analogically related to the perceptual states that produced them. (Barsalou 1999, p. 578)

In other words, to know what a chair is means to know what it feels like to interact with a chair. This means that linguistic knowledge is heavily impacted by the world that human beings collectively experience. This has been empirically accounted for by appraising the long-overlooked abundant existence of iconic (cf. Peirce 1903) linguistic signs and their role in both the expressivity of linguistic systems (Dingemanse et al. 2015) and language learning (Nielsen & Dingemanse 2020). Other empirical studies have elucidated how iconic graphical signs start as visual representations of the experienced world and how these signs then evolve into symbolic signs that are abstracted from their perceptual basis (Garrod et al. 2007). Neurological evidence also suggests that the human conceptual system, and by extension language, works based on simulating the corresponding perceptual states in memory (Barsalou 2003). This means that using the word 'to carry' means to re-live the action of carrying something. At the same time, this raises the question of how concrete, tangible experiences of physical objects of emotional states can translate into more abstract thinking and the conception of intangible things such as justice. Different proposals have been put forth to answer this question. One of the most famous mechanisms explained is the conceptual metaphor (Lakoff & Johnson 1980b) proposing that concrete meanings are extended via a metaphoric extension to apply to more abstract things. Typical conceptual metaphors are GOOD IS UP and BAD IS DOWN which the authors then account for with numerous examples from the English language. Such a metaphoric extension was encountered before when the metaphors THE MIND IS A COMPUTER and THE COMPUTER IS A MIND (Lakoff & Johnson 1980a; Gigerenzer & Goldstein 1996) were referenced. These examples explain how the experience of concrete things is used to conceptualise more abstract concepts. Properties of the former are applied to the latter to make them more tangible. Another proposed process is that of conceptual metonymy (Kövesces & Radden 1998) whereby properties of one concept are applied to another not by iconicity, but as a result of co-occurrence. For example, the metonymy LOVE IS WARMTH conceptualises love as the feeling of warmth that is physically associated with it (blushing, hugging, etc.).

All these advances in linguistic theory go to show that, while language is largely a result of interaction, the individual is important in so far as its perceptual and cognitive apparatus brings certain abilities and affordances to the table. These abilities lie in the possibility of interacting with the world and processing experiences from the outside world conceptually. What's more, theoretical papers (e.g., Beckner et al. 2009; Tylén et al. 2013) make explicit connections between the highly developed perceptual and conceptual systems of human beings and the way they mutually adapt in an effort after efficiency. Based on ancient engraved ochre and ostrich eggshells from the South African Blombos Cave and Diepkloof Rock Shelter, for instance, it was found that *homo sapiens* have been optimising their semiotic behaviour to fit the affordances of the visual and cognitive apparatus since some 100,000 years ago (Tylén et al. 2020). That is, perception and conception shape each other in a mutually adaptive process. This relationship results in the external world having an important impact on linguistic meaning-making strategies (Nölle et al. 2020) and the development of cognitive learning biases (Culbertson et al. 2012, 2013). Human interaction and the environment are thus intricately linked in the emergence of linguistic meaning. A striking linguistic example of this is the impact of ideational structure (in the sense of Halliday & Matthiessen 2014) derived from the perceptual characteristics of the environment, that is information structure, on the emergence of grammatical categories such as differential object marking that has recently been observed experimentally (Tal et al. 2022). Such evidence hints at the integration of the ideational and textual metafunctions of language and the contribution thereof to human navigation through their social, linguistic, and ecological environment (Halliday & Matthiessen 2014). That means that, while higher-order linguistic meaning-making such as Unlimited Semiosis (Eco 1990) does exist, language does optimise for grounded (cf. Barsalou 1999) aspects of meaning, and is never entirely self-contained.

This is not true for information on the Blockchain. It was laid out before how information on the Blockchain is rather restricted by the lesser semiotic abilities of network nodes on the Blockchain as compared to human beings (Section. 1.3.1). Parra-Moyano (2017) examines the relationship between the Blockchain and the information it contains in more detail. He recurs to the aforementioned definitions by Glaser (2017) distinguishing between closed distributed ledgers (Type 1) and open distributed ledgers (Type 2). Type 1 ledgers are those that, like Bitcoin, only contain self-generated information. Type 2 ledgers are those in which real-world information is encoded. Such information can be notarial records such as house and land ownership (e.g., Ismaev 2017). Such information exists *a priori* in the world and is generated by other entities and is then merely mirrored on the Blockchain. Remember that the strategy of Blockchains for providing security lies in providing optimal information for all nodes. That is, all relevant information has to be accessible to all nodes in the network to be checkable for veracity at any given point. When information is generated on the Blockchain itself, this is a trivial task and is solved by Bitcoin by broadcasting blocks of transactions to all nodes (Section 1.1.4). But recently, researchers have proposed the use of so-called oracles, that is entities that broadcast real-world information such as land ownership to the Blockchain (Antonopoulos & Woods 2018). Such oracles are trusted third-party objects that vouch for the veracity of information from the real world as it is broadcasted. While this can be a useful solution, it has been pointed out that this creates problems for the integrity of information on the Blockchain, which can in turn only be solved when the system is trusted (Caldarelli 2020); a condition that Blockchains such as Bitcoin originally try to circumvent.

When real-world information is encoded on the Blockchain, it can ultimately not be guaranteed that all nodes can check for the veracity of the information, because the access point of this information to the Blockchain is the oracle. The nodes have to trust that this information is true, to begin with. The oracle problem (cf. Caldarelli 2020) has been analysed and formalised by Parra-Moyano (2017) in terms of linguistic logic under reference to Russell's Paradox.

The verification of information on the Blockchain has been described in the following way: "every [information] is granted [veracity] by a verifying instance [that is the Blockchain] if and only if this entity cannot grant itself [veracity][25]" (Parra-Moyano 2017, p. 695):

25 Parra-Moyano himself speaks of "identity" in his article. In order to provide ease of reading "veracity of information" is used to paraphrase.

$$\forall x: \quad verify(x, instance) \leftrightarrow \neg verify(x,x)$$

(adapted from Parra-Moyano, p. 695)

To pinpoint the problem, this can be read as "any information *x* on the Blockchain is verified by an instance of consensus on the Blockchain, if and only if it doesn't verify itself". That is, information has to be verified via consensus in the network. But the principle of Bitcoin is to only contain information that was generated on itself, which implies that the instance of consensus is the same thing as the information,

$$x = instance$$

According to Parra-Moyano, this leads to the following implied paradox:

$$\forall x: \quad verify(x,x) \leftrightarrow \neg verify(x, x)$$

(adapted from Parra-Moyano, p. 695)

As the author points out, this is equivalent to the definition of Russell's Class, which is defined as:

$$\forall x : x \in X \leftrightarrow \neg x \in X$$

This means that an element x is an element of the set X if and only if x is not a member of the set X (Russell 1903). This definition of Russell's Class has been illustrated in different ways. Parra-Moyano himself uses the example "The barber is the one who shaves all those, and those only, who do not shave themselves. The question is, does the barber shave himself?" (Russell 1918; cited in Parra-Moyano 2017, p. 695). The answer is paradoxical because if the Barber doesn't shave himself, he doesn't abide by the sentence. After all, the Barber is required to shave anyone who doesn't shave themselves. If, however, the Barber does shave himself, he isn't a Barber because the Barber is required to shave only those who don't shave themselves. Russell's Paradox (1903) is used to reduce Cantor's (1897) definition of a set *ad absurdum* because it states that a "*set* is an aggregation of discrete individuals regarded as a whole" (Wall 1972, p. 1, original emphasis). This is nowadays also referred to as naïve set theory. To solve this problem, different axiomatic set theories have been devised, meaning that they make axiomatic presuppositions of things that can constitute sets.

The implication of this for the Blockchain is that its information cannot be regarded as a set or list of information that is contained in the world and which can be represented on the Blockchain at the same time. In principle, there is no way to allow any type of information to be put on the Blockchain unless it was generated therein. In this sense, self-reference is an axiomatic condition for information to be eligible for representation on the Blockchain; the information put on the Blockchain has to originate from the Blockchain itself. Empirically, this is only true of type 1 ledgers (Glaser 2017), while type 2 ledgers do not abide by this principle.

While various authors in line with formal theories of linguistics (e.g., Chomsky 1957; Montague 1970) entertain the idea that meaning in language can be reduced to formal and syntactical operations, many accounts for ecological theories of semantics were cited above. Regarding this ecological conception of language, there is a stark contrast between information on the Blockchain and information in language, because the former is completely contained in itself while the latter recurs to grounded meaning. But this is not an argument against formal accounts for meaning. An obvious example of sensibly splitting language from the outside world is second language acquisition. To L2 learners, a linguistic system is a set of rules that can be learned in a way that is completely detached from the complex levels of embedding described above. In this situation, language as a system can sensibly be reduced to a system in the structuralist sense. Thus, language does of course contain a level of semiotic self-containment where language is nothing but a reference to language and language alone. On the other hand, the proponents of the CAS approach to language do conceive of second language acquisition as a complex process and "because L2 learners are normally more cognitively mature, the social environment/conditions of learning are significantly different from those of a child acquiring an L1" (Beckner et al. 2009, p. 11). Hence, and in reference to the cognitive (Robinson & Ellis 2007), psycholinguistic (Kroll & de Groot 2005) and sociolinguistic (Lantolf 2006; all cited in Beckner et al. 2009) dimensions of L2 acquisition, this process can be regarded as even more complex than those of the L1 (ibid.).

The ontological semiotic status of information in language must thus be characterised as rather interactive with its environment, even though a core system can be modelled and extrapolated. Information on the Blockchain on the other hand is radically different. The points at which the information interacts with the real world are well-defined and rather restricted. The information on the Blockchain, beyond the entry points of being able to formulate and order transactions, is fully self-contained and predisposed by how it is programmed.

2. Graph Theory and Network Analysis – Formal Definitions

This chapter is dedicated to explaining the bases of network analysis. This will be largely based on concepts of graph theory. To maintain adequacy and readability, some concessions have to be made regarding formal definitions. Mathematical concepts will be established to the extent that they are necessary to review the code[26] used for data collection (Chapter 5) and experimental analyses (Chapters 6, 7 and 8). Many of the concepts that are encountered in this chapter apply to the conceptual explanations of Blockchain technology above. Some definitions extend the conceptual deliberations formally and provide proof for some of the claims made above. In particular, the formal descriptions of communicative problems that Blockchain technology attempts to solve provide evidence for the security of these systems. Where possible, examples from linguistic communication will be drawn such as to underline the relevance of these mathematical concepts for either body of literature. Furthermore, the application of the meta-theoretic vocabulary of Graph Theory to both domains of research helps to narratively support the claim that human and computer networks are functionally equivalent in an architectural sense, thus exhibiting diagrammatic iconicity (cf. Section 1.3). The definitions cited in Bender and Williamson (2010) are adapted to fit the terminology of the *networkx* library (Hagberg et al. 2008) for Python more closely, as this was used to program the code for data retrieval and representation (Chapter 5).

2.1. Graphs

Different types of ledger implementations will be described as graphs. This section will give a brief overview of the relevant concepts. To maintain the method of analysis as simple as possible, this section will solely be preoccupied with the description of undirected graphs. That is, the direction of interaction between two nodes will be disregarded. A connection between two nodes is merely the presence of an interaction, independent of the direction of communication. The distinction between information source and destination is thus ignored.

26 Available under https://github.com/TobiDschi/linguistic_network_structure

2.1.1. Graphs

A graph G is an ordered pair of two sets N and E.

$$G = (N, E)$$

(adapted from Bender & Williamson 2010, p. 148)

It is ordered (cf. Wall 1972, p. 104) because the first digit of the pair always indicates the set of nodes N and the second always indicates the set of edges E. A graph is thus nothing more than an ordered pair of two sets which is all that is needed to adequately describe a network. A good example of a graph is any computer network such as the Internet or more old-school Local Area Networks (LAN). In the same sense, society could be considered a network of citizens.

2.1.2. Nodes

The first digit N is a set of nodes n, often called vertices.

$$N = \{n_0, n_1, n_2, \dots, n_n\}$$

(adapted from Bender & Williamson 2010, p. 149)

A node n is an entity in a network. Real-world examples of nodes are servers, terminal devices (computers, mobile phones, etc.) or agents in a network. In a linguistic social network, nodes can be speakers. The set N is just the collection of all of these elements that are relevant to the network described.

2.1.3. Edges

The second digit in G is E, the set of edges e that describe connections between the nodes n.

$$E = \{e_0, e_1, e_2, \dots, e_n\}$$

(adapted from Bender & Williamson 2010, p. 149)

Edges e represent connections between exactly two nodes n. Consequently, they are unordered pairs of nodes n. This means that edges e contain exactly two nodes n. The order of the nodes is irrelevant to the description of the connection, as only undirected connections are considered (cf. Section 3.3). To sensibly describe a graph G, edges can only contain nodes that are in N. Furthermore, edges can only be established between two different nodes. As only undirected graphs are considered, reflexive edges which refer to the same node at both ends, are not allowed. The set of edges E is thus defined as a set of unordered pairs.

$$E = \{(n_i, n_j) | n_i, n_j \in N \; and \; n_i \neq n_j\}$$

Such edges can represent a direct connection between a terminal and an Internet server, or an interaction between two people by speech.

2.1.4. Paths

A path P is a set of edges between two nodes nodes n_i and n_j, such that it is possible to navigate from n_i to n_j and *vice versa*. A path thus contains all the edges necessary to connect these two nodes in the network.

$$P(n_i, n_j) = \{e(n_i, n_x), \ldots, e(n_j, n_y)\}$$

(adapted from Bender & Williamson 2010, p. 162)

If an edge exists between n_i and n_j, the path P is equal to the edge e between these two nodes. In the following, the term *shortest path* will play a role in describing the properties of graphs. The shortest path is, as its name suggests, the path P that expresses the possible connection between two nodes n_i and n_j with the fewest possible edges. To determine the shortest path, algorithms (e.g., *networkx.shortest_path*, Hagberg et al. 2008) construct all possible paths from n_i to n_j and then choose the path P that contains the fewest unordered pairs (i.e., edges). The longest path is defined as the opposite. It is the longest possible path between two nodes, such that no edge in the set of edges is repeated. However, this is only of marginal interest and will only reappear in the definition of the linear network typology (Section 2.3.1).

2.2. Ledger

The above informal definition of the term ledger is that of "a book in which things are regularly recorded, especially business activities and money received or paid" (Cambridge Dictionary). In the context of the Internet, the word book is metaphorical. More generally, a ledger is a physical or virtual object that can store information. This definition will be complemented with a formal definition. A ledger object L is "a sequence of *records*, supporting two basic operations: *get* and *append* […], where the get operation returns the ledger as a sequence S of records and the append operation inserts a new record at the end of the sequence" (Fernández-Anta et al. 2018, p. 3, original emphasis). Displayed as pseudo-code, the object is defined as follows (Tab. 2):

Tab. 2: Definition of the ledger object L. It starts as an empty sequence S of records r. The get method can return (display) the sequence S. The append function can concatenate (||) the sequence S with the new record r to return the updated sequence S. (Table adapted from Fernández-Anta et al. 2018, p. 3)

Ledger Object L
Init: $S \leftarrow \emptyset$
function L.get():
return S
function L.append(r):
$S \leftarrow S \mid\mid r$
return

This defines a ledger object L as something that can only do two things, be appended with a new bit of information, or be read by someone. Appending is here understood as concatenation (||), which is linking the new piece of information to the previously existing information. Understanding this principle is the first step to understanding DLT implementations such as Bitcoin (cf. Nakamoto 2008). In particular, note that there are no methods to delete or remove defined for a ledger object. Such is the case for Bitcoin too (cf. Nakamoto 2008).

Fernández-Anta et al. (2018) also supply a definition of a Validated Ledger Object VL. This is an important distinction because Blockchains cannot just be appended by any one user. The network has to approve the object through consensus. This means that a Validated Ledger Object VL is distinct from a Ledger Object L in that it doesn't just accept any given input r for concatenation with the sequence of records S. Only valid inputs are going to be accepted as appendices to S, otherwise, the input is rejected. What valid means is dependent on the consensus algorithm employed to validate information (Tab. 3).

Tab. 3: Definition of the validated ledger object VL. It requires records to satisfy validity requirements. This is expressed by the predicate Valid(). Otherwise, the input is not accepted and the sequence S will not be appended with the new record. (Table adapted from Fernández-Anta et al. 2018, p. 3)

Validated Ledger Object *VL*
1: **Init** : $S \leftarrow \emptyset$
2: **function** *L*.get():
3: **return** *S*
4: **function** *L*.append(*r*):
5: **if** *Valid*(S‖*r*) **then**
6: $S \leftarrow S \parallel r$
7: **return** ACK
8: **else return** NACK

This formally expresses the properties of any ledger such as a bank account. It can be appended and looked up. Note that a withdrawal from a bank account is not taking away information from it, but merely adding negative information. So, withdrawals and deposits can be expressed respectively as negative and positive values *r* to be added to the ledger *L*. The validation rule in VL is important in a situation where a person wants to make a withdrawal from their account. in this case, the record *r* would only be valid if the amount of money to be deducted from the account is smaller than the amount of money available in the account. If there is enough money to make the withdrawal, the *Valid*( ) predicate will return *TRUE* and allow the sequence *S* to be appended by the record *r*. Otherwise, *VL* will ignore the withdrawal and not append the sequence *S*. In the case of distributed ledger objects, the rules of validity depend on consensus. If consensus is reached, the ledger can be appended. If no consensus is reached, the input gets rejected.

2.3. Ledger Implementation – Network Topology

The implementation of ledgers, such as defined above (Section 2.1) is described as graph topology. DLT are not only ledger objects or validated ledger objects, but distributed ledger objects. Distribution refers to how the ledger is implemented in a system. Chapter 1 explained that Blockchains are inherently distributed implementations of information networks and that they oppose centralised implementations of these networks. Implementation, in a more general sense, refers to how the ledger can be accessed by users and defines which users have the right to append information to the ledger. Such levels of authorisation could, for instance, be implemented in validated ledger objects. If the *Valid* ( ) function detects certain user credentials, a transaction from such a user can be appended to the ledger object. Users without such credentials may only be able to use the *get* ( ) method.

In a specific sense, implementation refers to the arrangement of connections between nodes, which will henceforth be referred to as network topology. Topology is an important property of networks in that it determines the possible flow of information and affects the states of consensus that can be achieved in a network. Imagine a network consisting of fourteen nodes (Fig. 6). How does one implement a ledger, such that all of the fourteen nodes have optimal access to the information in the network? In the following, five different network topologies will be discussed.

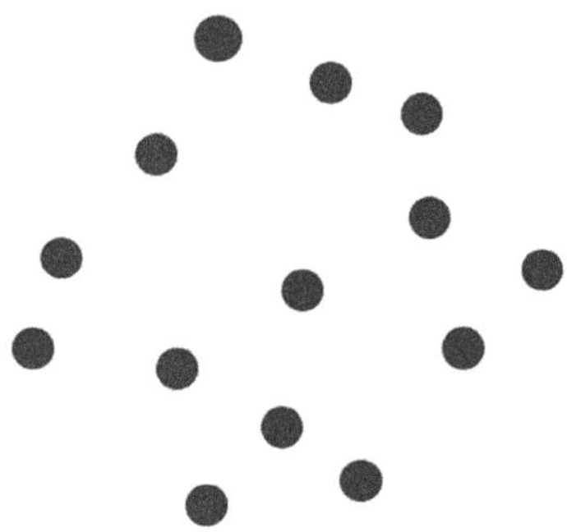

Fig. 6: A population of fourteen hypothetical users of the ledger object. Each node represents a user in the network.

2.3.1. Linear Topology

The first network topology is linear. This topology implements connections between nodes in such a way that each node is connected to exactly two other nodes, except for the two marginal nodes, which are only connected to one node (Fig. 7).

Let the marginal node at the top be denoted n_0 and the marginal node at the bottom left be denoted n_{13} (Fig. 7). A path can be defined that connects these two nodes as a set of unordered pairs, that is edges:

$$P(n_0, n_{13}) = \{e(n_0, n_1), e(n_1, n_2), e(n_2, n_3), \ldots, e(n_{12}, n_{13})\}$$

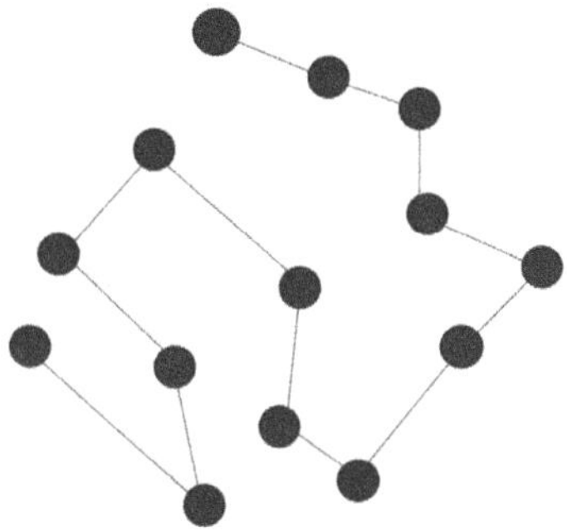

Fig. 7: Example of a linear network topology.

In a linear graph topology, all possible paths are a subset of the longest possible path, that is, the path from n_0 to n_n. So, if the graph contains fourteen nodes, as in the above example, a linear implementation is an implementation in which all possible paths (P) are a subset of the longest path (P_{max}). Formally, this is expressed as follows:

$$\forall P : P \subseteq P_{max}$$

In terms of ledger implementation, however, this would make for a rather poor setup. All nodes would only broadcast transactions to their nearest neighbour which, in turn, would have to broadcast the information to their next nearest neighbour, and so forth. This results in a Chinese Whispers[27] paradigm, where the correct transmission of information can never be secured. None of the nodes would be able to verify whether the information they transferred was faithfully reproduced upon reception, making information increasingly fragile. Similarly, the broadcasting nodes would have no control over the correct reproduction of the information down the line. Thus, the information could be tampered with at any given point, without any node ever knowing whether this has happened or not.

27 dt.: *stille Post*
es.: *teléfono descompuesto*

2.3.2. Centralised Topology

To secure information, networks are often centralised around a user *C* who is trusted and charged with the correction and broadcasting of all information. In this scenario, only one node has access to the ledger object's *append*() function, while all the other nodes have to turn to this node as an intermediary for the transactions. All nodes are grouped around a central node, which mediates all communication between any two given nodes unless it communicates information itself (Fig. 8).

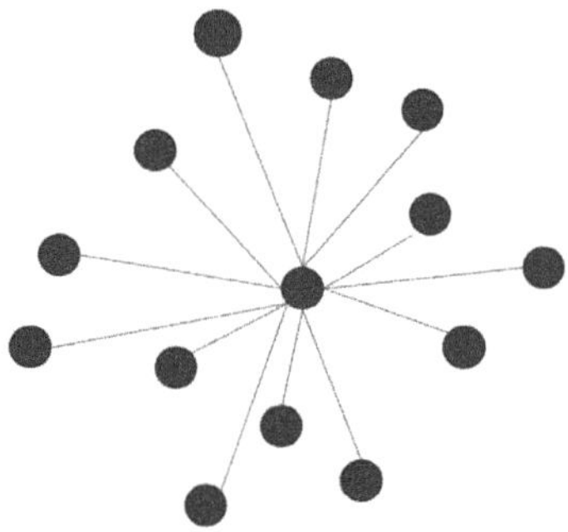

Fig. 8: Centralised network topology. Any given node has to turn to n_0 (C) to interact with the ledger, which is solely controlled by the node at the centre.

This centralised topology represents a graph in which each of the nodes in the network refers to exactly one other point in the network, except one. Moreover, the point that all nodes refer to must be the same, meaning that all nodes refer to one central node n_0. This can be formalised as follows:

$$\forall i : i \in \mathbb{N}$$

$$\forall n_i : !\exists e(n_i, n_0)$$

This reads as, for all nodes *n* with an index that is a whole number bigger than zero (i.e., the set of natural numbers $\mathbb{N}$) there is exactly one edge *e* that refers to the central node n_0 from any node n_i. Informally speaking, a centralised graph is then defined as a network in which all the nodes refer to the same central node and only the central node. Importantly, note that the edge $e(n_1, n_0)$ does not imply a directionality from n_1 to n_0 or from n_0 to n_1, since an undirected graph – as defined above – is described here. The edge *e* simply connects the two nodes.

Informally speaking, these kinds of networks rely on the parameter of trust (Klems et al. 2017) in the central node. The nodes which require access to the ledger *VL* have to trust that the validation rules are applied truthfully and that the central node will append the ledger object with the same information that the soliciting node intends. Also, the central node can only prevent the issue of double-spending it if processes transaction requests in the same order that they have been submitted.

Even if all the nodes decide that the central node is fully trustworthy, the information in the ledger object is not secure. If anyone other than the intermediary were able to gain access to the ledger object and modify it, an informatic attack on this single node would be enough to damage the information in the whole network. In other words, attackers only have to attack a single node of information in order to compromise the information of the entire network.

In conclusion, there is up and downside to centralised networks from an engineering standpoint. They are easy to maintain, the burden of work lies with one single node, and groups can store information in a common ledger collaboratively. However, the nodes do depend on the reliability of the central node and its capacity to protect the ledger from unwarranted access.

2.3.3. Decentralised Topology

Instead of a centralised topology, networks can also be arranged in a decentralised fashion. This means that the nodes in the graph are not all linked to the central node. Rather, the system exhibits a hierarchical structure. It may (or not) have a central node at its centre, while the peripheric nodes refer to intermediate nodes which, in turn, converge on the central node (Fig. 9).

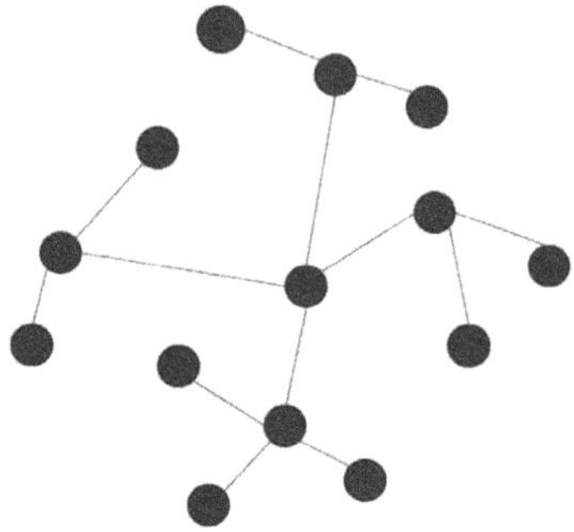

Fig. 9: Decentralised network topology. The peripheric nodes are connected to the central node not directly but mediated through nodes of higher hierarchical order.

A decentralised graph exhibits a topology in which not every node is connected to the central node, but where no connections between the resulting subgraphs (cf. Bender & Williamson 2010, p. 163) exist. In the above example (Fig. 9) four subtrees can be identified, one to the north, another to the west, one to the south and the last one to the east. Not having any connections between the subgraphs means that for each node that is not the central node, there is exactly one simple path from the node to the central node. This is formalised in the following way:

$$\forall i : i \in \mathbb{N}$$

$$\forall n_i : !\exists P\left\{e\left(n_0, n_{0+1}\right), e\left(n_1, n_{1+1}\right), \ldots, e\left(n_{i-1}, n_i\right)\right\}$$

This statement reads as follows: For each node *n*, which has an integer index bigger than one, there is exactly one simple path that describes the connection from the centre node n_0 to the peripheric node n_i. Note that, strictly speaking, this definition of a decentralised network applies to the definition of a completely centralised implementation because, in a decentralised setup, there is exactly one path from n_0 to n_i. This is the path *P* that contains only the edge *e* between n_0 and n_i.

$$P\left(n_0, n_i\right) = e\left(n_0, n_i\right)$$

Instead of formulating a caveat stating that a decentralised system must contain a layer of intermediate nodes, or that paths in a decentralised system must contain more than one edge, centralised topologies will be regarded as subsets of decentralised systems. A centralised topology is hence a decentralised topology with the additional restriction that there be only one edge for each peripheral node.

$$\forall i : i \in \mathbb{N}$$

$$\forall n_i : !\exists e(n_i, n_0)$$

2.3.4. Fully-Connected Topology

A fully connected topology exists in a network in which every node n_i is connected to every other node in the network (Fig. 10). This means that for each node n_i, there are $|N|-1$ edges[28] incident upon n_i. Thus, a fully connected graph is a network for which the following statement is true.

$$|E| = \frac{|N|(|N|-1)}{2}$$

This means that the size of the set *E*, the set of edges in a set of nodes *N*, is equal to the size of *N*, or the number of nodes, times the number of nodes minus one divided by two, equalling the set $E*$, the set of all possible edges given the set of nodes *N*.

28 $|N|$ refers to the size of the set of nodes, that is the number of nodes *n* contained in the set N.

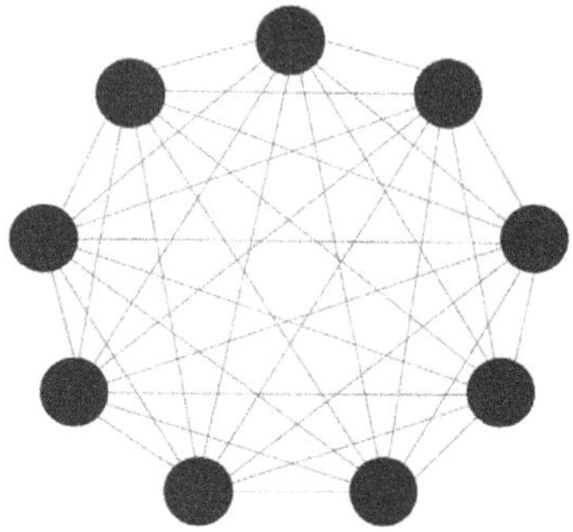

Fig. 10: Fully connected network topology. Each node is connected to every other point. Note that the nodes are not connected to themselves but only to each other.

Considering that edges are described as unordered pairs of the two nodes they connect, the table of pairs of nodes (Tab. 4) describes all the possible edges in a fully connected network. It hence describes the set of all possible edges $E*$. This object (Tab. 4) is constructed by arranging the set of nodes in the network in two opposite dimensions which can predict all possible combinations of nodes in *N*. This object is called the edge space $E*$. Since only undirected graphs are described, the pairs of nodes are commutative, meaning that the edge space is represented twice in the table, mirrored at the diagonal.

Tab. 4: The edge space E* is a set of nodes in a fully-connected network generating all the possible edges for the network. Note that the edges are not directed hence (n_1, n_2) is the same as (n_2, n_1). Hence, E* is represented twice in the table.

	N_1	**n_2**	**…**	**n_i**
n_1		$e(n_1, n_2)$	$e(n_1, \ldots)$	$e(n_1, n_i)$
n_2	$e(n_1, n_2)$		$e(n_2, \ldots)$	$e(n_2, n_i)$
…	$e(n_1, \ldots)$	$e(n_2, \ldots)$		$e(\ldots, n_i)$
n_i	$e(n_1, n_i)$	$e(n_2, n_i)$	$e(\ldots, n_i)$	

2.3.5. Distributed Topology

As the term *DLT* implies, this topology is neither centralised nor decentralised. Informally speaking, distributed networks are not bound by the restrictions for decentralised, centralised, or linear topologies formulated above. Instead, nodes can be connected unrestrictedly in a distributed network (Fig. 11).

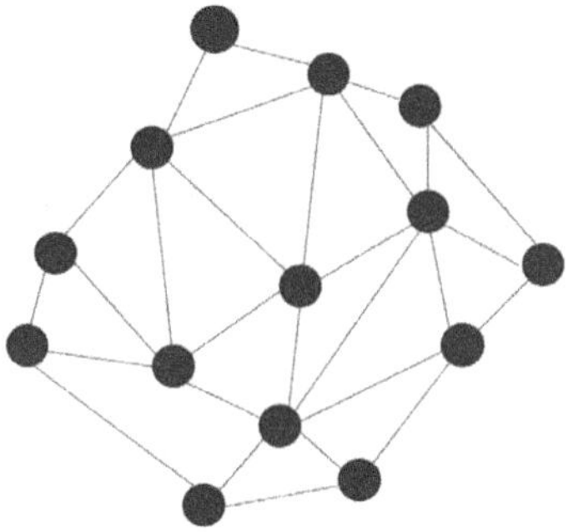

Fig. 11: Distributed network topology. No node has superior relevance to the network. In this implementation, the information can run rather freely from any given node to any other.

There is no central node to control the information. There are, of course, still nodes that are more central than others, such as the node in the physical centre of the network which is connected to five edges, while the uppermost node is only connected to two edges (Fig. 11). However, if either of these nodes were suppressed, the information running through the graph would still be accessible, because it can flow from any given point to any other given point by taking another path. This is possible because, unlike in decentralised topologies, there is more than one way to any other point in the network.

Formally, a distributed network is any network whose set of edges is a proper subset of $E*$, and which is not bound by the restrictions for central, decentral, and linear topologies, as stated above. A network has a distributed – as opposed to fully-connected – topology when the set of edges E of a network with $|N|$ nodes is a proper subset of the edge space $E*$ with $|N|$ nodes. Additionally, none of the aforementioned restrictions on either linear, centralised, or decentralised topologies can apply:

$$E(N) \subset E*(N)$$

A further distinction is in order. Distributed topologies are here distinguished from real distributed topologies, according to the definition above. By implication, a distributed topology is a topology in which there is more than one possible path from any given node n_i to n_0 (Fig. 12b), because it has more edges than a decentralised topology (Fig. 12a). But there are still nodes, which are dependent on a single node. If this node was to spread false information, some nodes could not access this information from other sources. They are hence single-node dependent. No alternative flow of information is possible. A real distributed network, then, has a topology in which no node has single-node dependency. Whichever node one was to suppress (Fig. 12c), no node or subgraph will be cut off from the rest of the network.

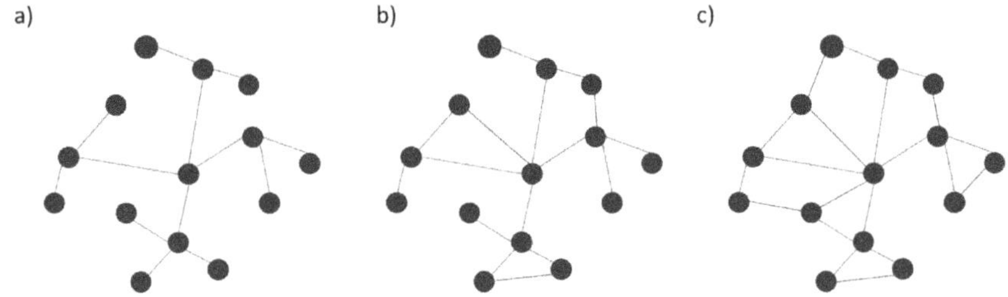

Fig. 12: Difference between decentralised (a), distributed (b), and real distributed (c) network topologies. A real distributed network is defined as a network in which no node has single-node dependence. Whichever node is deleted from the graph, the network is still able to provide all nodes with information.

The definition is extended to real distributed networks such that there can be no node in the system that has a dependency on a single node to find other nodes in the system, eliminating dead ends.

It is intuitive to describe a population of speakers, a social group, a linguistic group, or any other describable population, in terms of such a graph. The nodes represent the speakers, and the edges represent the interaction between two interlocutors with each other. A distributed topology intuitively appears to be most suitable for such a model because, in modern societies, people can choose to relate to any one person and are not bound by restrictions in their choice of interaction. Thus, there shouldn't be any restrictions *a priori* to the topology of a social network. Whether this is empirically true will be under investigation later on (Chapter 5). In general, the interest of this dissertation is to show the effects that network topology has on the language that happens in such social networks.

Distributed network topologies can solve interesting problems in communication from an informatics standpoint. At this level of implementation, the network and all of its participants gain strong independence from the potentially arbitrary power of a central node. This means that there is no actor in the network upon which anyone is so dependent that information can be altered without it being noticed. Even if certain nodes spread wrong information, there is still enough redundancy in the network connections that the correct information can flow to any point in the network. The question of how a network can be attacked by nodes that spread wrong information is important to quantify its security properties mathematically. This will be treated below (Section 2.5.1). This is the type of attack that the Blockchain attempts to solve. Before turning to these explanations, a little more terminology is in order.

2.4. Network Properties

Other than just network topology, several other properties can be measured in the description graphs. In the following, the concepts that are used for data collection and description (Chapter 5) will be described formally. All computer code generated for the description of the data will be according to these mathematical descriptions and are available for review in the online repository.

2.4.1. Degree Centrality

All types of networks, except for linear topologies, can be meaningfully described in terms of centrality. In graphs, degree centrality describes the degree to which a node is central to a system. Degree centrality is defined as the number of edges that a node is connected to (Nieminen 1974; cited in Freeman 1978, p. 220). The central node n_0 in the decentralised topology (Fig. 12a), for instance, has a degree centrality of four, while the central node n_0 in the real distributed topology (Fig. 12c) has a degree centrality of seven. This measure is a count measure and the centrality of a central node in a centralised graph increases infinitely, as long as new nodes are added to the graph.

To maintain this value comparable for networks of different sizes, degree centrality will not be defined as the absolute number of edges incident to a node, but as the fraction of nodes n in the network G to which the node is connected. The following definition applies:

$$C(n) = \frac{|E(n)|}{|N| - 1}$$

The centrality C of a node n is the size of the set E incident on the node n divided by the size of the set of nodes ($|N|$) minus one. This is the definition applied by the *networkx.degree_centrality()* function for Python 3 (Hagberg et al. 2008), which will be used in the analysis section. This definition allows for the description of the centrality of a node in a network irrespective of network size. Different definitions of centrality, such as betweenness and closeness centrality, are available (Freeman 1978) and have been applied in the exploration of the data (Chapter 5). However, only degree centrality has led to meaningful results, which is why it is the only type of centrality reported here.

2.4.2. Graph Centrality

While degree centrality is a measure of centrality for single nodes in a graph, this concept can be extended to describe the degree of centralisation of an entire graph. From the set of degree centralities of all the nodes in a given network, the graph centrality or network centrality as a measure of centralisation of the whole network can be obtained. Freeman (1978) defines graph centrality as:

$$C_D(G) = \frac{\sum_{i=1}^{|N|}\left[C_D(n*) - C_D(n_i)\right]}{|N|^2 - 3|N| + 2}$$

(adapted from Freeman 1978, p. 230)

The centrality of a graph G is the quotient of the sum of all subtractions of the nodes n_i from the most centralised node $n*$ divided by the number of nodes squared minus the number of nodes times three plus two. With these definitions in order, networks become describable for this thesis. Note that, most importantly, centralisation is a continuous variable that can be measured as a function of how the nodes connect. Even if central and decentral networks were here archetypically represented as two different groups, no actual implementation is fully centralised or maximally decentralised. Note that the definition of graph centrality is a quotient that approaches zero, hence there is no maximum degree of decentralisation of a network. Implementations of networks are thus always *more or less centralised*. These measurements can be applied to any given network topology, even though it is always equal to one for completely centralised networks.

2.4.3. Network Density

Any network with a set of edges $E(N)$ can be characterised by the ratio of the size of $E(N)$ to the edge space $E*(N)$. This expresses how many of the possible edges e in the set E are present in the network. This is termed network density $D(G)$. Network density is the number of actual connections divided by the number of possible connections and is also defined as such in the $networkx.density(G)$ function (Hagberg et al. 2008):

$$D(G) = \frac{|E(N)|}{|E*(N)|}$$

A fully connected network hence has a network density of 1, while any distributed network has a network density bigger than zero but smaller than one. This concept is most useful for distributed topologies, as one can describe the density of their connectivity. In the case of centralised or even decentralised topologies, where most nodes are connected to only one or two other nodes, network density decreases as the size of N increases. This means that the bigger the centralised (and to a lesser degree decentralised) topologies are, the lower their network density is.

2.4.4. P-Regularity

P-regularity is a property exclusively of real distributed graphs, as will become evident below. It is an important property in that it puts restrictions on some of the solutions that are proposed for distributed consensus, which will be explored formally below (Section 2.5.3). P-regularity refers to the property that each node n in the network is connected to exactly P other nodes. This means that the number of edges incident on a node must be the same for each node. Each node has the same degree. Compare the two networks below (Fig. 13). On the left side, each node is connected to exactly three other nodes, making the network P-regular, with $P = 3$ (Fig. 13a). In the other case (Fig. 13b), four of the nodes are connected to three other nodes, while the central node is connected to four other nodes. Hence, the graph is not P-regular.

2.4.5. Diameter

The "*diameter* of a graph is the smallest number [δ] such that any two nodes are connected by a path containing at most [δ edges]" (Lamport et al. 1982, p. 396). It can hence be described as the shortest possible, but the longest necessary path to connect any two nodes in a network. In the case of a centralized network, the diameter is fixed at two ($\delta = 2$), because it takes at most two edges to get from any peripheral node to any other peripheral node (first going from the origin to the central node and from there going to any peripheral node). In the case of a fully-connected network, the diameter is one ($\delta = 1$) because any given node n_i is directly connected to any other given node n_j. In the case of decentralized and distributed networks, the diameter is variable, and will hence be an important measure for the experimental analyses. In the examples below (Fig. 13). the diameters are both $\delta = 2$, because there is always a path constructed from two edges that leads from any node to any other node.

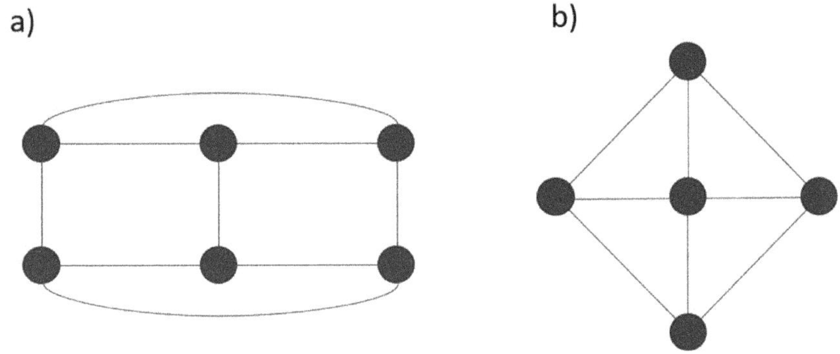

Fig. 13: A P-regular graph and a non-P-regular graph. In (a), each node is connected to exactly three other nodes, while nodes in the non-regular graph (b) don't have the same number of neighbours. (Adapted from Lamport et al. 1982, p. 394)

2.5. Achievement of Consensus in Distributed Networks

In the foregoing sections, the relevant terminology for the description of networks, as well as their topologies and different measurable properties were reported. Given the vast variety of different properties and possible topologies, there is not one single best solution to implementing a ledger object. Even within the specific and restricted class of Blockchain technologies, different use cases may have different affordances concerning network properties (Fridgen et al. 2018). The problem that all types of networks have to solve is the achievement of consensus. A conceptual overview of consensus in terms of communication and some of its semiotic properties were provided above (Section 1.3). This section will describe this concept from a more formal standpoint.

The overarching question is the following: How does a distributed network make sure that the information in the network is coherent? The term coherent mustn't be conflated with correct. The factual correctness of the information, in the sense that it represents truthful propositional values, is irrelevant to consensus. Information in the network is coherent as long as no unwarranted appendices are made to the data, and as long as the network "knows" this. The network has to guarantee that all nodes in the network share the same information. This problem is trivial in centralised network topologies. A central node can force coherence on the network by controlling which information is available to any other node. But how can the state of coherence be maintained in a distributed network? Practical answers to this were given above. Formal considerations follow below. The state of having a coherent set of information shared throughout a distributed network without a central entity is called distributed consensus.

2.5.1. The Byzantine Generals Problem in Fully-Connected Networks

In the foregoing sections, the processes of communication and the properties of communication networks were only considered descriptively. The conditions under which information in distributed systems is compromised were largely left out. The problem of distributed consensus was formalised by Lamport et al. (1982) as the *Byzantine Generals Problem*. The problem formalises possible attacks on distributed consensus based on the metaphor of the Osman siege of Constantinople in 1453.

In this thought experiment, Constantinople was besieged by nine Osman generals. Since Constantinople was heavily fortified, a coordinated attack on the city was necessary to take it. Every evening, a decision was made about whether or not the city should be attacked the next morning. If all generals managed to agree upon an attack, the city would be attacked. If they didn't reach consensus, they held out for another day and the decision was put off until the next evening, continuing the siege. If only a proportion of the generals attacked, the attack would fail and the remaining generals could not take the city later on. Therefore, consensus among the nine generals was indispensable to deciding whether or not an attack would be carried out.

To make their decision, the generals could only coordinate the attack via couriers sent freely from one general to another and stating either "yes" if they wanted to attack, or "no" if they wanted to hold out on the siege another day. Every general sent their vote to everyone else. Furthermore, every general sent everyone else a message about the answers they had received from other generals. In terms of the definitions provided above, this can be described as a fully connected network with nine nodes and a resulting edge space of $|E*| = \frac{9*(9-1)}{2} = 36$ edges, and a network density of $\frac{36}{36} = 1$. The problem that this thought experiment illustrates is faulty consensus. A Byzantine spy general could send out messages with conflicting information (Fig. 14), making some generals think that consensus on attacking had been established, while other generals would hold out on the attack. This would mean that only some generals would attack, but thinking that all other armies would join, while the remaining generals would think that no one should attack.

The Byzantine Generals Problem elucidates how many of the nodes in a fully-connected network can become faulty, that is propagate wrong information into the network, without consensus being compromised. Consider a situation where one of the nodes is malevolent and intentionally or erroneously spreads incoherent information into the system (Fig. 14). As a result of the metaphor in Lamport et al. (1982) this has become known as a Byzantine Attack.

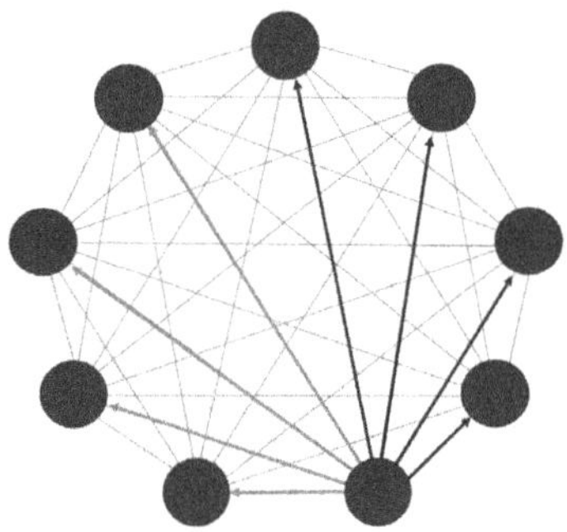

Fig. 14: Schematic representation of a Byzantine Attack. A node propagates conflicting information in the network. Grey lines indicate 'attack!', and black lines indicate 'hold out!'. The node tries to trick other nodes into thinking that consensus has been established, while nodes don't share the same information. This creates a situation in which the Osman generals behave differently and an attack on Constantinople will inevitably fail.

2.5.2. The Oral Messages Algorithm

Lamport et al. (1982) asked whether there was a communication algorithm that would reach consensus in the network even in the presence of malevolent nodes. The authors proved that the problem is solvable for two different types of algorithms. Importantly, they also proved that their solutions apply to non-fully connected networks. In the first part of their contribution, the authors refer to a solution with oral messages (OM) Every general sends word to the others by a messenger who delivers the message correctly. The messengers (i.e., edges) cannot be traitors meaning that, in Shannon's (1948) terms, the *channel* is working correctly. The generals can also report on the decisions of the other generals that they have heard from. What Lamport et al. (1982) demonstrate[29] is that there exists an algorithm for any fully-connected network as long less than a third of the nodes are faulty or malevolent nodes:

$$\forall n,m : n,m \in \mathbb{N}$$

$$\forall n \geq 3m+1 : \exists OM(n,m)$$

For any natural (positive, integer, non-null) number of traitors m there exists an algorithm with oral messages (OM) that achieves consensus in the network if and only if more than two-thirds of the nodes n are non-malevolent. In the case of the example network (Fig. 14), this means that the network could deal with no more than two malevolent nodes because the network consists of nine nodes. Hence, there exists an oral algorithm if and only if the number of traitors (m) times three plus one is minor or equal two the number of nodes in the network. For $m = 2$ the statement evaluates to true because $3*2+1=7\leq 9$ is smaller than 9. However, for three traitors ($m = 3$) the statement evaluates to false because $3*3+1=10\nleq 9$ equals ten and is therefore not smaller or equal to 9. In this case, no functioning algorithm can be constructed. That is because any general can compare conflicting information from different generals and infer which information is correct and which isn't. This works as long as the number of malevolent generals is smaller than ⅓ of the number of nodes. Hence, consensus can be achieved.

29 The actual prof involves a further simplification of the problem, where the generals, rather than taking tactical decisions on their own, act as Lieutenants receiving orders from their commander. This is a simplification in that it reduces the directions that decisions can take (otherwise all generals would have to be treated as commanders and Lieutenants at the same time, or could choose to ignore a given order, which would complicate the problem further). For ease of reading, this proof will not be reproduced here. Rather, the section is interested in characterising the formal problems that the achievement of distributed consensus entails.

2.5.3. The Signed Messages Algorithm

The authors then turn to a more sophisticated algorithm. The Signed Messages Algorithm (SM) uses unforgeable, signed messages, rather than just orally communicated messages. The feature that is added to the messages here is that each message "yes" or "no" is signed with an unforgeable signature by the general who sends it. Moreover, each time a message is received and resent (general 1 sends a "yes" to general 2 and general 2 resends this "yes" to general 3), copies are created and a further signature is appended under the already existing signature (meaning that the "yes" answer from general 1 arrives at general number 3 carrying both the signature of general 1 and the signature of general 2). In this way, any message can be traced through the network and its correctness doesn't have to be inferred from the comparison between different messages. Any message that doesn't carry a correct set of signatures under it can be rejected by any general. Applying this principle to the Byzantine Generals Problem, it is shown that consensus can be achieved through signed messages as long as there are more or equal loyal generals *n* than traitors *m*:

$$\forall n,m : n,m \in \mathbb{N}$$

$$\forall n \geq m : \exists SM(n,m)$$

In principle, the hashes that Bitcoin uses function as such unforgeable signatures (cf. Nakamoto 2008). Thus, it would seem that the Bitcoin network could never be attacked. But this solution is true only under the assumption that the network is fully-connected. This means that for each sending transaction there is necessarily an alternative route, such that each node has access to all the information from all the other nodes, being able to compare them. However, DLT cannot be presumed to be fully connected. Most networks are, empirically speaking, not fully connected. Therefore, Lamport et al. (1982) investigate cases of distributed networks and determine the conditions under which the OM and SM algorithms can still work.

2.5.4. Non-fully Connected Networks

The authors prove that an OM algorithm can exist if the network is not fully connected. However, the solution is restricted to P-regular (Section 2.4.4) graphs. The authors prove that an OM algorithm can solve the Byzantine Generals Problem if and only if *m* is an integer bigger than zero and if *P* is bigger or equal to $3m$. This results in the following formal definition:

$$\forall m, P : m, P \in \mathbb{N}$$

$$\forall P \geq 3m : \exists OM(m, P)$$

In the case of the P-regular network (P = 3) on the left (Fig. 13a), this means that the network can tolerate up to one traitor (m = 1). That is because P = 3, which when divided by 3 (inverting the product 3m) equals 1, resulting in the P-regular network (P = 3) being Byzantine Fault Tolerant up to one traitor. In the case of the right network (Fig. 13b), the theorem doesn't apply, because it is not P-regular.

More often than not, networks are a lot more variable than what is presumed by the assumption of P-regularity. For this, Lamport et al. (1982) extend their proof of SM algorithms to non-fully connected and non-P-regular networks. To express them formally, the diameter of the network (Section 2.4.5) is relevant. The authors prove that there is always an algorithm $SM(\delta, m)$ that solves the Byzantine Generals Problem as long as two conditions are met. Firstly, it is assumed that the subgraph (the proper subset of edges of the graph) of loyal generals is connected. This means that there is a way to get from one node to another without having to pass through a traitor node or, generally speaking, to move from one node to the other (Fig. 15a).

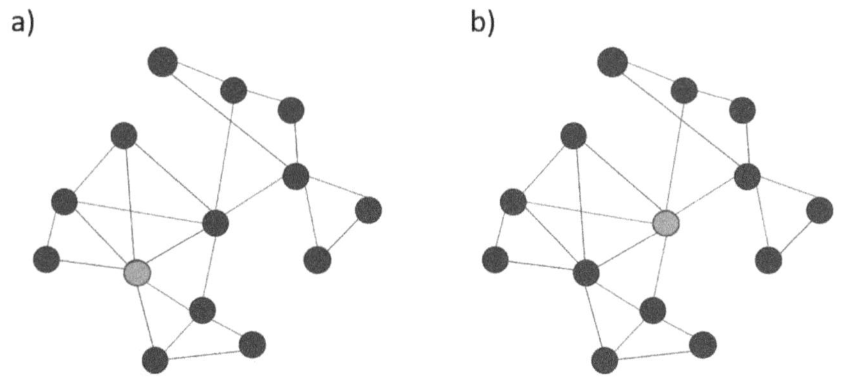

Fig. 15: Connected (a) and unconnected (b) subgraphs. The subgraphs of loyal generals to the northeast and southwest are connected in (a) and unconnected in (b) in the presence of a traitor (light grey) While the traitor in (a) and (b) have the same degree (C = 6), its presence in (b) disconnects the subgraph because no information can be shared between the subgraphs without passing through the traitor node.

With the assumption that the subgraph of loyal generals is connected (thus not completely shielded from each other by malevolent nodes), the Byzantine Generals Problem is solvable for any network, regardless of the number of traitors. Formally, the following conditions are obtained:

$$\forall m, n, \delta : m, n, \delta \in \mathbb{N}$$

$$\forall \delta < n, \forall m < n - \delta : \exists SM(m + \delta - 1)$$

This means, that there is an algorithm with signed messages that solves the Byzantine Generals Problem for any number of nodes and traitors, as long as the loyal generals are connected among each other. That is because the conditions $\forall \delta < n$ and $\forall m < n - \delta$ are always true within the connected subgraph of the loyal generals. However, as the authors point out (Lamport et al. 1982), the time to achieve consensus in such a case scales as a function of the number of traitors and the diameter of the connected subgraph of loyal generals $(m + \delta - 1)$. This means that while, in principle, consensus can be achieved in such networks, the time this takes can differ radically according to the number and position of traitors in the whole network.

This description concludes the formal considerations of graph theory. The following chapter goes on to explore how such concepts have been applied in language-related sciences (Chapter 3). From the merger of these two perspectives, testable hypotheses for the corpus work will be generated (Chapter 4).

3. Network Theories in Linguistics

Having established the conceptual and formal framework for the description of language and communication in networks, a review of the notion of networks in linguistics is in order. This review comprises a rather short period in the history of linguistics because the term has only gained traction in the past few decades.

In the pre-structuralist period, inquiry on language was more or less aimed at the contribution of scholars to their national identities. While this was the role of philologues throughout 19th century Europe, this circumstance had great repercussions in the Western Romanic countries, where a prescriptivist attitude toward language was (and is) sustained throughout the 20th century and the beginning of the 21st century. The socio-political importance of organisms such as the *Académie Française* and the *Real Academia Española (RAE)* to this day is reminiscent of such attitudes. In 2005, the *RAE*, together with the Spanish national news agency EFE and the bank BBVA, founded the FundéuRAE (*Fundación del Español Urgente*). This non-profit organisation has tasked itself with the "promotion of the good use of Spanish in the media"[30] (FundéuRAE 2021), which is a noteworthy investment of funds for a private enterprise. The importance of 'correct' language in these countries is also underlined by the fact that it stands in high regard as a uniting political force. Accordingly, the political constitutions of France and Spain regulate the official status of their national languages in Articles Two and Three respectively. Germany and the United Kingdom, as instances of an opposing tendency, do not regulate the official status of their languages at all, at least not at the level of constitutional or quasi-constitutional law. Studying 'good' language was long reflected in the works of the nations' authors of reference (e.g., Menéndez-Pidal 1908). Hence, prescriptive approaches to how to speak and write properly were the norm (e.g., Grevisse 1973) among scholars in these societies.

On the other hand, prescriptive tendencies have left their mark on the linguistic development of the corresponding languages. The study of certain grammatical or semantic nuances and their relevance for the expression of highly differentiated thought led to the systematic preservation of such nuances in language through institutionalised education. This was indeed very productive to maintain certain grammatical features, especially those which are considered

---

30 From Spanish: "impulsar el buen uso del español en los medios de comunicación". https://www.fundeu.es/Sobrefundeubbva/quienes-somos/

particularly difficult and are thus regarded as elements of the cultured norm. In the Romance languages, the widespread usage of the subjunctive mood, for instance, is quite directly linked to overt discussions on its 'correct' usage. In the case of French, it has been claimed that the subjunctive was first reduced to a grammatical requirement as opposed to an expression of nuanced meaning[31], and subsequently preserved as such a requirement, due to the surrounding discussions of 'correct' language (Hunnius 1976). The lack of actual expressivity of the French subjunctive results in widespread confusion about its usage. Usually, such confusion in French is simply resolved by resorting to lists of trigger verbs[32] (e.g., Soutet 2000), which are still mainly based on the reasoning of academics in the philological tradition of linguistic inquiry in the first half of the 20th century (e.g., Brunot 1922; Clédat 1923).

While this type of thought about language does persist to some extent, the end of the 19th century in European Academia is characterised by a positivistic revolution, for which Darwin's *The Origin of Species* (1859) was one of the most important impulses. While the idea of biological evolution was greatly inspired by historical linguistics and etymology in the beginning (Atkinson & Gray 2005), the discovery of the principles of evolution, in turn, promoted scientific rigour and meticulosity in other fields of academic activity. This 'scientification' also influenced Swiss linguist Ferdinand De Saussure, who, in his doctoral dissertation, applies the idea of evolutionary laws in language development to the study of vowels in the Indo-European languages (1879). While this relationship is by no means mono-causal, it exemplifies the *zeitgeist* and the connection between linguistics and other sciences at the time. The Geneva School and subsequent traditions in linguistics started to turn toward a more descriptivist approach to language, following the model of the sciences. This tendency went on throughout the 20th century. As cited above, Russian Formalism attempted to apply more formally rigid models to the study of poetics (e.g., Jakobson 1960). Formal syntax (Chomsky 1957) was an attempt at formalising structuralism even more. It was shown in the foregoing chapters that these approaches were also heavily impacted by technological developments at the time.

The focus of inquiry in both cases, the pre-structuralist prescriptivism and structuralist descriptivism, is always the linguistic system. Whether the system is characterised in terms of its correctness or functional setup, language is taken to be a thing that exists in the world and that can be described and analysed like a

31 From French: "servitude grammaticale" vs. "finesse d'expression" (Hunnius 1976, p. 22).
32 "verbes déclencheurs" (Soutet 2000).

clockwork, or – as is the most common metaphor in structuralism – the rules of chess. Under this conception, languages are treated as entities that exist in the world and whose structure or rules can be extrapolated from the observation of many instances; as if one observed many games of chess to extrapolate its rules. Such is the structuralist or generative approach to linguistic description. And indeed, in synchronic language studies, this approach leads to the development of extremely powerful grammars such as Dependency Grammars (e.g., Tesnière 1953) or Phrase Structure Grammars (e.g., Chomsky 1957, 1965). On the diachronic front, such structures can be compared to older versions of documented languages to establish continuity between stages in their development through laws of sound change. For instance, one sound law that characterises the development of Romance languages is the palatalisation of velar sounds as Vulgar Latin turns into modern Romance (e.g., /k/ → /ʃ/ in French: "canem" → "chien"). This law is viewed as a property of the 'things' called Romance languages.

It wasn't until after the cognitive turn that the concept of a network could become meaningful in the study of language. The cognitive turn casts the systematicity of language aside. Language is no longer a thing, but the result of human cognition. This means that the *Cognitive Study of Art, Language, and Literature* requires the integration of philosophical questions and methods from disciplines such as cognitive neuroscience (Turner 2002). Such claims move the linguistic sciences away from the object of language and focus them on the human being. The following review of the literature attempts to show the different levels on which networks have been applied to the study of languages. The reason that this review is embedded here in the broader history of linguistics is that the application of networks to language is only plausible and applicable under a scientific paradigm that considers the social and cognitive conditions for language.

Lastly, a caveat for this review is in order. It is important to underline that the term network often refers to different concepts. As will be shown, the notion is applied to different levels of linguistic phenomena. While some accounts use networks as models for different types of grammar, others apply them to communities of speakers. These different applications come with different implications for the resulting theories. Also, different bodies of literature make rather different assumptions about what constitutes a network. The following sections will elucidate the tendencies that exist in the literature.

3.1. Language Typology

The cognitive shift notwithstanding, there are of course still modern and valuable efforts in empirical linguistics or language typology to document and classify languages and their phylogenetic relationships. Even though networks are more pervasive in cognitive theories of language, they have been applied in purely descriptive studies. In language typology, networks are used as an extension of trees. A linguistic tree is a *graph*-ical (!) representation of the lineage of languages in the same sense as they can represent the lineages of species (Huson & Bryant 2006). While trees only allow for the branching off of nodes from the stem, networks allow more detailed connections in the description of such phylogenetic relationships. In language typology, the application of networks follows the following axiomatic assumptions:

1. A network is a model for the description of genetic relationships between languages.
2. Nodes in such a network represent languages, and the edges between them represent phylogenetic relationships.
3. The phylogenetic network is a representational extension of the genetic tree.

This notion responds to a significant problem in the application of family trees to both populations of animals and languages. Spanish, lions, and humanity are not just fixed entities that pass on their genes to the next generation with some random mutations that induce change. Rather, these entities are composed of large quantities of individuals that carry the genetic (or in the case of language memetic[33]) information and pass it on to the next generation.

This isn't to say that in singular cases a German household where the mother is French wouldn't adopt some sort of language mix which may not affect the evolution of German in general. But if this family setup became popular enough to affect the linguistic community as a whole, at which point would this result in a new language and would such a new language then be a daughter of German or French? This question also translates into anthropology, where usually *homo neanderthalensis* isn't regarded as a precursor to modern humans, but another ramification of the *homo* family that died out in competition with the *Cro-Magnons* – the earliest known *homo sapiens*. However, recent genetic discoveries have found that modern humans, especially in Europe, still carry DNA that used to be uniquely attributed to *homo neanderthalensis*, resulting in a different interpretation of the human lineage. Rather than being two fully

33 Richard Dawkins popularised the term *meme* in his book *The Selfish Gene* (1976) as a neologism to provide a metaphorical bridge between *genes* as biological units of information and *memes* as cultural units of information. His idea is that memes are subject to similar evolutionary pressures as genes.

separate branches of the *homo* family, of which only *homo sapiens* survived, it is argued that sexual relationships between both types of hominids have led to a shared gene pool, into which Neanderthal DNA has diluted (Sankararaman et al. 2012).

A similar argument has been made for the development of language. When discussing genetically less well-documented languages, such as the Australian languages, the problem with trees described above is usually not taken into account, and proposals of genetic relationships are still made in a tree-like fashion. Family trees are still made in this fashion (Fig. 16).

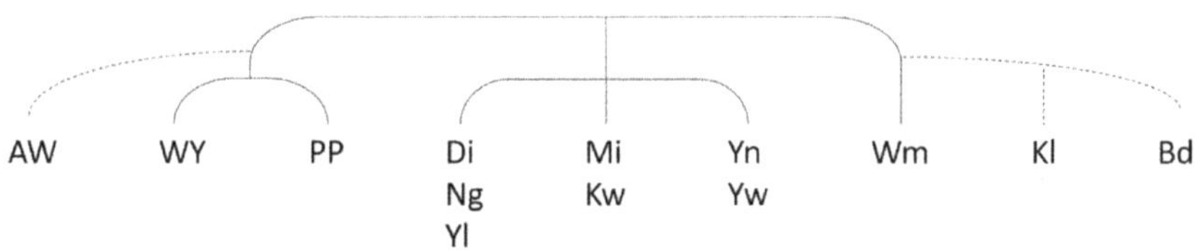

Fig. 16: A language tree proposal of the Karnic subgroup. Dotted lines indicate languages that have not always been regarded as part of Karnic by proponents of the grouping. (Adapted from Breen 2007, p. 178)

Bowern (2009) reviews the Karnic subgroup of Pama-Nyungan and assesses the methodological shortcomings of this type of tree-like representation. The critique stems mainly from the lack of agreement that researchers have had about the classification of this language subgroup after several attempts. This also concerns the concept of border languages which researchers have to resort to when caught in this straightforward interpretation of the tree model for genetic relationships between languages.

Bowern (2009) argues that conflicting attempts at classification are mainly interpreted in terms of contact between the languages that obscures a clear branching off from the mother language (e.g., Thomason & Kaufman 1988; Labov 2007; cited in Bowern 2010, p. 3849). She finds this argument unconvincing, because:

> It seems clear that there are cases where the same processes of language change that produce tree-like splits may also produce networks. In particular, a large area that was settled fairly quickly and where speech communities retained alliances with one another for some time is highly likely to produce a complex dialect area, and relics of the conflicting isoglosses in the earlier dialect area may persist after the languages lose mutual intelligibility (and cease to be regarded as dialects of one another). Arguments of this type rely on relative chronology of shared innovation. (Bowern 2010, p. 3849)

Bowern argues that, in the tree-like representation of linguistic genetic groups, researchers cannot account for similar lexical elements in otherwise very different languages, simply because language contact is regarded as a threat to the comparative method, rather than the norm in interaction. Thus, shared lexical items have to be regarded as shared archaisms rather than shared innovations. By applying network structure as a framework to lexical borrowings, this methodological restriction of the tree-based approach is overcome. Splits (in the representation of shared archaisms) and merges (representing shared innovation) of the genetic process and mutual adaptation of the lexicon can be accounted for in this way (Bowern 2010, p. 3852). Through the application of the NeighborNet algorithm (Bryant et al. 2005; Huson & Bryant 2006; cited in Bowern 2010) processing 770 lexical character sets and lexical closeness of 25 distinct taxa in the Karnic subgroup, a network representation of the loan paths for lexical items was generated (Fig. 17). Rather than being a clear-cut tree with discrete branches, this new representation is claimed to make the actual nature of the evolution of linguistic families more convincing.

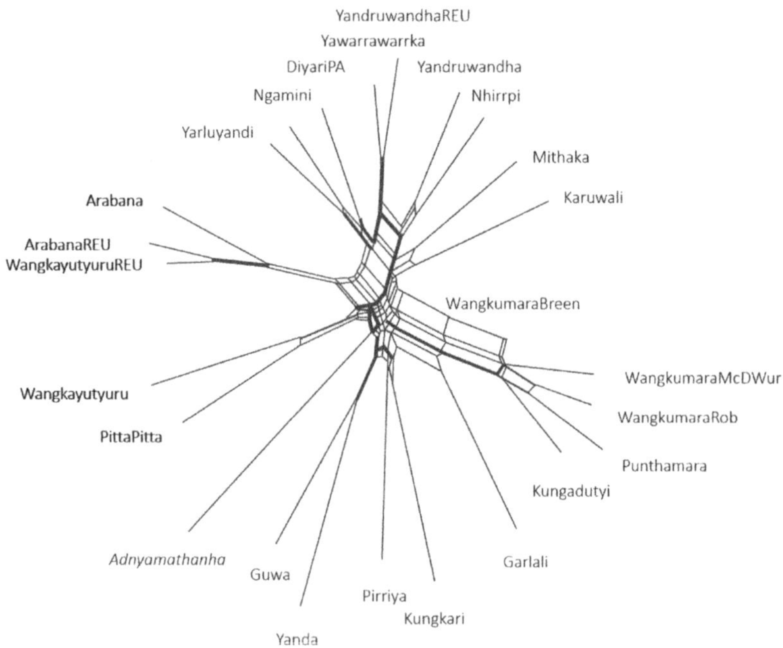

Fig. 17: The twenty-five taxa of the Karnic subgroup of Australian languages. (Adapted from Bowern 2010, p. 3850)

This representation is different from the tree-like representation in that it doesn't inherently map development over time. The time scale in the tree-like representation is implied in that one goes from older to younger languages from the trunk node to the leaf nodes at the bottom. In the case of a network, the temporal scale could be inferred going from the inside out, but it doesn't lie in the nature of this representation to make claims about the order of the temporal scale. After all, data for all analysed taxa is synchronic.

Bakker et al. (2011) state the problem of the historicity of phylogenetic trees more overtly and criticise the fact that they only regard

> [...] shared, historical features [such that] English will unequivocally belong to the Germanic branch, even though the language is significantly influenced by other languages, especially French. Any contact influence is ignored, and double inheritance (mixture) is not possible in this model. (Bakker et al. 2011, p. 11)

The authors claim that this historical way to look at linguistic data is not suitable for creole languages, which they deem a separate class of languages in its own right. That is because the emergence of these languages is fundamentally different from how European languages developed, given that they exist almost exclusively in colonial contexts. In such contexts, speakers from unrelated languages try to communicate with each other and establish pidgins which can then be systematised into more complex creole languages. In terms of typology, they also present a more technical problem in that the genetic relationship to other languages in a tree-like model depends to a high degree on whether or not one chooses the lexicon or the grammatical structure as a standard for comparison.

> In trees based on inherited vocabulary, creoles unsurprisingly cluster with the lexifier languages [...] Creoles typically show lexical continuity with their [lexifier languages], but only limited continuity in their structural make-up making it strictly seen impossible to consider a creole language a genetic descendant of its lexifier. (ibid., p. 14)

Therefore, the authors resort to an extended method, namely plotting phylogenetic relationships between languages in a network, in which they combined both lexical and grammatical features of 12 non-creoles and 18 creoles into a phylogenetic analysis. They find that, in this type of analysis, creole languages form a cluster that is distinct in its features from non-creole languages. Rather than creoles clustering around their lexifier languages, they cluster around each other and therefore form their own class (Fig. 18). This is an interesting finding in that the treatment of creoles as a separate class has often been advocated from various standpoints such as reduced complexity (Parkvall 2008; cited in Bakker et al. 2011) and similarity among each other rather than similarity to their lexifier languages (McWorter 1998; cited in Bakker et al. 2011).

The representation of these genetic relationships between language in terms of networks, rather than phylogenetic trees, has thus had a huge methodological impact on the documentation and classification of linguistic typologies, especially in those contexts which lack continuity in historical documentation. This is also the case in Australian languages (Bowern 2010). This also goes to show that an increase in the facility of access to computational resources and software that enables these types of mathematical analysis gives a whole new set of possibilities for linguistics researchers, as was stated in the introduction (Section 0.2).

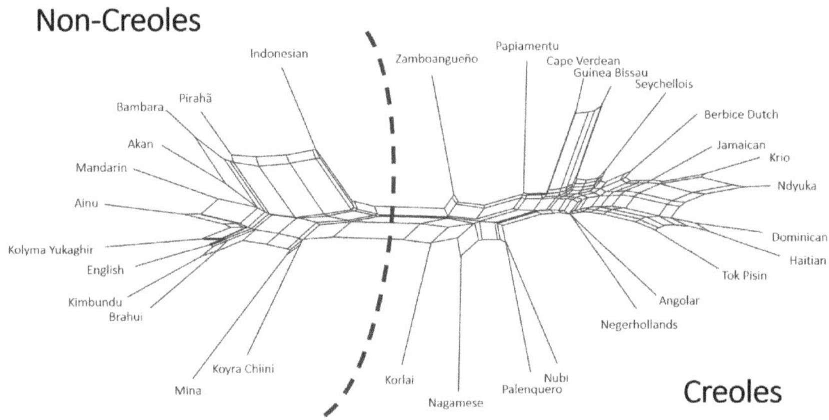

Fig. 18: Phylogenetic network of twelve non-creoles and eighteen creoles. (Adapted from Bakker et al. 2011)

To show the value of the notion of network for linguistic inquiry, it is interesting that a change in the representation of phylogenetic relationships (from tree to network) has such an important methodological impact and can ultimately produce new arguments to settle long-standing discussions about the formal and historical relationships between languages.

Another way in which the concept of networks has impacted the work on linguistic typology is the mapping of syntactic structures as networks. Such networks can then be used to classify languages according to their network parameters (Liu & Li 2010). For this, the authors arrange semantic dependencies of fifteen different languages from various example sentences into syntactic networks. This is similar to the two earlier contributions in that this method supposes a complexion from a tree-like structure to a network structure. In the previous examples, this meant purposefully complexifying the representation of linguistic phylogenetic relationships. In the case of Liu and Li (2010), the networks are a result of combining the tree-like dependency structure of various example sentences into one bigger structure. As the following section will show, this is a typical procedure for the induction of syntactic networks (Section 3.2). These are however more complex than what can be visually plotted. A simplified example of such syntactic networks is provided below (Fig. 19). The authors show that languages can then be classified according to the resulting network properties such as average degree of nodes, cluster coefficients, average path length, network centralisation, and diameter, among others (cf. Chapter 2 for definitions). The takeaway message from this example, together with the previous ones, is that the extension of the tree-like structure to a network structure has had an important impact on typological studies on language.

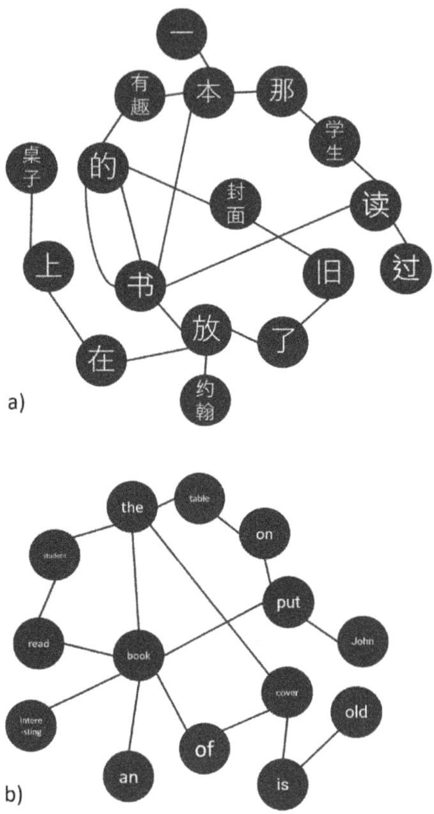

Fig. 19: Syntactic networks of three example sentences from (a) Chinese and (b) English. (Adapted from Liu & Li 2010, p. 3460)

While the concept of networks has illuminated the field of linguistic typology, as the previous examples show, this is not the focus of the current study. The references are interesting in so far as they show the profound theoretic impact that a methodological choice can have. In the following, this impact will be evidenced by cognitive and socio-linguistic theories.

3.2. Cognition and Linguistic Networks

It was reported earlier that science in the 20th century was characterised by several paradigm shifts. One of these, the cognitive turn, was the shift away from the observation of language as a systematic phenomenon toward its underpinnings in individual psychology. Such efforts begin early in the 20th century but don't become mainstream before the 1960s. For instance, to harness the vast variety of usages of the subjunctive mood in Spanish and bind them into a single, more comprehensive concept, the psychological subjunctive (Lemon 1927) was introduced. At the same time, Bühler's *Crisis of Psychology*[34] (1927) made the point of the importance of the psychological reality of humans in the analysis of humans' semiotic and, by extension, linguistic behaviour.

Noam Chomsky, whose approach was earlier characterised in terms of the underlying computer metaphor, gains traction during the cognitive turn, even though his early work is not concerned with cognition at all (e.g., Chomsky 1956, 1957, 1959b; Chomsky & Schützenberger 1959). However, Chomsky later incorporates a cognitive perspective to characterise language as a reflection of human thought (Chomsky 1965, 1968). This modernises the structuralist approach to language in that the structure of language now grants access to the structure of human thinking. While the conception of cognition in Chomsky's work is by and large equated with computation, the great achievement at this point in the history of linguistics lies in the appraisal of linguistic structure and the underlying substrate that is cognition.

With more recent psychological and neuroscientific knowledge, this approach was challenged by a newer approach to language (Harris 1996), still focused on the individual psychological reality of speakers, but with a less narrowly defined methodology and more adequate tools for the analysis of the psychological basis of human language. This development has given rise to modern areas of linguistic research such as psycholinguistics (e.g., Osgood & Sebeok 1954), neurolinguistics (e.g., Kutas & Hillyard 1980) and cognitive linguistics (e.g., Lakoff & Johnson 1980a), all of which have immense repercussions in the modern sciences and contribute to exploring the intricate relationship between the human organism, its cognitive capacities, and the language(s) that it produces.

It is in the avenue of these conceptions of language, that the term network is systematically applied to the study of languages and grammars. An insightful anthology on the subject was edited by Mehler et al. (2016) who shed some light

34 Original title: *Die Krise der Psychologie* (Bühler 1927).

on the structure of this scientific field. The volume is structured into Cognition, Topology, Syntax, Dynamics, and Resources. The first three sections share a common definition of what a linguistic network is and will be subject to review in this section. The contributions grouped into these sections abide by and large by the following axiomatic conception. The three common axioms of linguistic networks are:

1. Linguistic structure can be represented in graphs, where words are described as nodes and the (grammatical) relations between them can be mapped as edges,
2. Grammar is a product of exclusively human cognition (or is even equated with cognition), and
3. Cognitive processes take place at the level of the individual mind.

Many of these approaches are rather tightly linked to formal and generative work in linguistics (e.g., Čech et al. 2016; Ferrer-i-Cano 2016). Language as a network, in all of the literature considered in this section, is subject to the following conception: A "linguistic network is represented as a graph whose vertices denote linguistic units (e.g., words, sentences, or textual units) and whose edges model linguistic (e.g., syntactic, semantic or pragmatic) relations of these units" (Mehler et al. 2016, p. v). In the subsequent sections, different applications of linguistic networks will be reported, with the main distinction drawn between semantic and syntactic networks. These descriptions will be complemented with some comments on the limitations of such networks as identified in the literature. Please note that the descriptions of these applications of graph theory to the study of language, while useful and important, are not going to be of further interest to this study. They are reported in an effort to clarify the level at which networks can be and are used in linguistic studies and to extrapolate presumptions and methodological choices in the application of graphs in linguistics.

3.2.1. Semantic Networks

Semantic networks are best characterised as networks of semantic units which are connected by edges that express a semantic relationship. As Choudhury and Mukherjee (2009) point out, such semantic relationships can be induced by several parameters such as semantic similarity, hierarchical structure (relationships of hypernyms and hyponyms), and others. A rather simple example of such a language network is reported in Vitevitch (2008) and reproduced in Vitevitch et al. (2016), in which lexical units are modelled as a network of phonological similarity (Fig. 20). Each edge indicates a phonological minimal pair relationship. This type of network is used by the authors (Vitevitch 2008; Vitevitch et al. 2016) to model phonetic and phonological retrieval of lexical units and misperception of speech respectively. However, the arbitrariness of choice with regard to the nature of the plotted relationship (e.g., phonological similarity, hierarchical relation) between lexical units also raises the question of which types of relationships can be meaningfully plotted as networks.

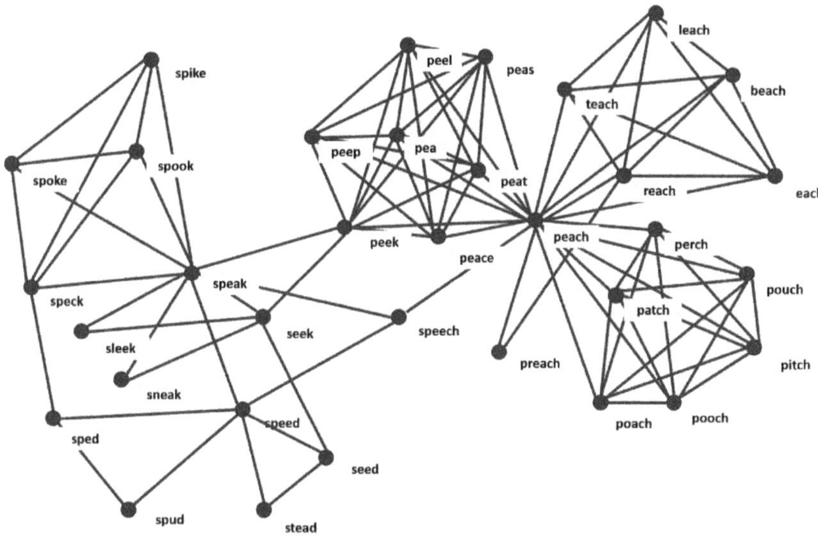

Fig. 20: A small portion of the English phonological network as analysed in Vitevitch. (Adapted from 2008, cited in Vitevitch et al. 2016)

It has been argued that the relationship between nodes shouldn't be induced by theoretical precepts (Araújo & Banisch 2016; Zweig 2016). Rather, graphs should be used to represent empirical relationships between identifiable lexical units. Hence, a great deal of attention in linguistic networks is placed on word co-occurrence networks or collocation networks (Choudhury & Mukherjee 2009; Araújo & Banisch 2016) in which the edges refer to the observable co-occurrence of two words in either the mental lexicon or in a corpus of text. This distinction is crucial in that the latter is preoccupied with methods of data analysis in corpora, whereas work on the mental lexicon makes specific claims about the cognitive reality of information retrieval.

Another way of inducing linguistic networks is based on semantic similarity (Choudhury & Mukherjee 2009). For instance, the WordNet® lexical database for English at Princeton University is built upon the word relation of synonymy:

> WordNet® is a large lexical database of English. Nouns, verbs, adjectives and adverbs are grouped into sets of cognitive synonyms (synsets), each expressing a distinct concept. Synsets are interlinked by means of conceptual-semantic and lexical relations. The resulting network of meaningfully related words and concepts can be navigated with the browser. (Princeton University 2010)

While such "conceptual-semantic and lexical relations" can be induced via expert evaluation, as in the above case, other proponents of such mental lexicons have used responses of large numbers of human participants in experimental association tasks to generate more empirically valid representations of such semantic networks (e.g., De Deyne et al. 2013).

In all of the reviewed literature, there is no specific convention as to how semantic relationships should be modelled in networks. Rather, different phenomena and research questions seem to warrant different applications of networks. For a more complete review of different applications of semantic networks see Beckage and Colunga (2016). In their contribution, the authors characterise different ways to construe and construct semantic networks. Two examples are given below (Fig. 21). Note that the network structure emerges from the extension of the tree structure by adding further dimensions. This diagrammatical extension is the same that was described earlier referring to Bakker et al. (2011).

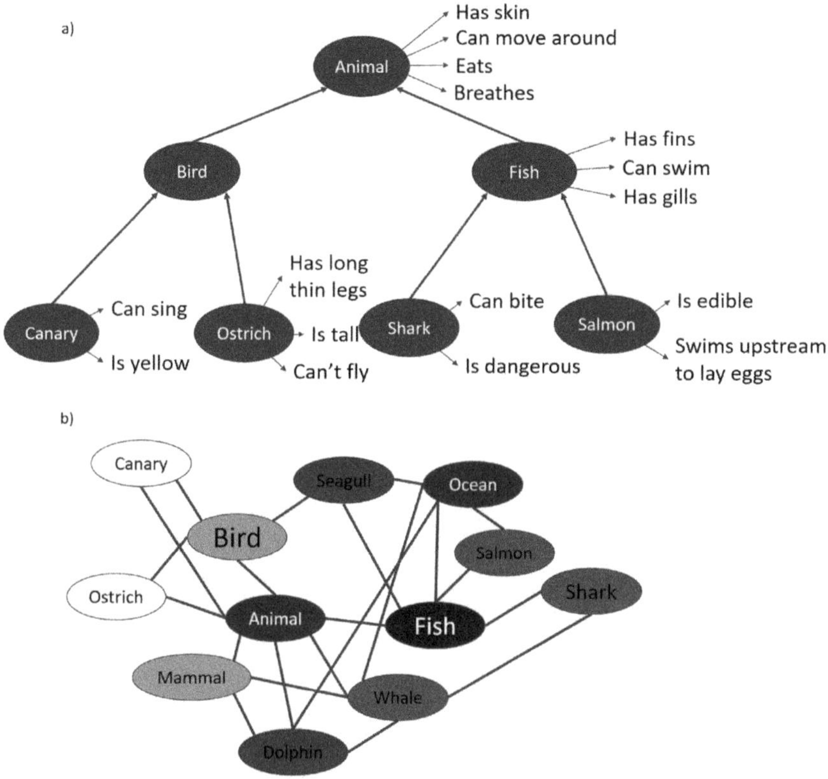

Fig. 21: Two types of semantic networks adapted from (a) Quillian (1967) and (b) Collins and Loftus (1975), both cited in Beckage and Colunga (2016). Note how the network structure emerges from additional dimensions in the hierarchical tree structure.

De Deyne et al. (2016) compare two different types of models of the *Structure and Organisation of the Mental Lexicon*. They compare corpus-induced semantic networks with word association networks, that is, networks that are induced upon cues and responses by participants in the lab. The authors argue that this type of network provides a "more direct way of assessing the mental content of the lexicon" (De Deyne et al. 2016, p. 47). They also report that word association networks and corpus-based networks exhibit different structural properties and that word association networks are better at capturing the relatedness between concepts that results from participants' answers in judgement tasks. This particularly shows the individual cognitive model of language that underlies semantic networks.

The references cited above are characterised by the aforementioned individualistic approach to language and cognition. Cognitive processes are conceived of as taking place in a single mind. This isn't trivial with regard to the limitations of these approaches discussed below (cf. Section 3.3.3). Beckage and Colunga (2016) make their individualist approach explicit when laying out their *Language Networks as Models of Cognition*.

> Here we choose to focus on language at the level of the individual – where cognitive processes occur. We focus on network representations that are inherently cognitive, derived from individual language knowledge or human performance. Specifically, for the sake of capturing the influence of cognition on language networks, we focus on two broad classes of networks that have influenced linguistics and psychology – 1) semantic networks […]. (Beckage & Colunga. 2016, p. 5)

This is also true for Choudhury and Mukherjee (2009) who revisit how linguistic networks can be used to model and explain the "mental lexicon" (Choudhury & Mukherjee 2009, p. 2), which is explicitly construed as an individual cognitive process, involving the storage and retrieval of lexical units in long term memory. The authors report on a plethora of different contributions (Sigman & Cecchi 2002; Vitevitch 2004; Gruenenfelder & Pisoni 2005; Tamariz 2005; Kapatsinski 2006; all cited in Choudhury & Mukherjee 2009) that construe the mental lexicon as a network. Each lexical item is stored as a node that is connected to other items through phonological or semantic similarity, frequency of usage, co-occurrence, syntactic dependency or other factors that can create a connection between nodes. To store and/or retrieve lexical units, the mind navigates these densely connected networks to access appropriate units. Rather than being mere computational models, these networks are often construed as cognitive processes that take place in an individual's mind (e.g., Solé et al. 2010).

Furthermore, Beckage and Colunga (2016) make an explicit claim as to the specific 'humanness' of language, which relates to their conception of semantic networks: "Language is inherently cognitive and distinctly human" (p. 4). As will be argued below (cf. Section 3.3) this also conflates individual cognition and language. A similar formulation can be found in Choudhury and Mukherjee (2009). This assumption does prove to be useful when challenging the mere behaviouristic or structural view of language as was pointed out earlier because is true that separating "the object of language from the human mind fails to capture the language system fully" (Beckage & Colunga 2016, p. 4). But it neglects the effects of the interaction of both language and the human individual with the environment and other individuals. This caveat notwithstanding, the representation of individual cognitive processes in networks allows for useful applications ranging from semantics and phonology to language acquisition. For example, language acquisition is described as the induction and growth of a semantic and syntactic network in a speaker's mind (Hills et al. 2009; cited in Beckage & Colunga 2016). This explicative power of networks in terms of individual cognition is tremendous because they are versatile in their application to various phenomena. However, the empirical validity of such induced networks has to be defended in each case where they are applied (cf. Araújo & Banisch 2016; Zweig 2016).

3.2.2. Syntactic Networks

Turning to syntactic networks, Choudhury and Mukherjee (2009) introduce the distinction between collocation networks and syntactic dependency networks (Ferrer-i-Cancho & Solé 2004; Ferrer-i-Cancho 2005; cited in Choudhury & Mukherjee 2009). While both types of networks are based on word co-occurrence, the former model semantic relationships, while the latter model syntactic relationships. Such syntactic dependency networks represent a different way of modelling syntactic relationships. Again, it can be observed that the network structure is an extension of the tree structure.

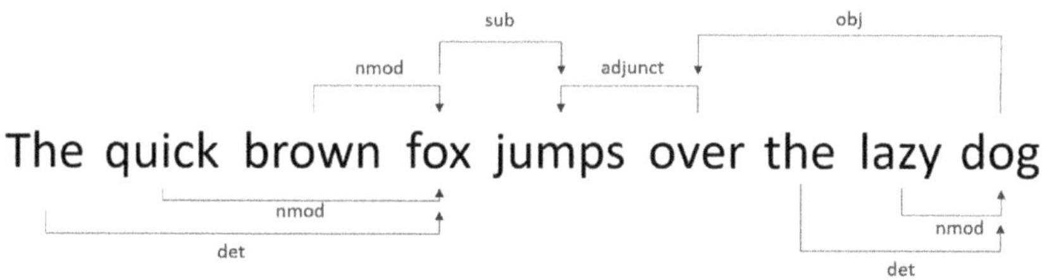

Fig. 22: Example of a dependency tree, modelled as a network of syntactic relations. The arrows are labelled according to the type of dependency relation. (Adapted from Choudhury & Mukherjee 2009)

While the above illustration shows the network for a single sentence, Solé et al. (2010) elaborate on the process of building more complex syntactic networks from corpora of texts. Built in this fashion, the syntactic network doesn't merely reflect the behaviour of single linguistic units *in situ*, but reflects general properties of the grammatical system, in so far it shows all possible syntactic dependencies in the corpus. The above example by Liu and Li (2010) works similarly. However, their approach is directed at the characterisation of linguistic families, rather than modelling cognitive processes (cf. Section 3.1). It appears, then, that the ontological status of such networks isn't well-defined. For a review of syntactic networks and their applications in language acquisition and typology see Čech et al. (2016). According to their exhaustive review, syntactic networks all represent words as nodes, whether they are lemmas or particular word forms, while edges represent semantic dependencies. They also report that such networks are based on dependency grammar (Čech et al. 2016, p. 169). The authors also state that approaches that use networks are far from uniform in their theoretical underpinnings. While syntactic dependency is sometimes claimed to be a deterministic rule (e.g., Solé et al. 2010; cited in Čech et al. 2016), the authors themselves emphasise a more probabilistic model of syntactic dependencies.

With such a range of different theoretic approaches, it is clear that not all authors in Mehler et al. (2016) sustain the axioms stated above to the same degree. Ferrer-i-Cancho (2016), for instance, does apply networks to cognitive processes, but ultimately argues that these grammatical networks are not grammatical in a strong sense. In his contribution, he alludes to Lecerf's (1960) and Hays' (1964) observation that grammatical dependencies, when drawn out in networks, usually do not cross (Fig. 23). This is often taken to be indicative of the 'designedness' of language or the innateness of grammar in the human brain.

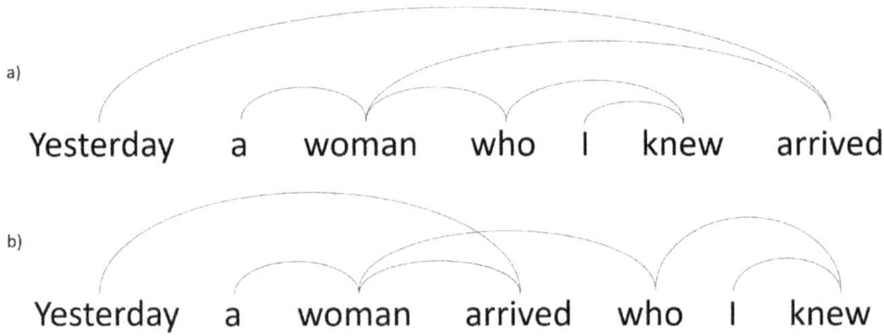

Fig. 23: (a) An English sentence with a relative clause ("who I knew"). (b) The same sentence with the right extraposition of the relative clause. (Adapted from Levy et al. 2012; cited in Ferrer-i-Cancho 2016). According to the argument, the upper sentence is more well-formed and more easily processable, because it avoids crossings, although it is less economic with regards to path lengths.

Ferrer-i-Cancho (2016) argues that the rare empirical occurrence and low grammatical acceptability of sentences with dependency crossings needn't be accounted for via innateness of grammar. Having excluded chance as a driver for this effect in various experiments, he argues that the reduction of dependency lengths and the avoidance of dependency crossings require less cognitive processing. That means, crossings don't have to be forbidden by cognitive rules but appear to be the more resource-efficient and hence desirable construction. Even though this account is grounded in a procedural model of language, it specifically argues against an explanation of grammatical effects that equates these processes with the underlying cognitive architecture.

This entails a caveat for the axioms mentioned above, as the strong version of such claims is contradicted by some researchers of syntactic networks. What this shows is that strong claims of innateness or the cognitive reality of syntactic processes in syntax-based theories of language are no longer uncontroversial. In a historical perspective on the relationship between generative linguistics and linguistic networks, Pater (2019) identifies various stages of confluence and discrepancy between connectionist (i.e., network) and rule-based models of language. Chomsky's syntactic theory (Chomsky 1957) and Rosenblatt's *perceptron* (Rosenblatt 1958), the basis for modern neural networks, appeared to be based on similar conceptions of human language processing (Pater 2019). But the connectionist and syntactic traditions collided in the past-tense-debate between Rumelhart and McClelland (1986) and Pinker and Prince (1988, both cited in Pater 2019). From the perspective of these authors, the idea of distributed representation clashed dramatically with the compositional nature of Chomskyan linguistics. In more recent approaches, Pater (2019) identifies pleas to the approximation between rule-based theories of syntax and network approaches, simply because the statistical explicative power of the latter cannot be ignored. The general trend seems to be that connectionist models and network representations of language are playing an increasingly important role in syntactic theories of language. While the 1980s are still characterised by very polemic rejections of connectionist models in defence of rule-based approaches (e.g., Fodor & Pylyshyn 1988), newer studies on semantic or syntactic networks (e.g., De Deyne et al. 2016; Čech et al. 2016, respectively) incorporate connectionist approaches while maintaining a strong theoretical grounding in generative linguistics.

The association of linguistic networks with the generative theory of syntax is relevant in so far as it concerns the cognitive status of these networks. Some authors are adamant about the cognitive reality of network processes in the human mind (e.g., Solé 2005; Solé et al. 2010; De Deyne et al. 2016). This means that they construe networks as being physically present in the human organism, or that the structure of thought is materially equivalent to networks. In this regard, some authors stand in the tradition of the strong version of the claims of generative grammar equating linguistic networks with mental networks. Other authors, however, use syntactic networks as models of the cognitive process. In this version, networks provide robust explanations for phenomena and allow to predict the outcome of previously unobserved data without generalising such processes to cognition. Ferrer-i-Cancho (2016) uses networks to argue for a principle of least effort because simpler network representations correlate with more acceptable sentences. He doesn't presuppose, however, that the network representation is therefore materially correspondent to the cognitive process. Čech et al. (2016) too, use syntactic networks for the description of language acquisition and typology but emphasise the probabilistic nature of these rules. Also, typology and acquisition are vastly different areas of research. The former constitutes a macro-phenomenon and the latter an individual developmental process. The authors hence emphasise the role of networks as models for these phenomena. While they do underline that networks are useful as generalising models, because they can be applied to micro-, meso-, and macro-level structures, they are careful not to equate these models with the processes modelled.

3.2.3. Limitations of Linguistic Networks in Individual Cognition

The literature itself provides some arguments to systematise the concerns about the application of linguistic networks to cognitive processes. Araújo and Banisch (2016) review a long list of different network models, ranging from typical linguistic tasks such as semantic co-occurrence to airport nets and nets of financial transactions (p. 125). Comparing these vastly different cases, they systematise the levels of abstraction on which the network framework is applied:

1. Abstraction Level-1: real networks of systems composed of elementary units which are explicitly linked or in between which real processes take place,
2. Abstraction Level-2: proximity networks of systems composed of elementary units and a well-defined measure of distance in between these units (shared features, correlation or similarity),
3. Abstraction Level-3: induced networks that are synthesised out of databases (probably the outcome of a complex system) and in which the definition of elements and links is not explicit in the data (Araújo & Banisch 2016, p. 109)

This means that networks have different semiotic statuses, depending on the ontology of the modelled phenomenon. Instances of abstraction level-1 networks are marriages in Renaissance Florentine or airport networks (Borgatti

2005; cited in Araújo & Banisch 2016, p. 125). In these cases, the connection is observable and not induced. Family members are legally bound to another family in marriage. Similarly, two airports are connected via a flight connection. On the other hand, linguistic networks such as vectorial semantics (Salton et al. 1975; cited in Araújo & Banisch 2016, p. 125) are classified as abstraction level-2, whereas syntactic or semantic networks are even classified as abstraction level-3 networks (Solé et al. 2010; cited in Araújo & Banisch 2016, p. 125). That is because the connections between nodes in the networks are by no means apparent. While vector-space semantic networks are clearly defined in terms of statistical properties of the co-occurrence of words in actual texts, other types of networks might be less well-motivated. Is, for example, homophony (Vitevitch 2008; Vitevitch et al. 2016, Fig. 20) a meaningful connection in a semantic network? Such questions render the concerns raised before (Section 3.2.2) relevant. If cognitive processes were physically structured in a network fashion, a network would undoubtedly be a reasonable model for such processes. If, however, networks aren't well motivated with regard to the level of abstraction, what information can be inferred from them?

For many purposes, a pragmatic argument might suffice. If it works, it is a good model. The introduction (Section 0.4.1.1) drew upon Artificial Neural Networks and their importance for linguistic modelling and practical application. It was stated that ANN were produced in the appraisal of human neurons but that the underlying computer metaphor was somewhat inadequate (Jain et al. 1996, Section 0.4.1.1). However, it cannot be denied that ANN are very successful in the modelling of human language. Products such as Google Translate[35] or DeepL[36] achieve amazing results in machine translation of colloquial language compared to just a few years ago[37].

Much of the theoretical work on ANN is agnostic with regard to the similarity between humans and linguistic networks (e.g., McCloskey 1991). Agnostic means that the development of ANN for natural language processing is – ideologically speaking – not concerned with the accurate modelling of the human mind, but merely measures the success of the neural network against the quality of translation (or other behaviour) it provides. Put differently, whether humans and machines produce and/or process language in the same way is not of concern, as long as both result in a use of language that is intuitively recognized by humans

35 https://translate.google.com
36 https://www.deepl.com/translator
37 Again, the body of this thesis was written even before the publication of ChatGPT.

as 'correct', 'natural', or 'adequate'. To employ a previous analogy, an aeroplane might not be a good model for the mechanisms that birds use to fly, but if flying at all is the goal, the aeroplane still does an adequate job of achieving this.

But the extrapolation of good modelling results to human cognition (e.g., Solé 2005; Solé et al. 2010; De Deyne et al. 2016, Section 3.2.2) appears, from the standpoint of the motivation of the underlying linguistic networks (Araújo & Banisch 2016) a stretch of argument. In semiotics, the transposition of material results (i.e., networks) onto immaterial phenomena (i.e., cognition) has been termed Material Derailment[38] (Eschbach 2015, p. 10) and is considered a fallacious argument regarding the status of representation.

Zweig (2016) is even more critical. She doubts that word adjacency networks (and by extension syntactic networks) *are* networks in a strong sense altogether. She claims that network representations are extremely useful to identify and describe effects that cannot be reduced to the effects of a single node; that is, effects that arise only through the interaction of these nodes. But such phenomena presuppose the existence of entities and connections between them in the first place. For Zweig (2016), network representations can only be applied to represent effects that are existent and observable. She gives the – now rather universal[39] – example of a virus spreading in a population. When people interact, physical closeness permits the actual transmission from one person to another. In terms of Araújo's et al. (2016) argument, this would correspond to an abstraction level-1 network. Zweig calls into question, whether word adjacency networks can be used to describe lexicon retrieval processes in the mind at all because word adjacency networks are ultimately statistical models constructed from corpora. Her position is that such induced networks cannot inform cognitive processes, because the network already is a model which needs an empirical basis to be mapped onto.

It is furthermore interesting to observe the role that network representations have played in the history of syntactic theories. The different points of confluence and collision between network theories of language and formal theory of syntax were briefly alluded to above (Pater 2019, Section 3.2.2). This relates to the assumptions of human uniqueness of language on the one hand and primacy of individual cognition on the other hand. While neither assumption is uncommon, it is not the topic of this dissertation to fundamentally argue against or in favour of such positions[40]. Much more interesting is the development that this

38 From German: "Stoffentgleisung".

39 This thesis was written to a large proportion during the COVID-19 pandemic.

40 Many researchers in both semiotics and biology – less so in linguistics – are challenging human exceptionalism, for instance in further developing the biosemiotics of Uexküll

theoretical opposition has undergone in the past decades. While the network view and the rule-based view appeared to be irreconcilable at the time of the past-tense-debate (Pater 2019), it now appears that the network representation is sometimes reinterpreted in order to uphold the assumptions extrapolated above. Baroni (2019) is a key example of how the relationship between network models and linguistic cognition has been turned upside down since the 1980s. Baroni argues that, while ANN are usually thought to exploit probabilistic effects in language processing, they are (or have to be) capable of generalising algebraic compositional rules. He concludes his review of the literature by suggesting that deep networks are capable of subtle grammar-dependent generalisations, while they don't rely on compositional rules as building blocks. With this argument, Baroni attempts to reconcile rule-based traditional syntax in reminiscence of Chomskyan (1965) linguistics and the computationally much more successful ANN.

It is within this rather complex panorama of positions that networks, both in the sense of ANN and linguistic networks, have their place in the syntactic and formal theories of language. The drawbacks that were reported for these approaches entail that the design of linguistic networks has to be well justified. Furthermore, robust definitions of entities (nodes) and their relationships (edges) have to be provided at the level of representation. This will also be of importance to the current study and will be laid out in the description of the dataset (Chapter 5).

Most importantly, networks can be applied to all sorts of linguistic phenomena, as long as they are in tune with Zweig's (2016) argument or Araújo and Banisch's (2016) definition of an abstraction level-1 network. For instance, the application of networks to the process of language acquisition (De Deyne et al. 2016) can be applied to the interaction dynamics of the infant with other speakers of the language (e.g., Gong & Shuai 2016) rather than to the growth of the infant's cognitive network itself. While the same phenomenon is under investigation, the application of a network framework moves to a different level. In the next section, applications of networks to social phenomena will be reviewed, where instead of modelling language as such, nodes and edges model human agents and the relationships between them.

(1974, 1984). This quarrel is most popularly fought on the fronts of Chomsky (1968) and Pinker (1994), who argue that language is innate, and hence an exceptional capacity restricted to humans alone, versus Tomasello (2003) and Sampson (2007), who argue that language isn't necessarily a special tool for communication in the animal kingdom.

3.3. Social Cognition and Social Networks

This section is chiefly occupied with the description of social networks in a framework of social cognition. Both terms require further definition. Social cognition is defined as those psychological processes and capabilities that are used not to make sense of the world, but to make sense of other social beings (Frith 2008). In a broader sense, social cognition includes phenomena of collective, rather than individual cognition. Linguistic meaning, for example, is by and large not an individual capacity, but a collective effort of interaction and mutual control that implies complex dynamics (Tylén et al. 2013). In this sense, social cognition is an emergent property of social interaction, and methods from this field are used to explain phenomena which cannot be sufficiently accounted for at the level of individual cognition. This conception plays an important role in fields like linguistic evolution, where language-internal factors of language evolution (Labov 2001; cited in Gong & Shuai 2016) are complemented by language-external factors and social factors, as the following sections will evidence. Many of the cited contributions referenced in this section (3.3) and the following chapter (4) subscribe – or can be attributed – to research efforts in social cognition.

Social networks, on the other hand, are models of agents that, according to the above-formulated assumption of social cognition, are embedded in social relations (Brandes et al. 2014). According to the authors, social network analysis investigates the effects that occur in such networks, which cannot be reduced to the behaviour of single actors. Furthermore, such networks are often described and analysed in terms of graph theory, as also the current study intends. This section will be concerned with the specific effects that network properties have on linguistic and semiotic phenomena. The contributions to social network analysis presented in this section subscribe, to varying degrees of explicitness, to the following axiomatic framework of social network theory:

1. Linguistic interaction can be modelled in networks, in which nodes are agents (i.e., speakers and hearers) and edges are linguistic interactions between these actors,
2. Language and linguistic structure are an epiphenomenon of communication and interaction, and
3. "cognition" isn't confined to the individual mind, but collective efforts can sensibly be described as social cognition.

It has to be pointed out that many of the following authors argue explicitly (e.g., Kirby et al. 2007) against the tradition of generative linguistics. The strong opposition between the social ("functionalist", Leech 1980) and cognitive ("formalist", ibid.) views had already been identified by Geoffrey Leech, who argued that the integration of these approaches under a unifying paradigm was a desideratum for linguistics (Leech 1980). That is, a linguistic theory cannot cast aside the meaning of social interactions and measurable effects therein as a product of pragmatics as opposed to the 'pure' linguistic description of syntax and semantics[41]. On the other hand, this also requires acknowledging the cognitive reality and autonomy of individuals. While the literature under review doesn't call the latter into question, it is clear that the focus lies on the former aspect.

3.3.1. Networks in Language Development

It has long been argued that structural elements in societies, such as institutional mechanisms that represent a centralised authority have an impact on social conventions, and therefore language (Merton 1938). This seems intuitive given the very high degree of supra-regional mutual intelligibility within the highly institutionalised Romance languages, in particular, Spanish and French (cf. Section 3.0). These languages can be spoken across various continents with relative ease of mutual intelligibility as opposed to more atomised dialect clusters such as Italian, where communication over a few hundred kilometres distance can result in serious problems for communication. While the centralisation of linguistic or political authority might have some degree of influence on the stability of languages, the argument does of course fall short. English is a widespread language with high mutual intelligibility, even compared to Spanish, while regulatory efforts of language fixation are minimal compared to Spanish. Also, from the impact of social institutions on social conventions, it is impossible to explain how social conventions come about without their presence. It is ultimately impossible to explain how these social institutions come about in the first place (Ungeheuer 1987; Centola & Baronchelli 2015).

41 The categorisation of semantics, syntax, and pragmatics goes back to Charles W. Morris (1938) and is not meant to suppose a harsh trichotomy between different areas of investigation. Rather, Morris defines these levels of inquiry to have different relational status with regards to the sign. Semantics is where the sign interacts with what it represents, syntax is where it interacts with other signs, and pragmatics is where it interacts with its user. From this definition, and especially with regards to Peirce (1903) and Spielman (2004) there is no reason *a priori* to grant primacy of syntax and semantics over pragmatics (nor vice versa).

Now, several accounts have established quite important correspondences between single properties of social networks and linguistic structure. For example, the connection between the number of individuals in a speech community does have a quantifiable impact on the evolution of the languages spoken in these communities. An observational study of over 2,000 languages from the World Atlas of Language Structures has shown that group size correlates with simpler inflectional morphology, while languages that are spoken in smaller communities exhibit more complicated case systems and verbal paradigms (Lupyan & Dale 2010). Such differences could be accounted for through confounding variables such as the age of the language. But an observational study on two sign languages of approximately the same age with different social structures suggests that these sign languages do develop differently according to the network properties of the culture they are spoken in (Meir et al. 2012). The independent variables measures were foremostly the interconnectedness between individuals and group size, reproducing the findings in Lupyan & Dale (2010) on a much smaller scale. Furthermore, Reali et al. (2018) have confirmed in agent-based simulations, that bigger population sizes lead to simpler grammatic structures and a larger vocabulary, further indicating that the age of the languages in Lupyan and Dale (2010) isn't the determining factor of the observed effect.

While the number of speakers (i.e., nodes) alone is a simple network property that doesn't take the specific connectivity of the nodes among each other into account, it appears that the number of speakers in a speech community is inherently related to network structure. Especially socio-linguistic accounts have investigated the empirical configurations of social networks. In particular, bigger speech communities are not only bigger but are typically also more sparsely connected than small communities (Trudgill 2009). While this is in itself an interesting finding with regard to the coherence of human groups and the interaction therein, it shows that the number of nodes in linguistic networks and their connectivity are co-dependent variables. Hence, more rigorous graph theoretic approaches might be able to disentangle the effects of the size and connectedness of a speech community for the resulting linguistic system.

But socio-linguistic accounts are typically more concerned with the local effects and the behaviour of individuals according to their connectedness in the social network. Labov (2001) for instance, is interested in the propagation of linguistic features in social networks from a variationist standpoint. The specific question that he addresses in his famous Philadelphia study is the relationship between social status and linguistic innovation in social networks. While he isn't able to simply correlate social status and linguistic innovation, his most relevant discovery is that linguistic innovation stems from well-connected individuals.

That is, highly connected individuals drive the spread of new linguistic variants because they sit at neuralgic points of the social network, through which these variants can propagate into the system. In terms of the Byzantine Generals Problem, this is a logical consequence. The more nodes are connected to a linguistic innovator, the faster linguistic innovation can be passed on to the other speakers.

This is contrasted by the view that it is not the socially well-embedded individuals that promote linguistic change, because a well-connected group converges on a dominant variant that is high in status and hence rather conservative (Labov 1969). This is also coherent with the Byzantine Generals Problem and its solution for connected subgraphs. If a conservative individual occupies a neuralgic point in the network (Fig. 15b) innovations cannot be passed on to other individuals in the network unless the node is circumvented. It is thus argued that outsiders in social networks, agents with high mobility and weak social ties, can bring new varieties into social networks more easily and are mostly responsible for such linguistic innovations (Milroy 2002). This ultimately leads Trudgill (2009) to argue that smaller and more tightly-knit social groups tend to preserve norms rather than innovate them, which is consistent with the finding that larger speech communities have less complex grammars (Lupyan & Dale 2010).

Milroy and Milroy (1992) attempted to integrate the notion of social networks into the stratification of social classes. They argue that other contributions in the field had seen theories of social networks and social classes as mutually exclusive because they produced irreconcilable and even contradictory observations for the study of language. They claim that theories emphasising social class were based on the idea of conflict and mutual out-grouping, while social networks emerge as a result of consensus. The authors then put forth a unifying model, where the social stratification of the classes is the result of network structures, in which subgroups are internally structured by strong ties, and where the distinctions between social groups arise through weak-tie connections between such subgroups.

Importantly, this view has enabled socio-linguistics to view linguistic variation both in terms of social class and in terms of paths of propagation. This argument enabled Eckert and Wenger (2005) to adopt a model of power in social networks, where the power relationship is modelled through directed edges. This unifies the ideas of social structure, which is by and large well-modelled by network approaches and socio-linguistic notions such as power and social class. While such studies have enormous theoretical implications, the field of socio-linguistic contributions to linguistic variation in social networks is characterised by many studies of particular phenomena. For instance, Schmidt (2019) has determined that exposure to speakers of Rio de la Plata Spanish changes the phonological perception of [ʃ] in non-Rioplatense listeners. While listeners with a low degree of interaction with Rioplatense speakers attribute [ʃ] to the phoneme /ʧ/, high connectivity with speakers of this variety changes the phonemic attribution to /j/, even if the speakers themselves do not produce the allophone [ʃ].

The socio-linguist literature thus contains several interesting contributions concerning the application of networks to the study of language. However, as has become clear, the underlying notions of networks do often not exploit the mathematical properties that networks provide to a high degree. For instance, the strong-tie weak-tie debate doesn't quantify which type of connections between groups are regarded as strong or weak. Also, Schmidt's study could well be executed without the notion of networks, because she is mainly interested in the exposure of speakers of one dialect to another dialect. This doesn't warrant the application of networks with all the mathematical possibilities they entail.

Lee et al. (2005) addressed the question of network topology in language evolution from a more formal point of view. The authors attempt to simulate the emergence of shared grammar in different populations of linguistic agents (i.e., nodes) and manipulate population structure to measure the effects of different topologies on shared grammatical conventions. Simulations up to that point had concentrated on fully-connected networks, which, according to Lee et al. (2005), is an unrealistic assumption. This assessment is also in line with the socio-linguistic literature (cf. Trudgill 2009). Lee et al. (2005) then compare fully-connected networks, linear topologies, von Neumann lattices, and bridge topologies, which connect two fully connected networks through bridging edges (Fig. 24).

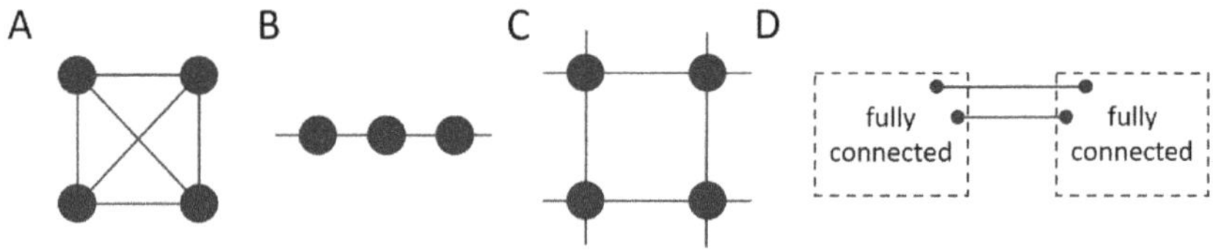

Fig. 24: Network topologies adapted from Lee et al. (2005). Fully-connected network (A), linear network (B), von Neumann lattice (C), and bridge network (D) (p. 25).

Their main findings suggest that the convergence of populations on a single grammar depends on the network topology in which communication takes place. Fully-connected networks behave the way the maths suggests, namely converging rather quickly on a single grammar, once the learning fidelity of each individual reaches the threshold of about 85 %. Importantly, this isn't the case for all scenarios. Linear networks fail to converge on a single variant altogether. The authors suggest that this might be indicative of a threshold in connectivity (i.e., number of neighbours) for global convergence[42]. Bridge networks, on the other hand, start to converge rather quickly on two grammars, one for each of the fully-connected networks. The authors argue that this is a more realistic representation of human speech communities. Lee et al. (2005) were the first to show that network topology plays a significant role in the development of language. Importantly, they can isolate this parameter experimentally from other factors such as learning fidelity in language acquisition and group size. Interestingly, such a difference between different network topologies couldn't be produced in the emergence of semiotic systems (Raviv et al. 2020) as will be discussed in more detail below (Section 3.3.3).

Another set of simulations (Segovia-Martín et al. 2020) pointed out the importance of network connectivity as opposed to network topology alone. This means that the time that a network requires to reach its final configuration may differ from one network to another. The authors run simulations on the transmission of cultural variants in agent populations of different sizes while manipulating content bias. Content bias refers to the probability of adoption depending on the quality of a stimulus (Tamariz et al. 2014). If a stimulus is inherently useful to a user, it is more readily adapted. In the experiment, this variable is manipulated by tweaking the probability of adoption of a cultural variant in a given interaction. Depending on network connectivity, the information (Fig. 25) of the cultural variant requires different amounts of time until it can potentially have propagated through the network. The authors model three situations for connectivity, early, mid, and late connectivity (Fig. 25).

---

42 The intuition expressed above (Section 2.3.1) states that linear ledger implementations are poor candidates for the transmission of information. Under the assumption that the convergence on grammar is similar to consensus on information (Chapter 4) this experimentally confirms the formal argument made on linear ledger implementations.

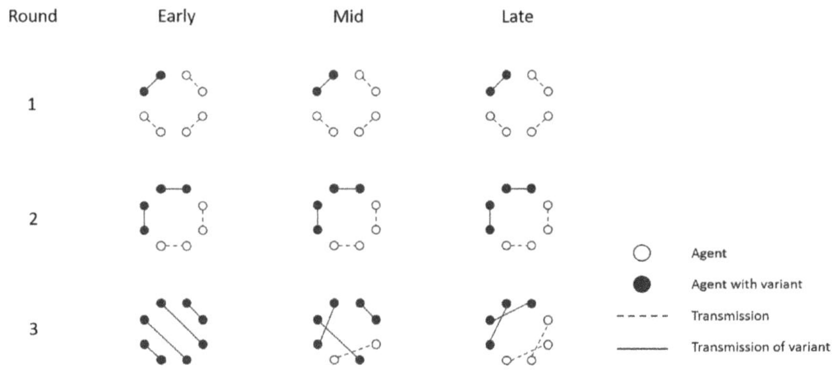

Fig. 25: Network connectivity (Adapted from Segovia-Martín et al. 2020). Depending on the order in which nodes connect, it takes potentially longer for the variant to be spread across the whole network. In this illustration, it is assumed that each contact with an agent with the variant automatically overrides the white variant (content bias = 1). In the simulations, the propensity of this to happen is dependent on the content bias. The higher the bias, the more likely the adoption of the variant.

The simulation runs various rounds of interaction and investigates the time it takes for the network to converge on a single variant. The authors diagnose that network connectivity plays a role in the convergence of the network on a variant, but only in populations with relatively high content bias. That is, in populations with high-quality variants, network connectivity effectively correlates with the speed of convergence. The faster the network reaches full connectivity, the faster the variant is spread through the network. However, when content bias is low, network connectivity does not appear to play a major role in the propagation of a cultural variant.

This finding is in line with the simulations by Baxter (2016), who investigates the impact of network structure on linguistic change. In his simulation, linguistic variants compete to be established in a given population. His astonishing finding is that network structure doesn't have an impact on the transmission of a dominant variant, as long as interactions between agents are symmetrical, that means, as long as each agent has an equal chance to pass on their variant to the next agent. If, however, social influence differs between the agents, network structure has an important impact on the time the network takes to converge on a dominant variant. The fixation time is mainly affected by the scale of the relationship between the influence and degree of a node. If highly influential nodes are well connected at the same time, the fixation time for the dominant variant is drastically reduced. Note that, while Segovia-Martín et al. (2020) and Baxter (2016) conceptualise their simulations rather differently, the biases modelled in the nodes are rather similar. The presence of a high-quality variant is mathematically equivalent to a high influence of a node that has an unbiased variety. The two setups do differ in the way they simulate the network itself, or the edges that connect the nodes. While Segovia-Martín et al. (2020) investigate communication between agents to achieve full connectivity of a fully-connected network, Baxter (2016) doesn't presuppose full connectivity for the network in the first place and treats edges as always being operative.

Baxter's (2016) conceptual approach to the simulation, namely the presence of popular individuals in the network is in line with several studies that assess the role of individual agents in social networks. Gong et al. (2008) manipulate no less than three different ways in which individual agents and their behaviour play a crucial role in the convergence of the network on a cultural variant. They simulate fully-connected networks in which the nodes have different weights. This means that the probability of two agents interacting is not completely random. Rather, the simulation models interaction between one randomly selected node and a popular node following a predefined probability. The more popular the node, the higher the probability that it is chosen as a node that the randomly selected node will interact with. The authors then measure the time it takes the community to develop a common language. A common language is modelled as a set of symbols for which the average rate of communicative success in interactions surpasses the threshold of 80 %. The interactions themselves and their success are modelled after a *Coevolution Model of Lexicon, Syntax and Social Structure* (Gong & Wang 2005; Gong 2008). Importantly, Gong et al. (2008) identify two competing principles concerning the role of popular agents within a network. On the one hand, the presence of popular agents can accelerate the convergence of a common language, because they potentially enhance connectivity. However, a high-degree agent is only beneficial when the information it spreads is stable. When interactions of the popular agent with other agents continuously change the language of the popular agent, conflicting information is spread into the system and the convergence of the network is decelerated. According to the authors, both acceleration and deceleration seem to compete with each other in the model. Empirically, they show that an overly popular agent leads to longer convergence times and lower understanding rates. Comparing their results against Gong and Wang (2005) however, they claim that there is an optimum popularity rate where convergence is maximally accelerated. They don't specify the value of this optimal popularity rate. Such contradictory roles of popular agents are in line with the contradictory findings in socio-linguistics (cf. Labov

2001; Milroy 2002), which were, in turn, earlier characterised in terms of the Byzantine Generals Problem, where the exact positioning of a node in a network gains importance for information transmission.

On a similar note, Maity and Mukherjee (2016) model the role of rigid individuals in the propagation of dominant opinions in social networks. They define rigid individuals as individuals which are "speaker-only" and hence never adopt the opinions of other speakers. The authors modelled this scenario as a naming game, in which digital agents had to agree upon the best football players. They manipulated the parameter of the fraction of agents which were speaker-only and went on to describe the impact of this fraction on the time it took for the network to converge on a dominant opinion, modelling this process for different network topologies. In the case of fully-connected networks, the authors find that rigid individuals can seriously affect how opinions propagate in a network[43]. Firstly, they show that an increase in speaker-only individuals leads to a loss of convergence of the network on a dominant opinion and leads to more atomic clusters of opinions, which is intuitive. More importantly, however, they determine that there is a specific cut-off value for this phenomenon depending on the size of the network. For example, in networks of size $|N| = 1{,}000$, the frequency of the dominant opinion abruptly falls at a value of around 50 % of rigid individuals. At $|N| = 5{,}000$, 30 % of rigid individuals are enough to make the dominant opinion lose importance abruptly, suggesting that bigger networks can more easily be influenced by rigid individuals. Moreover, the authors show that the most dominant opinions are often generated by these rigid individuals. At $|N| = 1{,}000$, less than 7.5 % of rigid individuals are enough to make their opinions dominant in 50 % of the simulations. At $|N| = 5{,}000$, 5 % are enough to make their opinions the dominant ones in 50 % of the simulations. At 25 % presence of rigid individuals and $|N| = 5{,}000$, 100 % of the winning opinions in the simulations are generated by these individuals, suggesting that a big enough fully-connected network can easily be influenced by a few speaker-only agents.

This is affected by network structure in so far as scale-free networks (i.e., non-homogeneous and non-fully connected networks) amplify the trends identified in fully-connected networks drastically. Smaller proportions of rigid individuals are needed in all of the aforementioned cases to produce the effects that were identified in the previous experiment. Maity and Mukherjee (2016) expand on

43 This finding is complementary to Baxter (2016) in that he finds network structure to be irrelevant as long as individuals have equal probabilities of passing on their information.

this paradigm by changing individuals over time, simulating the birth and death of individuals in a society. What they find is that the role of rigid individuals is highly important in static networks, but that their importance decreases when nodes are often replaced. Put differently, the faster a society changes (i.e., younger populations with lower life expectancy), the less important the presence of rigid individuals becomes concerning the convergence of the network on a dominant opinion.

The role of single agents in the diffusion of information in networks has also been studied from another standpoint. Rather than manipulating the connectivity of the innovator itself, Lev-Ari (2018) was interested in the network structure of the receivers of linguistic innovation. The rationale behind this simulation is that listeners who are embedded in small social networks are exposed to fewer stimuli and hence attribute greater importance to each stimulus. Under this premise, innovators should be more successful in diffusing their innovation into a network, if they expose less well-connected listeners to their innovation. In a simulation of linguistic agents, it was then shown that vowel merge diffuses more quickly across a network when the first agent exposed to the innovation was less well-connected (Lev-Ari 2018).

Such studies on network structure are hardly feasible in real speech communities because the interaction of individuals with one another is difficult to record outside of a total surveillance paradigm. On the other hand, this leads to problems with the external and ecological validity of the experiments reported above. These problems can be mitigated by the experimental approaches reported below (Section 3.3.3). However, most of the studies reported in this Section (3.3.1) are studies of simulation which are concerned with the synchronic interaction between agents in a network and the effects of their network structure. This means that certain features of languages, such as morphological complexity or, more generally speaking, the convergence of a speech community on a cultural variant, are measured against different properties of the networks in which interactions take place, with little regard for the generational transmission of information over longer periods.

3.3.2. Cultural Transmission

Complementing the aforementioned synchronic and data scientific approaches, Kirby and Hurford (2002) argue that cultural transmission is a key process for the generational propagation of cultural and linguistic information. In more general terms, they sustain that the emergence of language lies at the intersection between ontogenetic learning, cultural evolution, and biological evolution, all at once (p. 122). According to the authors, a well-formed linguistic theory has to be able to model all of these. In this avenue of investigation, Kirby and Hurford (2002) put forth their Iterated Learning Model (ILM), which describes the transmission of cultural information from one generation to the next. This is a way of exemplifying cumulative cultural evolution (cf. Boyd & Richerson 1996; Tomasello 1999). For a more recent discussion of the terminology also see Mesoudi and Thornton (2018). Cumulative cultural evolution explains how the accelerated expansion of human culture works at different levels, namely by assuming a model of culture in which one generation can rely on the information generated by the previous generation and innovate on top of this. In terms of Kirby and Hurford (2002), this means that the process of learning isn't restricted to the ontogeny of the learner, but that learning processes involve cross-generational social interaction which impacts the evolution of a cultural artefact such as language.

To empirically account for the power of this model, the authors provide evidence from a simulation of agents. Agents are simulated as ANN (artificial neural networks) and have to produce several signs for different types of meanings. The question the authors ask is whether or not simulated agents will systematise meaning without being taught any specific rules for the use of the resulting proto-language. The first 'generation' of ANN creates this proto-language by creating:

> strings for 50 simple meanings (i.e., with no embedding ["John loves Mary"]), 50 degree-1 meanings (with one level of embedding ["John knows that Mary admires Gavin"]) and 50 degree-2 meanings ["John knows that Mary knows that John admires Gavin"]. (Kirby & Hurford 2002, p. 130).

Cultural transmission is then simulated by training a second "generation" of ANN on the output of the first generation. The third generation is then trained on the output of the second generation, and so on. The network aspect of this type of cultural transmission is minimal, as only transmission from one artificial agent to the next is modelled. This results in the simplest possible network G consisting of two nodes and an edge that connects them:

$$G = \left(N\{speaker, hearer\}, E\left\{e\{speaker, hearer\}\right\}\right)$$

Regarding the question of syntax, this rather simple ILM results in the spontaneous emergence of recursive syntax, seemingly out of thin air. But the transmission of information from one agent to the next represents a sufficient pressure of comprehensibility to systematise the information over time. The initial stages of the simulation result in completely unstructured meanings and no apparent representation of the embeddings:

(1) ldg
"Mary admires John"
(2) xkq
"Mary loves John"
(3) qj
"Mary admires Gavin"
(4) axk
"John admires Gavin"
(5) gb
"John knows that Mary knows that John admires Gavin" (Kirby & Hurford 2002, p. 130)

However, after only a few iterations of simulating cultural transmission, the following structure emerges:

(6) qj h   f tej   m
John   Mary   admires
"Mary admires John"
(7) gj h   f tej   wp
John   Mary   loves
"Mary loves John"
(8) gj qp   f tej   m
Gavin   Mary   admires
"Mary admires Gavin"
(9) gj qp   f h   m
Gavin   John   admires
"John admires Gavin"
(10) i h u   i tej   u   gj qp   f h   m
John   knows   Mary   knows   Gavin   John   admires
"John knows that Mary knows that John admires Gavin" (Kirby & Hurford 2002, p. 131)

The latter examples (6–10) emerge after a few iterations of generational cultural transmission. The chain of ANN had already structured the language to a degree, where a simple OSV structure with some sort of 'ergative' case marking could be distinguished. The authors claim that this assessment of regularity holds even when considering the complete grammar that emerges in the experiment. Interestingly, the resulting grammar thus exhibits some very typical aspects of human languages, such as compositionality and recursive structure, a correlation of high frequency and grammatical irregularity in case marking and verb infliction[44], and linguistic generalization. All of this is achieved by modelling iterated social interaction over generations, with no change in the cognitive dispositions between generations of speakers and hearers.

This argument is confirmed by Smith et al. (2003) who also model linguistic actors and the linear transmission of their linguistic systems over various generations. They show that compositionality is directly linked to the properties of the stimulus and that poor stimuli lead to more compositional language. This means that language isn't systematic *despite* the "poverty of stimulus" (Chomsky, 1959a) but *because of* the poverty of the stimulus; systematic language is more easily adopted than non-systematic language. Another experiment by the authors expands on the argument of systematization without predefined grammatical dispositions. Kirby et al. (2007) developed a formal framework that incorporates learning, culture, and evolution into a model of cultural transmission based on Bayesian Inference. The authors report that weak cognitive biases can result in strong linguistic universals when cultural transmission is properly modelled. This ultimately means that linguistic universals needn't be directly innate in cognition, but that the polygenetic development of different languages can converge on very similar forms even when they share no genetic origin. These expansions of the argument (i.e., Smith et al. 2003; Kirby et al. 2007) harness previous work (Kirby & Hurford 2002) more directly against arguments of innateness.

Cultural transmission based on the ILM has become quite important in the past decades. A more recent review (Kirby et al. 2014) provides further evidence for the consistency of this model and reports on the reproduction of predictions made by the ILM in formal mathematical models (Griffiths & Kalish 2007; cited in Kirby et al. 2014), experimental studies with humans (e.g., Kirby et al. 2008, Section 3.3.3), and even with chimpanzees (Horner et al. 2006; cited in Kirby et al. 2014). In the context of structuralist philology and Romance Studies, Verhoef (2012) makes an important effort in providing evidence for the emergence of the

44 An example for this in Spanish are high-frequency high-irregularity words such as *ir* which inflect as *v(a)-* (present tense), *fu(i)-* (simple perfect tense) and *ir-* (future tense), as opposed to low-frequency words such as *apostar,* which are perfectly regular and only inflect on the grammatical bound morpheme: *-o, -as, -a, -amos, -áis, án* (present tense), *-é, -aste, -ó, -amos, -asteis, -aron* (simple perfect tense), and *-aré, -arás, -ará, -aremos, -aréis, -arán* (future tense) without irregular changes to the radical semantic morpheme *apost-*, even when considering the allomorph *apuest-* which is determined by the tonicity of *-o* or *-ue* respectively.

duality of patterning[45] (Martinet 1949) through iterated learning. In a laboratory experiment, participants had to communicate meanings to one another using slide whistles, from one generation to the next. The resulting sets of sounds exhibit such doubled patterning, that is combinatorial structure of meaningful units (second level of articulation: morphemes) which are distinguished by discriminatory units (first level of articulation: phonemes).

Mind that this model doesn't suppose any application of social networks at all. Rather, the ILM is based on the concept of a transmission chain, more closely related to a linear ledger implementation (Section 2.3.1). But the model is central to subsequent studies and experiments, which do consider network structure in cultural transmission. This is why the development of the ILM has crucially contributed to informing the role of social networks in cultural evolution.

3.3.3. Experimental Semiotics

The literature review in this section is aimed at reconstructing how the linear notion of cultural transmission (ILM) has been extended such that the role of network structure in diachronic language evolution could be meaningfully investigated. The extension of transmission chains to transmission networks can be understood analogously to the extension of language or syntax trees to linguistic networks (Section 3.1, 3.2). Here, the focus lies on studies in experimental semiotics[46] (Galantucci 2009). In this approach, human semiotic behaviour is studied either by conducting "controlled studies in which human adults develop novel communication systems [...] or impose novel structure on systems provided to them [...]" (Galantucci et al. 2012, p. 1). A specific avenue in experimental semiotics is the type of generational experiments in which diffusion chains are used to model cultural evolution (Cornish 2010). It is in this specific branch of experimental semiotics that the development from chain to network can be shown most convincingly.

As mentioned above, the first experiment was presented by Kirby et al. (2008) and served as the direct experimental expansion of the arguments formulated beforehand (Kirby & Hurford 2002; Kirby et al. 2007). In the experiment, participants were asked to learn a fictional language that provided them with twenty-seven words to describe objects according to $3 \times 3 \times 3$ properties: colour (black, blue, or red), shape (square, circle, or triangle), and movement (straight

45 From French: "Double articulation".

46 For the most exhaustive review of the systematicity of experimental semiotics, see Galantucci et al. (2012).

line, zigzag, or circular movement). Out of the twenty-seven possible stimuli and corresponding lexical expressions, only fourteen were provided for training. Participants subsequently had to name all of the possible twenty-seven shapes, as they were presented to them on a computer screen. The cultural transmission of the language was modelled in the way that the output names for each of the twenty-seven shapes from each generation were given as learning input to the next generation. After ten generations of learning, the linguistic system had been simplified to contain only between two and five words, resulting in systematic underspecification. Out of the three dimensions of meanings (i.e., colour, shape, movement), only one would usually be encoded.

This tendency could be broken by biasing the system toward expressivity. In concrete, the experiment forbade the training data from containing the same word for two different figures under this condition. This modelled a bias for the full specification of every possible figure. If a word was included twice in a generation's output, only one of the meanings would be included in the training data for the next generation. This pressure for expressivity resulted in languages with more structure, but also slightly more attribution errors. First and foremost, it led – in some cases – to rather complex morphology in the emergence of structure (Fig. 26), where the first morpheme could be interpreted as a code for colour (<n> = black, <l> = blue, <r> = red), the second morpheme as encoding shape (<eho> and <aho> = circle, <ere> and <ane> = square[47]), and the third as the encoding for motion (<pilu> = circular motion, <plo> = zigzag, <ki> = straight line).

47 Many of these morphemes also exhibit exceptions or allomorphs, depending on the phonotactical context and the adjacent morphemes. So this is just a small collection of morphemes.

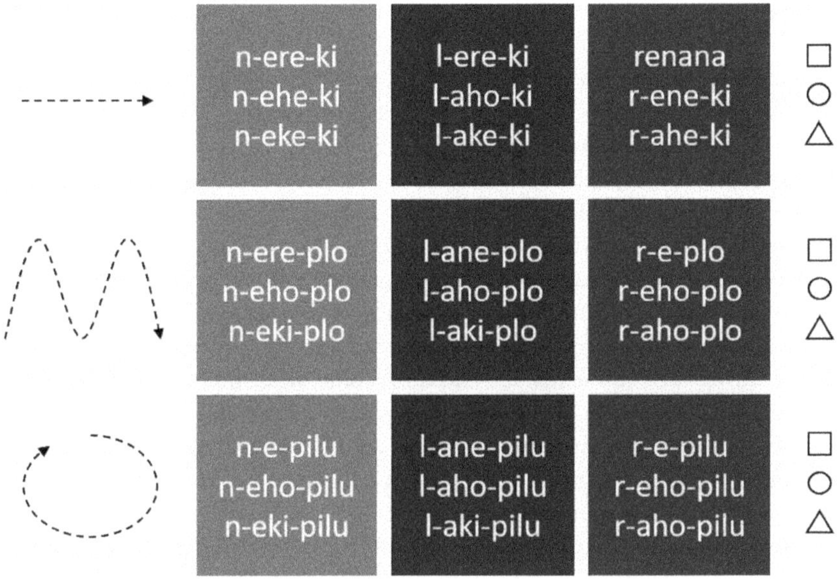

Fig. 26: An experimentally generated example language (second experiment). The language is structured: the string associated with a picture consists of substrings expressing colour, shape, and motion, respectively. The hyphens represent one way of analysing the substructure of these strings and are added purely for clarity [...] (Kirby et al. 2008, p. 10684).

Even though this experiment does not yet contain an element of network structure, it shows experimentally what Segovia-Martin et al. (2020) have modelled in simulations. Even in the simplest case of information transmission (i.e., from one agent to another), biases and assumptions about the quality of stimuli represent an important criterion for the transmission of information. In this case, the quality of the stimulus is biased toward uniqueness; a word cannot represent two objects at the same time. The experiment is interpreted as indicative of the structures that can emerge from cultural transmission, even without direct interaction. In the literature, this process of cultural transmission has been termed vertical cultural transmission (Scott-Phillips & Kirby 2010), where vertical refers to the sequence of different generations of laboratory participants.

Horizontal cultural transmission, then, refers to the transmission of information in synchronous interaction processes. Garrod et al. (2007) for instance, present three experiments on the repeated usage of signs for reference in communication. Their participants play Pictionary while their performance is assessed over various rounds of play. A director has to convey concepts from a finite set of elements ($n = 16$) through drawings on a screen. The director conveys concepts in several trials to a matcher, who has to guess the meaning of the drawing correctly. Both the communicative success and the graphical complexity of the pictures drawn are measured. To measure graphical complexity, the Perimetric Complexity Measure (Attneave & Arnoult 1956; Pelli et al. 2006; cited in Garrod et al. 2007) is adopted. The authors find that the degree of interaction between the players affects both the evolution of the signs and the success of the matchers. The more interaction and feedback there is between players, the more their drawings become schematic and non-iconic, while high rates of success in guessing are maintained. The authors also find that those users who haven't been exposed to these signs and their semiosis are not as good at recognising their meaning. This provides grounds to argue that iconicity is being reduced through the repeated use of a sign in the interaction between players. The authors relate such processes to the evolution of Chinese characters (Garrod et al. 2007), which developed from iconic representations into more conventionalised forms.

Importantly, the study of horizontal cultural transmission motivates the question of the role of networks. That is because the authors systematically vary between conditions of single directors without feedback (SD-F), single directors with feedback (SD+F), and double directors with feedback (DD+F). In the SD-F condition, a single director repeatedly draws concepts for an imaginary audience without feedback. In this condition, no development from iconicity toward convention was identified. By including a matcher in the SD+F condition, thus expanding the network by one node, where this node gave feedback on the identifiability of the concept, the tendencies described above were identified. In the DD+F condition, the functionality of each 'node' was expanded by alternating between the functions of director and matcher, making for a more varied and thus more performant communication.

This is of course a primitive network – if a network at all – because there are only two nodes and one edge. But, the expansion from $|N| = 1$ to $|N| = 2$ does have an identifiable impact on the semiotic processes in the network, whereby speculation about the effects of other parameters in such networks and their large-scale effects becomes meaningful.

Mesoudi and Whiten (2008) develop a taxonomy of cultural transmission which allows the appraisal of the different aspects of cultural transmission and motivates further interest in the study of network structure in this particular context. The aforementioned experiments include vertical transmission in chains and horizontal cultural transmission in dyads. These are complemented in Mesoudi and Whiten (2008) with the replacement method and the closed group method. The closed group method includes collaborative tasks or individual learning tasks in closed groups. Under laboratory conditions, researchers can study the relevance of different social factors. Do participants, for example, copy more behaviour from a popular agent? What makes a given cultural variant successful in a group in general? The question of network structure in such experiments appears to be rather obvious since experimenters can manipulate the structure or order of interaction between participants. This has however been relatively unexplored until relatively recently, as we will address below (e.g., Centola & Baronchelli 2015; Raviv et al. 2020). The replacement method (Mesoudi & Whiten 2008), on the other hand, relies on both vertical and horizontal transmission of cultural variants at the same time. Instead of simulating generations by single agents, groups of participants are used to produce cultural signals. These are then not merely plugged into a completely new generation, but participants are replaced one by one in the interaction (Fig.27), simulating steady life-and-death cycles and the gradual replacement of societies, similar to Maity and Mukherjee (2016).

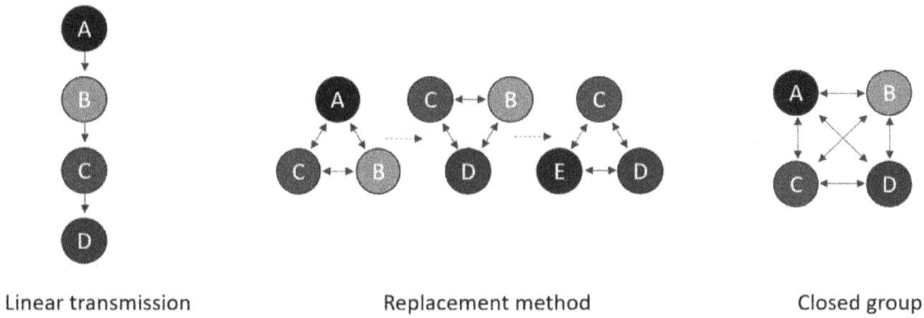

Fig. 27: Methods of simulation of cultural transmission (Mesoudi & Whiten 2008). (Visualizations adapted from Scott-Phillips & Kirby 2010)

The horizontal and vertical cultural transmission was then integrated experimentally by Theisen-White et al. (2011), who replicated the Pictionary experiment (cf. Garrod et al. 2007) and added an element of vertical cultural transmission. Instead of letting participants think of signs for listed items on the spot, they taught them selected signs from previous generations of players to use in their round of gaming. Note, however, that there was no direct interaction between a generation and the preceding generation, the signs to use were acquired by the participants in a situation of formal learning. They describe interesting interactions between features of horizontal and vertical cultural transmission. For instance, the systematic compositionality within generations doesn't increase significantly, as individuals recur to idiosyncratic signs that emerge in the shared communicative history of participants. However, the increase in systematic compositionality is significant across generations, simply because individuals replace unsystematic and idiosyncratic variants of previous generations and introduce their own, which then may or may not be systematized and adopted by the subsequent generation. The authors entertain the possibility that this can be interpreted as "a feature of cumulative cultural evolution, in which possibly very small changes at the generational level are amplified (Kirby, Dowman, & Griffiths 2007)" (Theisen-White et al. 2011, p. 960).

Now, it has to be pointed out, that the aforementioned experimental semiotic accounts of cultural transmission are not explicitly concerned with network structure as such. However, it should have become clear that these models of interaction and/or cultural transmission between agents can well be explained in terms of networks and that the corresponding accounts operate within the framework of the axiomatic assumptions laid out above (Section 3.3). Furthermore, the literature revised above directly precedes the following experimental accounts. The concepts that are elucidated by research in experimental semiotics are thus fundamental for the following studies, which tackle the impact of network structure on communicative systems more explicitly.

Centola and Baronchelli (2015) were the first to adopt a network-based approach to the study of the emergence of social conventions. Their main argument is the infinite regress that the explanation of social conventions by central authorities (cf. Merton 1938) represents. That is, how do social institutions, which provide collective conventions for communities, come about without there being collective conventions in the first place? In a laboratory experiment with human participants, the authors try to observe the emergence of social conventions in a naming game[48]. The question is whether or not conventionalised arbitrary terms can generalise in the global population of participants ($n = 24$) only through local interaction. Participants played rounds of a game in which they had to converge on a single name for a given entity. These interactions took place in dyads, but the dyads changed throughout the experiment such that the

48 In terms of the terminology proposed by Galantucci et al. (2012) this is termed a semiotic referential game.

interactions induced different types of networks. However, participants weren't aware of the network condition they were in. The authors then compared how the structure of each network condition affected the convergence of the group on a dominant name for an object. Three types of network structures were compared. The authors compared spatially embedded networks, exemplified by a one-dimensional p-regular lattice of degree $P = 4$ (Fig. 28a) with a random network (Fig. 28b), and a homogenous network (Fig. 28c), most closely resembling a fully-connected network.

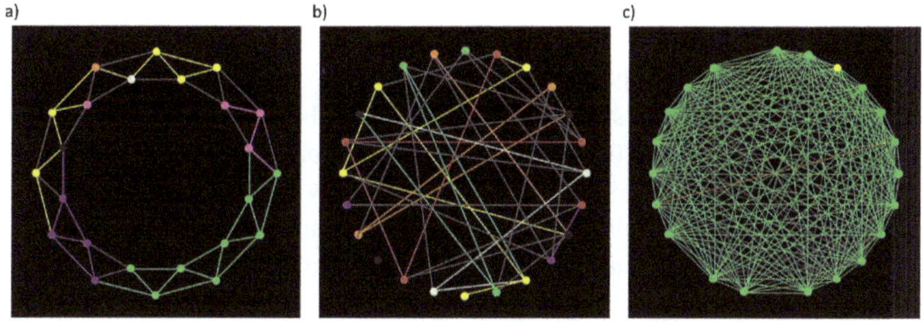

Fig. 28: Network structures examined by Centola and Baronchelli (2015) (a) one-dimensional p-regular lattice (P = 4), (b) random connectivity network, (c) homogenous network with near full connectivity. Differently coloured edges represent different agreed-upon terms in the interaction between two nodes. Grey edges indicate that no term was agreed upon.

Centola and Baronchelli (2015) identify interesting network dynamics depending on how the interaction is structured in terms of the underlying network. They find that in the spatially embedded network (Fig. 28a), local groups of connected agents agree upon different terms, with no term ever propagating dominantly throughout the network. Analogously to the linear topology simulated in Lee et al. (2005), there are "extended 'patches' of individuals with the same […]" (ibid., p. 4) name for an object. While Lee et al. (2005) simulate the convergence of simulated agents on different grammars instead of words, it seems that Centola and Baronchelli (2015) replicate the impact of a linear (or quasi-linear) transmission of a linguistic convention. Furthermore, the authors point out that conversion on a single dominant variety only occurs in the homogenous condition, which confirms the findings of Lee et al. (2005) experimentally. To avoid a bias in terms of population size, Centola and Baronchelli (2015) then replicate their experiments with networks of size $|N| = 48$ and $|N| = 96$, finding the same effects. This is interpreted as an effect of local coordination. Participants are rewarded for converging on the same name locally. The optimisation of local success rates in converging on the same name for an object corresponds to the drift toward a single dominant variety. Consequently, the success rates of non-fully connected networks fluctuate, while the success rate in the fully-connected condition tends toward 100 % after a sufficient number of trials. For the authors, this answers the question of the emergence of linguistic conventions without centralised institutions. As long as enough interaction is possible and connectivity in the population is sufficiently high, the coordination bias (i.e., successfully converging on a single name for a given object) on the local level leads to global coordination without a coordinating entity.

Raviv et al. (2020) extend their previous paradigm on group size (Raviv et al. 2019) by looking at group structure. This approach also extends the approach by Centola and Baronchelli (2015) in that it includes a more complex communicative task. While the latter experiment focussed only on the convergence of participants on a single cultural variant, the former analysed the emergence of a more complex communicative system, including words for different shapes with systematically varied properties. This semiotic referential game (cf. Galantucci et al. 2012) is based on the paradigm by Kirby et al. (2008), although it includes far more complicated shapes and more subtle shading and patterning instead of full-fledged colouring. The authors had participants name and guess visual items in dyads, with one participant being the producer and the other being the guesser. The producer produced a term for a shape that appeared before them, while the guesser had to select the shape out of a finite set of shapes. However, instead of repeatedly playing this game in the same dyad, interactions alternated between different participants, such as to simulate changing interactions in a micro-society. The structure and order of these interactions were modelled such that different network structures could be observed for each micro-society. Just as in Centola and Baronchelli (2015), participants weren't aware of the network structure in which they were immersed. In concrete, they investigated three different types of micro-society according to network structure (Fig. 29). They distinguished fully-connected networks, small-world networks, and scale-free networks. The difference between small-world networks and scale-free networks is that the degree distribution over all nodes is homogeneous in small-world networks and resembles a power-law distribution in scale-free networks. In this study, all nodes in a small-world network had either three or four out of the possible seven neighbours. In the scale-free network, one more centralised node had five neighbours, while all others only had three. The assignment of participants to each of these three network conditions was manipulated as the independent variable. As dependent variables, the authors assessed different properties of the resulting semiotic system; linguistic structure, communicative success, stability, and convergence of the words used to communicate the different shapes.

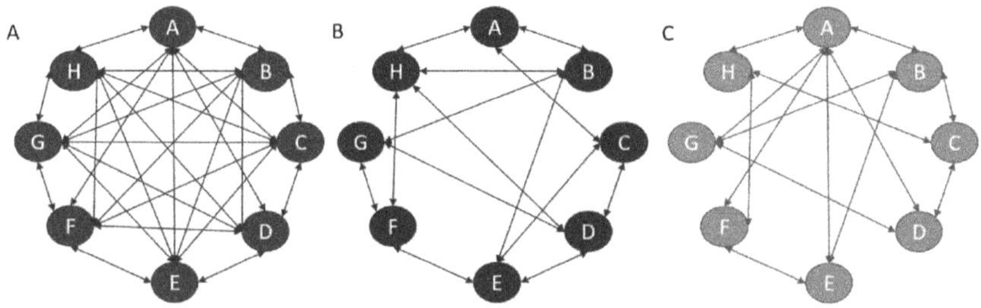

Fig. 29: Figures from Raviv et al. (2020) (a) The three different network structures employed for the interaction of their participants: fully-connected network (A), small-world network (B), and scale-free network (C). In small-world networks, nodes had either three or four neighbours, while the scale-free network exhibited a power-law node degree distribution. One node has five neighbours, while the rest have only three. Note that, formally speaking, all of these are distributed networks.

The authors predicted that these variables would develop differently according to the network structure that participants were subject to. Contrary to these predictions, the authors didn't find any significant differences for any of the four dependent variables, even though the revised literature suggests differently. In the face of the reported literature, both in the reported study and in this dissertation, this is rather odd. The authors do however report some exploitable findings. For instance, it appears that fully-connected networks present much better linguistic convergence on shapes that were introduced early in the game, while later introduced shapes were more variable. In the other network types, there was no difference between old and new shapes with regard to the familiarity of participants and subsequent naming conventions. Furthermore, small-world networks present measurable differences as compared to other network types. While the overall tendency in all of the linguistic variables was the same, the authors report that the variance in these behaviours was bigger for small-world networks than for the other two. According to the authors, this suggests that sparser contact leads to more linguistic diversity, which is also suggested by the observational data from Lupyan and Dale (2010).

Concerning their main hypotheses, the authors offer a variety of reasons for the absence of significant effects between networks. They explore reasons such as the small group size $(|N|=8)$ and a lack of exploitation of the potential differences of network properties. Given the differences between this and the other reported studies, it appears that these reasons are palpable. With regards to differences in network structure it could for instance be argued that, formally, the three network types investigated by Raviv et al. (2020) are not too different in their setup. All of them are distributed networks. In terms of the Byzantine Generals Problem (Section 2.5.1) only the fully-connected network is solvable with an oral algorithm for a maximum of two traitors (cf. Lamport et al. 1982). The scale-free and small-world networks exhibit the same formal requirements and can only be solved with the adapted signed messages algorithm $SM(m+\delta-1)$ under the assumption that the loyal generals be a connected subgraph. It could be tested whether more differences could be identified if the formal properties of the networks were more diverse and the number of nodes increased.

These contributions from experimental semiotics are complemented by studies from other fields of research, most notably, behavioural economics. Even though such studies are not preoccupied with the evolution of language *per se*, two studies elucidate the global and local dynamics of consensus in different network structures. They are therefore reported in this section. The first study (Kearns et al. 2009) expands on the experiments reported hitherto because it introduces conflicting experimental biases in the setup. While the overarching goal for the network is still to converge on a single variant, that is to achieve consensus in voting between variants, different individuals are provided with different incentives for either variant. In the experiment, participants are expected to colour their node either red or blue, but some participants are awarded more money if they colour their node blue, while others receive more if they colour it red. After one minute of deliberation, however, the whole network has to be coloured in one colour. Otherwise, no one is rewarded. Thus, there are conflicting pressures, one where individuals try to maximise their own profit while acting in the interest of the whole group (in so far as this is the condition to make any profit at all). In the experiment, participants could only ever see their direct neighbours, not the whole network. Out of the present 36 nodes (network density for all different networks: $D=0.160\pm0.002$), they could thus see between one and nine other nodes, depending on how many nodes they were connected to.

The authors created three types of networks for this experimental setup. Firstly, they designed two types of cohesion networks. In these networks, the authors varied whether any given node had more neighbours of the same preference (red vs. blue incentive, intra-group cohesion) or more neighbours of a different preference (inter-group cohesion). From these cohesion networks, they derived two types. The first type was the random attachment type. That means that each node had approximately the same number of neighbours. The distribution of centralisation was thus rather even, with networks sometimes being P-regular. In the second type, the preferential attachment cohesion networks, centralisation followed a power-law distribution. Thus, few nodes had many neighbours and many nodes had few neighbours. Such networks were thus highly centralised. The last type of network in this experiment was the power minority network. Power minority networks are networks in which one minority of nodes is highly connected and where this minority shares an incentive for one of the two variants (red vs. blue). However, this variant is not shared by anyone outside this minority, meaning that the incentive of the highly connected minority group has to compete with the much more present, but less well-connected, incentive of the majority population.

The authors report findings on both the global and individual levels. Globally, the authors find that both types of preferential attachment networks (power minority networks and preferential attachment cohesion networks) are much better at reaching consensus, while the more evenly distributed random attachment cohesion networks perform rather poorly. Interestingly, this finding is related to the experimental task. Random attachment cohesion networks hinder global consensus (Kearns et al. 2009), but when the task is social differentiation (colouring one's node in a colour that no other neighbour uses) such networks outperform the preferential attachment networks (Kearns et al. 2006; cited in Kearns et al. 2009; Judd et al. 2010). With regards to consensus, however, preferential attachment networks achieve consensus more easily. What's more, not only do power minority networks arrive at consensus more often but the minority variant is mostly chosen for consensus. This shows that a well-connected incentivised minority can easily override the efforts of a loosely connected majority. When comparing only the random attachment networks, however, neighbourhoods with higher inter-group cohesion are more likely to reach consensus.

The authors summarise their findings stating that "it appears most beneficial to have extremists present in a relatively indifferent population and most harmful to have 2 opposing extremist groups" (Kearns et al. 2009, p. 1350). The authors report that stubborn individuals usually make higher profits over all rounds played, as long as they don't compromise the success of the entire group. That means that "successful players managed to be 'tastefully' stubborn" (Kearns et al. 2009, p 1352). Similarly, Maity and Mukherjee (2016) have pointed to the role of rigid individuals in the formation of dominant opinions. For consensus to emerge in the network, the principles of stubbornness on the one hand and collective alignment, on the other hand, are competitive principles that modulate each other. This corroborates other contributions reported earlier, in which the opposition of competing factors was pointed out as a key feature for linguistic change (Gong 2008) and in which the role of popular agents can be both hindering and beneficial for the communicative success in the network (Gong et al. 2008). As briefly alluded to above, it is also important to point out that the role of network topology hinges on the communicative task and other contextual parameters (Judd et al. 2010).

3.3.4. Concluding Remarks on Social Network Theories

The previous paragraphs (Section 3.3) explored some key components of social networks and social cognition. Given their strong empirical foundation, both in behavioural experiments and simulations, these approaches will be used for the motivation of the experimental hypothesis for the current study. Before doing so, some elements of the literature shall be highlighted, because the method of review has brought forth some interesting findings in its own right. Instead of following a subject-based division of the literature, it was attempted to compile information such that they elucidate the development of social networks in their application to linguistic questions in the history of their respective disciplines. This has brought forth some interesting parallels between vastly different corpora of literature, which shall be laid out in a more pinpointed fashion below.

On the one hand, networks represent a more complex way to use transmission chains in the study of cultural and linguistic evolution. This is represented by the line of investigation starting at Kirby and Hurford (2002) and extending to Theisen-White et al. (2011), who integrate vertical and horizontal cultural transmission. Investigation of cultural transmission and communication has furthermore shown that communication alone isn't sufficient for the type of systematization that was observed in the aforementioned studies. Rather, for the systematization of communicative systems to happen in the long run, communication must be accompanied by cultural transmission (Silvey et al. 2019). This implies that these processes have to be described in terms of complex, three-dimensional networks, with the first two dimensions describing the horizontal, that is spatial connectivity between actors and the third dimension intersecting this plane as time goes by. Networks of cultural transmission would thus have to be characterised as a three-dimensional lattice of sorts. In a proper network model of cultural transmission, generations of transmission would not be described as discrete, but contingent on the actual interactions that take place in the network (Fig. 30).

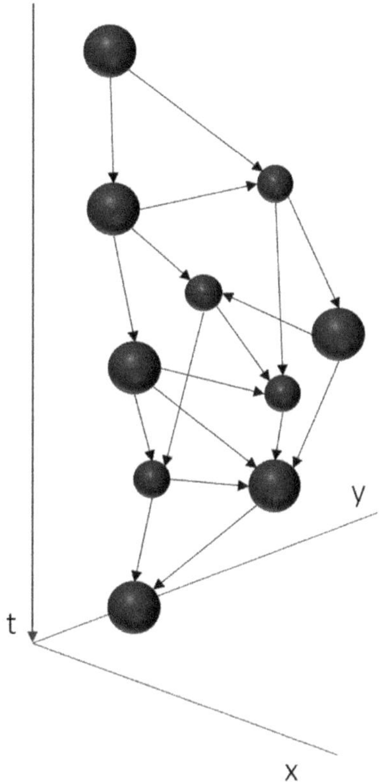

Fig. 30: A simple lattice representation of cultural transmission that incorporates both the vertical axis of time and the horizontal interaction among agents. Axes x and y represent spatial dimensions, while axis t represents the elapse of time between interactions and the physical presence of actors in the network.

Although such a model isn't put forth by any of the reviewed authors, it would be the subsequent level of conceptualisation for the integration of the axes of vertical and horizontal cultural transmission proposed before (Mesoudi & Whiten 2008; Scott-Philipps & Kirby 2010). What is more striking, however, is that the combination of contributions from rather different fields has led to the simple but meaningful observation, that the vastly different bodies of literature combine well on two different levels.

Firstly, it was shown that the application of graph theory can help to inform the linguistic discussion about social structure with a meaningful meta-language. The chapter attempts to describe different network structures in two ways. While the terminology from each study was reported as used in it, the application of the formal language provided in Chapter 2 was used to make some of these contributions more comparable and to find analogies between the reported studies where possible. With a more formal understanding of graph theory, it was also possible to point out where one study (Raviv et al. 2020) fell short in its design from a formal perspective. While the study is of unquestionable relevance and an important advance in the development of experimental semiotics with the methods of graph theory, it was shown that formal arguments from graph theory, notably the *Byzantine Generals Problem*, can pinpoint the shortcomings of the experimental setup. This finding was ultimately possible due to the analogy between language and the Blockchain because it motivated a linguistic framing of the *Byzantine Generals Problem*.

Secondly, the review of different methodological approaches based on simulations and experimental data with human research participants has shown that the role of network topologies in linguistics is described similarly across different disciplines. The most notable complementary findings were found in the works of Kirby et al. (2008) and Segovia-Martín et al. (2020) who both identify the importance of content biases in the transmission of information from one linguistic agent to another. While the former is an experimental approach, the latter is based on agent simulations. Other examples are convergent findings by Raviv et al. (2019, 2020), Reali et al. (2018) and Lupyan and Dale (2010) who each identify, with experimental, simulational, and observational data respectively, that sparser connections within linguistic groups lead to more complex and/or less systematised linguistic variety. Whether this is due to network size or connectivity, which are co-dependent variables (Trudgill 2009), will be explored in the data of the current study. Finally, Kearns et al. (2009), with behavioural data from human experimental participants, and Gong et al. (2008), with simulation data, converge on some interpretations of the role of well-connected cliques and popular agents respectively. Both of these contributions are interested in the degree distribution of networks and find evidence for competing phenomena in networks. While popular agents or cliques can have a positive effect on consensus in networks, they can also represent a hindering factor. The same opposing relationship is true for stubborn (Keans et al. 2009) or rigid (Maity & Mukherjee 2016) individuals. These opposing effects modulate each other according to different factors such as the experimental task (Judd et al. 2010), the ratio of popular agents to the overall population (Gong & Wang 2005), and potentially other factors.

While the summary of these comparisons doesn't do these approaches justice, the previous paragraphs (section 3.3.3) point out the findings and corresponding interpretations in more detail. This is here merely reproduced to show that the multi-disciplinary integration of such approaches is a rather valuable research effort in its own right. To conclude the review of literature on networks of language, the aforementioned global contributions shall be complemented by a short review of philological studies. While experimental and simulation data are very controlled and statistically viable, it is important to consider real-world data to understand how the experimentally isolated phenomena and effects play out in real-world scenarios and to check for their ecological validity.

3.4. Online Social Networks

Most philological data on the network effects on language stem from online social networks. It is important to distinguish the analysis of *social networks* from *online social network* services, also known as *social media*, such as Twitter, Instagram, Facebook, YouTube, etc. In the following, it will be shown that studies in this avenue, for the most part, have very little in common with the accounts laid out thus far. However, online social networks are of course networks in a strong sense of abstraction level-1 (cf. Araújo & Banisch 2016) in that accounts or posts can be represented as nodes that are connected via friend requests (in the case of accounts) or interactions (in the case of posts), which are in turn represented as edges.

Most of the linguistic literature about online social networks, however, isn't concerned with the analysis of these structures on a macro level. For the most part, analyses of online social networks exploit them as a source of linguistic data, which helps to characterise Internet speech as a linguistic variety (e.g., McCulloch 2019). This new linguistic variety has been argued to drive language evolution and the development of other linguistic varieties (Crystal 2004).

In the case of Spanish and Latin American Studies, accounts in the linguistics of the Internet in general (Yus 2008; Tascón 2012) are mostly concerned with the description of the Spanish language in the context of Internet usage. Apparent differences in linguistic usage on a pragmatic level (Yus 2001) and even diverging grammatical features are identified, leading to a classification of online Spanish as a linguistic variety in its own right (Urrutia-Cárdenas 2009). In the specific case of online social media, different observations are put forth. For example, different authors have described diverging norms of the lexicon (Torrego-González 2011a) or orthography (Torrego-González 2011b) of Spanish. Such tendencies have been claimed to be indicative of the construction of a proper identity of Internet users, specifically in online social media (Mancera-Rueda 2016). While some researchers have expressed themselves as sceptical about this type of identity construction (Ellison & Boyd 2013), others have pointed out the opportunities that this new identity provides, for example in the context of language learning. Identities that are detached from the purely physical realm of proximity and shared community offer a great opportunity for language learning in online social media contexts, at least as far as services dedicated to this end go (Harrison & Thomas 2009). Other studies have claimed that the mixture of languages in the use of the Internet has even given rise to mixed forms of communication in Internet language. For instance, Laghos et al. (2012) show that "Greeklish" (Greek language written in Latin characters) is the predominant form of written communication for Greek users on Youtube. Such a quasi-creolization of linguistic and para-linguistic systems hasn't been identified in the case of Spanish. That is, Spanglish isn't a predominant variety of Spanish on the Internet, even though the Internet does contribute to the development of this variety in the physical world (Montes-Alcalá 2009). This might be due to the Greek language being in a more exposed position to linguistic contamination, simply because it uses a writing system that has relatively little importance in online communication.

In any case, studies (across languages) for specific online social network services such as Facebook (Pérez-Sabater 2012), Youtube (Laghos et al. 2012), Tuenti (Torrego-González 2011b), Twitter (Zappavigna 2011) and the specific linguistic conventions therein have especially been under investigation during the first half of the 2010s. The relevance of such studies to the analyses in this dissertation, however, is rather reduced, in that none of the features identified can directly be linked to the network structure of social media. Such attribution has at least not been provided by the authors.

Additionally, online social networks have been under investigation concerning more specific phenomena, in a less language-specific fashion. For instance, hate speech (with corresponding definitions ranging from verbal assault to a type of terrorism) and its typology have been major topics in the linguistic analysis of social media (Chetty & Alathur 2018). More recent studies have linked the concept of identity in online social media expressed above to these specific phenomena, such as Hardaker and McGlashan (2016), who investigate the role of group identity and online affiliation with the phenomenon of misogynist hate speech. However, it should be noted that this linguistic phenomenon finds much more attention in the fields of criminology and penal law (e.g., Miró-Llinares 2016), and machine learning (e.g., Miok et al. 2019) than in philology and the study of specific languages. On a more technical front, computational approaches are used to model pragmatic phenomena such as irony (Barbieri & Saggion 2014) or sentiment (Agarwal et al. 2011)[49] exploiting the possibilities of online social networks as a source of corpus material.

While the aforementioned contributions are of interest to linguistic and philological inquiry, they aren't directly relevant to the kind of network analysis envisioned for this study, precisely because they don't investigate the network properties of social media. Other related works, however, try to tackle the question of network structure in more or less formal detail. Conceptually, the notion of hypertext (Larrondo-Ureta 2008; Pujolà et al. 2009) lays the groundwork for the conceptualisation of text linguistics on the Internet and online social networks. Hypertexts are defined as interconnected texts, which refer to one another and are technically linked. In this sense, any body of scientific literature could be considered a hypertext, because they are densely connected texts that form some sort of thematic unity. In online social networks, the easiest way to think of hypertext is the connection of entries in Wikipedia. In the online encyclopaedia, one can navigate a dense network of entries, thanks to an easy-to-use referencing mechanism through links. A hypertext is thus also a sort of network, where texts are nodes and connections between texts are edges. Wikipedia can and has been readily described as a network of entries (Bellomi & Bonato 2005). Even collaboration on Wikipedia in the sense of an online social network has been described in terms of network structure and organisation (Brandes et al. 2009).

More typical online social networks, such as Twitter, can also be conceived of as hypertext. Micro-texts on the site are linked to one another, either through direct quoting or via the connection of their authors through the *follow* function. In the case of the online social network Twitter, hashtags (#) play an important role in the structuring of the hypertextual network. Hashtags can be and are used to reference certain topics of interest in the social space that is the network, and other users can filter their feeds by hashtags, such as to only read contributions

49 Since it is irrelevant for this contribution, this chapter will not include more detail on the overwhelming body of literature that exists on sentiment analysis in the year 2023. Suffice it to say, that this discipline in NLP has grown to significant repute, to an extent where entire libraries of programming languages, such as *R* (Rinker et al. 2014; Rinker & Spinu 2016), are dedicated to the extraction of linguistic sentiment from text.

made under this specific hashtag. Some of these hashtags can even be indicative of social movements as the *#MeToo* movement has shown (Jaffe 2018). On a more technical note, however, this structuring serves two purposes. On the one hand, hashtags render online discourse searchable. On the other hand, hashtags serve the purpose of affiliation to such movements as *#MeToo* or to affiliate with the evaluative collective behaviour that is expressed under these hashtags (Zappavigna 2011). This structure of cyberspace can also be plotted in terms of networks, where hashtags and users are plotted as nodes and where mentions of a given hashtag by a user are represented as an edge between the user and the hashtag. Cunha et al. (2011) have used this conceptualisation of Twitter (although without actually representing it as a graph) to investigate the distribution and propagation of linguistic innovation in terms of hashtags. They analyse the popularity of three different hashtags of relevance at the time, *#MusicMonday, #MichaelJackson,* and *#SwineFlu*, each reminiscent of a socially relevant event. They argue that the creation of hashtags is similar to the creation of linguistic innovation, in the sense that it is the result of a need for expression. That is, whenever individuals feel the need to organise their knowledge or opinions around a certain topic, specialised linguistic strategies emerge to express this. Depending on contingent circumstances, these strategies, then, may or may not be adopted by other individuals. While the authors don't explicate what these contingencies are in terms of network topology or other properties, they do find some striking similarities with linguistic systems. Referring to Easley and Kleinberg (2010, cited in Cunha et al. 2011), they argue that the propagation of linguistic trends in online social networks follows the "rich-get-richer phenomenon" (p. 61). This is the idea that, while popular hashtags get more popular faster, the increase in popularity of less popular hashtags is slowed down.

The authors don't specifically address how this is tied to network structure but confirm the rich-get-richer phenomenon by comparing the relative popularity of the aforementioned hashtags to their absolute number of occurrences. They find that the correlation between the absolute occurrence of hashtags and the hashtag's rank in a Twitter-wide popularity rating is governed by the Principle of *Relative Frequency* (Zipf 1929), which states that the frequency n of an item is correlated to its rank R in a ranking of all items:

$$n = \frac{1}{R}$$

This principle has been identified in all kinds of linguistic contexts and was linked to a principle of human least effort (Zipf 1949). The principle has gained popularity under the term *Zipf's Law* ever since. The resulting curve can be described in terms of a power function[50] with a negative exponent and represents the relationship that Cunha et al. (2011) found for the popularity of hashtags. But again, they do not link this concretely to the structure of network space. However, such a distribution is consistent with findings in simulations (Maity & Mukherjee 2016), where the relative frequencies of dominant opinions in scale-free networks with a low number of rigid individuals also follow a power-law distribution.

An interesting account that is more dedicated to network structure and linguistic features investigates the propagation of rumours on Twitter on three axes: temporal, structural, and linguistic (Kwon et al. 2013). The authors find that all three elements contribute to the description and classification of rumours. For instance, rumour topics such as *#Bigfoot*, *#FanDeath*, or *#HIVKetchup* exhibit different properties from topics such as *#Summize*, *#ObamaFly* or *#District9* on the three mentioned axes of analysis. As such, the rumour topics exhibit various spikes of popularity over time and keep bouncing back, whereas the non-rumour topics usually have one single spike of popularity, which then cools down according to the Zipfian power law described above.

Concerning network structure, the authors identify that non-rumours are best classified as those tweets which flow from low to high-degree nodes. This means that non-rumours, even though initiated by individuals with fewer followers, are quickly picked up on by better-connected users, which then pass on the message to the rest of the network. Another indicator here is that rumours are more likely spread by singletons or users whose tweets are barely retweeted.

In terms of linguistic measures, the authors single out three aspects of the reaction of users toward the tweet containing the rumour. In concrete, these responses are far less likely to contain positively affected words, while, on the other hand, users were very likely to include negating words (*not, no*) and references to cognitive action (*cause, know*) in their responses (Kwon et al. 2013). Most interestingly, it could be speculated about the interplay of these three factors with regard to non-rumour language, and how certain linguistic devices propagate in (online) social networks. A possible example to generate hypotheses for further research is the effect of the emotive content of tweets on the propagation of fear of crime in hashtags such as *#StopIslam* (Castro-Toledo

50 This distribution is also known as the 80-20 rule in popular culture.

et al. 2020). While not based on a specific framework for network analysis, their findings suggest that more aroused tweet semantics lead to a higher perception of danger, but also a high engagement with the tweet. This could ultimately lead to a better propagation of negative and aroused stimuli in social media networks.

4. A Linguistics of Social Networks

As a result of the previous considerations, one could make an argument to support pragmatic primacy in language. This means that language is only meaningful when it is used to communicative ends. The meaning of any signifier is dependent on its being used with a particular intended meaning. Furthermore, the social network has to agree with the usage of a signifier (i.e., the Saussurean principle of conventionality) and on the other hand, the signifiers that circulate through the social network depend on the individual usage decisions that actors take when solving communicative problems on the micro-level. The following case is an anecdotal example of this circumstance.

The word "quizzaciously" is defined by the Oxford English Dictionary, but according to Stevens (2015) doesn't appear on Wikipedia, in the Gutenberg Corpus, the British National Corpus, or the American National Corpus. One could claim that, since it wasn't used at all, it didn't mean anything. When Stevens' video was produced (2015), Google allegedly returned only one single occurrence of this word on all of the Internet upon search. However, the decision to publish this piece of trivia about the word "quizzaciously" led to Google now finding around 12,200 occurrences in less than 0.4 seconds (last query: 15.03.2021). The moment when Google's findings for the word "quizzaciously" included two findings for the first time was recorded almost in real-time by Stevens himself, in a Tweet on September 15th 2015[51]. This tweet was, in turn, retweeted over a hundred times, meaning the term could henceforth also be found on Twitter, which increased the count of Google occurrences of "quizzaciously" by another point almost instantaneously. This means that, by the time the current study is edited, the term "quizzaciously" has gone from being meaningless to almost every English speaker in the world to being somewhat meaningful for people who follow Stevens' content on the Internet. This is relevant to the study of networks in linguistics because it exemplifies how the connectivity of a speaker can affect linguistic change (cf. Labov 2001) and that the production of collective meaning is highly dependent on the properties of the social network in which such collective meaning is generated. In other words, the local choices of speakers can have important implications across wider parts of the network, which means that the local and global levels of networks are highly interwoven. It is argued

51 https://twitter.com/tweetsauce/status/643905654646771713

that this connectedness can only be accounted for by a systematic appraisal of the role that social networks play in language usage and, by extension, development.

Having established the notion of network as used in the linguistic and other relevant literature, the formulation of testable claims and expected observations is now in order. The present chapter is thus dedicated to entangling the arguments from the three previous chapters in a novel way, thus compiling some of the properties of social networks in the context of language. This is far from the formulation of a cohesive theory of social networks in language. But it is attempted to explore some of the key features of such a theory, which can be tested in three experimental approaches reported below (Chapters 6, 7, and 8).

To achieve this objective, the chapter will be divided into two sections. The first section will attempt to provide a network conceptualisation of language in terms of *Complex Adaptive Systems* (CAS). The CAS approach to language is chosen because it provides a notion of language that is compatible with the network approach. The reason for this is that CAS foregrounds the interconnectedness of agents rather than focusing on the individual. The second section of this chapter will then present some of the most pertinent properties of linguistic consensus in CAS as identified in the literature reported above (Chapter 3). These properties will then be used to generate testable hypotheses for the study of social networks in linguistics.

4.1. Language as a Complex Adaptive System

The issue of the impact of social network structure on language leads to the question of what (a) language is. This is why different axiomatic assumptions about the application of networks to languages (cf. Sections 3.2 and 3.3) lead to fairly different approaches. The reason for this is that the conception of language is usually a methodological question that is answered prior to investigation, rather than its result. If a language is considered a system, the network is applied to the level of individual cognition, such as to model the dynamics of the cognitive system called language. If, on the other hand, language is fundamentally understood as a social phenomenon, then the application of the network takes place on the level of society. This is the meta-theoretic finding of the literature review in a nutshell.

Now, if the latter interpretation is to be modelled into a cohesive network approach, this poses some problems for traditional definitions of structural linguistics. First of all, the structuralist concept of the linguistic system (De Saussure 1916) has to be called into question. For the structuralist school following the *Cours de Linguistic Générale*, language is a system of linguistic signs guided by structural, that is, syntactic rules which govern possible relations between the linguistic signs. Importantly, these rules are not motivated but arbitrary, as is the relationship between the signified and the signifier. Such a conception of language is counterproductive to the approach taken in this dissertation because it construes the structure of language as an ontological object that exists in the world. This is why Coseriu (1962) is able to argue that language is stratified into *system*, *norm*, and *speech,* with the linguistic system determining the minimal scaffold for the language to exist, and specific norms for the use of this system to determine the actualized speech of the individual. This is also inherently linked to the Chomskyan dichotomy of *competence* and *performance* (Chomsky 1965) as Maria Azucena Penas-Ibáñez (2005) points out. The ontological argument in both cases is that the system of language precedes its usage.

The structuralist definition then assumes that the usage of language is subject to the system of language. The rules of the system determine (with some room for variation) which linguistic norms are possible and which, in turn, determine the actual usage of language (Coseriu 1962). But it was shown with ample reference to linguistic experimentation (cf. Section 3.3) that the linguistic system is shaped by the circumstances of its usage, which is why the opposite route for the systematic fixation of the linguistic is proposed in the context of network theory.

System > Norm > Speech

Speech > Consensus > System

This means that language, rather than being the prerequisite of communication and the creation of consensus, is the result of communication and the achievement of consensus. This is of course not a genuine contribution of this thesis. Previous contributions have shown extensively that the linguistic system adapts to the needs of communication.

Fusaroli and Tylén (2012) review several experimental studies in the field of linguistic coordination, raising the argument that the use of symbolic forms emerges and stabilizes in local interaction while the refinement of these systems, in turn, enables the tackling of more complex social tasks. This idea is sustained by experimental evidence for the increase in collective performance on perceptual tasks under selective linguistic alignment (Fusaroli et al. 2012). This means that dyads of participants have more success in solving perceptual problems if they converge on more aligned linguistic practices. This means that goal-directed interaction benefits from linguistic coordination and the refinement of semiotic structure through this interaction. This idea has later been pinpointed as "interpersonal synergy" (Fusaroli et al. 2014) with special emphasis on dialogue as an emergent and self-organising system, in which goal-directedness, or "functional coordination" (ibid.) is a driver for the emergence of linguistic structure. Importantly, the authors argue explicitly that the description of language from an individual standpoint is insufficient.

This doesn't mean that there is no linguistic system that individuals have to follow to make themselves understood. It merely implies that the use of language shapes the system rather than the other way around and that the interaction between individuals is the locus of language. Applying this to Chomsky's (1965) terminology would amount to stating that performance precedes competence, instead of the other way around. In this line of argumentation, Schoenemann proposes that the

> specific rules and structures in a given language represent simply conventionalizations that allow languages to accurately communicate between human semantics. Grammar and syntax would in this case be seen as behavioural adaptations that take advantage of different possible (i.e., pre-existing) cognitive abilities to accomplish the task of representing higher-order conceptual complexity. (Schoenemann 2005, p. 70)

Now, these two perspectives aren't necessarily mutually exclusive but have to be understood in terms of their complementarity. Saying that linguistic structure doesn't exist without language being used, does not amount to saying that it isn't there; it just means that the structure emerges from interaction and cultural transmission (cf. Silvey et al. 2019). On the other hand, the structure does, of course, put constraints on the usage of language on the individual level. In the acquisition of modern and full-fledged languages, it would be impossible to argue that learners are not subject to the rules of their speech community. The circumstance that each generation learns based on the previous generation makes linguistic and cultural evolution (Kirby et al. 2008) so powerful. The reason for this is that there is no need to reinvent the discoveries of past generations, precisely because the structure *does exist*.

The aforementioned Fusaroli and Tylén (2012) refer to the circular relationship between the processes of local adaptation and conventionalisation. Locally adaptive behaviour can, given the right circumstances (Baicchi 2015), give rise to conventionalised structure, which feeds back into the community. This feedback enables speakers to solve more complicated linguistic problems while, at the same time, constraining their possibilities for linguistic expression. These constraints then, lead to new communication strategies when needed and the cycle starts anew. In the words of the authors: "coordinative needs motivate linguistic alignment leading to the emergence of stable symbolic patterns, which in turn guide and constrain the interactive dynamics in an iterative process" (Fusaroli & Tylén 2012, p. 114).

This model feeds into the idea that in the relationship between language and social coordination, none precedes the other. Rather, they are intrinsically linked in a sort of "circular causality" (Kelso 1995, p. 9) like hen and egg. None of either was there first[52], but their complementary nature brings them into existence. Such a conception aids the explanation of the emergence of language and cognition as a result of the interaction between them. As language structures cognition, cognition becomes enhanced and can produce even more nuanced language, resulting in a positive feedback loop that characterises cognitive evolution (Deacon 1997). When applied to the notion of networks, such dynamic processes can be claimed to take place between the local and the global level. That is, while the local behaviour structures the network and its structural properties, such as its topology, these structural properties can in turn have an impact on the local interaction between nodes.

The complementary principle can be illustrated by looking at the discussion of word order universals. It has been argued (Chomsky 1965) that the predilection of languages for either SVO or SOV structures for the most fundamental parts of speech subject (S), verb (V), and object (O) hints at the innateness of these structures in the human brain. An alternative explanation is that SOV and SVO are not hardcoded into the brain, but that they reflect more closely on the structure of actions as they are observed in the world. They are thus better adapted to the representation of facts as they are observed in the world. Since the subject is the most active part of any given action, it makes sense – from the perspective of distributing information over the sentence – to name it first and name the object second. The adaptive pressure of the described scene on the preference for word order can be shown experimentally. In phrases that represent object manipulation events, people are more inclined to use the SOV structure (Christensen & Tylén 2013). The subject and the object as preexisting entities are presented and then the action carried out by the former on the latter is specified: "(S) The person (O) the ball (V) kicks". If, however, the object is the result of the action as in construction events, the SVO structure is more commonly used since the object doesn't exist prior to the action: "(S) The person (V) makes (O) a pizza" (Christensen & Tylén 2013). It appears that there is a more habitual way for people to order phrases such that event structure

52 If we restrict our argument to chicken eggs. Dinosaur eggs were of course there before hens.

is somehow mapped onto the grammar of the sentence. However, this doesn't mean that innateness is a meaningless category for the predilection of SOV or SVO languages across the world. If this structure is so predominant in its use it can fossilize to a degree where it is innate. That means that the innate inclination of doing something in one way or another is determined by what is functionally viable for a long time; at the same time, functionally viable forms are boosted if they coincide with the innate inclination.

Conceptions of language that foreground the dynamic adaptation of language, cognition, and behaviour are often described as emergentist theories. That is because the structure of language emerges from interaction and cognition rather than it being the precursor of the latter. The idea of emergence has ever since had great success in the linguistic sciences. Määttä (2000) identifies a phalanx of emergentist linguistic theories around the end of the past millennium. Beckner et al. (2009) in their seminal position paper make their case for a conception of language as a complex adaptive system (CAS). This conception of language is ultimately the conception that the reported studies on social cognition and language subscribe to. This is a conception of language that, as opposed to the structural view of language, is more compatible with the notion of language as a product of consensus achievement. Language as a CAS is construed as follows:

> (a) The system consists of multiple agents (the speakers in the speech community) interacting with one another. (b) The system is adaptive; that is, speakers' behaviour is based on their past interactions, and current and past interactions together feed forward into future behaviour. (c) A speaker's behaviour is the consequence of competing factors from perceptual mechanics to social motivations. (d) The structures of language emerge from interrelated patterns of experience, social interaction, and cognitive processes. (Beckner et al. 2009, p. 2)

Point (a) sums up the aforementioned arguments that the ontological locus of language is not the Platonian world of ideas (cf. Tylén et al. 2013) but the interaction between people who communicate with each other (Kirby & Hurford 2002; Schoenemann 2005; Fusaroli & Tylén 2012; Silvey et al. 2019). This property reproduces the axiomatic underpinning of the texts reviewed above (Section 3.3). In these approaches, the network systems are modelled with agents as nodes and the interaction between them as edges to capture the dynamics of agent networks and their impact on language. These studies also subscribe, to a higher or lesser degree, to a conception of language where language is an epiphenomenon of interaction and cultural transmission (Silvey et al. 2019) which is contingent on biological evolution, learning biases and cultural evolution (Kirby & Hurford 2002). This view is central to the body of literature described above. It is important to point out that, while cognitive learning biases are contingent on biological evolution and cultural evolution is contingent on such learning biases, this doesn't convert these evolutionary pressures into a one-way street. In adaptive systems, the systems influence each other and there is no primacy of one over the others. While the biological system of course precedes the cultural system in that it is older, the biological system is affected by the cultural system just as much as the other way around.

The adaptiveness (b) of language refers to its propensity to change. As was pointed out earlier, very useful or conventionalized forms can be grammaticalised and incorporated into the system if they are functionally adaptive (Baicchi 2015). One of the key properties of CAS is that the different interacting systems adapt to each other rather than one simply building upon the other, even if one layer emerges from the previous one. To illustrate this, consider a study by Gillings et al. (2016) who argue that the evolution of evolutionary substrates amounts to leaps in information processing capacity. They conceptualise evolutionary substrates as information carriers of different sorts. Through combination, each level can store, reproduce, and process more information than the previous one. Genetic information in the form of DNA allows for multicellular life which, in turn, can give rise to neural nets in multicellular organisms with increasing brain sizes which, in turn, increase their memory by inventing different stone- or paper-based and later digital information technologies. While each level emerges from combinatory effects on the lower level (RNA > DNA > multicellular life > cognition > technology) the upper levels can impact back on the lower levels of information. If certain multicellular organisms develop immune systems against certain viruses, then these organisms create new evolutionary pressure for the RNA-based virus, even though the development from RNA into DNA allowed for the existence of multicellular organisms in the first place. Similarly, it was argued above (Section 3.4) that the existence of the Internet has an impact on certain conventions for language, even though conventionalised language certainly is a pre-condition for the existence of the Internet in evolutionary terms. Without a highly advanced linguistic system including also highly codified habits of scientific communication and collaboration, the Internet couldn't have been created. But it does now affect its condition, because of the mutual adaptation of systems within a CAS.

Furthermore (c), the processes that lead to the emergence of new forms are the result of competing pressures. This means that evolutionary pressures, which appear to be counterproductive to each other, actually complement each other. Consider the experiment in Kirby et al. (2008) in which one pressure for expressivity and another for comprehensibility together result in emerging systematised linguistic forms. Expressivity and comprehensibility are opposed in nature. While expressivity drives a system of linguistic expressions toward exuberance, comprehensibility produces simpler and smaller communication systems. The systematisation of signs into dually patterned symbols (cf. Martinet 1949; Verhoef 2012) then ensures comprehensibility by recurring to only a few unique morphemes and expressivity by allowing for relatively free combinations of these morphemes. A recent example of research on complementary pressures in linguistic systems models linguistic politeness as a result of the interaction between strategic (i.e., trying to get something) and social (i.e., group belonging) elements of linguistic interaction (Gretenkort & Tylén 2021).

Finally, point (d) refers to the absence of *a priori* structure in language; the structure is a consequence of its usage, as was also pointed out by researchers emphasizing the concept of usage-based grammar (Beckner et al. 2009, p. 5). This is the case for the rebuttal of the structuralist conception of language. Speech isn't a token of a linguistic system, but the linguistic system emerges from speech through the integration of "experience, social interaction, and cognitive processes" (Beckner et al. 2009, p. 2). Newer accounts have updated this list of "interrelated patterns" (ibid.) to "1) the physical constraints and affordances of our surrounding material environment, 2) biological constraints of our human bodies, 3) social normative constraints of culture and society, and 4) the local history of social interactions" (Tylén et al. 2013, p. 39).

As an example of such a process of linguistic evolution, consider the case of the Romance synthetic future tenses. The synthetic future tense *iré* is a result of the Latin analytical form *ire habeo* > *ir he* > *iré*. The process lends itself to a description from a CAS perspective. First of all, the process is adaptive. Latin already had a future to *ire* namely *ibo* . For reasons of adaptation, however, the Latin future didn't survive the transition to Romance and was ubiquitously substituted by *ire habeo* resulting in the modern Romance vocabularies *j'irai* and *iré* (Leumann 1962) But, as Schon (2011) points out, the contraction of the analytical to the synthetic form resulted in diverging degrees of analyticity. While the Spanish and French forms are completely fossilised and can't be broken down into unbound semantic morphemes, Portuguese allows the infixation of the complement of the indirect object. Consider the following example from Portuguese:

$$dar - \mathbf{lhe} - ei \left(give - \frac{him}{her} - I\ have = I \frac{have\ to}{will} give\ it\ to \frac{him}{her} \right)$$

This adaptive process can be interpreted in terms of competing pressures, where one pressure drives grammatical fossilisation and another one drives the conservation of analytical features for expressivity. The degree of analyticity is dependent on surrounding contingencies that can be found both in the linguistic system itself and extra-linguistic circumstances (like the interaction patterns of speakers of Portuguese as compared to Spanish). At the same time as the synthesis of *iré* and *j'irai* occurs, all three linguistic systems start to use a competing future tense, that is the going-to future. This is an analytical form based on the auxiliary verb *to go* as in *je vais(y)aller, voy a ir*, and *vou ir,* which competes since the Middle Ages with the synthesized form of *irai, iré*, and *irei* (Schon 2011). The particularity of this form is that it allows adding an indirect object between the finite form and the infinitive: *je vais lui donner* and *vou lhe dar.* In French, this makes for two distinct future tenses with different expressive connotations and different grammatical degrees of analyticity. While the more analytical form is more suitable for the written language modality, it is still conserved to some degree in speech, because it is different enough from the competing form to be conserved. In the case of Portuguese however, *dar – lhe – ei* has been completely abandoned in informal oral discourse, as a result of a lack of difference in comparison to the competing form (Schon 2011). Thus, the principles driving the development of analytical and synthetic tenses in the Romance languages could be considered competing pressures that modulate each other and lead to different results under different conditions. In some situations, the analytical, and in other cases, the synthetic forms come out on top. This is subject to conditions in the grammatical system. In the case of Spanish, for instance, the analytical form frees up the infinitive (*daré* vs. *voy a dar*) for usage. Thus, clitics can be added to refer to complements such as the indirect object (*le daré* vs. *voy a darle*). But the analytical form can also be conceived of as a synthetic form (*le voy a dar*) making the *ir + infinitive* form the grammatically more versatile one. It can be conceptualised as either a synthetic or an analytical form, given the communicative context, which explains the slow but steady substitution of the simple *infinitive + habere* form in favour of the more analytical form *ir + infinitive* in Romance languages since the Middle Ages, which Schon (2011) reports.

This example shows how many different adaptive processes in language evolution modulate each other and influence the adaptation of the linguistic system to the communicative needs of its speakers. This thesis maintains the hypothesis that the network dynamics in the interactions between speakers of languages have an impact on this type of development as well. After all, the choice between one future form or the other isn't dictated by a central authority, but the choice is made locally, given the affordances of communication with the interlocutor.

4.2. Language as a Solution to the Consensus Problem

As indicated, a network view of language is most compatible with the conception of language as a CAS. The previous section has pointed out some of the properties of language as a CAS and has exemplified this view with an example of the development of tense in the Romance languages. Having established this conceptual framework, this section proceeds to explain how language can be framed as a solution to the consensus problem.

The claim sustains the idea that language is the result of communication, a view for which the previous sections have provided the necessary framework. The problem of consensus was earlier characterised as the necessity to provide all nodes in a network with the same information. According to the axioms laid out earlier (Section 3.3), speakers of a language can be characterised as nodes of a network; a social network. The problem of consensus, then, is to make sure that all people share the same set of information. While this is possibly not the main – and by no means the only – adequate way to describe human interaction, it is an important feature when turning to situations of collaboration (e.g., Fusaroli & Tylén 2012). That is, whenever a pragmatically defined goal requires the collaboration of different agents in a network. This extends to the creation of collective narratives and social conventions (Centola & Baronchelli 2015). For example, the question of whether or not Bitcoin is a suitable means of payment is not determined by its actual legal and informational status but by the readiness of a big enough group of people to adopt Bitcoin as a method of payment, which in turn depends on the usability and convenience of the payment system.

Consensus in a linguistic sense however isn't easily defined mathematically, unless there is a specific goal against which consensus can be measured. The construction of a building or a coordinated attack on Constantinople (Section 2.5.1) are good examples of such goals. If the structure of the building is stable or if the attack on Constantinople succeeds, there is reason to argue that consensus was achieved. Without such a pragmatic measurement, however, the definition is a lot more difficult. The closest account to quantifying consensus under such circumstances is provided by Herrera et al. (1996). The model is dedicated to the analysis of human consensus and its application in decision support systems. It is based on methods of fuzzy logic and explores how to quantify consensus on a set of different options. Hence, Herrera et al. (1996) don't define consensus without recurring to a pragmatic goal either. In their model, consensus is measured as a collective choice from a fixed set of options. They recur to the specific situation of decision-making. The authors define consensus on two different parameters. The consensus degree represents how close the group as a whole is to achieving consensus, with the highest degree of consensus being one. This is different from the view of consensus in information systems because any divergence from full consensus is regarded as non-consensus. In the present model, consensus can be attained to a higher or lesser degree, which is more useful for the description of social processes. The linguistic distances represent pairs of distances between each person in the group. That is, based on linguistic labels, the authors try to determine how aligned two individuals are in their inclination to choose one alternative over another. In the further development of this model (Herrera et al. 1997), the authors apply this analysis of the state of consensus to different relationships of the closeness of opinions between the different individuals involved in the decision-making process as well as the closeness between opinions expressed by the same individual. The main component of consensus, on which all types of measurements are based, is linguistic proximity. This means that people using similar terms for the quantification of their preference (e.g., "most", "at least half", "as many as possible") also have similar attitudes toward the available alternatives. This is corroborated by human experiments, most notably the contribution with the cunning name *Coming to Terms* (e.g., Fusaroli et al. 2012), in which it has been determined that the alignment of groups on task-relevant vocabulary is a relevant predictor for the outcome of the collaborative task. This means that selective alignment (Fusaroli et al. 2014) rather than low-level priming (cf. Pickering & Garrod 2004) plays an important role in the optimisation of language for consensus. A caveat to the method by Herrera et al. (1996, 1997) has been proposed by Cabrerizo et al. (2009), claiming that quantifiers of linguistic consensus (e.g., "low", "middle", "high") might not be evenly distributed. This means that "low" might not have the same distance to "middle" as "high" has. The authors thus try to incorporate their assessments of the distribution of linguistic quantifiers into a fuzzy model of consensus which is otherwise quite similar to Herrera et al. (1996, 1997).

Importantly, these contributions indicate that linguistic proximity can be used as a measure of linguistic consensus. Hence, linguistic proximity will be the basis upon which the experimental data on the consensus in interaction will be operationalised. The more similar contributions are linguistically the more closely related they will be deemed conceptually (cf. Section 6.2), that is in terms of consensus. The concept of consensus put forward for analysis is hence much broader than what can be mathematically assessed. But based on the CAS literature, consensus is here argued to be the overarching goal of communication (lat.: "communicare" → "to make something common"). While this is a claim of considerable magnitude, it does appear to be in line with the CAS literature, especially given the pragmatic primacy that is attributed to language. But it does stretch the arguments of the reported literature to a certain extent. Under the consensus view, language becomes a tool that under the described selective pressures becomes optimised for whatever task is at hand during communication, while the communicative tasks in the reported literature were always more neatly defined. This argumentative stretch is an assumed risk for this study.

What the current study tries to contribute is the identification of pressures that are inherent in networks, expanding the list of reported pressures in the emergence of language. Under the consensus view, it is argued that embedding these pressures in different network topologies, or nodes with higher or lower relative connectivity, has a different impact on the use and development of language. One of the most important features of consensus in social networks is the dependency of the local level on the global level and vice versa. This builds upon the foundation laid out in previous experiments (Kirby et al. 2008; Centola & Baronchelli 2015; Segovia-Martín et al. 2020). In the following, some features and biases of languages in social networks are going to be explored.

4.2.1. Parallel Fixation of System and Information

One of the most important features of social linguistic networks is the parallel fixation of the system and information. This means that, while the linguistic system is used to fix meanings in a given context, the language itself is fixed through the achievement of consensus. A successful interaction thus not only leads to a fixation of the pragmatic meaning (i.e., agreeing on what to do) but that the linguistic system itself can be impacted by successful communication. This follows from the theoretical conception of language put forth in Halliday and Matthiessen (2014) for whom language integrates ideational, interpersonal, and textual metafunctions. The former two are at the level of information, that is, the question of *what* is being said either about an object or the relationship with an interlocutor. The latter relates to the question of *how* something is said. This was earlier alluded to (cf. Section 1.3.2) in a much more radical fashion as overcoming the "absolute distinction between representation and things" (Latour 1996, p. 375) which ANT tries to achieve. This conception now gains significance as it refers to the necessity of having to settle on both *what* is being communicated (i.e., information) and *how* it is being communicated (i.e., system) at the same time.

The present network approach to language agrees with the aforementioned authors' conception in that both levels are interwoven and subject to the same dynamics of interaction. This was exemplified in the studies of selective alignment in collaborative tasks (Fusaroli et al. 2012), which, in and of itself, doesn't represent a driver for linguistic change. But the experiment describes local adaptation in a specific context, which speaks to the impact of communication on both languages and the pragmatic objective of the communication. However, it was also shown that cultural variants, which can arise in such specific contexts, can propagate in social networks and alter the macro-consensus of the system on the linguistic feature in question (Segovia-Martín et al. 2020). That is, the concept of networks enables researchers to look at both local behaviours and how such local behaviours can affect the larger-scale community. Thus, if a feature is locally highly adaptive (Baicchi 2015), then a network view of language can plausibly account for the propagation of such communicative strategy throughout the whole linguistic community. The term parallel fixation then means that, while language is used to settle on and communicate certain sets of information, the language itself is also fixed in its grammatical system through the act of communication, which is the argument of usage-based grammar (cf. Beckner et al. 2009).

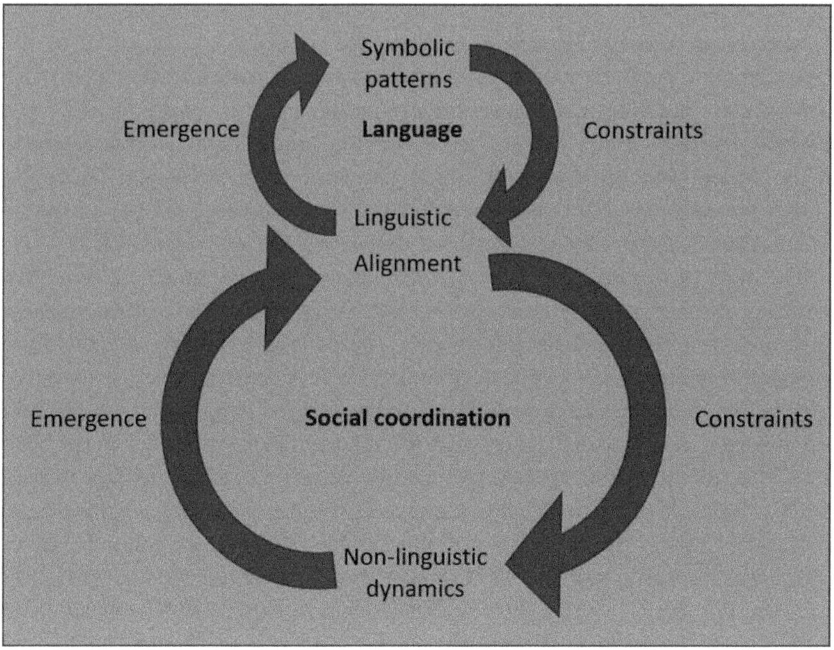

Fig. 31: Interaction of social coordination and language. (Adapted from Fusaroli & Tylén 2012)

Fusaroli and Tylén (2012) argue that this is possible through the interaction of the levels of communication and language that goes both ways. That is because the influence of language on coordination and vice versa are complementary directions of impact, where there is no primacy of one over the other (Fig. 31). In concrete, social coordination affects linguistic alignment which in turn is influenced by the linguistic system constraining the possibilities for linguistic alignment. The possibilities for linguistic alignment, on the other hand, put constraints on what can and cannot be achieved. This double fixation of information and the linguistic system is, in the present study, embedded into a bigger network structure, which informs the model further.

This is in line with the CAS position on language, for which the element of "distributed control and collective emergence" (Beckner et al. 2009, p. 14) is paramount. That means that even though "language exists both in individuals (as idiolect) and in the community of users (as communal language)" (ibid.) and these levels and their behaviour are not governed by the same principles, there needn't be a central entity that coordinates these levels. Rather, frequent interactions (Pickering & Garrod 2004) and mutual adaptation (Baicchi 2015; Lupyan & Dale 2016), as mentioned before, can lead to convergence on a shared self-organised system. Furthermore, language as a CAS is sensitive to and dependent on network structure. While it was first assumed that real-world networks are random, it was later shown that the structure and connectivity of the network interactions can and do have an important impact on the dynamics of the system and the emergent effects (Beckner et al. 2009, p. 17). Various studies have also argued that the architecture of social networks has an impact on language development and linguistic diversity (Lupyan & Dale 2016).

The study by Fusaroli and Tylén (2012) explains in detail how both directions "from coordination to language" (p. 104) and "from language to communication" (p. 109) are at work and that this is widely accounted for in the linguistic literature. This would make the issue appear as though there is no primacy of content over form or vice versa. Rather, it would have to be assumed that in interactions, both the messages and the ways to account for the messages are fixated at the same time. This notwithstanding, there is of course already a linguistic system in place (such as 'English' or 'Spanish') which one can presume to be widely agreed upon. Thus, adaptions to the system would have to be extremely useful, not only on a local but also on a global level, to make them spread out through the entire network. But this is in principle possible and can be explained when conceiving of linguistic communities as networks.

While the analogy to Blockchain technology is at this point less relevant for the production of concrete research hypotheses, this principle loops back to a major difference between consensus in language and consensus on the Blockchain (Section 1.3.3). While the communicative system and procedure (i.e., the algorithm) of the latter are stable and pre-defined (i.e., hard-coded into the system), the linguistic system can adapt to the needs of reaching consensus. This point mustn't be underestimated because it shows that consensus in language cannot rely on a perfectly stable system. It appears relatively stable in that it enables local interaction with other nodes that one node has no previous knowledge of, but according to the principle of fallibility (Ungeheuer 1987), it cannot be assumed that the linguistic system is always a suitable tool to agree upon something. Dos Santos (2017) comes to a similar conclusion about the Blockchain in saying that DLT are not complex chaotic systems.

4.2.2. Network Topology as a Typology of Interaction

According to the definitions (Section 2.3) and evidence (Section 3.3.3) provided above, it is hypothesised that the typology of both local and global interaction has an impact on what and how a given topic is talked about in a network. It was reported that network structure does have a palpable impact on the emergence of social conventions, seemingly out of thin air (Centola & Baronchelli 2015). Furthermore, it was shown that global network structure (even if the nodes are unaware of the structure) does have an impact on reaching consensus in different experimental tasks (Kearns et al. 2006, 2009; Judd et al. 2010). Even though such differences couldn't be replicated in lab experiments on the emergence of more complex communicative systems (Raviv et al. 2020), both the authors themselves and Chapter 3 have provided a variety of reasons why the experimental setup as such was flawed, rather than the influence of network structure on language development not being the case.

This is interesting because the above-described principle of parallel fixation would predict that the same principles which enable nodes to agree on something would hold for changes in the linguistic system. Circumstantial observational evidence on the other hand hints at a possible impact of network structure on the linguistic system. Lupyan and Dale (2010) have pointed to differences in grammatical systems between languages contingent on population size which, in turn, has been connected to social network structure (Trugdil 2009; Lupyan & Dale 2016). Thus, such an impact should be detectable with a suitable experiment.

The evidence thus raises the hypothesis that aspects of the topology of communicative networks have an impact on the degree of consensus that is reached in local interaction. This hypothesis will be tested in the first experiment below (Chapter 6).

4.2.3. Degree Bias

The reported literature elucidates the role of popular or well-connected agents in networks. It has been shown in various experiments and simulations that popular agents have an important impact on the information that propagates in a network (Gong & Wang 2005; Gong 2008). On the opposite side, there are studies about the role of rigid individuals that hinder the flow of information rather than benefit it (Maity & Mukherjee 2016). As was pointed out earlier, small and well-incentivised cliques or powerful individuals can also have an important impact on the network in terms of reaching consensus (Kearns et al. 2009; Judd et al. 2010).

The different roles of individuals in social networks have been extensively discussed in the opposing views of strong-tie (Labov 2001) and weak-tie (Milroy 2002) theories in socio-linguistics. More generally speaking, it can thus be argued that the connectivity of an agent in a network can have an important impact on the global consensus in the network. Similar claims can be made based on formal deliberations. For example, the considerations of the *Byzantine Generals Problem* have shown that nodes that sit at neuralgic points in a network can seriously affect the reaching of consensus (Section 2.5.1) because they act as either gatekeepers or promotors of information.

It is thus hypothesised that more highly connected nodes contribute more to the propagation of information in a system than less well-connected nodes.

4.2.4. Identity Bias

The socio-linguistic literature argues that different agents pass on their linguistic memes to other agents in the social network (Labov 2001). Even if they aren't well connected, people who imitate their behaviour pass their linguistic variants on to other agents, which can eventually spread through the network (Milroy 2002; Lev-Ari 2018). The identity bias can thus be characterised as the influence of the social reputation of agents on the network properties, regardless of the connectivity of such a node. In particular, content from more highly reputed nodes can potentially be adapted more frequently, if the source of the content is known. This is related to the notion of authority or power within social networks (Milroy & Milroy 1992). The behaviour of such popular nodes (Gong 2008) or their aversion to innovation (Baxter 2016) can affect the propagation of information in such networks to an important degree.

Identity bias poses a rather big problem to the analysis of networks on a macro-scale because it has to be taken into account that edges in social networks might not be of the same quality (Milroy & Milroy 1992). The identity bias is also at odds with the degree bias. After all, even less well-connected nodes could potentially impact the propagation of information or linguistic habits in a system (Milroy 2002). That is because the information coming from nodes with a good reputation might be more trusted. Such effects are notoriously hard to measure in large-scale networks because the specific reputation of a node from a purely graph-theoretic standpoint can only be assessed in terms of node degree. Other information about the popularity of a node is usually not available. This will have to be methodologically corrected for the collection of data (Chapter 5). The study will have to account for the effect that different identities of nodes can have on the propagation of information and the network topology.

4.2.5. Degree Distribution Bias

Degree distribution bias refers to the skew in the degree distribution of social networks. This means that the degrees of nodes, rather than being evenly distributed, follow a distribution closer to the rich-get-richer principle reported above (cf. Easley & Kleinberg 2010; Cunha et al. 2011). Under the assumption of such a distribution, there are few very popular and many unpopular nodes. If the degree distribution bias holds true, social networks should empirically more closely resemble scale-free (Fig. 29c) rather than small-world networks (Fig. 29b) in the sense they are reported in Raviv et al. (2020). This means that networks are on a macro-scale biased toward a distribution in which most edges are incident on a few nodes. Thus, some nodes are inherently better connected than other nodes. As reported above, this has massive consequences for how information can propagate through such networks (Gong & Wang 2005; Gong 2008; Kearns et al. 2009; Judd et al. 2010). For the description of the data (Chapter 5), it will thus be of relevance to describe the degree distribution that networks have.

4.2.6. Content Bias

Several studies reported that the quality of the content of a message impacts its propensity to propagate in a network (e.g., Tamariz et al. 2014; Segovia-Martín et al. 2020). Thus, it is here hypothesised that the content of a message contributes to the generation of direct neighbours on a local level. This is useful for a linguistic study because successful contents can be analysed in terms of the linguistic properties that they present. In particular, it can be measured whether or not certain contents generate more neighbours for any given contribution.

Now, the content bias is at odds with the identity bias. While certain contents could enhance the success of a communicative contribution, it is easy to conceive of a node that contains high-quality content but it isn't a node with an important enough identity to spread the content. At the same time, this interacts with the degree bias in that good content from poorly connected nodes cannot spread this information while well-connected nodes can propagate low-quality stimuli.

4.3. Concluding Remarks and Experimental Predictions

This chapter is rather short because it merely harnesses the reviewed literature into a more structured account of certain properties of linguistic social networks. It is however an important chapter in that the condensed information allows for a clearer view of these properties and allows to motivate experimental claims which can then be tested empirically. In summary of the aforementioned properties of social linguistic networks, the following hypotheses will be put forth.

Experiment one (Chapter 6) will seek to elucidate the discussion of the topology of linguistic social networks from a macro point of view. The study is interested in the effect that network structure, and particularly graph centrality, has on the local agreement on a conversation topic. According to the parallel fixation of system and information both the level of agreement on linguistic forms (e.g., selective alignment) and conversation topics could be measured. This experiment will focus on measuring the level of consensus on the conversation topic and the importance of network structure for this type of consensus. From the principle of distributed control (Beckner et al. 2009) and the call for more secure information systems through more widely applied decentralisation, the following prediction is formulated:

> H1: More decentralised interaction topologies lead to a higher degree of consensus on conversation topics compared to centralised interaction topologies. Furthermore, the more distributed the interaction topology is, the more consensus about conversation topics is achieved.

Experiment two (Chapter 7) tries to tackle the problem of the interaction between identity, node and content bias. It was argued that popular agents contribute to the information in the network by controlling the information flow to some degree. What the experiment aims to show is that in networks where the identity bias is precluded from nodes in a network, alternative strategies to gain reputation in the network have to be put in place (cf. Bernstein et al. 2011). This means that, when the identity of a person isn't available to readers, individuals seek other linguistic means to signal their trustworthiness to the network. Such agents thus try to skew information through secret handshakes that replace identity bias in the form of content bias, leading to better connectivity of the node and enabling it to reach more people. This results in the following hypothesis.

H_2: Certain linguistic features, that indicate knowledge of the communicative conventions of a group, signal trustworthiness to other nodes in the network and thus lead to higher connectivity of nodes containing these linguistic features. Which linguistic features have to be adopted in any case is contingent on the circumstances and conventions of the given social group. The specific linguistic features under investigation will be identified in the introduction of the corresponding experiment (Chapter 7).

Experiment three (Chapter 8) is concerned with content bias proper. The experiment is focused on identifying those linguistic features which correspond to the high connectivity of nodes and which help to predict the propensity of information propagation. Such content biases are potentially abundant and there can be many different ways in which the content of a contribution can affect its connectivity. Strictly speaking, experiment two already identifies such content in the form of secret handshakes. The third experiment, however, will draw upon literature on emotion, therefore generating an exemplary hypothesis for a less domain-specific content bias. Based on Ströbel (2014), it is argued that expressivity in the form of sensorimotor strategies is an important predictor of the connectivity of nodes in a network. Thus, experiment three is going to tackle the following hypothesis:

H_3: The connectivity of a node in an interaction network is contingent on the expressivity of the content present in that node. This expressivity can be measured in terms of the dynamicity of the sensorimotor content of the word. This is only one example of how content can affect the connectivity of a node. The exact motivation for this claim will be explained in more detail in the corresponding experiment (Chapter 8).

While these hypotheses are by no means an exhaustive analysis of all the different aspects of the linguistics of networks, these experiments contribute to three exemplary features of the described type of networks. On the macro-level, the role of network structure for consensus in a linguistic sense is investigated. On the micro-level, two selected types of biases in linguistic networks are investigated. This leaves a lot of room for future investigations. Not only is the totality of identified biases in linguistic networks not exhaustively analysed, but especially content bias can take many different forms of local strategies, which leads to a myriad of small-scale local studies of the relevance of certain linguistic features in networks. On the other hand, it is argued that the three proposed experiments exploit gaps in the literature and elucidate more or less under-investigated phenomena while binding them together under a more generalisable paradigm. That is, while local phenomena are of interest for single studies, the theoretical framework provided in this thesis does allow to subsume studies of local behaviour under a network framework where the findings of local studies aren't only not contradictory but can explain the emergence of networks effects on the macro-level.

5. Data

This section is dedicated to the description of the dataset. The dataset forms the basis for all statistical experiments that were run. Also, the specific properties of the dataset will be considered in light of the interpretability of the data.

Considering the literature revised in Chapter 3, it has been shown that there is ample evidence for linguistic usage and evolution through cultural transmission in simulations and experimental accounts. While these are valuable sources for the exploration of network effects, it could be argued that they lack ecological validity, meaning that these works have to be complemented by observational data showing how theoretic accounts play out in existing languages and authentic linguistic material. The existing observational data on the development of the Spanish language on the Internet lacks a formal consideration of network properties. While they're valuable for the documentation of large-scale linguistic developments within the language, they don't allow for the observation of local linguistic behaviour systematically. This means that claims about the impact of the Internet on linguistic features can be made on a general level, while specific phenomena cannot be linked to specific properties in which Internet communication differs from physical communication. This thesis, therefore, proposes observation of a Spanish dataset, to determine how network structure affects linguistic behaviour. With regard to the revised literature on cultural transmission and experimental semiotics, two key differences have to be pointed out. First of all, the Internet doesn't provide long-term linguistic data, thus direct observation of linguistic evolution is not feasible. This forces the current study to investigate communication on a local level, with data that can be meaningfully represented as an abstraction level-1 network (cf. Araújo & Banisch 2016; Zweig 2016) in the Spanish language.

For these reasons, the dataset will be comprised of posts and comments on an online social network platform, where contributions to a thread are plotted as networks, with the original post (OP) at the centre, and comments being plotted around this central post. In principle, this can be achieved with content from any online social network. The resulting networks are not proper social networks because nodes aren't user accounts. The networks at the basis of this thesis will hence be referred to as linguistic interaction networks, where posts' responses are plotted as nodes, while the edges represent references between them.

The dataset had to conform to a set of requirements that are important for the presented research. First of all, the dataset should allow researchers to disentangle the aspect of network structure from other elements. The literature suggests that network structure is easily conflated with different other elements such as group size (Trudgill 2009; Lupyan & Dale 2010). This will be a question to empirically address in the dataset. Furthermore, the presence of popular agents (Gong & Wang 2005; Gong 2008) and rigid individuals (Maity & Mukherjee 2016), subsumed under the term identity bias (4.2.4) needs to be solved to disentangle actual network properties and effects of reputation. The data needs to isolate network structure from other aspects so that network properties can be presumed to be the main variable for analysis.

As a means of eliminating these biases in the dataset, the data was collected from an online social network that doesn't have any account structure, and where communication takes place solely on a local level, without any underlying 'social' structure.

5.1. Hispachan – Anonymous Linguistic Interaction Networks

Hispachan[53] was chosen as the most suitable platform for the analysis of linguistic interaction structure. The reason for this is the elimination of the aforementioned identity bias (Section 4.2.4). Hispachan doesn't have any possibility of following, liking or sharing content. The only way of interacting with content on Hispachan is to read a message (which doesn't leave a digital trace and is thus irrelevant to this study) or to reply directly to it. One can also write an original post (OP) that doesn't reply to any other content. The website hence allows for exactly one way of plotting a level-1 network (cf. Araújo & Banisch 2016), namely by modelling posts as nodes and references between them as edges. One cannot log onto the

---

53 I have to report that https://www.hispachan.org went offline in 2022, that is, at some point between the defence and the publication of this doctoral dissertation, as the reader will be able to confirm under the aforementioned URL. However, the html structure of similar websites such as https://4chan.org, should be similar enough that reproducibility of the reported experiments with the code provided in the annex should still be achievable with relatively little effort. One drawback of resorting to 4chan is that its content is entirely in English while my own corpus is in Spanish. Hence, language specific steps of data processing (e.g., special characters, data cleaning, etc.) may have to be adjusted to a bigger extent. Also, there's no guarantee that the user populations of these websites operate and communicate in the same way, so my findings may not generalise to other websites (cf. Chapter 10).

website with a user profile. Rather, anyone can post to the website and comment on other posts anonymously. A random ID is generated for each post, such that it isn't even possible to identify whether two posts in the same thread stem from the same person. Therefore, no likes and no following are possible, and interaction is entirely local (Fig. 32). This is helpful in the elimination of conflating identity bias, such that knowledge about other users cannot overshadow the effects that network properties have on the communication itself (e.g., the popularity of the interlocutor).

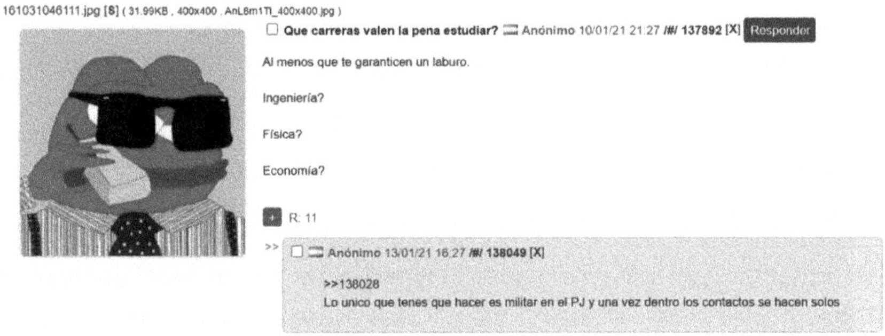

Fig. 32: Example of a post to Hispachan AR. Observe that both the original post and the comment are titled "Anónimo" as the username. A hashtag (#) number serves as an identifier for each post (#137892 and #138049, respectively). Note that only the most recent interaction with the post can be observed (#138049), while 11 more replies are hidden, as the sign "+ R: 11" indicates. The thread (even though heavily memefied through the use of "Pepe the Frog", who is here depicted as a hustling 1980s entrepreneur) appears to be a rather conventional discussion of job chances and career choices in Argentina. The only hint to a person's identity is the flag next to "Anónimo", which indicates the country in which a user's IP number is located (and which can be easily rerouted using a VPN client).

While the complete anonymity on Hispachan does erase the methodological problems of identity bias, which is highly relevant on online social networks such as Twitter, the anonymity of posts on Hispachan presents a structural problem that wasn't considered in choosing it. On a technical note, it has to be pointed out that Hispachan is anonymous and not pseudonymous. One could achieve pseudonymity on YouTube or Twitter by creating a username that masks one's identity. However, posts under the same account and certain behavioural patterns would lead to a cohesive identity, independently of whether or not this can then be traced back to the physical person behind the post. The only way to evade identification on either of these two levels would be to post under a different profile, which entails creating new accounts for each interaction. Masking one's identity on these social networks would be going to great lengths, especially given the fact that most people, especially on Twitter, nowadays tweet under their clear name and use the platform as a digital outlet for their physical personality and personal brand. However, posts on Hispachan aren't linked to a cohesive profile, giving true anonymity to users, especially when these resort to technically masking their physical location by VPN clients or accessing via other protocols such as the TOR network. A study on *4chan*[54] – the Anglo-Saxon equivalent to the Spanish-speaking Hispachan (Escandell-Montiel 2016) – has shown that 90 % of users are fully anonymous. Posts are extremely ephemeral and only exist for seconds on the main page of a given imageboard. They take only five minutes to expire and be deleted completely from the website (Bernstein et al. 2011). This is a huge difference from Twitter, where popular publications – even though still rather ephemerally – can be trending for a couple of days, and are stored indefinitely on the platform's servers.

This technical difference gives rise to some quite fundamental differences between Hispachan and other types of online social networks. For example, to gain repute on the website, or at least show pertinence to the core community on the website, users use alternative ways to signal their group identity (Bernstein et al. 2011). They establish, either overtly or covertly, secret handshakes that indicate whether or not a user has understood the specific conventions for communication on the imageboard.

Furthermore, the – quite literal – absence of face (cf. Goffman 1955) in the sense of a personal, attackable, and protection-worthy identity, leads to the proliferation of texts and opinions that would otherwise not be suitable for expression in the public sphere (Escandell-Montiel 2016). The mechanism behind the proliferation of this type of content, however, doesn't merely appear to be a consequence of anonymity but also seems to be a consequence of a certain content bias (Section 4.2.6) on the website. Different researchers agree upon the fact that 4chan (Nagle 2017; Torres-Nabel 2017) and Hispachan (Torres-Nabel 2017) were previously

54 Note that the literature quoted on this topic is mainly centred around the imageboard *4chan*. It has been argued that *Hispachan* is the Spanish language version of *4chan* and that they can be sensibly compared to one another in terms of political profile and aspects of radicalisation, such as the proliferation of pseudo-apolitical and taboo topics (Escandell-Montiel 2016). However, this shouldn't be regarded as an empirical fact because the populations do not appear to be the same. However, literature on Hispachan in particular is scarce, so resorting to the literature on 4chan appears sensible, as long as empirical claims on the latter are checked for the former.

rather apolitical. But the influx of apolitical and overly satirical content has led to an effective radicalisation of content both on these websites and in the physical world. The mechanism has been linked to anonymity in a rather loose way. Utterances (or hashtags) such as: "#QuemaYMataUnGato", "#SéFelizYGolpeaAUnaMujer", "#2017SinNegros", "#GaysNoMerecenNavidad", "#SaqueaUnWalmart", or "#MásMasacresEnMéxico" (Torres-Nabel 2017) are effectively 'apolitical' in the sense that they are so unthinkable and politically incorrect that no one would ever say them in public. In exculpating themselves from being radical, users who use these hashtags can always resort to the argument of "satire", precisely *because* these utterances are so extremely unthinkable – not *despite* this fact. However, the aforementioned hashtags have led to incidents of violence in the real world, such as the looting of Walmart outlets in 2017 in Mexico (Torres-Nabel 2017). Pseudo-satire and pseudo-apolitical talk have been used as effective tools for radicalisation ever since. Firstly, according to this strategy, there is no harm in making overly and 'obviously satirical' claims about minorities and social movements such as feminism. Secondly, the use of a language that challenges societal standards and mainstream etiquette is appealing to younger Internet users, especially boys and young men (Nagle 2017; Greene 2019). Interestingly, even before the political relevance of this communication strategy was empirically identifiable, it was already argued that the anti-systemic, anonymous and contingency (i.e., nowness) based interaction, made it political (Knuttila 2011) because the *improper*[55] usage of satirical anti-establishment language leads to the normalisation of such content. It appears that anonymity doesn't only enable users of these imageboards to say things they think but wouldn't say in public, but that their being anonymous gives them the possibility to think things they wouldn't normally think. While entertaining *improper* ideas isn't a problem in and of itself (Knuttila 2011), anonymous communities on 4chan use content such as the antisemitic "(((they)))" meme to construe themselves as political collectives (Tuters & Hagen 2020). Anonymity thus complicates the picture. While the current study is mainly interested in mechanisms of linguistic interaction and not in the description of political radicalization strategies, the political implications of anonymity on Hispachan will have to be taken into account in the interpretation of the data.

Furthermore, there is no moderation present on Hispachan, while this is usual on other online social networks such as Twitter. On the board *reglas*[56], users are

55 From German: "uneigentlich". The word „improper" does not mean „inappropriate" in this context, but refers to the detachment of the user from the meaning of the word.

56 https://www.hispachan.org/reglas/

asked to adhere to certain standards in communication. For example, users are asked not to violate legislation in their countries of origin or the legislation in the Netherlands, and to avoid so-called "shitposts" which reduce the "quality of the boards". Furthermore, divulgation of identity (self or others) is prohibited, further cementing anonymity, as discussed above. Furthermore, "orthographic horrors" are considered unacceptable and can lead to a ban. However, it is not clear how these bans are enforced in light of anonymity. Possible IP bans can easily be circumvented by VPN clients, the use of proxies, or the TOR network. It is interesting that, while content is informally regulated, these regulations do not contain a ban on hate speech on the board. There is no information on the number of bans that are pronounced and/or enforced on the board. These technical aspects underline the problematization reported above.

5.2. Data Collection

In order to gather data from Hispachan, a scraper was built to gather posts from the Hispachan subsites *Argentina (AR)*[57], *Bolivia (BO), Centroamérica y Caribe (CC), Chile (CL), Colombia (CO), España (ES), México (MX), Perú (PE), Uruguay (UY), Venezuela (VE), Humanidades (HU), Economía (K)*[58], *Política (POL), LGBT+ (Q), Tecnología (T)*, and *Meta (M)*[59]. To navigate the html structure of

57 https://www.hispachan.org/ar/
https://www.hispachan.org/bo/
https://www.hispachan.org/cc/
https://www.hispachan.org/cl/
https://www.hispachan.org/co/
https://www.hispachan.org/es/
https://www.hispachan.org/mx/
https://www.hispachan.org/pe/
https://www.hispachan.org/uy/
https://www.hispachan.org/ve/
https://www.hispachan.org/hu/
https://www.hispachan.org/k/
https://www.hispachan.org/pol/
https://www.hispachan.org/q/
https://www.hispachan.org/t/

58 Abbreviations according to the ones used in Hispachan's URL.

59 It has to be pointed out that, originally Ecuador (EC) was also part of the programme. However, the board seems to have been suspended at some point during 2020. By 2021, Bolivia (BO) too seems to have been suspended from the website.

the website, the Python library *BS4: BeautifulSoup 4.4.0* (Richardson 2019) was used. To navigate the website, the program first accessed the addresses of all the pages on a given imageboard and compiled a full list of subpages on each board (Fig. 33).

Fig. 33: Screenshot of the page navigation at the bottom of each page. The scraper accesses each of the numbered pages via the Html structure of the website to make a full list of pages on each country/region's imageboard.

Then, the *html* document for each URL was downloaded and parsed with the *BS4 html.parser* . By accessing the *div* -tag *thread*, data collection for a thread was started. For each thread, the *original post* (OP) was collected containing four data points: (1) Its URL, accessing the *span* tag *reflink* at its *href* position; (2) its text body, accessing the *div* tag *thread* at the position *blockquote* and stripping the text of its whitespace; (3) its community by copying the first twenty-nine digits of the URL (thus cutting the URL of after the position where the sub-board (*AR, BO, CC, CL, …*) is mentioned; and (4) the point in time of the collection via Python's *time* (Python Foundation 2021) libraries *localtime*() function. The same was then done with all the comments of a given thread in a similar fashion[60].

60 All code relevant to this dissertation can be accessed under https://github.com/TobiDschi/linguistic_network_structure

```
▼<form id="delform" action="https://www.hispachan.org/board.php" method="post">
   <input type="hidden" name="board" value="ar">
   <title>Manejar los Celos</title>
  ▶<div class="moculto" style="float:right; margin-left: 4px;">…</div>
  ▼<div id="thread137658ar" class="thread">
     <a name="s"></a>
    ▶<span class="filesize">…</span>
     <br>
    ▶<a target="_blank" style="display: block;" href="https://www.hispachan.org/ar/src/16099
    5628367.jpg" onclick="javascript:expandimg('137658', 'https://www.hispachan.org/ar/src/16
    0995628367.jpg', 'https://www.hispachan.org/ar/thumb/160995628367s.jpg', '2000', '1000',
    '250', '125');return false;">…</a>
     <a name="137658"></a>
    ▶<span id="threadinfo" class="threadinfo">…</span>
     <span id="dnb-ar-137658-y"></span>
     <br>
    ▼<blockquote style="max-width: 422px;">
       "

       Nada, me estoy viendo con una piba y ella sale con las amigas, creo que algun otro
       chongo debe tener tambien.
       "
       <br>
       "Como copeo con eso? Sé que no nos vamos a casar, pero no puedo evitar sentir celos.
       Mientras estoy con ella estoy en el cielo, pero los días que no estoy o que ni
       siquiera me responde el wp me siento re mal.
       "
       <br>
       "Ayuden a un negrito romantico."
       <br>
       <br>
      ▶<div style="margin-top: -3px;">…</div>
     </blockquote>
     <a href="#top" onclick="javascript:
```

Fig. 34: Example of an Html file from a thread on AR, where an Anónimo asks for relationship advice. BS4 allows navigation through the file by searching for the tags 'div', 'a', 'span', 'blockquote', and so forth. Different objects such as the URL can be accessed through parameters such as "href", "id", or "class".

The data of these threads were not only stored in a datasheet but as a network reflecting the structure in which posts interacted with one another. Using the *Networkx* library for Python (Hagberg et al. 2008), threads were stored as networks. All posts (OP and comments) were stored as nodes in the network. To distinguish between OP and comments, a fifth metadata point was created. The datapoint *central* was set *True* for OP and *False* for comments. Depending on which other post each post referred to, an edge was created to represent the reference from one post to another. This is possible because a reference to specific comments (thus creating a comment on a comment) can be explicitly stated in each comment. If no explicit reference is stated, the comment defaults to OP. With this information, a network of all existing threads at a given point in time could be generated. A possible network *G* of an OP and three hypothetical direct comments on OP would thus contain the following information:

$$N(G)=\begin{Bmatrix} n0 = data(central = True, text = \ldots, retrieved = \ldots, URL = \ldots, community = \ldots), \\ n1 = data(central = False, text = \ldots, retrieved = \ldots, URL = \ldots, community = \ldots), \\ \ldots, \\ n3 = data(central = False, text = \ldots, retrieved = \ldots, URL = \ldots, community = \ldots) \end{Bmatrix}$$

$$E(G)=\{(n0,n1),(n0,n2),(n0,n3)\}$$

Note that "…" indicates some fictitious value corresponding to anything that makes sense in the given context. In programming, some further steps had to be included for processing. They will be reported as they become relevant, like the exclusion of problematic data points. In principle, however, the aforementioned steps reflect the logic that was applied in structuring the data.

5.3. Data Pre-processing

To run calculations and statistical tests on the data, network data was pre-processed to obtain two different CSV datasets. The first contained information on each node and the second summarised information for each thread.

5.3.1. Node-specific Dataset

As the first step in processing, the different subgraphs had to be separated from one another by the *networkx.connected_components*() function, which identifies connected graphs within a bigger network. At this point, networks consisting of only a single node were excluded from further analysis. Then, each subgraph was analysed and information for each node was generated, and then stored in a data frame and exported to a CSV file. The data for each node contained the following data.

1. *Thread:* Each thread was identified by the identifier of its central node. In some cases, no central node could be identified, and an exceptional ID was created for this thread. This happened when OP was suppressed, either because they

didn't contain any text, or because the text body contained characters that couldn't be coded in the utf-8 code that was used by the Html parser.

2. *Node:* The ID from Hispachan was copied to the dataset to obtain a unique identifier for each node in the dataset.
3. *Text:* This information was copied from the previously existing datapoint in the network.
4. *Community:* This information was copied from the previously existing datapoint in the network.
5. *Central:* This information was copied from the previously existing datapoint in the network.
6. *Retrieved:* This information was copied from the previously existing datapoint in the network.
7. *Neighbours*: Each node was analysed for the number of direct neighbours it had in the network. This measure is otherwise termed degree and is a measure of centralisation or decentralisation of a node. However, it was dubbed neighbours to avoid confusion with the normalised measure of degree centrality.
8. *Degree centrality:* The degree of a node, as a measure of its centrality, is usually defined as the number of edges that are incident upon this node (i.e., the number of its neighbours, since this specific data doesn't allow nodes to be connected to themselves). However, to be able to compare measures of degree centrality across different graphs with different numbers of nodes, degree centrality was normalised using the $networkx.degree\_centrality()$ function (Hagberg et al. 2008). This function normalises the degree through the division by the maximal possible number of neighbours in the network, which equals $|N|-1$. Since this network doesn't allow for self-reference of a node to itself, the maximum normalised degree centrality equals 1, while the lowest possible degree-centrality is $\frac{1}{|N|-1}$.
9. *Betweenness centrality:* Shortest-path or betweenness centrality is an alternative measure of centrality of a given node, that measures its centrality as the sum of the fraction of all-pairs shortest paths that pass through *n* (Hagberg et al. 2008):

$$betweenness - centrality(G) = \sum_{s,t \in G} \frac{\sigma(s,t|n)}{\sigma(s,t)}$$

As for degree centrality, this measure is normalised by the *networkx.betweenness_centrality()* function, such that nodes from different networks with a different number of nodes can be compared to one another. The normalisation through the quotient $2/((n-1)(n-2))$ again results in a maximum value of 1 and a minimum value that approaches 0 as $|N|$ is increased. Betweenness centrality was calculated but didn't yield any meaningful statistical results. Thus, it is not conceptually introduced in Chapter 2 and won't reappear in any of the analyses.

10. *Distance from central:* This measure indicates the length of the shortest path from the given node to the central node. Subsequently, all central nodes have a distance from central of 0, while direct comments on OP have a *distance from central* of 1. The Distance from central, conceptually, indicates how many comments are nested into one another, and how far the interaction has moved away from the OP.

5.3.2. Subgraph Dataset

The subgraph dataset includes some more data columns and summarises some of the information present in the node-specific dataset. The information in one data entry refers to a subgraph as a whole:

1. *Thread:* The nodes are no longer pointed to individually. Instead, the thread ID is used to refer to the summarised information on the thread.
2. *Community:* This information is copied from the other dataset and indicates in which of the communities the thread has been published.
3. *Retrieved:* This information is copied from the other dataset and indicates the point in time at which the data has been collected from Hispachan.
4. *p_regular:* This value is coded as *TRUE* or *FALSE* and indicates whether a given subgraph is P-regular, according to the definition given above (Section 2.4.4).
5. *p_mean:* This value is coded as numerical and indicates the mean value of P according to the definition above (Section 2.4.4). The value is meaningless unless the subgraph is P-regular. When this is the case, P is an integer, indicating the number of nodes that every node is connected to. This value was calculated but ultimately useless for analysis because no P-regular networks could be identified in the network.
6. *Diameter:* This value is a whole number, expressing – according to the definition above (Section 2.4.5), the extensiveness of the graph. Conceptually, it expresses how long it takes to get from the relatively most remote point of the graph to its most remote counterpart.

7. *Incomplete subgraph:* This variable is coded as *True* or *False* and expresses whether or not the information about the nodes that comprise the subgraph was complete. If any data points were missing during pre-processing up to this point, this variable would indicate this, enabling us to exclude incomplete information from further analysis.
8. *Network density:* According to the definition provided above (Section 2.4.3), network density expresses the connectivity of the network as compared to the highest possible value of connectivity. Network density was calculated, but ultimately useless for data analysis because no real distributed networks were identified.
9. *Graphtype:* This variable codes for the network topology of the subgraphs according to the definitions given above (Section 2.3). The variable codes for *linear*, *centralised*, *decentralised*, and *distributed* networks, where *real distributed* networks aren't distinguished from *partially distributed* networks.
10. *Graph_centrality:* This variable gives an overall measure of the degree of centralisation of the graph. It is based on the number of neighbours of each node and normalises the centralisation of each graph according to the following equation:

$$Graph\,Centrality(G) = \frac{\sum_{i=1}^{|N|}\left(neighbours(most\,central\,node) - neighbours(n_i)\right)}{|N|^2 - |N|3 + 2}$$

(adapted from Freeman 1978, p. 230)

11. *Centre equals most central:* This value is encoded as either *True* or *False* and indicates whether OP is the post with the most neighbours.

5.4. Dataset – Descriptive Statistics

Data collection took place at two points in time. The first collection took place on the 25th of April 2020, and the second, for replication, on the 18th of January 2021. Across the thesis, only those results that could be replicated between both datasets will be considered. Data collection at the two points in time differed in the sub-boards that were considered for data collection, again, for replication of the results. The boards *HU*, *K*, *POL*, *Q*, and *T* were only included in the second run of data collection, such as to identify possible discrepancies in the results across communities.

The thusly obtained dataset was comprised of 54,393 comments (nodes) across 2,695 threads, from 16 different communities. In the first data collection, 23,653 nodes across 1,078 networks were collected, whereas 30,740 nodes were collected across 1,617 threads at the second time of data collection. A short description of the general statistical properties of the dataset will be provided. Further steps in data processing and statistical description will be supplied for each experiment separately.

Note that the dataset for this study is composed rather differently from the ones that were reviewed in the literature. Rather than modelling agents and their interactions, the dataset models the contributions to an instance of communication (i.e., a thread) where edges represent the connection to the post that a newer post refers to. Since Hispachan has fully anonymous linguistic interaction networks, there is no way of determining whether the posts are indicative of individual agents. This goes to the credit of this study because it attempted to achieve the description of such network effects in local behaviour.

5.4.1. Thread Length and Diameter

Threads differ greatly in the number of nodes they contain, with thread lengths ranging from 2 to 281. The distribution shows a heavy right skew (Fig. 35) peaking at a median of twelve comments (including OP), with a power-law resembling distribution. Typical descriptive measures of distribution mean and standard deviation ($ø = 20.18$, $\sigma = 24.84$) are rendered meaningless. Thread length is hence not normally distributed, as would be expected of this value. Communications on Hispachan tend to be shorter rather than longer and are typically between 6 and 24 interactions long (IQR, Tab. 5).

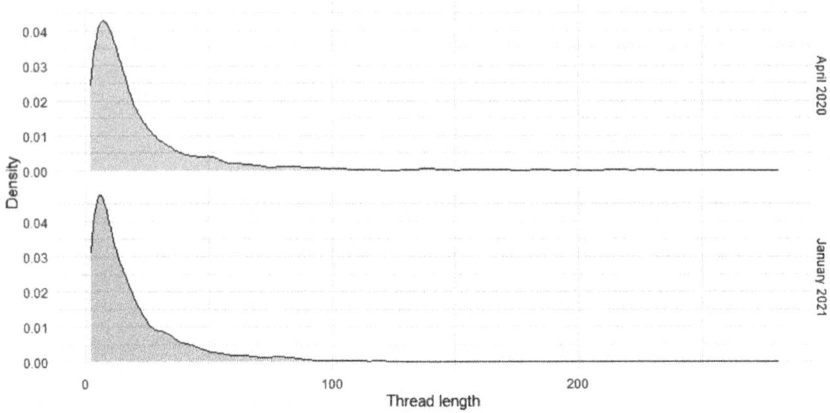

Fig. 35: Length of threads according to the dates of data collection. Both distributions are heavily right-skewed and peak at about twelve interactions per thread, with small amounts of extremely long conversations up to 281 comments (including OP). Differences between both points in time are marginal and can be accounted for by differences in community samples (Section 5.4.2).

Tab. 5: Descriptive summary of the distributions for both dates of data collection.

Date	Minimum	1st Quartile	Median	Mean	3rd Quartile	Maximum
Apr 2020	2	7	13	21.94	25	229
Jan 2021	2	6	12	19.01	23	281
Combined	2	6	12	20.18	24	281

In the upcoming interpretation of data, this fact will have to be taken into account. Since most statistical tests for this thesis are based on linear models, they rely on normally distributed data. Possible normalisation techniques for the data will be addressed in the given contexts.

Furthermore, the diameter of the threads was considered. It was found that the distribution of diameters of threads behaves similarly to thread lengths, with a highly right-skewed distribution, meaning that typical diameters range from 2 to 8 (median = 5, mean = 6.28), while diameters as big as 68 do occur, albeit very seldomly in the dataset. There are visible differences between the two points in time in which data was collected (Fig. 36). But these can be accounted for by considering the different communities, as will become apparent in the following section, where a higher occurrence of centralised topologies was found to be present in the topic-related communities as opposed to regional communities (Section 5.4.2).

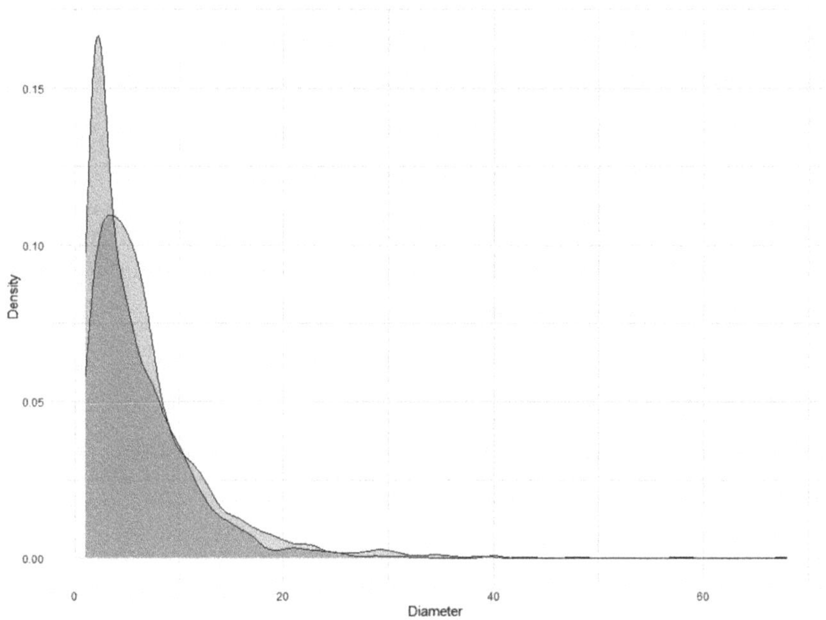

Fig. 36: Density plot indicating the occurrence of different diameters across all graphs. The difference between the 2020 dataset (lower) and the 2021 dataset (taller) can be explained by more commonly occurring centralised graphs in the case of topic-related communities (Section 2.4.2), which weren't present in the first data collection.

Furthermore, thread length and graph diameter are correlated, which is trivial. Smaller graphs, by definition, cannot have a diameter that surpasses the number of nodes in the graph, and this can only be achieved in a linear graph. However, bigger graphs do not necessarily have a bigger diameter, because even if there are infinite nodes, there is – in principle – no reason why the nodes shouldn't all refer to the same central node. Empirically, however, it can be observed that while smaller graphs exhibit small diameters, the scattering of small and big diameters increases as the number of nodes in the network increases (Fig. 37). However, there still appears to be a correlation between thread length and diameter. As the thread length increases, so does the diameter.

The relationship appears to be best described as a logarithmic relationship, where the rate with which the diameter increases, decreases as the thread length augments. To describe the statistical relationship between the variables, a generalised linear model using the *glm*() function was used, assuming a Poisson/log-normal distribution for natural numbers (Miller 2007), including a logarithmic transformation on thread length. The logarithmic model expressed as $diameter \sim tread\ length + I(\log(thread\ length))$ appears to be better suited to explaining variance in the data, especially the more scattered data points of bigger networks and is hence the one reported. Note that the model only includes datapoints from decentralised topologies, as centralised topologies have a fixed diameter at $\delta = 2$. R^2 was determined using the variance function (Zhang 2017). Chi-squared test on the deviance table revealed a highly significant linear effect of thread length on diameter (χ^2 (1, N = 1865) = 18.75, p < 0.001). The model explains around 63 % of the variance ($R^2 = 0.63$).

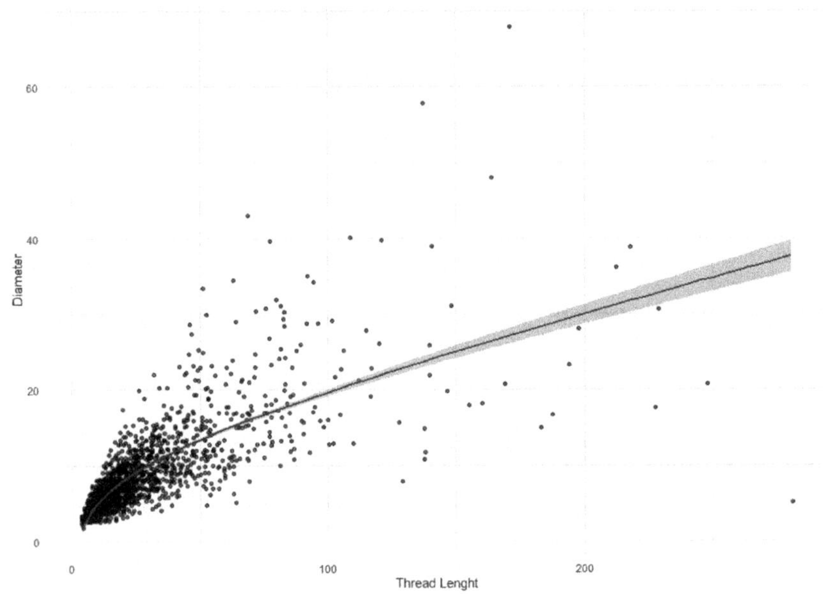

Fig. 37: Jitterplot describing the correlation between thread length and diameter. Note that the rate of increase of the diameter by thread length decreases as the thread length augments. Note also that only decentralised graphs are analysed as centralised graphs have a fixed diameter of 2.

5.4.2. Representation of Communities

According to the procedure in data collection, the different communities in the dataset are relatively equally distributed with regard to the collected subgraphs. In each case, just over 100 threads were collected from each community per collection, which has to be expected given the hard-coded limits of threads that are featured on each page of the imageboard.

Closer examination of nodes in each community, however, reveals that certain communities are overrepresented and others underrepresented with regard to the mere number of interactions that are present on these boards.

Tab. 6: Descriptive statistics of the number of nodes for each Hispachan community across both times of data collection.

April 2020		**January 2021**	
Community	**N° of nodes**	**Community**	**N° of nodes**
AR	1,436	AR	1,347
BO	1,031	BO	NA
CC	1,972	CC	2,216
CL	2,207	CL	1,873
CO	1,976	CO	1,908
ES	3,057	ES	2,756
HU	NA	HU	1,661
K	NA	K	794
M	NA	M	1,192
MX	2,820	MX	2,880
PE	2,352	PE	3,010
POL	NA	POL	2,944
Q	NA	Q	1,391
T	NA	T	2,220
UY	1,377	UY	1,279
VE	5,425	VE	3,269

Descriptive Statistics											
Min	1st Q	Med	Mean	3rd Q	max	Min	1st Q	Med	Mean	3rd Q	max
1,031	1,570	2,092	2,365	2,703	5,425	739	1369	1,908	2,040	2,818	3,269

To check for overrepresented values, the Shapiro-Wilk normality test (Shapiro & Wilk 1965) is employed. The test bares different results for the data from 2020 and 2021 because more values were considered in the 2021 sample, and because the topics treated on the boards included are different in nature, while the 2020 data only compares different regions.

Shapiro-Wilk test on the 2020 data yields $W = 0.84$ with $p < 0.05$, meaning that the data is non-normal. Upon visual inspection of a *qqPlot* from the R package *car* (Fox & Weisberg 2019), the outlying data point at 5,425 nodes in the case of VE could be identified (Fig. 38). This indicates that the number of contributions in the community *VE* is disproportionally high, given the assumption of normal distribution in the interaction on these boards.

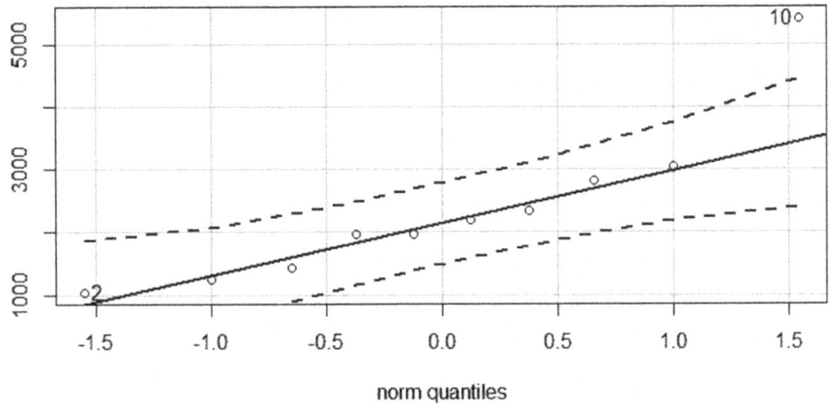

Fig. 38: Theoretical quantiles for the number of nodes in the different communities on Hispachan. The dotted lines indicate the 95 % confidence interval for theoretical quantiles. The outlier labelled 10 at 5,425 nodes corresponds to nodes in the network of comments on the board VE.

When investigating engagement on the January 2021 dataset, the Shapiro-Wilk normality test reveals a perfectly normal distribution of values ($W = 0.94$, $p = 0.41$). Visual inspection of a Q-Q plot did not lead to the identification of any outliers. To formulate a criterion for high and low representation of communities respectively, a corridor of the most typically represented communities can be defined to lie within one standard deviation from the mean of values:

$$upper\,limit = mean + \sigma$$

$$lower\,limit = mean - \sigma$$

For the January 2021 dataset, this corridor is defined between 1,270 and 2,828 nodes in a given community, which roughly coincides with the IQR. Lower limit outliers are the communities *K* and *M*, indicating that these communities are engaged with less than expected given the assumption of normally distributed data. The communities MX, PE, VE, and POL are out of the upper bounds, indicating that these are more popularly used boards. Finally, only VE appears to be a consistently overused board, with more engagement than other communities on Hispachan.

5.4.3. Graph Topology

It was assessed which network topologies exist in the dataset, that is whether interactions are structured in a centralised, decentralised, distributed, or linear way. Some interactions with other variables, that will be of interest, will be described as well.

First of all, the dataset is comprised of 2,695 graphs, of which 673 are centralised, 1,865 are decentralised, 31 are linear, and 126 do not fit the predefined definitions. These contain partially distributed networks, which do not contain exactly one shortest path from any given node to the central node but don't exhibit real distribution either.

Tab. 7: Summary of the distribution of network topologies across both times of data collection.

Graph Type	Centralised	Decentralised	Linear	None
Count (April 2020)	153	854	14	57
Percentage (April 2020)	14.19 %	79.22 %	1.30 %	5.29 %
Count (January 2021)	520	1003	17	69
Percentage (January 2021)	32.32 %	62.34 %	1.06 %	4.29 %
Count (Total)	673	1865	31	126
Percentage (Total)	24.97 %	69.20 %	1.15 %	4.68 %

This shows, that decentralised interactions are by far the most common on Hispachan, with 69.20 %, meaning that it is rather normal than exceptional, that conversations move away from direct responses on OP and that comments on comments are the norm. Technically, however, a network is classified as decentralised if only one comment on OP is commented on. This finding thus warrants further description, taking other measures of decentralisation than the classification of typology into account. The second most common type of topology is the centralised one with 24.97 % overall, that is, threads in which only OP is commented upon. Linear networks very rarely arise and are almost irrelevant with 1.15 % of the collected threads being in this layout. The unclassifiable networks average around 4.86 %.

However, fluctuations between the two points of time in data collection warrant a more nuanced picture. The differences in proportion between the 2020 and 2021 data are due to the inclusion of different communities, which appear to behave differently with regard to centralisation. In concrete, the decentralised topography is much more prevalent in the regional communities (e.g., AR, BO, CC, etc.) than in the topic-based communities (i.e., K, Q, M, and T). Contrary to what would be expected, topographies in these communities tend to be much more centralised, that is the most common topology for conversations is the centralised topology (Fig. 39). Testing this difference for the independence of variables with a Pearson's Chi-squared, a strong and significant dependence of network topology on community is diagnosed (χ^2 (1, 45) = 1325.9, $p < 0.001$). It is worth noting, that those communities with the most exceptional residuals are also all topic-oriented communities, whereas all regional communities are structured similarly across network topologies, with decentralised topologies as the most typically occurring network type.

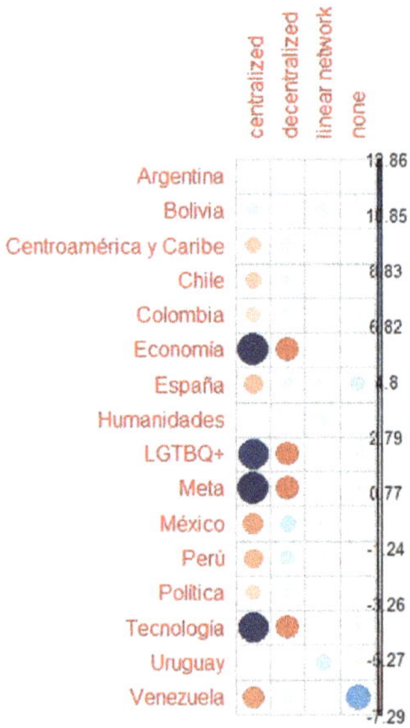

Fig. 39: Plot showing Chi-squared residuals for different network topologies across communities. The residuals indicate that the communities K, Q, M, and T contain a much higher number of centralised interactions.

Another interesting observation with regard to the occurrence of different network topologies in the dataset is the interaction of network typology with the number of nodes in a thread. It can be observed that the length of a thread correlates rather strongly with network topology. In concrete, longer threads tend to be decentralised, while shorter threads tend to be organised in centralised topologies. In concrete, centralised, linear, and non-classified topologies have a median length of 5, 3, and 3 respectively, while decentralised networks have a median number of 17 nodes (Fig. 40).

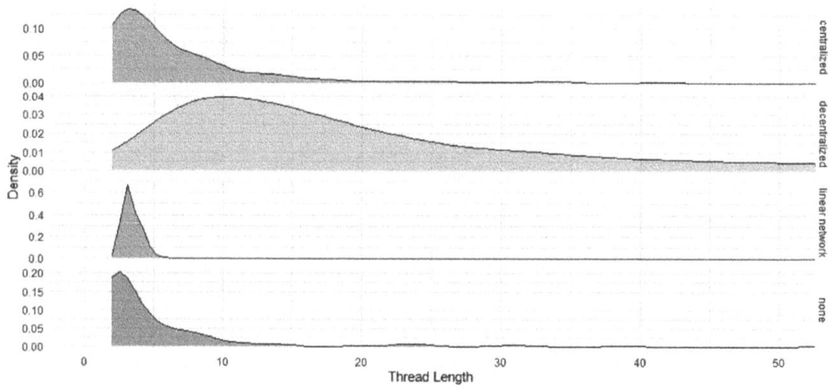

Fig. 40: Thread Length distributions by network topology. Note that y scales are freely varied to make differences in means and medians apparent. The area under each curve is thus not representative of the volume of threads represented.

To test whether this difference in distribution is incidental, a Kruskal-Wallis test is carried out. ANOVA cannot be used due to the heavily skewed nature of the data. The Kruskal-Wallis test doesn't presume normally distributed data and can be carried out on distributions stemming from more than two ($k > 2$) samples (Kruskal & Wallis 1952). Its null hypothesis is that all four ($k = 4$) samples stem from the same population. Given a significant result, the alternative hypothesis, that at least one sample (k) differs from the others, is adopted. Execution of Kruskal-Wallis resulted in a highly significant difference for at least one of the samples (χ^2 (1, 3) = 824.82, $p < .001$). By visually inspecting Fig. 40 it is henceforth assumed that decentralised topologies tend to contain longer threads than other network topologies. The models for each time of data collection will not be reported here, it suffices to say that the test replicates for both samples individually.

This observation will have to be taken into account in the further analysis of linguistic differences that are contingent on network topology because thread length must be regarded as a confounding factor in all corresponding models.

5.4.4. Node Degrees

It was laid out above that the distribution of node degrees is skewed toward a Zipf'ian power-law distribution and that this is characteristic of natural interaction networks. This theoretical assumption has been termed degree distribution bias (Section 4.2.5). The empirical distribution of node centralities is therefore explored at this point. The distribution of node degrees in the dataset is highly skewed in two different ways.

Firstly, when ordering the node degrees by rank, it can be seen that the numbers of neighbours as compared to the previous rank drop rapidly at first, and then stabilising the rate which with node connectivity drops going down the ranks (Fig. 41).

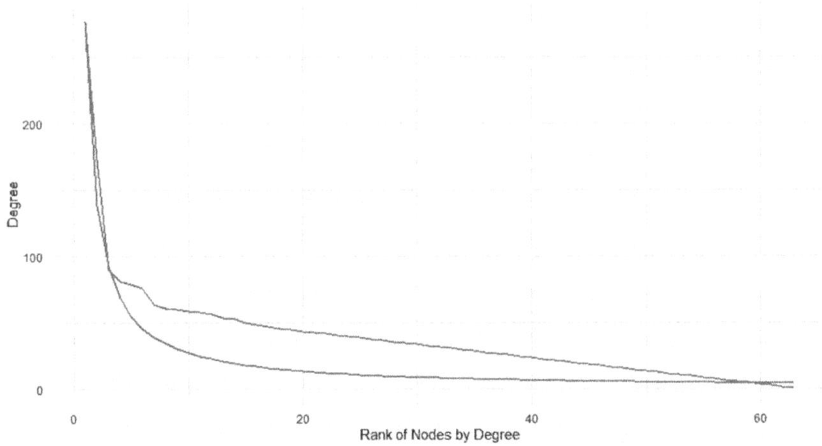

Fig. 41: Degree distribution of nodes by rank. The upper line indicates the number of neighbours (degree) of a node according to its rank. The lower smooth line indicates the expected degree of a node according to its rank under a theoretical Zipf distribution.

While the distribution appears power-like at first, a comparison to the expected distribution of values under a Zipf distribution shows that the empirical distribution and expected distribution stem from different samples. A Mann-Whitney U test was carried out to determine, whether this difference in distribution is significant. Conceptually, the test is similar to the Kruskal-Wallis test, with the difference that the independent variable is assumed to be a binary variable, rather than testing for more than two groups (Bauer 1972). Execution of the test using R stat package *stats'* (R Core Team 2020) *wilcox.test*() function revealed a significant difference in these distributions (W = 3027.5, $p < 0.001$). This is unsurprising because the degree of nodes is a discrete distribution with very closely occurring values. In the lower ranks (rank > 20) the degree of nodes decreases by exactly one per rank, making the relationship between rank and degree exactly linear. However, in the higher ranks (rank < 5) it can be seen that the drop in connectivity from one rank to the next very closely resembles what would have to be expected under a Zipf distribution. While the empirical distribution is statistically different from a power-law distribution, the distribution at least approaches what would have to be expected under the degree bias or "rich-get-richer" principle.

Furthermore, there are extremely few nodes with such high connectivity. The distribution of frequencies of degrees across the data is extremely skewed. While node degrees range from 1 to 277, the second and third quartiles range from degrees 1 to 2 (median = 1, mean = 1.901). 95 % of nodes have a degree equal to or lower than 4, and 99 % of the data have a degree equal to or lower than 12. Any nodes with higher connectivity are in the 99th percentile of occurrence in the data, meaning that very few nodes are very well connected while most of the nodes are only sparsely connected, as the degree distribution bias would predict for such networks (Fig. 42). While the Mann-Whitney U test reveals a significant difference between the expected Zipf distribution and the empirical distribution (W = 233.5, $p < 0.001$), the view is maintained that this distribution follows a power-law, that results in an even stronger overrepresentation of poorly connected nodes than Zipf's law would predict. The 'rich-get-richer' principle roughly applies to the distribution of degrees across nodes and the ranks of degrees, albeit with different exponents, which were not calculated here.

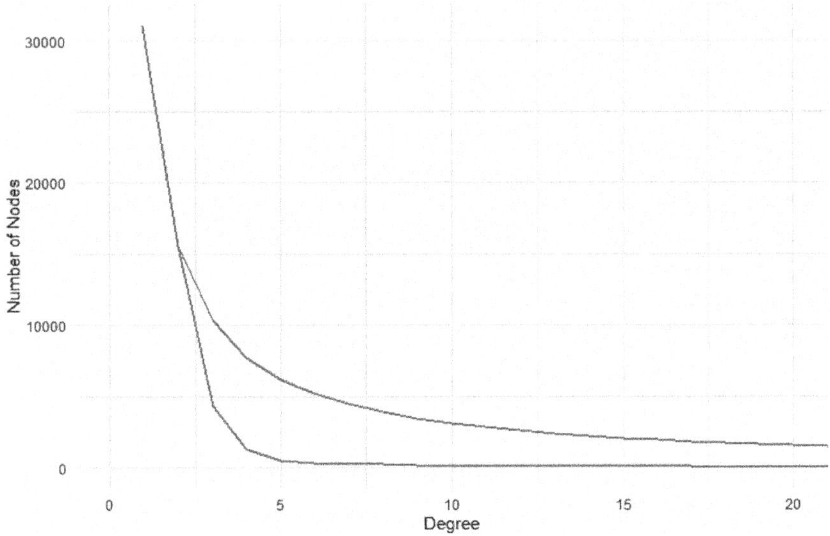

Fig. 42: Occurrences of degrees across nodes. The lower line shows the empirical count for each degree, the upper line shows the expected count assuming Zipf's law. The lower line illustrates that 95 % of nodes have only 4 neighbours or less, while degrees up to 277 exist. Note that for the sake of visual representation, the x-axis is cut off at 20, while the data model includes higher-degree nodes.

5.4.5. Graph Centralities

As was pointed out, graph centralities play a major role in the summarised data for each subgraph. In the following, some descriptive statistics on graph centralities will be reported. Graph centrality was calculated for each subgraph according to the formula reported above (Section 2.4.2). By definition, graph centralities are distributed differently depending on the network topology at work. The graph centrality for centralised network topology is universally equal to one because all nodes in the network refer to a single central node, which makes this node the highest-ranking node. The numbers of linear networks (n = 31) and unclassifiable network topologies (n = 69) are too small to follow any statistically meaningful distribution. Decentralised networks on the other hand, follow a slightly right-skewed distribution (mean = 0.42, median = 0.4, σ = 0.20), while a normal distribution grouping around the centre value (mean = 0.5) would be assumed (Fig. 43).

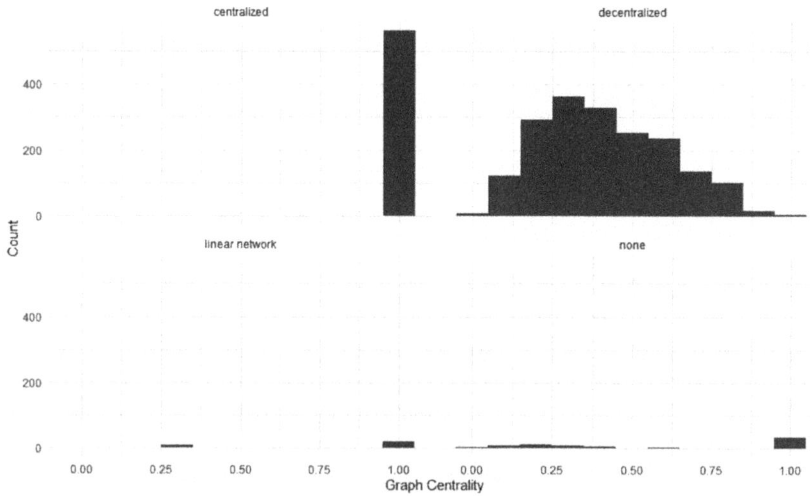

Fig. 43: Distributions of graph centralisations according to the network topology of each thread. Note that linear networks and unclassifiable networks are not to be meaningfully interpreted due to their rare occurrence. Centralised networks behave as expected while decentralised networks present a right skew in distribution.

The right skew in the graph centralities of decentralised network topologies can be accounted for when taking a look at those networks where OP isn't the most centralised node in the network. Conceptually, those networks in which a comment is more commented on than the original contribution behave abnormally and don't follow the same distribution as others. Generally speaking, those linguistic interaction networks tend to be a lot more decentralised (Fig. 44). A Wilcoxon rank-sum test with continuity correction was carried out to determine, whether this difference in distribution is significant. Execution of the test using R stat package *stats*' (R Core Team 2020) *wilcox.test*() function revealed a significant difference in these distributions (W = 94310, $p < 0.001$). Thus, the null hypothesis, namely that both distributions stem from the same sample, is rejected and it will henceforth be assumed that threads in which the original post is not the most centralised behave differently from other threads in terms of graph centrality.

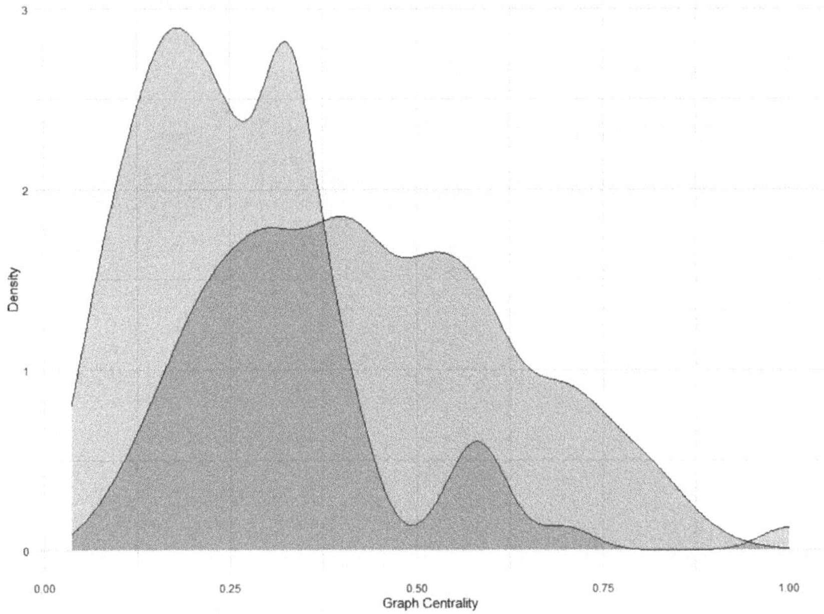

Fig. 44: Distribution of graph centralities according to the relevance of OP. The leftmost area indicates threads in which OP isn't the most central node. The lower-peaking area indicates those threads in which OP is also the most central node.

The right skew in the graph centralities of decentralised network topologies can furthermore be accounted for by a confounding variable. This variable is here postulated to be the diameter of the network, which has previously been identified to correlate logarithmically with thread length (Fig. 37). To show the relationship between centrality and diameter, a linear model was created, predicting graph centrality from the logarithm of the diameter: $graph\ centrality \sim diameter + I(\log(diameter))$. The model was constructed using R's *stats* (R Core Team 2020) package *lm*( ) function. Assuming the different distribution of graph centrality in threads where the most centralised node isn't OP, the model was exclusively created for data points that belong to decentralised threads in which OP is also the most centralised node (Fig. 44). It was shown that the graph centrality of graphs for which the original post is also the most central node in the graph correlates logarithmically with the diameter of the graph. The bigger the diameter of the graph, the less it is centralised. However, this effect softens as an increase in diameter contributes less and less to the centralisation of the graph (Fig. 45). This model of the relationship explains significant parts of the variance in the data ($F(2, 1604) = 1375$, $p < 0.001$, $R^2 = 0.63$).

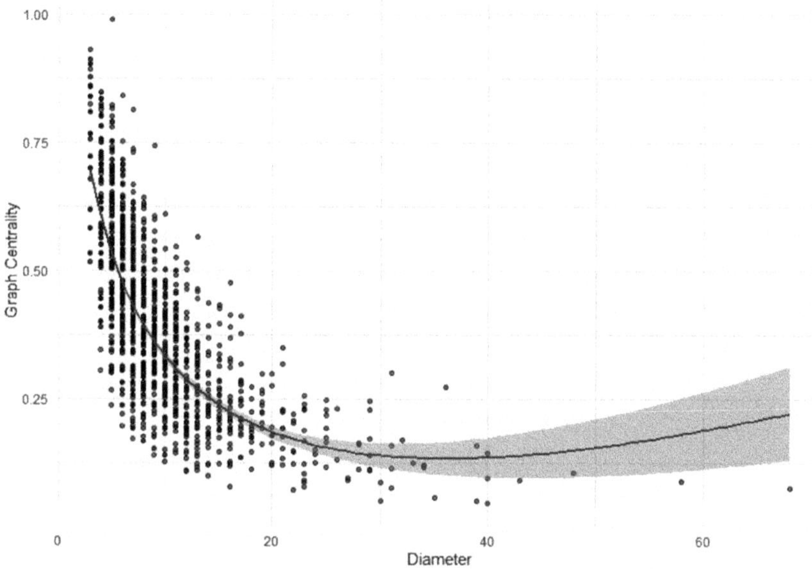

Fig. 45: Scatterplot and logarithmic model of the relationship between diameter and graph centrality. Shadows indicate the standard error.

The model is useful in explaining the non-normal behaviour of graph centrality. However, the variable of diameter violates the assumption of normal distribution (Section 5.4.1) and couldn't be normalised in other ways. Regression on Poisson distribution wasn't possible due to the continuous distribution of graph centrality. It was thus tested *post hoc* whether the residuals of the model itself follow a normal distribution, such as to estimate whether the model can be used to supply meaningful interpretations of the data. Visual inspection of a *Q-Q plot*, made with R's *car* (Fox & Weisberg 2019) package reveals that the residuals are rather normally distributed, although some of the lower quantiles do occur with irregularly high frequency (Fig. 46). Given this distribution of residuals and the other confounding variables previously identified, the null hypothesis is rejected. As an alternative hypothesis, it is assumed that the diameter of a network acts upon its graph centrality as a confounding variable.

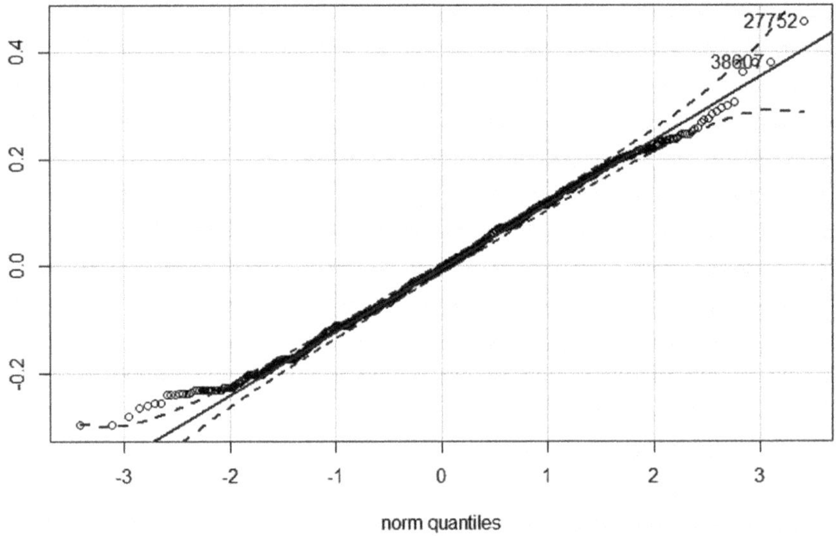

Fig. 46: Scatterplot indicating the distribution of residuals in the model. The x-axis represents the theoretical quantiles, and the y-axis the empirical quantiles of residuals from the reported model. The dashed lines indicate a 99 % confidence interval. Lower quantiles are slightly overrepresented.

The most relevant variables in the dataset are hereby sufficiently described. An overview of the number of nodes and threads was given, and some small differences between subgraphs in different Hispachan communities were described as well as graph topologies and their interaction with the first two. Furthermore, the unusual distribution of graph centralities was described and accounted for wih two confounding variables, which the upcoming experiments will have to take into account in their analyses.

6. Experiment One – Influence of Network Topology on Consensus

It was reported that the influence of network topology on language has been investigated in various linguistic contexts such as the emergence of novel communication systems (Centola & Baronchelli 2015; Raviv et al. 2020), the propagation of cultural artefacts such as linguistic varieties (Gong & Wang 2005; Gong 2008; Maity & Mukherjee 2016), language evolution (Lee et al. 2005), and for the classification of types of linguistic information such as rumours (Kwon et al. 2013). Although different results are reported in terms of the relevance of network topology in these cases, and many confounding variables have been identified such as community size (Lupyan & Dale 2010; Reali et al. 2018; Raviv et al. 2019), connectivity (Segovia-Martín et al. 2020), quality of stimulus (Tamariz et al. 2014), and reputation of single, strong individuals (Baxter 2016) or cliques in the network (Kearns et al. 2006, 2009), community size and connectivity can be modelled in the dataset, as there is access to this information. The interference of highly reputed individuals is excluded by definition, due to the highly anonymized nature of the data that was obtained for the experiment. To operationalise the linguistic phenomena that can be expected to change depending on the aforementioned conditions, the notion of consensus (cf. Section 4.2) will prove itself useful. Silvey et al. (2019) have pointed out, that the systematization of linguistic change cannot be achieved through communication alone, but must be accompanied by cultural transmission. The dataset however is not longitudinal, which is why linguistic change in the described networks isn't to be expected. However, the notion of consensus elaborated above (Section 4.2) allows one to look at language from two distinct angles. While communication determines consensus in the sense of convening on the forms of communication, communication – quite trivially – also regulates the content of what is being said. The caveat formulated by Silvey et al. (2019) only applies to the first level of consensus. Consensus on the content of a conversation, however, can also be operationalised locally, as has been done for dyads (cf. Fusaroli & Tylén 2012; Fusaroli et al. 2012).

This first experiment will thus produce some insights into how the dynamics of different network topologies in a given conversation affect the stability of a topic in a given thread. In other words, it will be investigated how different topologies and degrees of centralisations within these typologies affect a thread's ability to converge on a concrete topic. It is expected that network topology, thread length, centralisation, and diameter play a crucial role in the convergence of participants on a topic.

6.1. Materials and Methods

To assess the effect of network topology on topic conversion, the variables thread length, graph centrality, and diameter, along with graph type and community type were used as independent variables. The goal was to assess the effect of these independent variables on the similarities of the texts in each node across threads.

To this end, a topic model was created for each thread, from which similarities between texts could be drawn. Using Python's *gensim* (Blei et al. 2003) library, a latent Dirichlet allocation (LDA) model was used to identify different topics in each thread, such that computations on similarity could be done on the model. LDA have previously been used for topic modelling on a very similar platform, *4chan* (Papasavva et al. 2020). While the authors use LDA to characterise topics and analyse them in terms of their content, it is here tried to use LDA to measure the thematic proximity of threads as a measure of consensus. LDA is an unsupervised learning algorithm. *Unsupervised* refers to previously known information. Unsupervised machine learning models do not 'know' previously which topics they will identify, as opposed to supervised machine learning, where the categories into which data will be classified are known beforehand, and only the rules for classification have to be 'learned' by the model. In LDA, the topics which will be identified are not known beforehand but are constructed only from the observations of the words as a bag of words. Bag of words (BoW) means that syntax is disregarded. Rather, a *topic* is a collection of words that co-occur across different documents. This bares the assumption that documents are constructed of topics, which in turn, are constructed from words. By checking the co-occurrence of such topics across different documents, their similarity can be assessed. The most important presumption to be made by the investigator in the use of this model is the number of topics, which the algorithm cannot choose on its own. In other words, the LDA cannot assess how many topics are present in a text, but it needs to be told into how many clusters the vocabulary has to be grouped. This is crucial because, as will become evident below, the number of topics is inherently linked to the similarity of nodes in a given thread.

In order to automatise the production of LDA modes for each thread, each thread was separated from the dataset and treated as a corpus of documents. Each comment was treated as one document for topic modelling. It was already pointed out that the number of topics k to be identified has to be chosen for each model. Since both text lengths in each node and the number of nodes in each thread differ significantly (Sections 5.4.1 and 5.4.4), k cannot be assumed universally for all models. Hence, a programme was implemented which created a great number of models for each thread. Assuming that each node contains at least one topic, the programme created between five and fifty models for a thread. The programme created five models for threads with less than five nodes and fifty for threads with more than fifty nodes. Otherwise, the programme would create a number of LDA models that was equal to the number of nodes in the thread. To choose the most suitable model for each thread, the programme considers two measures, the number of topics modelled and their *coherence*.

Coherence is a measure of quality for LDA models. While the original publications (Blei et al. 2003) propose perplexity, that is the "surprise" that a model shows in the face of new data, as a measure of quality, newer contributions measure the quality of topic models measuring how semantically similar the high-ranking words in a given modelled topic are (Newman et al. 2010), resulting in the coherence measure for the quality of LDA. Semantic similarity in this case means context or co-occurrence with other words in the documents. Many methods to measure coherence are available. For this experiment, coherence will be calculated using the cosine-similarity-based *c_v* coherence as provided by *gensim's* (Blei et al. 2003) *CoherenceModel()* function by default.

To choose the most useful model for further processing of the data, however, coherence had to be traded off with the number of topics. Increases in topics can occasionally lead to slightly better coherence, but at the cost of having to account for more topics (Fig. 47). For this experiment, it was intended to have high-quality models (i.e., high coherence), while maintaining the number of topics relatively low, such as not to overfit the precision with which topics are described.

To automatise the choice of the best model, a function had to be found that would identify models with relatively high coherence and a relatively low number of topics modelled. This amounts to identifying a function that returns the data point at the triangle (Fig. 47) rather than the square (Fig. 47), even though the latter has a higher absolute coherence. The quotient ratio was excluded as this would skew the resulting decisions too much in favour of a very low number of topics modelled. Instead, the first derivation was used, expressed as:

$$optimality\,of\,model = \frac{\Delta coherence}{\Delta n^{\underline{o}}\,of\,topics}$$

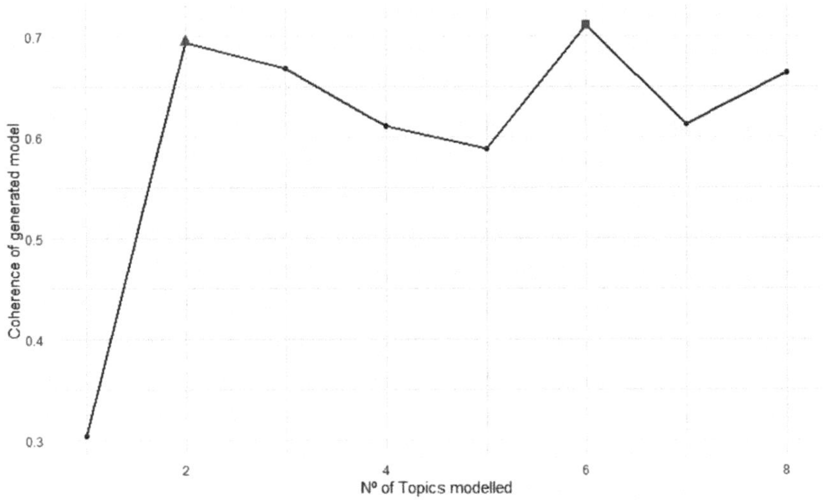

Fig. 47: A typical function of coherence by topics modelled. Coherence increases sharply when the threshold to a useful number of topics modelled is crossed (triangle at x = 2, y = 0.69). An even higher coherence is identified as the number of topic models is increased (square at x = 6, y = 0.71). For the experiment, the most useful model is indicated by the triangle, because the coherence of the model is high without having to assume too many topics.

The function divides the difference in coherence between subsequent data points through the difference of two subsequent data points in the number of topics modelled. This means that the function maximises the outcome value for a high increase in coherence compared to the next value. Hence, the data point at the triangle (Fig. 47) isn't chosen due to its relatively low number of topics modelled ($k = 2$), but because its increase, compared to the previous data point ($k = 1$) is higher than the increase at the square ($k = 6$ compared to $k = 5$). With this criterion in place, big amounts of models were generated for each thread, from which the most suitable model could be easily drawn.

Inspection of the distributions of the generated variables shows that the programme behaves as expected. Model coherence across threads is not normally distributed (Fig. 48). Coherences, defined as a value between 0 and 1, exhibit a mean of 0.61. Distribution parameters are not given, because they are meaningless for non-normal distribution. As a visual inspection of the histogram (Fig. 48) shows, better models are overrepresented, speaking to a bias toward better models than what would result from a random distribution. This is confirmed by a Shapiro -Wilk normality test ($W = 0.99$, $p < 0.001$).

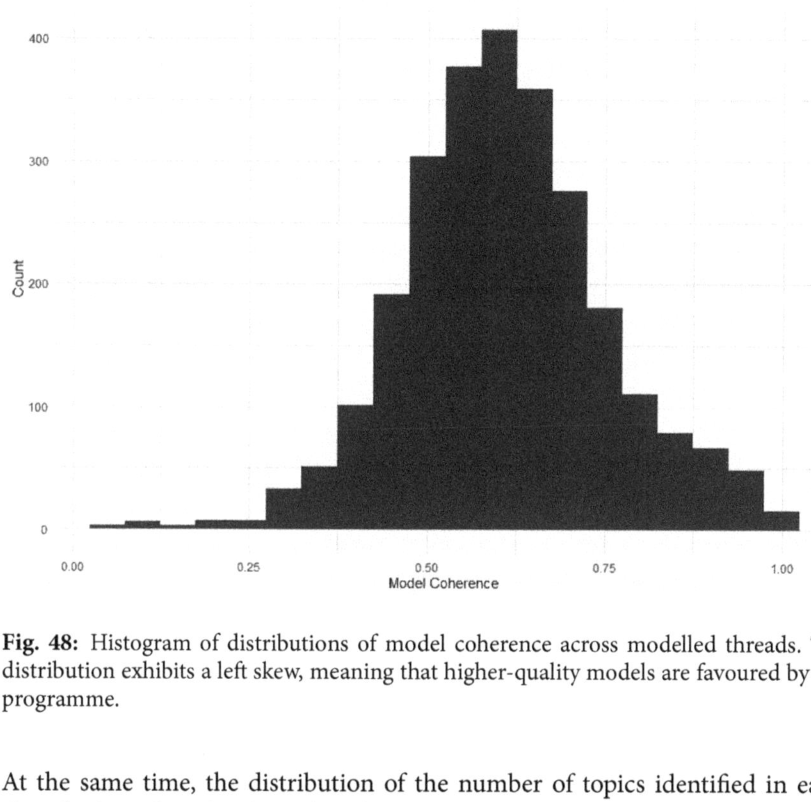

Fig. 48: Histogram of distributions of model coherence across modelled threads. The distribution exhibits a left skew, meaning that higher-quality models are favoured by the programme.

At the same time, the distribution of the number of topics identified in each thread is heavily right-skewed, with two models being the most typical case. The rest of the topic numbers follow a power distribution (Fig. 49), meaning that low topic numbers, as intended, are favoured over overfitted models. Models containing only one topic are a special case. These appear to be untypical, and may only occur in rather short corpora (i.e., threads).

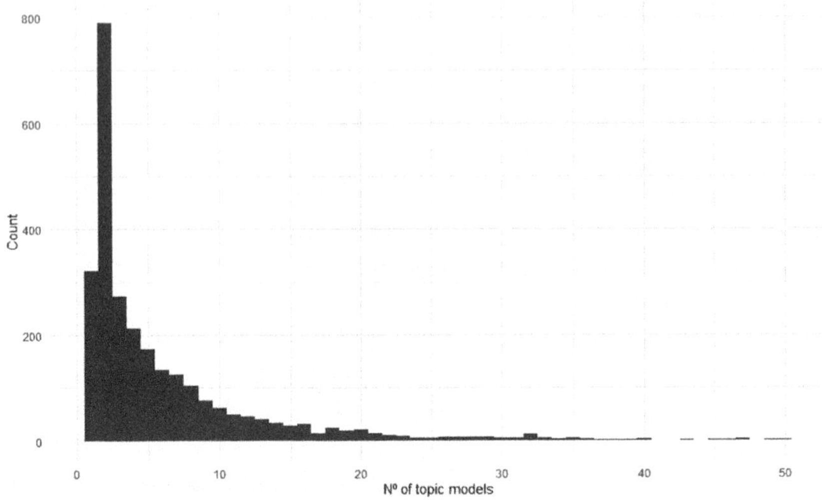

Fig. 49: Histogram of the number of topics modelled in each thread. The data is heavily right-skewed and resembles a power distribution, with exception of k = 1. This means that the programme favours models with relatively low numbers of topics and avoids overfitting the models.

From each model (now one topic model for each thread) a similarity matrix was constructed, using the *gensim* (Blei et al. 2003) function *MatrixSimilarity*() . This function produces a value of similarity for each pair of documents in the corpus, that is for each pair of nodes in the thread and the texts contained therein. The thusly generated value is the cosine similarity of a document when compared against any other node in the thread. From this, two further values were created. First, a mean value of similarity was created for each node, indicating how similar it was, on average, to all the other nodes in the text. From the mean similarity for each node, a mean of means was created for each thread, indicating how similar texts within each thread were to one another. This was the final measure of interest to assess how stable conversation topics were within each thread.

However, it was found that the mean of means similarity behaved in a manner that didn't allow for further processing, given its non-normal distribution (Fig. 50). While the relatively high occurrence of a mean of means similarity equal to one can be accounted for by those threads in which only one topic was modelled, the rest of the distribution still appeared to be dependent on a confounding variable.

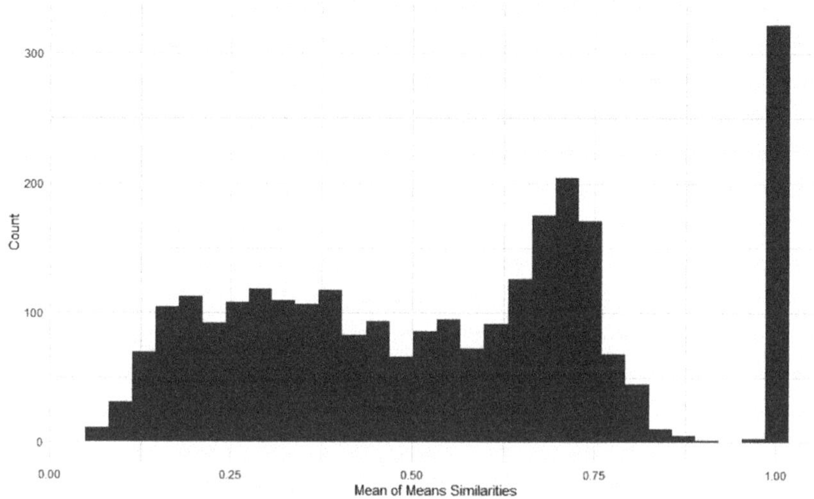

Fig. 50: Histogram of the mean of means similarities for each thread. The high incidence of values equal to one corresponds to those topics in which only one topic was modelled. The rest of the distribution is contingent on a confounding variable.

This confounding variable was identified to be the number of topics itself. It appears that the mean of means similarities are dependent on the number of topics modelled in each thread. The more topics were identified in a thread, the less similar the topics were within a given thread. Conceptually, this is a trivial finding. However, the very strong association between these variables allows the argument that not the mean similarity of nodes, but the numbers of topics modelled in a given thread are a more suitable variable for the subsequent measurements of topic stability in a thread of posts.

The association appears to be logarithmic, meaning that the higher the number of topics modelled is, the lower the mean of means similarities are. This trend is dampened as the number of topics modelled increases. In other words, the higher the number of topics in a model, the less an additional model contributes to the loss of similarity (Fig. 51). The association was tested by creating a linear model with the *stats* (R Core Team 2020) package's *lm*() function. The dependency of the mean of means similarities on the number of topics modelled was tested, including a logarithmic parameter for the number of topic models. The model was plotted as a continuous curved line in the scatterplot (Fig. 51).

$$lm(mean\ of\ means\ similarity \sim topics\ modelled + I(\log(topics\ modelled)))$$

The application of the linear model revealed a high association between variables, with a low standard error of residuals ($SE = 0.059$ on 2,687 degrees of freedom) and high accountability for variance in the data, as well as a highly significant p-value ($F(2, 2{,}687) = 2.49 * 10^4$, $R^2 = 0.95$, $p < 0.001$).

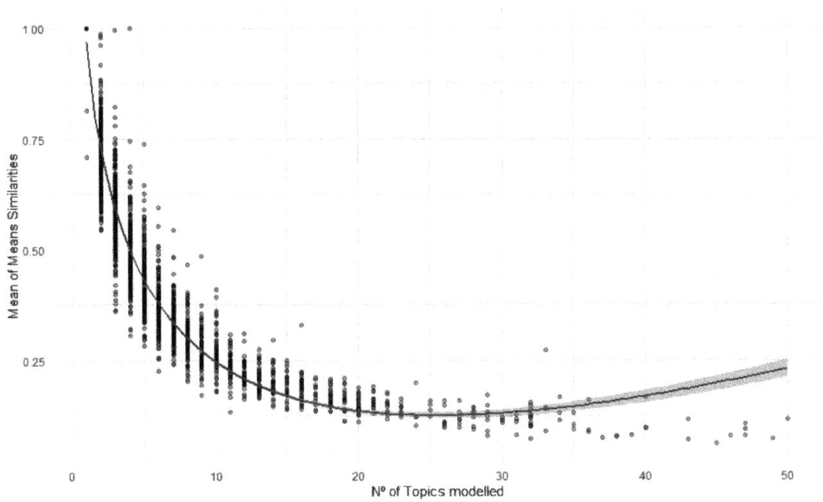

Fig. 51: Scatterplot and logarithmic model for the association between the number of topics modelled in a given thread and the mean of means similarities of nodes in threads.

6.2. Analysis

Summarising the aforementioned ponderations, it is assumed that different graph-theoretic properties of linguistic interaction networks on online social networks have an impact on the stability of the topics as a measure of consensus. As a dependent variable for this experiment, the number of topics modelled *k* was identified. Network topology, the number of nodes, the diameter of the networks, and the coherence of the generated models are hypothesised to be the main contributors to the dependent variable *k*. However, associations between the independent variables have to be taken into account. It was shown that network topology is contingent on diameter and the number of nodes, with bigger threads predominantly forming decentralised graphs. Also, the diameter of centralised graphs is fixed at $\delta = 2$, meaning that the topology can be described in terms of diameter. Thus, different configurations modelling the independent variables thread length and diameter were tried out, and only the most performant model will be reported.

To account for the nature of these variables, a generalised linear model (Nelder & Wedderburn 1972) assuming a Poisson distribution was used. Poisson models are used to model count data, that is variables that are integer in nature and may exhibit a log distribution. As shown before, this is true for all of the three variables: number of nodes, diameter, and *k*. Due to the covariate nature of possible random effect variables, the model only exhibits main effects. For this R's *stats* package's (R Core Team 2020) *glm* ( ) function was used. An interaction effect (*) between the number of nodes and diameter was included, as it resulted in lower residual deviance:

$$glm(n^{\underline{o}}\, of\, topics \sim number\, of\, nodes * diameter, family = "poisson")$$

All models which tried to include random effects of either community, the type of community (topic-based vs. region-based), or the subgraph in question failed to converge. To allow simpler testing methods such as linear regression, it was attempted to normalise the distribution of the variables. Attempts with power transformation or logarithmic transformation failed to produce normalised variables. The hypothesis to be tested in this context is that the number of topics modelled in a given thread as a measure of the stability of the topic treated therein is dependent on the number of nodes in the network and that this effect interacts with the diameter of the network:

H_0: The number of nodes in a graph and the diameter of this graph are not correlated with the number of topics in the network of comments.

6.3. Results

Running the model specified above resulted in highly significant effects for the length of threads ($p < 0.001$), the diameter ($p < 0.001$), and their interaction ($p < 0.001$). The null hypothesis is thus rejected. Effect sizes, on the other hand, are very small. The intercept of 0.94 is influenced by the number of nodes at $coef = 0.016$, the diameter at $coef = 0.084$, and the diameter modulates the effect of the number of nodes at $coef = -0.00071$. The dispersion parameter equals one, speaking to the adequacy of the Poisson family for the modelling of the data presented above. The model produces high residual deviance of 8,478.8

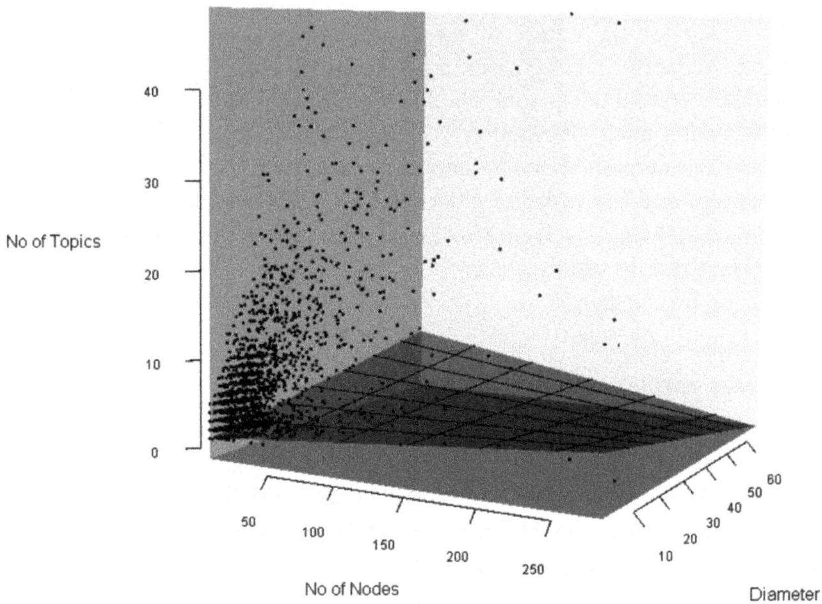

Fig. 52: Three-dimensional scatterplot of the association between the number of nodes, the diameter and the number of topics modelled. The curved grey plane and grid indicate predictions of the generalised linear model. The model produces high residual deviance, especially for threads with many topics.

on 2,691 degrees of freedom. Especially for those threads that exhibit many topics, the model falls short in making precise predictions (Fig. 52).

A post hoc ANOVA test executed on the model reveals the contribution of the different parameters to the explanation of the variance. All three parameters (i.e., n° of nodes, diameter, and the interaction thereof) contribute significantly ($p < 0.001$). Chi-squared analysis of the deviance table revealed differing likelihood ratios (LR) for each parameter, which expresses the ratio of the observed to the expected values. The most contributing predictor is the interaction effect between the number of nodes and diameter ($LR = 1{,}639.58$) followed by the number of nodes ($LR = 907.82$), and eventually the diameter itself ($LR = 502.90$). The model here reported is the best one that could be identified (minimizing residual deviance) given the variables present in the dataset. Attempts to normalise the data to execute linear regression failed. Attempts to include random effects in the model failed to converge.

6.4. Discussion

The model shows that the number of nodes in a thread as a measure of the number of speakers in a local interaction and the diameter as a measure of centralisation both contribute significantly to the explanation of the similarity of the topics within the thread. Conceptually, it is shown that an increase in the number of nodes and an increase in the diameter independently lead to an increase in the number of topics that have to be modelled, meaning that topics become less stable when more agents join the conversation or do so in a more decentralised fashion. However, the model shows that when many agents interact in a very decentralised way, or when the number of nodes and the diameter increase together, conversations become more uniform and fewer topics have to be generated to model what the agents talk about in these threads. On the one hand, this is surprising. On the other hand, it does match the expectations of what one would expect based on the deliberations on distributed networks, where big numbers of mutually regulating nodes lead to more informational stability within systems. However, a caveat is in order. Even though the model produced significant and interpretable results, it does include a great deal of error, especially in those extremer cases, where very big threads with big diameters need many topics to be accounted for. This may be a simple consequence of the underrepresentation of these threads in the dataset, or they might be actual outliers. Further detailed inspection of these threads could produce some insights as to how they are different from smaller threads. However, the data description showed that it is in the nature of these variables to be right-skewed. That is, shorter threads and smaller diameters as well as threads with small topic numbers, are more typical in the data. The overrepresentation of smaller linguistic interaction networks is also the reason for the small effect sizes. That is, the behaviour of bigger interaction networks isn't captured by the model, producing these large margins of error.

With this caveat established, some arguments for discussion can be put forth. First of all, the argument of community size (Lupyan & Dale 2010; Reali et al. 2018; Raviv et al. 2019) seems to be of utter importance. The similarity of topics in a given thread does seem to be dependent on the number of speakers in the thread. Of course, this argument is different from the aforementioned authors, in that they refer to the structural properties of the grammars of big populations and over generations respectively. However, it is here argued that network topology effects in linguistic contexts are relevant in both long-term development and contextual communication because the former is ultimately dependent on the latter. Whether or not these two effects can be equated will be addressed in further discussions. Here, it suffices to point out, that the numbers of speakers in anonymous linguistic interaction networks affect the ability of the network to maintain thematic consensus. The more individuals there are in such a network, the harder it is to maintain a stable conversation topic.

Furthermore, a significant relationship with the diameter as a measure of centrality is identified. This means that network topology – here approached as a continuous property rather than a categorical one – does have an impact on the convergence of groups on a topic. This opposes the findings of other researchers (e.g., Raviv et al. 2020). Again, their experimental task is quite different from the observation made in this experiment and their measurement of topology is also different. In any case, it does appear that not only the number but also the structural organisation of agents in terms of network topology does have an impact on the conversational local scale. This study thus complements – by observation – experimental evidence from a study by Centola and Baronchelli (2015). Their study is more concerned with the emergence of social conventions rather than conversational adequacy, but it will be discussed further down whether or not these two aspects can be consolidated into a similar argument.

The importance of the interaction effect is of special interest. This means that a high number of nodes in combination with a high diameter led to more similar topics in the corpus, which opposes the effect that they produce when occurring separately. According to the literature on graph theory, it would have to be expected that a high degree of similarity between contributions would be present in cases where networks are highly distributed, that is where nodes can mutually influence and correct each other with frequent interactions. However, as the data description showed, there are no real distributed networks in the corpus. Furthermore, due to the rather unequal distribution of graphs across different network topologies, it wasn't possible to account for this variable directly. Rather, the diameter had to be taken as a proxy to network topology, where a bigger diameter also speaks to a bigger degree of decentralisation (Section 5.4.5). It does appear that bigger and less centralised networks do maintain a great deal of similarity of topics across nodes, even without mutual regulation of the nodes. The reason for this isn't entirely clear. It can't be ruled out that this is a bias in the method, that is in the way that models generated from the LDA algorithm tend to identify fewer topics when more documents are compared. On the other hand, it can be speculated that topics that are bigger and more decentralised require more effort in reading by the contributors on the network, who in turn condensate their contributions more toward a shared, bigger topic. The mechanism behind this isn't clear, but the usual mechanism, namely the mutual regulation of nodes among each other doesn't hold as an explanation, simply because the networks aren't structured this way.

7. Experiment Two – Identity Bias and Secret Handshakes

Under the term identity bias, it was explored that individuals in a network can have a rather important impact, either because they are very well-connected (Kearns et al. 2006, 2009) or because their reputation is of high quality despite their low connectivity (Milroy 2002). For a theory that foregrounds the mathematical properties of such connections, this variable is an important confounding factor. In analysing, for instance, the impact of sensorimotricity on political language (e.g., Ströbel 2018), the statistical comparison between two politicians (e.g., Ströbel 2019) is easily overshadowed by the general popularity of the politician in question. That is, once a given identity is established, a sudden change in linguistic habitus won't result in higher popularity. Or, in the case of political discourse on social media, while one linguistic strategy may result useful for one politician, it might not produce as many mentions and likes for another one. This can be either because the linguistic strategy doesn't match the identity of the politician, or because the number of followers (i.e., degree) of their account is different, and represents a different baseline for network phenomena to take effect. Hence, there is a complex interplay between identity bias, degree bias and content bias that makes measurements extremely difficult.

As was pointed out above (Section 5.1), the dataset has a special disposition in that it is completely anonymised (cf. Escandell-Montiel 2016). While this is characterised as a problem (Section 5.1) for the online community in terms of potential radicalisation (Nagle 2017; Torres-Nabel 2017), such anonymity is useful from a methodological standpoint, because it allows researchers to disentangle identity bias from degree and content bias. However, identity bias still plays an important role in the verbal behaviour of participants in linguistic interaction networks. It appears that users on such imageboards still try to gain reputation in the community by signalling to belong to their peers through linguistic secret handshakes (Bernstein et al. 2011), which is an alternative way of communicating their identity and reputation.

Bernstein et al. (2011) examine specifically anglophone communication strategies to signal identity, thus their findings cannot be used to directly produce predictions. However, the word *anon* is often reported to be the self-denomination of users on 4chan (Bernstein et al. 2011; Papasavva et al. 2020; Tuters & Hagens 2020) and represents an integral part of slang on 4chan, specifically on the imageboard /pol/. Upon qualitative inspection of the corpus from Hispachan, it can be seen that the word *anon* is also pervasive in the Spanish version of the medium. It is mostly used as an appellative as in ">>119460 Concuerdo, anon" or "Hacelo, anon"[61]. Its diminutive, *anoncito,* is also frequent in the interaction between nodes. Another key component of slang on Hispachan is the word *negro.* In its English form, *nigger*[62], it is an important component of topics as identified by Papasavva et al. (2020, p. 891), but the authors do not attribute any pragmatic force to it. In the Hispachan corpus, however, the word *negro* is used widely in appellative contexts and in conjunction with imperative verb forms: ">>119350 Se te ardió el ano, Negrín?", ">>11315 Dame tu boypussy, negro. Nada es gratis". Variations of the use of *negro* include two different diminutives on an *-ito* suffix and an *-ín* suffix, resulting in *negrito* and *negrín*. While interactions usually take place within the bounds of the orthographic norm, *negrin* (without the *tilde*) does occur. Finally, different authors agree on the importance of *kek* as an element of *4chan* slang. It started as a variant of *lol*[63] and then became the "God of memes, via which they influence reality" (Papasavva et al. 2020), meaning that the expression has developed into an expression of allegiance and subscription to certain elements of the fuzzy political ideology defended on 4chan, even in real life. *Kek* on 4chan appears to be used in the context of God-like iconography, for example by depicting *Pepe the Frog* (Section 5.1) as a God (Hine et al. 2017, p. 2).

---

61 *Hacelo* (also *hacélo*) is the Spanish imperative to *hacer* which corresponds to the verbal paradigm of the addressing form *vos*. The use of this form has been discontinued in Iberian Spanish since the 16th century, but is still in use in some varieties of the Americas, most notably in Central America and in the Rio de la Plata area.

62 I am sorry to reproduce the use of this word, together with other opressive vocabulary, in the description of this experiment, and will only do so this once. I do believe, on the other hand, that it is necessary to be absolutely precise in the description of the object of study.

63 Although this could not be corroborated in the academic literature, the beginning of *kek* may lie in the MMORPG World of Warcraft published by Blizzard Entertainment in 2005. In the game, players can choose from different factions, each with their own culture, mythology and language. The linguistic aspect is simulated in the game in such a way that, when players within the world use the chat interface to communicate, messages are converted to more or less meaningless squiggles, unless the players belong to the same faction or have "learned" the language (they obtained the ability to see messages in game). While the modified text wasn't understandable, the conversion wasn't entirely random. The common Internet term *lol* (laughing out loud) was always converted to *kek*, which became a common word for players to use jokingly on the platforms and in their everyday lives at the time. Whether the word carried a political meaning at the time already can hardly be reconstructed in hindsight.

On Hispachan, on the other hand, the word seems to be used more along the lines of *lol*, although it carries a lot more degrading and resentful connotations than the general expression *lol*. Examples in the corpus are ">>2641 kek, tremendo down" mocking a photograph of a person with trisomy 21, the so-called 'Down Syndrome', and ">>133142 Esas habilidades sociales, kkk" mocking the conversation style of another poster. *Kkk* was identified as a variation of *kek*. Its use appears to be similar in context but presumably alludes to the *Ku Klux Klan*, a more or less consolidated group of different American organisations that engage in White Supremacist, Neofascist, Antisemitic, Antifeminist, and other Ultraright ideologies, sometimes resorting to quasi-terrorist means. This enhances the derogatory character of the expression as opposed to *kek*.

As other authors point out, there are also other strategies to signal identity on such imageboards, such as the triforce-meme (Fig. 53):

> the three-triangle icon of popular video game The Legend of Zelda [...]. Newcomers will be taunted by a challenge that 'newfags can't triforce.' Uninitiated users will then copy and paste an existing triforce into their reply. It will look like a correct triforce in the reply field; however, after posting, the alignment is wrong. (Bernstein et al. 2011, p. 56)

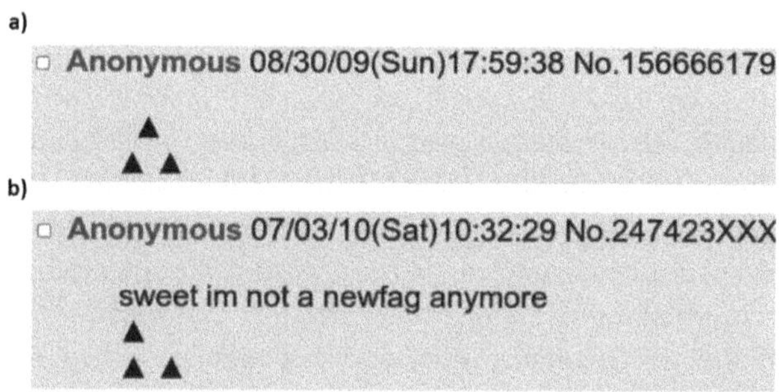

Fig. 53: Correct (a) and incorrect (b) depiction of the triforce meme (Bernstein et al. 2011, p. 56).

Since the correct depiction of the triforce-meme on 4chan requires a rather sophisticated manipulation of Unicode characters, the authors argue that this meme is an index (cf. Peirce 1903) of particular skill or knowledge. But such engagements are difficult to analyse in an automated manner, also given the fact that the data scraped from Hispachan contains exclusively linguistic material and none of the images uploaded to the platform. With regards to the more suitable expressions *anon*, *negro*, and *kek* (and their variations) it is argued here that such signs are used as indices to demonstrate intricate knowledge of the conversational conventions on the imageboard Hispachan. The index as a semiotic category allows the interpretation of such words as alternative communication strategies or secret handshakes.

Embedding such a signal in the network theory formulated above, the question is whether or not the creation of networks depends on the usage of such signals. In particular, the question is whether or not the use of secret handshakes leads to more adjacent nodes or direct neighbours. That is, are nodes that contain expressions of secret handshakes more likely to generate a response than others?

7.1. Materials and Methods

For this experiment, instead of working on heavily pre-processed data, a series of simple variables were created to carry out simple, but expressive statistical analyses. The text column from the node-specific dataset (Section 5.3.1) containing the raw text material from Hispachan was converted to lower case only, using the *stringr* package (Wickham 2019). Since the utf-8 encoded data doesn't support the relevant Spanish characters <é>, <á>, <ó>, <ú>, <ñ>, and <í>, their utf-8 equivalents were manually replaced with the *str_replace_all*() function.

Afterwards, a variable was created to signal the presence of a word in the text of each node. Using the *str_count*() function and assigning each node with a value unequal to zero the value *TRUE*, while assigning each node with a value equal to zero the value *FALSE*, a variable was obtained for each node and searched word, identifying whether the word was contained in the text. To count the occurrences of each word in the non-pre-processed text, the different variations of the words *anon*, *negro*, and *kek* were searched manually. The following variations were then included in the automated search in the corpus:

a. *Anon*: <anon>, <anons>, <anoncito>, <anoncitos>, <anona>, <anonas>, <anoncita>, <anoncitas>
b. *Negro*: <negro>, <negrín>, <negrin>, <negros>, <negrines>, <negrínes>, <negra>, <negras>
c. *Kek*: <kek>, <kkk>

To create a baseline for comparison of the functioning of these presumable secret handshakes, another semantic field was identified. The Covid-19 crisis has been identified to be one of the strongest topics fuelling right-wing extremism and populist tendencies both in alternative and regular media (Vieten 2020). It was thus hypothesised that this topic would draw attention to a node and create more responses than nodes not containing this word, but that the mechanism would differ from the one to be identified in the three aforementioned cases.

d. *Corona*: <Corona>, <coronoso>, <coronosos>, <coronosa>, <coronosas>, <covid>, <covid-19>, <covid 19>

For each concept, the variable indicating the absence or presence of the concept in a given node was grouped by the number of neighbours of the node. In this way, the proportion of nodes containing the concept compared to the number of nodes not containing the concept could be obtained for any given number of nodes. Finally, probabilities equal to either zero or infinity were removed from the data, such as to prevent working with data obtained from the non-defined zero division or the division with missing values. The following variables were then used for analysis.

a. *Concept Probability*: The probability that a word was present in a node as measured by the proportion of nodes of a given degree containing the concept.
b. *Degree*: The degree by which nodes were grouped to calculate the ratio of nodes containing vs. nodes not-containing any given concept.

7.2. Analysis

In summary of the above considerations, the following analysis was executed. To determine the role that a concept plays in the generation of neighbours of a node, several linear models were created using the *lm*() function from R's *stats* (R Core Team 2020) package. Node degree was used as a dependent variable and concept probability as an independent variable. For each concept, different models were attempted, comparing clean linear functions, linear functions with a logarithmic term, and linear functions with quadratic terms. In each case, only the most performant model will be reported. As the most performant model was defined the model which explained the most variance in the data in each case, thus maximising R^2.

For the three secret handshake concepts, the following model was applied. Note that the presumption of a gaussian distribution was not checked previously. To argue for the applicability of a gaussian family test on the data, the distribution of model residuals will be reported in the results (Section 7.3).

$$lm(degree \sim conceptprobability, family = "gaussian")$$

For occurrences of Corona, the following model was applied. Note that the time of data collection (April 2020 and January 2021) was included in the model to account for differences in the popularity and of the topic at different stages of the pandemic. In this case, the assumption of a Gaussian distribution will be tested on the distribution of model residuals.

$$lm(degree \sim concept\,probability + time + I(\log(concept\,probability)), family = "gaussian")$$

Again, only the most performant models are reported. This means that the secret handshake concepts were best modelled with linear regression models, while the inclusion of the logarithmic term in the case of the Corona topic led to a higher R^2. In the analysis, the following hypothesis was tested.

H_0: The probability for a given concept to appear in any node doesn't change across different degrees of nodes.

7.3. Results

The prevalence of the four concepts in the dataset lies more or less in the same order of magnitude. Out of the 54,393 nodes in the dataset, the concept *anon* appears in 3.18 % of the nodes (n = 1,728), the concept *negro* appears in 5.94 % of the nodes (n = 3,232), the concept *kek* appears in 1.24 % of the nodes (n = 677), and the concept *Corona* appears in 1.20 % of the nodes (n = 654).

The linear model for the concept *anon* yielded highly significant results for the linear relationship between concept probability and the degree of the corresponding nodes (Fig. 54). The values are positively correlated with a coefficient of 75.423. That is, for each 10 % in probability increase of the concept occurring, the degree rises by 7.54, explaining 68 % of the variance in the data ($F(1,23) = 51.1$, $p < 0.001$, $R^2 = 0.68$).

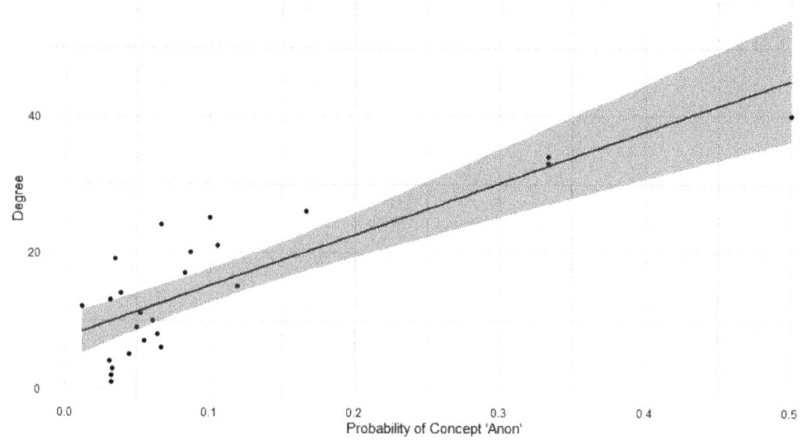

Fig. 54: Scatterplot and linear regression model for the relationship between the probability of the concept anon in a node and the corresponding degree of the node. The grey area indicates the model standard error.

To test the assumption of normal distribution post hoc, visual inspection of a normality plot generated with the *qqPlot*() function from R's *car* package (Fox & Weisberg 2019) showed that the model residuals are well aligned with the expected normal distribution. A corresponding Shapiro-Wilk normality test didn't find any significant difference between the residual distribution and a hypothetical normal distribution (W = 0.954, p = 0.31). Normal distribution for the model's residuals is assumed. The null hypothesis is just rejected. The alternative hypothesis is put forth, that the degree of any given node from the corpus is dependent on the probability of the concept anon appearing in this node.

Running the same analysis investigating the concept *negro* yields similar results. The application of the aforementioned model results in a strong linear association between the dependent and the independent variable with a correlation coefficient of 54.02 (Fig. 55). A 10 % increase in the probability of the concept *negro* in a given node thus increases the degree of this node by 5.40 and accounts for 41 % of the variance in the data ($F(1,31) = 23.19$, $p < 0.001$, $R^2 = 0.41$). These results are highly significant, the null hypothesis is thus rejected. The alternative hypothesis is that the use of the concept *negro* in nodes has an impact on the generation of neighbours and thus leads to higher degrees of nodes.

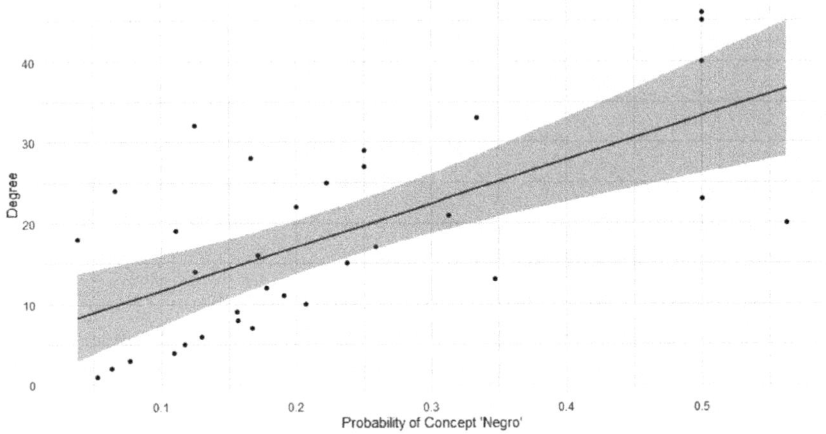

Fig. 55: Scatterplot and linear regression model for the relationship between the probability of the concept negro in a node and the corresponding degree of the node. The grey area indicates the model standard error.

To test the assumption of normal distribution post hoc, visual inspection of a normality plot generated with the *qqPlot*() function from R's *car* package (Fox & Weisberg 2019) showed that the model residuals are well-aligned with the expected normal distribution. All residuals fall within the envelope of normal distribution at a significance threshold of 95 % (Fig. 56). However, the Shapiro-Wilk normality test yields a slightly significant deviation of the empirical distribution from a normal distribution ($W = 0.935$, $p < 0.05$). The methods of checking for a normal distribution of model residuals are thus at odds. The normality of residuals is thus neither assumed nor rejected.

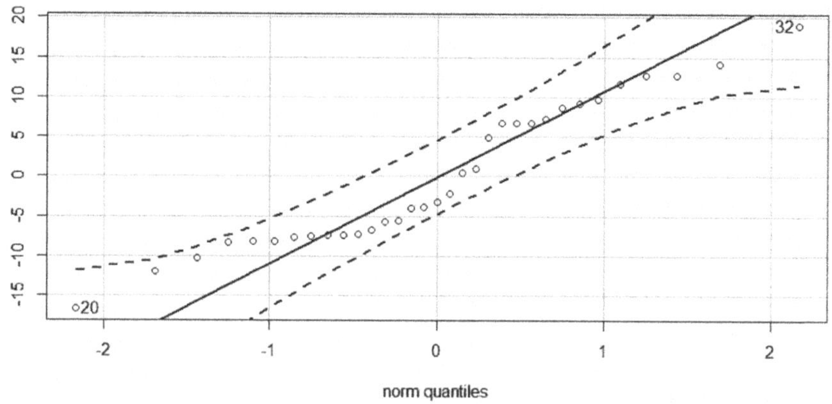

Fig. 56: Residuals of the model predicting the degree of the node from its propensity to contain the concept negro. The x-axis represents the theoretical quantiles, the y-axis represents the observed residual quantiles. The dashed line envelope represents the confidence Interval at a 95 % threshold.

Analysis of the concept *kek* yielded similar results. The application of the aforementioned model results in a linear association between the degree and probability of the concept *kek* with a correlation coefficient of 198.9 (Fig. 57). A 10 % increase in the probability of the concept *kek* in a given node thus increases the degree of this node by 19.9 and accounts for 50 % of the variance in the data ($F(1,11) = 13.14, p < 0.01, R^2 = 0.50$). These results are significant, the null hypothesis is thus rejected. The alternative hypothesis is that the use of the concept *kek* in nodes has an impact on the generation of neighbours and thus leads to higher degrees of nodes.

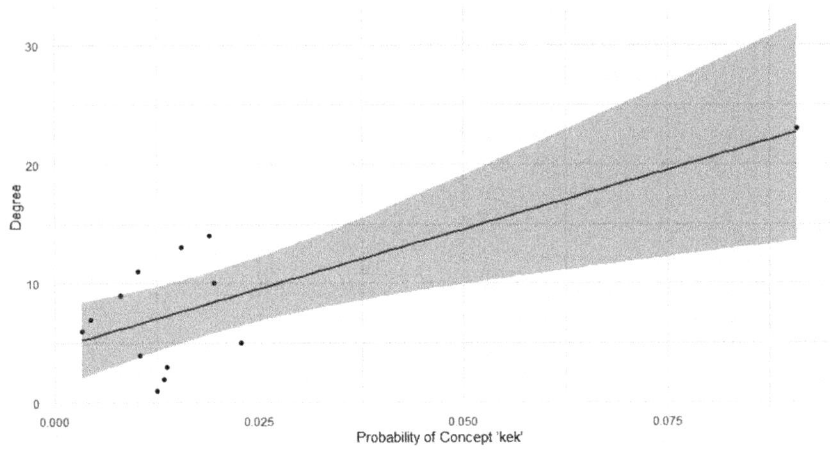

Fig. 57: Scatterplot and linear regression model for the relationship between the probability of the concept kek in a node and the corresponding degree of the node. The grey area indicates the model standard error.

To test the assumption of normal distribution post hoc, visual inspection of a normality plot generated with the *qqPlot*() function from R's *car* package (Fox & Weisberg 2019) showed that the model residuals are well aligned with the expected normal distribution. A corresponding Shapiro-Wilk normality test didn't find any significant difference between the residual distribution and a hypothetical normal distribution (W = 0.926, p = 0.30). Normal distribution for the model's residuals is assumed. The null hypothesis is just rejected. The alternative hypothesis is put forth, that the degree of any given node from the corpus is dependent on the probability of the concept *kek* to appear in this node.

Finally, the same test was carried out on the concept *Corona* but included a term to distinguish between the two points in time of data collection and a logarithmic term. These terms didn't enhance the performance of the other models. In the case of *Corona*, the model yielded highly significant results for both the factor of data collection time ($p < 0.001$) and for the logarithmic term of concept probability ($p < 0.001$). There is thus a strong and highly significant association between the logarithmic probability of the topic Corona appearing in a node and the degree of this node (Fig. 58). The model is very explicit and accounts for 86 % of the variance in the data ($F(3,31)$, $p < 0.001$, $R^2 = 0.86$).

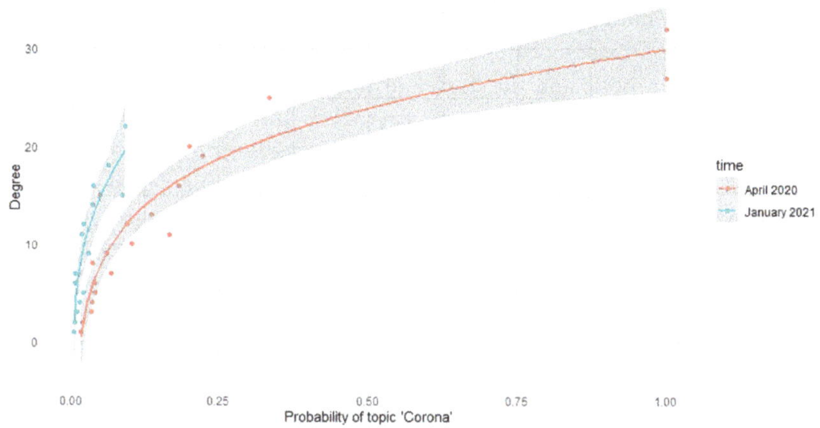

Fig. 58: Scatterplot and logarithmic model for the association between the probability of the topic Corona appearing in a node and the degree of the corresponding node. The model distinguishes between the two points in time of data collection. Grey areas indicate the models' standard error.

Post hoc testing of the model residuals included visual inspection of a *Q-Q plot*, which showed that all residuals fall within the expected normal quantiles. A corresponding Shapiro-Wilks normality test yielded no significant results (W = 0.98, p = 0.75), meaning that a normal distribution of model residuals is assumed. The overall null hypothesis can thus be rejected. As an alternative hypothesis, it is suggested that the degree of a node is contingent on its propensity to contain the concept *Corona*. The relationship is characterised by a steep increase of degree at low probabilities, while an additional increase doesn't contribute to the effect to the same extent.

7.4. Discussion

The experiment set out to analyse whether or not certain concepts from the corpus can be conceptualised as secret handshakes, and whether or not such secret handshakes enhance the degree of this node, that is the interaction with this node by other nodes. This question is embedded in the analysis of the identity bias in networks; the tendency of nodes to signal group belonging linguistically and thereby gain higher connectivity in the network. Having revised the literature, the concepts *anon*, *negro* and *kek* were identified as possible secret handshake strategies. As a baseline for comparison, these specific concepts were compared to the rather general but politically relevant topic *Corona*.

The analysis of the association between the propensity of a given concept to appear in a given node and the degree of this node yielded significant results for all four investigated concepts, *anon, negro, kek,* and *Corona*. However, subtle differences between these concepts and their associations can be described. The association of the concept *anon* with an increase in the degree of a node is straightforward. The higher the probability of the concept appearing in a given node, the higher the degree of the node. To illustrate this relationship, the highest value in the scatterplot (Fig. 54) has 40 direct neighbours and a probability of 50 % to contain the concept *anon*. This means that one out of two nodes with degree 40 contains the concept. On the lower end of the scale, nodes with only one neighbour have a probability of less than 5 % to contain the concept, although they are far more abundant. This is here interpreted as indicative of the fact that users who manage to engage a lot of other users to reply to their posts are more inclined to use the concept of *anon* to generate interaction. This would confirm the argument put forth by Bernstein et al. (2011) about alternative group-belonging signalling strategies.

The analysis of the concept *negro* shows similar results. However, the analyses are not conclusive with regard to the applicability of the linear model architecture to the data, because of the unconfirmed normal distribution of model residuals. While the *Q-Q plot* (Fig. 56) indicates that residuals fall along the line of normal distribution and within a 95 % confidence interval, the corresponding Shapiro-Wilks test reveals a slightly significant deviation from the normal distribution. At p equal to 4 % and no specifically justified threshold for significance, there is still a good chance that the null hypothesis holds (cf. Lakens et al. 2018). While the model for the concept *negro* explains less variance in the data, the probabilities are more evenly distributed between 0 % and 50 % (Fig. 55). This speaks to the strong linear relationship between the variables. Regarding the theoretical implications of this finding, it adds to the arguments put forth in the previous paragraph. The concept *negro* seems to be associated with a higher engagement with nodes containing it, thus empirically confirming the argument by Bernstein et al. (2011) and showing how their argument can be empirically informed through graph-theoretic measurements in the corpus.

As for the concept *kek*, the case is slightly different. Although *kek* presents the same sort of relationship between its probability of appearing and the creation of additional nodes, it seems to appear less overall. Instead of ranging from 0 % to 50 %, the maximum probability of *kek* appearing in a node of a given degree is 1 %. This seems to indicate that the concept is much more obscure than the other two, while at the same time contributing a lot more to the creation of new nodes. With a coefficient of 198.9, the same increase in the probability of *kek* arising contributes almost four times as much to the increase in degree as the increase in the probability of *negro.* But it is unclear if the relationship expands as far because *kek* doesn't appear as often. In tendency, *kek* appears to confirm what has been argued with regard to *anon* and *negro.*

Concerning *Corona,* another element becomes apparent. While the relationships between concept probability and degree for the other concepts is linear, it appears that it is logarithmic for *Corona* (Fig. 58). It was hypothesised that Corona doesn't contribute to the creation of higher degree nodes in the same way that the other concepts do as secret handshakes. The logarithmic association between the variables appears to be indicative of such a difference. But the relationship requires explaining. The degree of a node seems to grow proportionally in the case of secret handshakes. In the case of *Corona,* an increase in the probability of this concept leads to higher degrees at low probabilities, but at higher probabilities, an increase doesn't lead to much higher engagement. In other words, the effect wears off after it has passed a certain threshold. Put differently, the strong presence of the topic *Corona* is important for the identification of very high-degree nodes, while low-degree nodes concentrate on extremely low concept probability nodes.

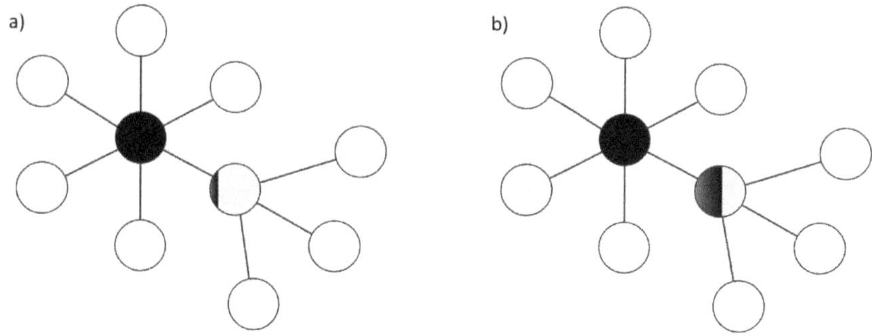

Fig. 59: Representation of the contribution of concept probability to the creation of high-degree nodes. The gradient represents the probability of a concept being present in that node. (a) represents the relevance of the concept of Corona, and (b) represents the relevance of the secret handshakes. Note that in (b) the probability is proportional to its degree, while in (a) also low probability nodes can generate rather high amounts of neighbours.

This difference could be explained by different network mechanisms (Fig. 59). A topic, even though very relevant to the community in terms of its occurrence, doesn't contribute as much to the generation of high-degree nodes as secret handshakes do. The latter does appear to be a better predictor of the communicative success of nodes in the networks at a local level unless concept probability is very high. It is argued that secret handshakes constitute a more stable communicative signal to create engagement. One caveat is in order about the statistical modelling of the data. In all four cases, the density of high concept probabilities is rather low compared to the low concept probabilities. That means that while many data points cluster close to the lower bounds of the x-axis and y-axis, there are fewer values as x increases. The missing values might make the linear models appear more performant. Also, the x-axis in the case of *Corona* extends to x = 1, while the maximum values for x in the other cases are x = 0.5 and x = 0.1 respectively. The relationship between the variables might appear linear in the lower bounds of the function, while these descriptions might collapse in the presence of higher empirical values. This is a possibility to consider. However, this alternative explanation for the difference between the concepts isn't pursued further, because logarithmical modelling for the effects of *anon*, *negro*, and *kek* in no case provided a more efficient model of description. The models reported above (Section 7.3) are the best in each case.

In terms of the more general aspects of the linguistic network theory laid out above (Chapter 4), it could be argued that identity bias outweighs content bias in this particular case, although this finding doesn't have to generalise. This finding shows that identity is an important pressure in the formation of linguistic interaction networks and that alternative strategies can move identity signalling into content-based strategies. Since the identity bias here outweighs the content bias in the form of the pertinent topic *Corona*, it is argued that the pressures modulate each other. Further investigation will have to compare different scenarios both with visible and invisible identities, such as to disentangle the role of both biases in the formation of communicative networks. These biases are possibly complementary, although this experiment isn't able to provide evidence for such a claim.

8. Experiment Three – Content Bias: Expressivity and Local Engagement

It was argued at various stages that spreading information is partly dependent on the quality of the stimulus. This has been termed content bias (cf. Tamariz et al. 2014; Segovia-Martín et al. 2020). The third experiment aims to inform the role that certain linguistic features play with regard to the creation of higher-degree nodes. This is similar to the previous experiment in that it seeks to elucidate the relationship between the occurrence of certain words and the degree of the node as a result of such an occurrence. However, the theoretical framework and the implications of the measurements are quite different. Instead of focussing on the specific vocabulary of websites such as Hispachan, this experiment is based on more general linguistic notions.

It was pointed out earlier, that network structure is one of the important drivers of linguistic change and diversity (Labov 2001; Milroy 2002; Trugdil 2009; Lupyan & Dale 2010; Lupyan & Dale 2016). While the present study cannot elucidate linguistic change, because of the synchronic nature of its corpus, one important factor of linguistic change can be tracked on a local level, namely expressivity. Ströbel (2014) argues that the expressivity of linguistic forms is a key feature of linguistic change. That is because linguistic forms lose expressivity through syntactical or cognitive synthesis and give way for new expressions to arise. As was pointed out above (Section 3.4.3), such processes of synthesis or systematisation take place especially in well-distributed networks (Raviv et al. 2020) through communication and cultural transmission (Silvey et al. 2019). Expressivity could thus represent a prime candidate for the creation of high-connectivity nodes in local interaction networks.

However, a myriad of techniques and definitions of expressivity in linguistic expressions is available. Some approaches of sentiment analysis and linguistic measurements (Castro-Toledo et al. 2020) were mentioned above, also with regards to their specific application in radicalised online discourse and its psychological impact on Twitter users (Gretenkort et al. in press). Attempts to correlate node degrees with such techniques didn't result in any meaningful findings.

However, Ströbel (2014) herself points out that the expressivity of linguistic forms is intricately linked to the underlying sensorimotor strategies conveyed by them. She has furthermore identified the role of such strategies in the engagement of political speakers with their audience (Ströbel 2018), meaning that highly expressive strategies in terms of sensorimotricity may lead to higher engagement. This is possibly also reflected in the fact that pre-election speeches in the political sphere appear to be more penetrated by projective sensorimotor strategies (Ströbel 2019). This conception is consistent with the theory of embodied cognition (Varela et al. 1991). While it doesn't necessarily follow that an increase in sensorimotor concepts leads to higher engagement of the hearer with what is being said, evidence from cognitive narratology also suggests that sensorimotor imagery and the resulting cognitive simulation of the narrative in the reader lead to higher degrees of immersion (Kuzmičová 2012). Ströbel's (2018) findings on political discourse do furthermore suggest that similar effects can be observed in non-fictional texts. Importantly, sensorimotor expressivity has a double function: it heightens engagement and promotes linguistic change in that more expressive linguistic forms start to occupy functions of already grammaticalized forms (Meillet 1912, 1926; cited in Ströbel 2014). This principle can be characterised as a perpetual replacement of formerly expressive forms, which upon grammaticalization lose their expressivity and then have to compete with newer, more expressive forms. Whether this can be integrated into a CAS approach to linguistic change with expressivity and grammar (i.e., linguistic economy) as opposing evolutive pressures may be discussed in more detail elsewhere.

In this particular context, however, it can be argued that the embedding of such a process in a network helps to argue why this mechanism is in place. It was argued that stimuli have to be very expressive to locally increase engagement. On the other hand, previous accounts on distributed control and consensus in such networks explain why the same expression requires grammaticalization as it propagates through the network. For the network to maintain consensus on the form, the form needs to be systematised. The bigger and more distributed the network, the more systematised the form has to become. This appears to be contradictory but feeds exactly into the principle of competing pressures in the CAS approach. While forms need to be very expressive to be locally adaptive, they need to be highly structured to maintain usability across the whole network. Thus, local and global adaptation warrant opposed properties of a stimulus.

For this experiment, the question of interest is whether the general tendency of expressive and thus more locally engaging linguistic forms eventually leads to the creation of high-degree nodes in a local interaction network. Such an effect doesn't prove the propagation of more expressive forms in a social network, but the local high connectivity of nodes containing such expressions is a condition for the subsequent propagation of such expressions across the network. Based on the considerations by Ströbel (2014), expressivity in local interaction networks should be measurable in terms of the concepts underlying sensorimotor strategies.

The author supplies two domain unspecific concepts and their hierarchical development in terms of expressivity as a function of their sensorimotricity (Tab. 8). This experiment relies on domain unspecific concepts because the Hispachan-specific lexical level was already covered in the previous chapter. This experiment is interested in the general biases of engaging with content, irrespective of the thematic properties of the website.

Tab. 8: Sensorimotor hierarchies and directions of linguistic development. (Adapted from Ströbel 2014)

Sensorimotricity *'Expressivity Chains'*		**Static**	**Dynamic**	**Directed**
Starting point: (to) BE (Speaker's Existence)	*"Hands"*	(to) HAVE (to) HOLD	(to) DO (to) MAKE	(to) GIVE (to) TAKE
	"Legs"	(to) STAND (to) STAY	(to) GO	(to) COME (to) RETURN

Ströbel (2011) argues that sensorimotricity of concepts can be divided into three phases, all starting from the same base assumption, namely the bodily existence of a speaker, that is embodied cognition (Lakoff & Johnson 1980a). On the level of their hands and legs, this mere existence is actualised in different levels of activity, *static*, *dynamic*, and *directed*. Ströbel (2014) argues that the expressivity of these concepts increases with increasing motricity, which, in turn, leads to the directed verbs being freer (cf. Lehmann 1995; cited in Ströbel 2014) in their compositionality and being less relevant in more grammaticalized forms and compositions. Over time, however, also formerly more expressive concepts such as *to go* can eventually be grammaticalized (Ströbel 2011), as in the going-to-future or its Romance homologues *aller + Inf* (*fr.*), *ir a+ Inf* (*sp.*), *anar a+ Inf* (*cat.*).

Now, the question is whether this type of expressivity correlates with a higher local engagement in the form of the creation of high-degree nodes in a local linguistic interaction network. The experiment will thus try to identify the contribution of these concepts to the degree of the corresponding node and find differences in the engagement with nodes depending on the degree of motricity.

8.1. Materials and Methods

Like in experiment two (Section 7.1), the *stringr* package for R (Wickham 2019) was used to show occurrences of words in the text data for each node in the corpus. Instead of tokenizing the data, the conjugations for each word were explicitly stated in the code, such as to maximise the chances of finding all the occurrences in the raw texts. For each word a Boolean variable was created that indicated the presence (*TRUE*) or absence (*FALSE*) of the word in the text of the corresponding node.

Following Ströbel (2011, 2014) twelve domain-unspecific words were searched. According to Tab. 8, these words were: *agarrar, coger, dar, estar, hacer, ir, llegar, quedar, regresar, ser, tener,* and *tomar*. To capture the biggest possible number of occurrences, the verbs were conjugated in *presente, imperfecto, perfecto simple, futuro, presente de subjuntivo, imperfecto de subjuntivo, condicional,* as well as including *gerundio* and *participio* to capture the analytical verb forms. In the identification of the concepts, different spelling versions[64] were included in order to cover common orthographic errors such as missing and additional accents (unless the missing accent would result in another word as in *sería* → *seria*). Also, for the verb *coger* all possible forms included a systematic variation of the graphemes <g> and <j>, because both can be and are used for the representation of the phoneme /x/ in spellings on the Internet (Torrego-González 2011b). Furthermore, all allomorphs of the subjunctive preterits *fuera* and *fuese* were excluded from the analysis of the concept *ser* for two reasons. Firstly, *fuera* and *fuese* are forms of both *ir* and *ser* and it is difficult to disambiguate which concept the form stems from. To gain a certain amount of disambiguation, tokens of the allomorph *fuera a* were collected and attributed to the concept *ir*. Furthermore, both *fuera* and *fuese* are oftentimes used in South American Spanish as an auxiliar verb to construct the past tense conditionals as in: "si yo le *fuera/fuese* dicho quién soy, no me habría contado lo que me contó".

Like in the second experiment, the propensity of each word occurring at a given node degree was calculated by grouping nodes according to their degree and dividing the number of nodes in which the word occurred by the number of nodes in which it didn't, expressing the concept probability for this word. Furthermore, the degree variable was used for the analysis.

64 To review the conjugations, check annex 3.10_experiment3.R In the code, the conjugations for each word are fully stated.

Furthermore, the concepts were grouped according to the theory put forth in Ströbel (2014), resulting in the following grouping of concepts according to dynamicity (Tab. 9).

Tab. 9: Grouping of concepts according to the dynamicity of the verbs as indicated by Ströbel (2014).

Dynamicity	**Concept**
Static	*estar, quedar, ser, tener*
Dynamic	*dar, hacer, ir*
Directed	*agarrar, coger, llegar, regresar, tomar*

Note, however, that the referenced account doesn't consider the particular semantic configurations of these verbs in Spanish, which is why the classification includes more concepts than the ones that would be obtained by mere translation. The verb *(to) take* in Spanish can be translated as either *coger, agarrar,* or *tomar.* It was chosen to include all three because *coger* in Latin American Spanish has a variety of other meanings, most notably the concept *(to) have sex*, although it is the most commonly used word to translate *(to) take* in Iberian Spanish. *Tomar* is a more usual way of expressing *(to) take* in Latin American Spanish, although it collides with the meaning *(to) drink* in many cases. This is why all three alternatives were collected.

Note furthermore, that this classification diverges with regards to the concept *dar,* which Ströbel (2014) classifies as directed, however not specifically in the case of Spanish. In fact, she argues that the sensomotricity of concepts is language-specific as her recent contribution on Portuguese *verbos leves* shows (Ströbel 2020). It is here argued that the verb has lost a great deal of its dynamicity in Spanish, specifically because it appears in many expressions which are not properly directed in a spatial sense. Such uses of the verb *dar* include for example *dar positivo* ("to indicate a positive result"), *dar miedo* ("to frighten"), *dar sueño* ("to tire"), *dar vergüenza* ("to embarrass"). It is argued that, while the change of state or causation (in the last three examples) can indeed be conceptualised as a directed sensorimotor process ("to put someone *from* one state *into* another"), this collocation is so prevalent that it can be conceived of as an almost grammaticalized feature of Spanish. That is, *dar* has replaced many other historical possibilities for causative collocations such as *hacer vergüenza* in the history of Spanish due to frequency effects, which is why it has also been described as the "causative dar" (García-Salido 2017). *Dar* is thus classified as a dynamic rather than a directed verb in this terminology.

8.2. Analysis

To investigate the impact of dynamicity on the expressivity of verbs in the corpus, the analysis was run in two steps. Generalised linear models for Poisson distributions were created for each concept using the *stats* package's (R Core Team 2020) *glm*() function. In this case, generalised linear models were used because linear regression models didn't yield normally distributed residuals. The Poisson family was chosen to predict the integer degree variable. This analysis was executed to obtain the relevance of each concept for the creation of high-degree nodes. The viability of the models for each concept was assessed by checking the p-value and applying Shapiro-Wilk normality tests to the model residuals. The models were constructed as follows:

$$glm\left(degree \sim conceptprobability, family = "poisson"\right)$$

To assess the feasibility of the model post hoc, the dispersion parameters for each model were checked and expected to be equal to one. A Shapiro-Wilk normality test was executed to check whether the model residuals were normally distributed. To obtain model descriptors, a chi-squared test of independence was performed post hoc on the model residuals, yielding the residuals' χ^2, degrees of freedom, and p-value to describe the performance of each model. Only if all three conditions were met, the models were included in the final analysis, which was conducted as follows. The null hypothesis for this part of the analysis was:

H_0: There is no association between the probability of a word occurring in a node and the degree of this node.

The main method of analysis was the comparison of the model coefficients. To assess whether dynamicity impacts the degree of nodes, the generalised linear models were grouped by the underlying dynamicity of each concept according to the previous ponderations (Section 8.1). The model coefficients of each model were normalised by dividing the coefficient by the maximum node degree in the model, thus creating the slope of the model. The slopes were then grouped by the dynamicity of the underlying concept and compared with an ANOVA test. It was thereby attempted to compare which concepts and underlying types of dynamicity contributed the most to the creation of high-degree nodes in the linguistic interaction networks.

$$anova\left(slope \sim dynamicity\right)$$

The null hypothesis for this test was the following:

> H_0: The dynamicity of a concept doesn't affect the effect size of a word contributing to the creation of high-degree nodes.

Furthermore, it was predicted that dynamicity had an impact on the quality of the model as expressed in the R^2, meaning that the models of directed and dynamic concepts should explain more variance in the data because the impact of concept probability on node degree is more clearly established. An ANOVA test was used to compare the impact of concept dynamicity on models' R^2:

$$anova\left(R^2 \sim dynamicity\right)$$

The null hypothesis was that concept dynamicity wouldn't have an impact on the quality of the models in terms of explained variance:

> H_0: The dynamicity of a concept doesn't affect the variance explained by the model.

8.3. Results

All concepts are positively correlated with the creation of high-degree nodes (Fig. 60). All models have a dispersion parameter equal to one, speaking to the adequacy of the Poisson family to test parameter distribution. Furthermore, post hoc Shapiro-Wilk normality yielded insignificant results for all models, indicating that the residuals are normally distributed. Chi-squared tests on the models yielded significant results for eleven out of the twelve original concepts. The chi-squared tests yielded significant results for the concepts *agarrar* (χ^2 (1, N = 13) = 38.50, $p < 0.001$) with normal residuals (W = 0.96, p = 0.68), *coger* (χ^2 (1, N = 17) = 27.19, $p < 0.001$) with normal residuals (W = 0.96, p = 0.60), *dar* (χ^2 (1, N = 33) = 73.89, $p < 0.001$) with normal residuals (W = 0.96, p = 0.22), *estar* (χ^2 (1, N = 35) = 43.49, $p < 0.001$) with normal residuals (W = 0.94, p = 0.06), *hacer* (χ^2 (1, N = 36) = 77.24, $p < 0.001$) with normal residuals (W = 0.98, p = 0.62), *ir* (χ^2 (1, N = 34) = 43.04, $p < 0.001$) with normal residuals (W = 0.64, p = 0.33), *llegar* (χ^2 (1, N = 25) = 43.78, $p < 0.001$) with normal residuals (W = 0.96, p = 0.48), *quedar* (χ^2 (1, N = 24) = 28.01, $p < 0.001$) with normal residuals (W = 0.97, p = 0.67), *regresar* (χ^2 (1, N = 13) = 28.77, $p < 0.001$) with normal residuals (W = 0.95, p = 0.64), *ser* (χ^2 (1, N = 37) = 4.17, $p < 0.05$) with normal residuals (W = 0.97, p = 0.37), and *tener* (χ^2 (1, N = 36) = 51.47, $p < 0.001$) with normal residuals (W = 0.95, $p < 0.14$). Thus, the null hypothesis for all these concepts is rejected. The alternative hypothesis is put forth, that the appearance of these concepts in a node contributes to the degree of that node.

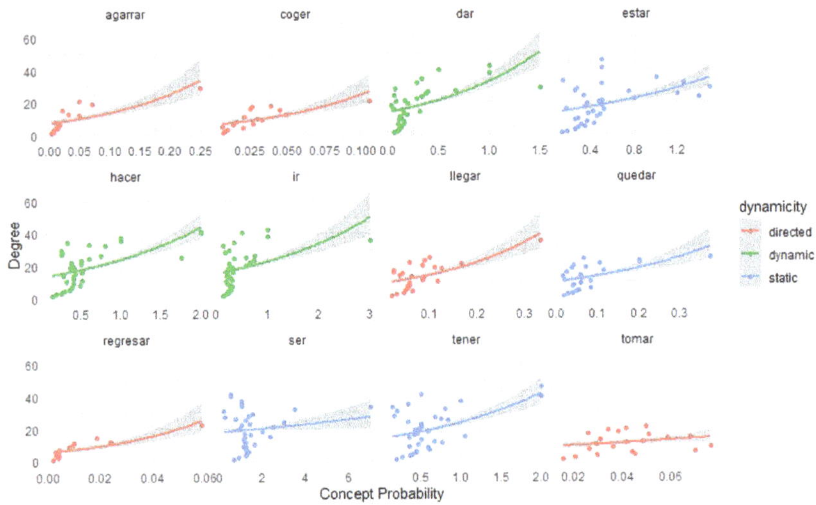

Fig. 60: Generalised linear models for each concept in experiment three. The x-axis represents the probability of the concept appearing in a node and the y-axis the corresponding node degree. Note that the scales are free to make a visual comparison possible, curved slopes may be misleading.

For the concept *tomar*, however, the model didn't yield significant results (χ^2 (1, N = 21) = 3.73, p > 0.05) although the model is adequate in that residuals are normally distributed (W = 0.93, p = 0.15). The null hypothesis is maintained for the concept *tomar*. It was excluded from the subsequent analyses.

The ANOVA test for the analysis of the impact of concept dynamicity on the model coefficient was thus executed on eleven concepts, namely *agarrar, coger, dar, estar, hacer, ir, llegar, quedar, regresar, ser,* and *tener.* The properties of the models are reported below (Tab. 10).

Tab. 10: Coefficients from the models for each concept. The slope is inferred for comparison in the subsequent test.

Concept	Coefficient	Max Degree	Slope[65]	R-Squared	Dynamicity
AGARRAR	6.08	29	0.210	0.55	Dynamic
COGER	14.05	21	0.670	0.43	Directed
DAR	0.89	42	0.021	0.30	Dynamic
ESTAR	0.661	46	0.014	0.18	Static
HACER	0.612	41	0.015	0.35	Dynamic
IR	0.400	42	0.010	0.17	Dynamic
LLEGAR	4.490	35	0.130	0.43	Directed
QUEDAR	3.140	25	0.120	0.29	Static
REGRESAR	26.290	22	1.194	0.69	Directed
SER	0.06	41	0.002	0.02	Static
TENER	0.562	46	0.012	0.25	Static

Significant differences between slopes according to the dynamicity are found (Fig. 61). The estimate for directed concepts is at 0.55 (SE = 0.15), which is modulated by dynamic concepts by -0.53 (SE = 0.23, $t = -2.31$, $p < 0.05$) and by static concepts by -0.51 (SE = 0.21, $t = -2.39$, $p < 0.05$). However, The ANOVA test comparing the model as a whole didn't yield significant results ($F(2,8) = 3.79$, $p = 0.06$). Therefore, the null hypothesis is maintained, meaning that no impact of concept dynamicity on the slope is assumed.

65 Coefficient of the model relative to the maxmium node degree. This renders coefficients comparable on a normalised scale.

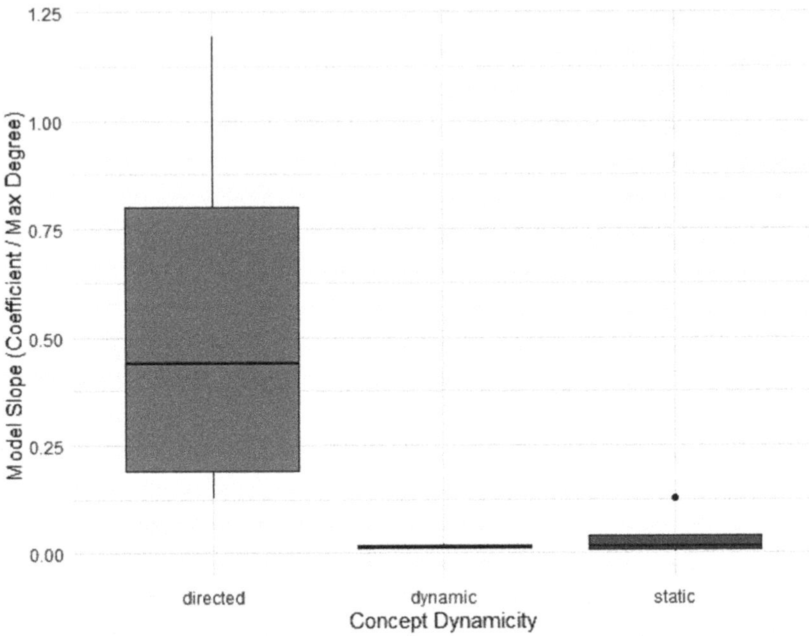

Fig. 61: Comparison between slopes by concept dynamicity. The directed concepts yield higher (and more spread out) slopes. The model didn't yield significant results at a threshold of α = 95 %.

The ANOVA testing the differences between concepts models' R^2, on the other hand, yielded significant results ($F(2,8) = 9.2$, $p < 0.01$). The null hypothesis is thus rejected. The alternative hypothesis is that concept dynamicity impacts the amount of variance in the data that is explained by each concept model (Fig. 62). Furthermore, the model estimate indicates that the R^2 of directed concept models is at 0.52 (SE = 0.05) and that it is modulated by dynamic concepts by -0.25 (SE = 0.09, $t = -2.89$, $p < 0.5$) and by static concepts by -0.34 (SE = 0.08, $t = -4.18$, $p < 0.01$).

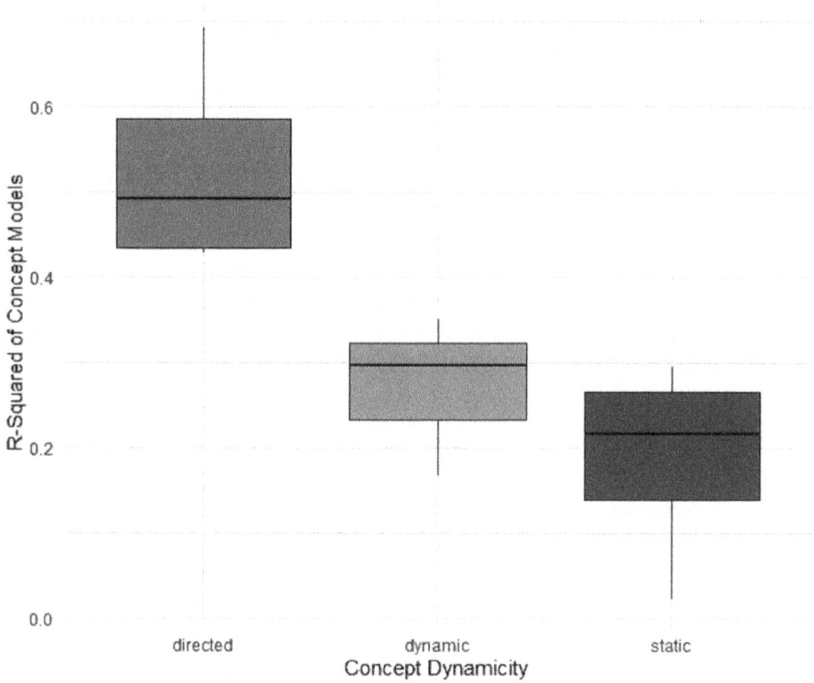

Fig. 62: Comparison of R squared values of models according to concept dynamicity.

8.4. Discussion

The third experiment has brought forth a series of insights into the lexical or semantic mechanisms by which information is spread through networks on a local level. It was found that different non-domain-specific verbs contribute with different strengths to the creation of high-degree nodes, that is nodes that have many neighbours. The underlying assumption is that nodes with many neighbours contain content that other users on social media platforms like Hispachan want to engage with. It was shown that the degree to which the appearance of domain-unspecific words contributes to such an enhanced engagement diverges, sometimes strongly. However, for all the verbs that were investigated, *agarrar, coger, dar, estar, hacer, ir, llegar, quedar, regresar, ser, tener,* except for *tomar,* did to more or lesser extent contribute to this. This corroborates other findings (e.g., Ströbel 2018) in that sensorimotor concepts can be and are used for persuasion or the creation of engagement. While her study offers an account of political language and persuasion techniques, it can still be argued that content on sites such as Hispachan is highly politicised and penetrated by persuasion techniques (Escandell-Montiel 2016). The analogy might therefore not be altogether inadequate. More importantly, a network approach to measuring such lexical effects on an anonymised platform that doesn't offer users ways to engage with the identity of a post rather than its content renders such effects measurable as a function of a node's degree. The embedding of such lexical approximations in a network-based framework has thus proven to be rather useful, while the network aspect is less obvious in this experiment than in the first one. This experiment is, after all, focused on local-level interactions in linguistic interaction networks.

Not only could it be determined that non-domain-specific sensorimotor concepts affect the creation of high-degree nodes to varying degrees, but it was in part shown that grouping the verbs by their dynamicity as proposed in Ströbel (2014) does affect these differences. The first ANOVA test on the models, comparing the percentages by which an increase in concept probability would affect the increase in node degree, didn't yield significant results. However, the test was conducted on a limited number of twelve data points, namely the verbs that could be generated based on the previous work (Ströbel 2011, 2014). Furthermore, the verb *tomar* had to be excluded from this analysis as its initial model wasn't significant, reducing the final analysis to eleven data points. Comparison of distributions of three and four values respectively are rather unlikely to yield significant results. Given this low number, a p-value cut-off at 90 % might have also been justifiable (Lakens et al. 2018). In any case, the data come close to statistical significance and the distributions appear to be rather different. In particular, it appears that the directed verbs are the most likely to enhance engagement with posts in the network. This is corroborated by comparing the models' R-squared which did yield significant results on all accounts. In particular, a significant difference is found between directed concepts and the other two categories, dynamic and static. Since R-squared expresses the variance explained by the model, it is assumed that the models for the directed concepts have less variance and that the contribution of these networks for the enhancement of engagement is stronger than in the case of the other two types.

The direct interpretation of this empirical finding is that only directed sensorimotor dynamicity sets itself apart as a mechanism for degree enhancement in this comparison, meaning that the dynamic mode has no (or very little) upside as compared to the static mode. In the bigger scheme of things, this could be indicative of the fading[66] (Ströbel 2014) of sensorimotor strategies as they become more grammaticalized, and therefore lose their power to provoke more local interaction. This was also the reason why *dar*, in the classification of the words under investigation, was placed into the dynamic category. The particular reasons for this in the case of the Spanish language were the reported frequency effects on *dar* (García-Salido 2017) in Spanish which have turned it into a causative construction. While this deviates from the classification put forth by Ströbel (2014), it doesn't contradict her findings as language-specific effects can modulate the dynamicity of verbs (Ströbel 2020). The effects found comparing models under the established classification suggest that this is indeed the case and that furthermore, neither the engagement heightening phenomena of sensorimotor concepts in local interaction nor the fading of the efficacy of such strategies are contradicted by the data of this experiment.

Now, the account of sensorimotor dynamicity (Ströbel 2011) is particularly connected to issues of grammaticalization, as she points out in her later work (Ströbel 2014). She argues that the fading expressivity of sensorimotor concepts in linguistic evolution is linked to more grammatical expressions. More grammatical expressions are more widely used and yield less expressivity, leading to lower engagement by participants in linguistic interaction networks. This is consistent with the higher number of occurrences overall of static and dynamic expressions in the experiment, as opposed to directed sensorimotor concepts. Invoking a network account of language, it can be argued that linguistic expressions in such interaction networks are functionally adapted (Baicchi 2015) to the augmentation of interaction on a local level. This is the stance that the data from experiment three supports. However, the data doesn't address the question of how locally adaptive communication strategies then grammaticalize. For grammaticalization to take place, the expressions would have to be propagated into the entire system. While local adaptation is the first step toward propagation, the stabilisation of a phenomenon across a bigger network warrants the opposite pressure. Grammatical forms have to be systematic, rather than locally expressive. This is the point for both the language-specific evidence from Romance (Meillet 1912, 1928; Ströbel 2011, 2014) and from the cross-linguistic observation which states that bigger communities (i.e., networks) create more systematic languages (Lupyan & Dale 2010), which has also been corroborated experimentally (Raviv et al. 2019). Furthermore, the data that is offered in this account is entirely local and synchronic, because the verbal behaviour of participants in linguistic

66 From German: "Abnutzung".

interaction networks is confined to a very tight time window of a couple of hours or even minutes (cf. Bernstein et al. 2011). Even with contributions stretching various days, weeks, months or even years, the interpretation of such data in terms of linguistic change, let alone linguistic evolution, is not externally valid. At least, the data doesn't contradict the predictions in that the locally identified behaviour would in principle allow for subsequent processes of linguistic change and evolution to take place.

A particular issue that has to be addressed is the provenance of the data, just as much as in the case of experiment one. The reason to base the experiment on data from Hispachan was its anonymity. It was thus possible to separate identity bias from topology and content bias. However, this means dealing with data from a highly specific context, which is highly politicised (Escandell-Montiel 2016) and where political radicalisation, in particular right-wing radicalisation, often takes place (Knuttila 2011; Nagle 2017; Torres-Nabel 2017; Tuters & Hagens 2020). This is, at least in part, a result of the anonymous nature of this imageboard. It is therefore difficult to extrapolate findings to other types of interactions. One argument in favour of such extrapolation could be that experiments two and three disambiguate linguistic expressions that are confined to this political space (*negro*, *anon*, *kek*) from domain-unspecific verbs which are frequent in any type of interaction. Findings from responses to terrorist attacks on Twitter, on the other hand, have suggested differences between the emotional structure of responses to such events, according to the political affiliation of users. In particular, tweets under the islamophobic hashtag *#StopIslam* have been shown to be more negative and aroused as compared to tweets of solidarity under hashtags such as *#PrayForBarcelona* (Castro-Toledo et al. 2020). The same group reported that arousal and polarity (i.e., positivity vs. negativity) of tweets also affects the perception of readers on social media, most notably that high-arousal tweets can drive readers toward a higher propensity to fear of crime or fear of terrorism (Gretenkort et al. in press). Now, while linguistic sentiment isn't the same as sensorimotor concepts, it has been suggested that language integrates both emotive and sensorimotor processes into semantic processes (Newcombe et al. 2012; Davis et al. 2017). Thus, the findings from this experiment might well be confined to the political realm or more generally speaking to types of discourse in which opinions are more opposing and controversial in nature. Also, the predictions of this experiment are based on a sensorimotor account (Ströbel 2011, 2014), which in its concrete application to text corpora was hitherto confined to political speech (Ströbel 2018, 2019). It is, in any case, encouraging that the postulation of sensorimotor mechanisms in linguistic change in conjunction with a theory of linguistic change in networks yields interesting results on a local level. Future investigations could deepen insights into such mechanisms by tracing the use of sensorimotor concepts along network paths, that is, by investigating how exactly the use of a given word moves along different nodes and whether or not they are picked up on by direct neighbours as well. This, however, entails expanding the paradigm used in this study, because it requires the use of directed networks rather than undirected networks. Hopefully, this paradigm will be of enough interest to generate subsequent research in this direction.

9. General Discussion

This dissertation set out to investigate network effects in linguistic interaction networks. In other words, are there phenomena that cannot be accounted for without representing linguistic interaction in the form of networks? And do the interaction networks behave as would be suggested from the simulation and experimental literature? To solve these questions, some elements of a network theory of linguistic interaction networks were proposed and attempted to be observed in linguistic data that is available online, specifically on the Spanish-speaking imageboard Hispachan. While the experiments were already discussed in isolation in each of their corresponding chapters, the general discussion will examine the overall success of the research project. Firstly, the success of the underlying analogy between DLT and linguistic processes will be evaluated, along with the question of whether or not it contributes novel information to the study of language(s). Secondly, the most relevant identified effects will be discussed, that is network effects on a local and global level, highlighting avenues for further investigation on the same, or similar datasets. In the description of these effects, the arguments from the discussions above will be contrasted with other elements, such as information from the data description. Afterwards, a short conclusion will highlight the value of this contribution to the field of linguistics.

9.1. Adding to the Network Approach to Language – Ecological Validity

This study set out to investigate the use of network theory for the study of linguistic phenomena. As the literature review revealed, this is by no means a new endeavour. Four major fields of relevance were described: Formal Linguistics, Linguistic Typology, Socio-Linguistics, and Linguistic Evolution. In all of these fields, applications of network theory are to some degree or another a relevant part of the existing literature. Where this study differs from other approaches, is its application to corpus data, structuring the corpus in terms of linguistic interaction networks, modelling each post and comment as a node, while an edge indicates which other node the comment is a reply to. The method adds to the existing body of literature, the relevance of which will be expanded on in the conclusion (Chapter 10).

More importantly, the study of networks on linguistic phenomena has shown that there are phenomena that cannot be reduced to the description of individual linguistic agents. In particular, the emergentist and CAS literature (Beckner et al. 2009) has already widely suggested that the emergence of social artefacts such as grammars (Lee et al. 2005), lexical conventions (Centola & Baronchelli 2015), and combinatorial linguistic structure (Raviv et al. 2020) is dependent on the graph-theoretic properties of the network in which these social artefacts emerge. In this particular case, such effects were also shown on a small scale, namely in interaction networks in the anonymous (Bernstein et al. 2011) online social network Hispachan. This differs significantly from the other paradigms in that the language in this corpus is already pre-established and not meant to emerge as a result of the experiment. Since Spanish already exists as a language, such a corpus can give more ecologically valid insights into how the effects described in the literature play out 'in the wild'. One important difference is that Spanish, as a natural language, is far less prone to observable effects of linguistic evolution on the spot because the constraints that the linguistic system puts on its usage are bigger than in the case of laboratory languages (Roberts 2017). While the latter are designed to change under laboratory manipulations, the former are characterised by a great deal of systematicity and stability. It is hence important to show that network effects, as predicted from graph theory, simulations, and human experiments can be found in natural language(s). This circumstance is underlined by the fact that the interactions recorded in the corpus are entirely local, while most of the cited literature (except Raviv et al. 2020) involves large-scale simulation and/or experimentation, with many trials and iterations. The current study is focused on the network properties of local interactions, and two of the experiments were designed to specifically dig into the mechanisms of local strategies for enhancing engagement. As the following section will show, even the global effects of the number of nodes and network diameter can be accounted for in terms of the effects of consensus in the direct vicinity of nodes. This study, therefore, supplies interesting hints for connecting the large-scale effects of different network topologies with the local behaviour of nodes in terms of natural language.

9.2. Internal and External Validity – Adequacy of the Blockchain Semiotics

Now, the bigger question is whether an approach ranging from an analogy to DLT to measurements of the creation of high-degree nodes in local interaction networks is adequate. That is, does this analogy contribute to the study of language at all, or is such a perspective adding unwarranted baggage to explaining linguistic phenomena? In terms of scientific history, it was shown for two pertinent examples, the Poetic Function of Language, and Generative Grammar, that such technological analogies are not only common but highly productive for the generation of new linguistic theories. The question is whether the analogy to DLT can achieve something similar.

As reported above, many researchers have incorporated methods from graph theory into models of linguistics. A wide range of linguistic subdisciplines has taken up the task of modelling linguistic data in such a way. But by reporting these contributions under the umbrella of a technological analogy, the following question could be addressed meaningfully. How is the notion of networks plotted onto linguistic phenomena? *Grosso modo*, three tendencies were identified. Firstly, networks are used as more sophisticated versions of trees. Both can be explained in terms of graph theory, and both are useful for plotting phylogenetic relationships between different languages. In such networks, languages are plotted as nodes, and edges represent phylogenetic relations between these languages (Bowern 2009, 2010; Bakker et al. 2011). Cognitive theories of language make use of networks by plotting lexical items as nodes and syntactic relationships between these items as edges, attempting to model linguistic cognition in terms of networks (Beckage & Colunga 2016). Since the connectionist models have gained a lot of territory in psychological sciences in the past decades (e.g., McCloskey 1991), it was natural for a cognitive theory of language to incorporate such network or connection models into their theory (Pater 2019). This comes naturally to a theory such as generative grammar because, again, syntactic trees had already been an accepted model for grammar, and networks merely represent a more complex version of such models. But in these theories, it is not always clear what is meant by "relationship" that is, what network edges represent. While some studies use edges to represent phonetic similarity (e.g., Vitevitch 2008; Vitevitch et al. 2016), others use them to represent dependencies (e.g., Ferrer-i-Cancho 2016).

Lastly, theories of socio-linguistics (e.g., Labov 2001; Milroy 2002) and social cognition (e.g., Centola et al. 2015; Raviv et al. 2020) use networks to plot agents as nodes and interactions between these agents as edges. While these theories mostly follow this assumption, there are still important differences. For instance, in modelling the interaction on social media, should accounts be modelled as nodes and friend requests as edges, or should single posts be regarded as nodes and replies to these posts as edges, with a new node at the other end? These types of networks were differentiated as social networks and linguistic interaction networks for this study, while the current study itself makes use of the latter.

Invoking an analogy between language and DLT, and working out this analogy to a degree of fine granularity, ultimately permitted this level of scrutiny of the reviewed literature. That is because the analogy itself forces the researcher to assess the adequacy of the metaphor in any given instance. As such, the analogy has been rather successful in enabling this level of metaphoric analysis of network models.

Furthermore, the analogy between DLT and language forced the study to ponder some of the more fundamental semiotic properties of human language and computer systems. While some commonalities were found, such as the assumption of distributed control (cf. Beckner et al. 2009) to achieve consensus in a strong or a weak sense, differences were found at the level of individual semiotic capacities. In particular, it was argued that human semiotic behaviour cannot be reduced to less than a triadic form of representation (Spielmann 2004), while computer systems, on which DLT operate, are sufficiently well characterised by a dyadic model of representation (Section 1.3.1). In pursuing this argument further, it was also determined that information in DLT is entirely self-contained and that meaning emerges from operations within the DLT and within the DLT alone (Section 1.3.3). Language on the other hand, while certainly capable of immense semiotic leaps in the form of self-contained phenomena such as Unlimited Semiosis (Eco 1990), does present an important element of grounding. Language is first and foremost a tool for collective navigation in the world and linguistic phenomena are hence contingent on ecological (Nölle et al. 2020), cultural (Tylén et al. 2013), and cognitive properties (Culbertson et al. 2012, 2013). This means that linguistic arbitrariness, under careful examination isn't absolute anymore (Dingemanse et al. 2015). While these are theoretical considerations, they are deeply relevant for this study, because they allowed for the selection of those elements that were to be investigated in terms of network structure. Rather than choosing to represent unconscious matter in terms of networks, these arguments provided reasons to choose a social approach over a cognitive mechanistic approach to language. The examination of networks in terms of meaning-making was thus an important requirement for the adequate design of this study.

What's more, the analogy between language and DLT has provided concrete tools for the study of language. In concrete, the notion of consensus and its achievement in different types of network topologies allowed for a comparison of such topologies (or proxies thereof) in concrete communicative situations (Chapter 4). Furthermore, knowledge of the *Byzantine Generals Problem* and the formal requirements of consensus enabled a criterion for the lack of systematic differences in the study conducted by Raviv et al. (2020), which could hopefully be elucidated by the formal argument made above (Section 3.3.3). What was mostly gained from the study of an analogy between language and DLT in conjunction with CAS approaches to language is the strong interaction between the local and the global level in such networks. The mechanisms that govern local strategies can influence outcomes for the whole of the network, while global phenomena such as the makeup of the network itself put constraints on the possibilities that are given to users at a local level.

9.3. Global Graph Topologies and Lack of Distributed Control

One of the strongest claims to be generated from both the linguistic and informatics literature on networks is that graph topology has an impact on the information that flows through a network. In particular, graph topologies affect how consensus can be achieved (Lamport et al. 1982) and have an impact on the emergence of social and/or linguistic conventions without centralised control (Centola & Baronchelli 2015). One of the initial goals of this thesis was to determine such differences between network topologies. Specifically, it was assumed that centralised, decentralised, linear, and distributed network typologies would differ in terms of the number of topics that are entertained in these networks. Such a test, however, wasn't feasible due to the empirical makeup of the data.

Data from online social networks such as Hispachan shows that certain network typologies in interaction are more prevalent than others. In particular, centralised and decentralised network topologies of interactions appear with similar relative frequency, while there is only a small number of linear networks, and no instance of a properly distributed network could be found. While this was a hindrance to the above-formulated intuition, this is a finding in its own right. Comments on Hispachan are usually made in reply to one other comment (or the original post), instead of replying to various other posts at a time. This is not as trivial a finding as it seems. While online social networks such as Twitter, utilizing the *reply* function, only allow directly replying to one tweet, comments on Hispachan can refer to more than one previous post at the same time by including the post ID manually in the comment text (Fig. 63). This possibility, however, is rarely used in the corpus that was generated for this study. So, the local verbal behaviour of participants in this particular instance of linguistic interaction networks is mostly directed toward one other person, resulting in interaction networks lacking distributed control.

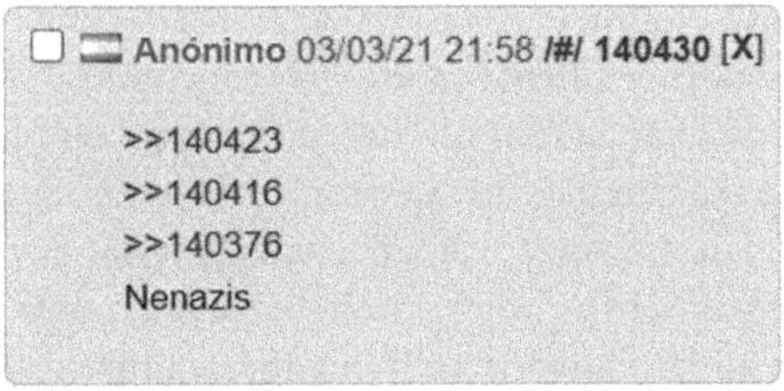

Fig. 63: Example of a node with degree > 1 in an interaction network. By manually including the IDs (140423, 140416, 140376) of previous contributions to the interaction network, this user (140430) creates a node in reply to not only one, but three other users whom he insults as "nenazis". This contraction of "nenas" (i.e., babies (f.)) and "nazis" (or also as a contamination of "nenazas" or "cry-babies") is here used against individuals that project racist and anti-semitic resentment onto their surroundings out of pity for their own life.

It is an open question whether this type of network typology is the default in online communication. Taking into account that *reply* functions in online social networks are usually designed such that one can reply to one post, this might be the case. But it still is an empirical question. If this was the case, it could be hypothesised that the lack of distributed control allows for phenomena such as hate speech and violent communication, as reported in the case of Spanish (Miró-Llinares 2016) and English (Chetty & Alathur 2018), or other anomalies of Internet communication. It was shown that distributed control is one of the main characteristics of social networks and that it allows for the creation of social rules that are agreed upon by participants (Centola & Baronchelli 2015). It is reasonable to assume that networks that lacked this distributional property would differ in the way that social norms and conventions are enacted by and enforced on individuals in these networks. In the literature, it was argued that the main difference between *4chan* (and thus Hispachan) and other online social networks is its highly anonymised nature (Escandell-Montiel 2016). To rephrase the argument in terms of linguistic network theory, the identity bias in non-anonymised online social media networks mediates the behaviour of participants in such networks, because they know they can be made accountable for their expressions under their identity. Hence, in order to exercise successful reputation management (cf. Tennie et al. 2010), users cannot afford to cross too many communicative lines. However, violent communication in online social media under clear names can also be observed (Miró-Llinares 2016; Chetty & Alathur 2018). It is thus posited that another effect is at work when disinhibiting the use of radicalised language, namely the absence of distributed control. It is proposed that when interactions are frequent, distributed, and have a high network density, the steady mutual correction and interaction among participants in linguistic interaction networks could lead to the containment of such expressions because it is confronted with more opposing opinions. It appears that studies from behavioural economics support this argument. Well-connected minorities can tilt consensus in a whole network in their favour (Kearns et al. 2009). It is possible that interaction networks lacking distributed control altogether are susceptible to adapting to extreme stimuli, which are not mitigated by interaction and contrast with other opinions, or that they don't adapt to anything within a social norm, whatever the shape of this social norm. In other words, non-distributed networks, and therefore Internet communication, by and large, might just be unsuitable for attaining social norms, not solely due to the absence of face (i.e., anonymity), but also due to the architecture of the communication in terms of network properties itself. While proving this idea is out of the scope of this study, it is an interesting avenue for future research, especially concerning the specific question of whether or not political radicalisation in communication can be prevented by incentivising more distributed modes of communication.

While the observation of the lack of distribution in online linguistic interaction networks is meaningful on its own, it was a hindrance to the analysis. The direct comparison between different network topologies and the number of topics in the corresponding network didn't yield any meaningful results. The different topologies don't appear in similar frequencies, making the comparison unfeasible. On the other hand, the different network topologies are co-occurrent with the number of nodes, as was described in the descriptive statistics (Section 5.4). In particular, networks with more nodes tended to be decentralised while smaller networks tended to be centralised (Fig. 40). But a significant problem here is that centralised and decentralised topologies are formally not too different from one another. Thus, instead of treating centralisation and decentralisation as categories, proxies had to be found to quantify centralisation and disentangle it from the number of nodes. The number of nodes and diameter were identified as useful proxies for the investigation of network typologies, and a significant relationship between these variables and the number of topics was identified (Fig. 52). In particular, it was shown that an increase in either the number of nodes or an increase in diameter leads to a higher number of topics when the other measure doesn't increase. However, when increasing both the diameter and the number of nodes, the number of topics in the network doesn't increase. This finding corroborates the argument made above, namely that nodes in non-distributed networks only agree locally on the topics that they talk about. This corroborates the findings of Lee et al. (2005) and Centola and Baronchelli (2015), who identify patches of local agreement in linear networks (Fig. 24b) and one-dimensional lattices (Fig. 28a) respectively. In this sense, both centralised and decentralised interaction networks can only maintain topic coherence in close vicinities. The illustration below (Fig. 64) then explains why this phenomenon reduces the number of topics in networks with a high number of nodes and a high diameter. While a small number of nodes converging on one central node (a small number of nodes with a small diameter) converge on fewer topics, an increase in either nodes or diameter means the addition of topics. When both variables increase at the same time, fewer additional topics are identified. This can be explained in terms of local topic alignment alone, as the circles in the figure indicate. No circle covers an area of more than six nodes or a diameter bigger than two. Thus, local topic alignment alone is sufficient to account for the relationship between the variables.

Again, while the study didn't set out to observe these relations, these observations are rather insightful with regard to the type of agreement that dialogue in Internet forums allows for. While distributed communication networks are known to work, it is interesting to see how decentralised control works in online social networks. It appears that patches of local agreement (Lee et al. 2005; Centola & Baronchelli 2015) are sufficient to explain global effects on centralised and decentralised communication architectures. Again, this feeds into the above-formulated idea that Internet communication might be unsuitable for the creation of social conventions altogether, at least at the level of linguistic interaction. This, however, would contradict sociological contributions which claim that the enhanced connectivity among people over the Internet effectively creates new shared identities (Mancera-Rueda 2016). This claim, however, hasn't been uncontested (e.g., Ellison & Boyd 2013). Furthermore, the arguments might not be incompatible. Wherever Internet communication allows for distributed control in interaction, social conventions might be feasible. But it appears that a lack thereof in local interaction networks effectively leads to higher toxicity in communication.

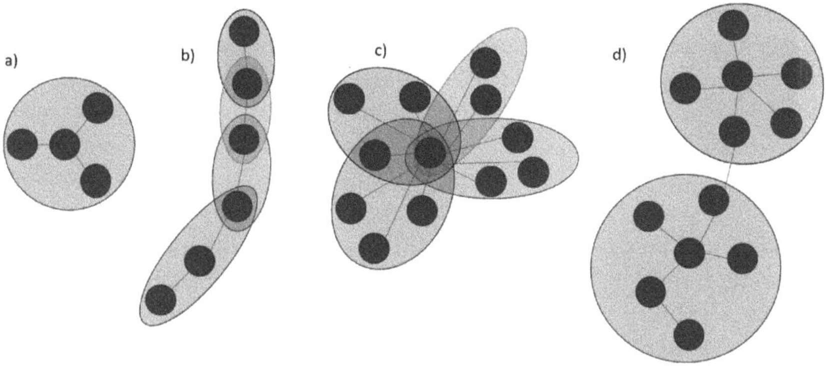

Fig. 64: Topics (circles) in different network topologies as described by the number of nodes and diameter. (a) few nodes ($|N| = 4$) with low diameter ($\delta = 2$) present few topics ($|T| = 1$) (b) few nodes ($|N| = 6$) with high diameter ($\delta = 6$) present many topics ($|T| = 4$) (c) many nodes ($|N| = 12$) with low diameter ($\delta = 2$) present many topics ($|T| = 4$) (d) many nodes ($|N| = 12$) with high diameter ($\delta = 7$) present few topics ($|T| = 2$). This figure is based on the statistical relationship to be found between the variables in the model and serves the purpose of illustration.

It is not clear how the rather divergent representation of communities with regard to network topology fits into the picture. It was shown that in certain communities, in particular in K, Q, M, and T, a centralised communication architecture is much more common than in other communities on Hispachan. It is noteworthy that these communities are based on specific topics rather than Spanish-speaking regions. While the effect of this circumstance on the network topology is significant (Section 5.4.2), the mechanism behind this isn't clear. However, this information is highly relevant for the interpretation of the role of network topology on communication and *vice versa*. It appears that the networks which occur in communication are not randomly distributed, but that certain affordances of the topics that are treated in such communities do have an impact on how the communication is structured. This speaks to the relevance of content bias also identified elsewhere (Tamariz et al. 2014; Segovia-Martín et al. 2020). While these contributions are concerned with the propagation of content across networks that already exist, here the content appears to determine how the network turns out to be structured. Something similar was observed by Kwon et al. (2013). They observe that the propagation of rumours creates different network structures from non-rumours. Apparently, not all types of content create the same network structures, also on Hispachan. While the presence of this effect in the data can be comfortably reported, the specific mechanism behind this is still unclear and opens up new avenues of research. Why do participants in networks about topics such as Economy, LGBT+, Meta (i.e., the imageboard itself) and Technology generate interactions that are more centralised and shorter, while the overall number of nodes in these boards doesn't differ significantly? This question cannot be answered by the data generated from this study. Hopefully, future investigations will clarify this point.

Most importantly, the different distributions of topologies in different communities speak to the relevance of network topology. While the correlation between network topology and the number of nodes could be taken as an argument to reduce the effects of network topology to effects of network size, two important findings speak against this. First of all, pairing network size with diameter yielded a more powerful model to predict the number of topics in an interaction network. Secondly, the differences in distributions of topologies across different types of communities suggest that topology represents a phenomenon in its own right since it is dissociated from the number of nodes in such communities. It is therefore suggested that the properties of networks, even when lacking distributed control, have an impact on the communication that takes place in such networks. In particular, these effects are attributed to the importance of local agreement. While distributed control over the networks (Beckner et al. 2009) could allow for more stable consensus, the networks under investigation only present local consensus, leading to the effects observed in the data, the implications of which for Internet communication, in general, were discussed in the previous paragraphs. In particular, it is highlighted that anonymity is not the only reason for the type of communication that takes place on such imageboards, but that the lack of distributed control plays an important role in Internet communication as a whole.

9.4. Local Effects and Alternative Communication Strategies

Global network effects make an excellent case for the use of network approaches in linguistics because they exemplify phenomena that can only be explained in the light of a network framework. But local communication strategies benefit from a more general framework of networks in linguistics too, as experiments two and three have shown. Both experiments were based on the identification of lexical items that enhance the local connectivity of nodes. The underlying question is whether certain lexical items enhance engagement with its content, and therefore increase the degree (i.e., number of neighbours) of the corresponding node in the network. This perspective only takes into account the direct environment of the node, and hence it might be argued that a network approach is an additional baggage to effects that can well be accounted for on a local level. The preceding section on global network effects (Section 9.2) has also pointed to the possibility that, in the absence of distributed control, all phenomena can be accounted for through the local cohesion of interaction, thus rendering an overly emphasis on global network structure more complicated than necessary. It is argued, however, that this is not the case as the local and global levels are intricately connected and that phenomena which spark on the global level necessarily originate on the local level, while not being reducible to the latter.

In particular, local competition for engagement with the published content leads to a network effect that is consistent with the 'rich-get-richer' principle which has been abundantly described in the literature (e.g., Zipf 1949; Easley & Kleinberg 2010; Cunha et al. 2011). In particular, it was shown that the distribution of degrees in the network follows a power-law distribution, with very few nodes accounting for much of the connectivity (Section 5.4.4). This descriptive finding is consistent with the degree distribution bias that was formulated above. Also, in linguistic interaction networks, few nodes appear to be highly connected while many nodes are poorly connected (Section 5.4.4). It appears that this is an effect of the competition of content for the attention (and thus engagement) of other participants on the imageboard. The result of such attention-seeking strategies is that only a few nodes succeed in generating high engagement, as is expected in social networks. This finding is important because it speaks to the reality of human social networks. For example, Raviv et al. (2020) attempt to find differences in semiotic behaviour between groups with very subtle experimental manipulation. They try to identify differences between networks in which node degrees are evenly distributed and those in which nodes follow a power-law distribution. Independently of their findings, the results from the current study seem to indicate that the latter case is the one that emerges naturally in interaction and that this is the situation under which human languages develop.

Having said that, there are of course important differences between linguistic interaction networks in data from online social networks and actual social networks and human interaction. It isn't clear *a priori* whether the finding can be extrapolated to local, let alone global interactions between humans outside of cyberspace, or even outside of online social networks with such special affordances as *4chan* and Hispachan. But it is reasonable to assume that empirical social networks follow a process of preferential attachment (cf. Kearns et al. 2006) rather than tending toward equal connectivity.

This empirical finding is in itself an important hint for further research and helps generate future hypotheses for the formation of networks. But most importantly, this is a network effect that is intricately linked to local behaviour. Whether a node engages with another node is not a question of global effects. A node doesn't seek to find a free node to attach to in the network. Rather, it attaches to the node with which it aims to interact based on content. After all, there are human agents behind these nodes, which make decisions of engagement with the text. The identity of a user is precluded from another user, which is why the primacy of content in the decision of node attachment is assumed here. Also, unlike other online social networks such as Twitter or Facebook, Hispachan doesn't show any metrics for the previous engagement with a piece of content. The 'rich-get-richer' principle can be explained on Twitter quite easily on a local level. Users tend to retweet or respond to tweets that already have generated a lot of engagement. On Hispachan, this sort of behaviour is not possible, because the platform doesn't nudge users with such metrics. Only the central comment is slightly more visually salient in a thread, which explains the relatively high number of centralised comment topologies. However, a big number of decentralised interaction networks, especially in the region-based communities (Section 5.4.2) is recorded. Thus, it is argued that the local decision for interaction is mainly based on node content. Hence, effects like the power-law degree distribution cannot be explained only in terms of local behaviour and engagement decisions.

Rather, specific content mechanisms need to be at work to generate this type of effect on a global scale. From a linguistic standpoint, especially one that focuses on a specific language, a vast array of possible analyses is possible. In discovering these possibilities, it was decided to follow one pragmatic and one lexical approach. The pragmatic approach was used to investigate domain-specific signalling of identity. The use of words such as *anon*, *negro*, and *kek* was interpreted, based on the literature (Bernstein et al. 2011; Papasavva et al. 2020; Tuters & Hagens 2020) as a pragmatic marker of identity signalling. It is highly context-sensitive in that it is only useful on this particular online social network and is, as was argued above, a pragmatic reaction to the absence of identity, thus disabling facework (cf. Goffman 1955) and reputation management (cf. Tennie et al. 2010) through personal information or accumulated behaviour. As Bernstein et al. (2011) point out, this circumstance forces users to signal their belonging to the community in other ways.

To investigate whether such strategies contribute to the type of degree distribution observed above, their local success was investigated. Experiment two thus measured whether the use of the terms *anon*, *negro,* and *kek* led to higher engagement. Clear correlations for all three concepts, but with different effect sizes, were identified. In particular, it was shown that nodes with higher degrees had a higher probability of containing such lexical items. Most of the very few nodes with high degrees contain these terms, especially *anon* and *negro*. This is taken as an indication that this signalling technique contributes to the preferential attachment of further nodes to the node containing this signal, even though it may not be reproduced in the commenting node. Again, it is underlined here that this effect is not just a question of 'rich-get-richer' in the sense that many replies to nodes will attract more nodes. Rather, the content of such nodes determines high engagement with them. Furthermore, there is a difference in the workings between these domain-specific terms and other popular topics such as *Corona*. This topic appears with a similar relative frequency to the domain-specific pragmatic signals but behaves rather differently. While an increase in the topic *Corona* also potentially increases the number of neighbours, the effect wears off with increasing probability. That is, even high-degree nodes have a relatively low probability of containing the topic *Corona*. The logarithmic nature of this relationship indicates that the topic doesn't contribute in the same way to the creation of high-degree nodes as the other words do. Still, a stable and statistically significant relationship is detected. This might be indicative of the propagation of this topic. While high-degree nodes do contain the topic, thus creating highly centralised interaction networks with the *Corona* topic at the centre, the word might not be picked up to the same degree as it is present in the original contribution. This makes sense in so far as *Corona*, once established as a topic in a given interaction network, needs no further explicit mentioning, while the absence of accounts for users does push users to reiterate their belonging to the imageboard's community by signalling their identity.

These findings do not extrapolate to any other platform, because the terms under investigation are native to Hispachan and its Anglophone counterpart *4Chan*. But these contextually embedded strategies do shed some light on the contribution of local communication strategies for the entirety of the network. In particular, the differences in the quality of content lead to a degree distribution in which very few nodes are responsible for most of the connections in the networks, meaning that immense communicative power lies with individuals who manage to manipulate content in this way. Furthermore, the study by Kearns et al. (2006) has shown that such small numbers of powerful individuals can hugely affect consensus, or discourse for that matter, when they are well connected among each other and when few connections exist between the other individuals. In light of the findings discussed above (Section 9.2), this ultimately appears to underline the fact that communication on the Internet is not suitable for balanced communication shielded from the influence of radicalised individuals. It appears as though such networks, both in terms of their network architecture (lack of distributed control) and in terms of the role that few individuals with great skill for the manipulation of content and the resulting engagement, are very susceptible to influence by well-connected extremist groups. *Extremist* is here used in a rather neutral way. Extremist can mean a small group that carries a cultural variant that is very different from the variants that otherwise exist in the network (cf. Kearns et al. 2006). But it is clear to the author that extremism in this particular dataset is to be taken literally, as such tendencies have been reported for the dataset under investigation (e.g., Knuttila 2011; Hine et al. 2017; Nagle 2017; Tuters & Hagen 2020). One plausible mechanism is the fact that extremist groups have an important incentive to be well-connected and attract a lot of attention, while individuals that don't want to engage with their positions can just abandon the network or move toward other platforms, further handing power to extremist groups.

Experiment three concentrated on a similar type of phenomenon but without tapping into the specifics of the imageboard Hispachan. In this experiment, it was attempted to measure the effects of domain-unspecific words, specifically verbs with underlying sensorimotor concepts on the creation of high-degree nodes. It was found that verbs that represent directed movement, in particular *agarrar, coger, llegar,* and *regresar*, contributed more to the creation of high-degree nodes in local interaction than other nodes. This was linked to theories of linguistic variation and change (Ströbel 2014), which argue that the underlying expressivity of such verbs, as opposed to static verbs, leads to a higher engagement with these verbs. This is based on the assumption that more expressive verbs engage more responses, which leads them to be successful communicative tools. This is of relevance, not only in linguistic change but also for the engagement of political audiences (Ströbel 2018, 2019). To the extent that this argument concerns local interactions, this could be verified in the corpus. But the arguments put forth by Meillet (1912, 1926) and subsequently Ströbel (2011, 2014) go a lot further. The authors claim that very expressive verbs propagate and generalise in a linguistic community, which then leads them to fade in their expressivity and grammaticalise and systematise over time, as usage increases. Since the data of the current study is highly synchronic, there is no way to address this question directly, but some arguments can be formulated based on this data, by contrasting the data with the arguments put forth in the literature. In particular, this conception of grammaticalisation processes sustains the idea that there are two competing pressures (cf. Beckner et al. 2009) at work, which can only be accounted for if the local and the global level of interaction are distinguished from one another. For linguistic forms to be locally adaptive (cf. Baicchi 2015), the aforementioned authors and the data analysed in this study suggest that expressivity is a key factor. But this concerns only the local level. On the global scale, linguistic expressions have to be the opposite, namely systematic to be sustainable in terms of learnability and regular usage. This is also suggested by observational data which attributes higher systematicity and lower complexity to larger groups of speakers (Lupyan & Dale 2010). This idea has been confirmed in experimental semiotics, where larger groups were shown to develop more systematic combinatorial language systems (Raviv et al. 2019). It thus appears that the local pressure, namely expressivity, and the global pressure, systematicity, compete and regulate each other in the fixation of linguistics systems in groups. While the data from Hispachan only hints directly at the pressure of expressivity on a local level, a CAS approach to language allows for both pressures to be present in linguistic change in social and interaction networks at the same time. But for this conception to hold, any approach to linguistic variation and change needs to disentangle the local and global levels. A network approach to the study of social groups does provide the possibility to distinguish local and global effects, as this study has shown.

This argument is ultimately able to explain why the expressivity of sensorimotor strategies in local discourse fades as a function of time. A hint of this fading effect being at work is provided in the results of experiment three. Only directed sensorimotor concepts are significantly different from dynamic and static concepts, while no difference could be found between dynamic and static concepts. This would indicate that, as Ströbel (2014) proposes, sensorimotor strategies lose weight as one moves down the hierarchy of dynamicity, of which only the highest degree meaningfully contributes to a higher engagement in terms of node degree. The reason that this is measurable is through plotting posts and replies as networks. It is therefore sustained that measuring network properties in interaction is a useful technique for uncovering effects in linguistic data, which can otherwise not be accounted for. Particularly experiment one has shown that the sheer size of communities is not a sufficient predictor of linguistic consensus, because the inclusion of other network parameters such as diameter in this particular case, show to be more explicative of the data in terms of statistical significance. On the other hand, the effects of network size and network structure are difficult to disentangle. As was observed by Trudgill (2009), there is an inherent correlation between network size and social structure, which is also true for the data in this study. In the descriptive analysis of the dataset, it was shown that bigger interaction networks tend to be decentralised, while smaller networks are typically centralised. This has prevented the study from comparing network topologies directly. Thus, it was resorted to constructing a proxy by including network diameter.

In the previous discussion of global effects (Section 9.2), it was already shown how this links back to local effects. An explanation was put forth that connected these global effects to the local behaviour of nodes. It is suggested that interactions with content on online social networks are only planned on a local level, forming strategies for engagement enhancement while this produces large-scale effects. The two levels are intricately linked. Further studies in this direction will have to show whether this paradigm can be expanded on, for instance by tracing the local alignment with a given concept (either sensorimotor or secret handshake) across networks, and evaluating whether linguistic signals are repeated and aligned along network paths in this interaction. What has been shown thus far is that similar quantitative effects of engagement on the local level can have rather different conceptual bases. While both secret handshakes and sensorimotor concepts enhance local engagement with content, the underlying strategies are different. This finding underlines that local strategies while resulting in similar measurable effects in a network on a global scale have to be highly adaptive in their given context.

What's more, it was shown that Hispachan behaves differently from other types of online social networks in terms of the large-scale effects that emerge on this platform. In particular, it was shown by other researchers that such platforms are a breeding ground for radicalised political views (e.g., Knuttila 2011; Hine et al. 2017; Nagle 2017; Tuters & Hagen 2020) and that the lack of control is destructive in terms of political identity. However, this has been largely attributed to anonymity alone, and it was shown here that such networks work very differently from other social networks in terms of technical capabilities (absence of likes and retweets) for local interaction. When communication is bound to such a local realm of communication, where one can only interact with what is put in front of them without further contextual knowledge, this might have an important effect on large-scale phenomena such as radicalisation. It might hence be important to connect the conditions of local interaction to the more global effects that emerge in such media.

10. Conclusion

The use of methods for network analysis is nothing new in linguistics since it has been applied to sociolinguistic phenomena since the 1980s. This study, however, didn't set out to connect previously unconnected fields of investigation. The added value of this doctoral dissertation lies in reviewing and reporting the application of the notion network in the many linguistic subdisciplines and binding them together under a common framework of description. Instead of confining this framework to the exclusively mathematical realm, it was attempted to draw an analogy to DLT, because these technologies are conceptually well-studied and of important societal relevance, especially regarding the fast expansion of such technologies that have already taken place and are to be expected in the future as well. As insights into the study of language and technology from a science historic perspective have shown, such analogies aren't improper, or at least not unusual, in that both Chomsky and Jakobson have taken great inspiration from the works of Turing and Shannon respectively. But human behaviour isn't the same as machine communication, which is why a point was made to assess the semiotic properties of consensus in human groups and distributed systems, to judge if and how far the analogy between these very different types of systems carries.

As for the review of the literature, it is argued that the very basic notions of graph analysis that were put forth in Chapter 2 are of immense utility in disentangling and disambiguating the different types of approaches that are collected under the umbrella network. It was argued that semantic and syntactic networks, although positioned under rather similar axiomatic assumptions in the great scheme of things, can hardly be compared to one another. While both types of networks model lexical units as nodes, it is not homogeneously defined what an edge is – a minimal pair relationship (Vitevitch 2008), semantic similarity (Collins & Loftus 1975), or syntactic dependency (Levy et al. 2012)? Entering the realm of socio-linguistics and social cognition, it was shown that social networks are more well-defined. People are modelled as nodes and interactions between them are edges. It was shown that such a conception of social networks has proven to be very useful for the study of the emergence of social conventions without centralised control (Centola & Baronchelli 2015) and the emergence of linguistic structure and combinatorial syntax in groups modelled as networks (Raviv et al. 2020). There is even a large body of literature that is not concerned at all with social networks as such, but for which the underlying assumptions are of immense importance. The question stands whether different experimental paradigms in cultural evolution (cf. Mesoudi & Whiten 2008; Scott-Philipps & Kirby 2010, Fig. 27) only differ in their quality of modelling human interaction in groups over time, or whether the network properties of these paradigms (i.e., linear cultural transmission, replacement method, closed-group paradigm) affect experimental findings, to begin with. These important experimental findings are accompanied by simulation data, which reveal that agent networks are hugely impacted by global network structure in converging on grammatical (Lee et al. 2005) or cultural items (Segovia-Martín et al. 2020). Such simulations have also shed light on the role of single agents in such networks either for being very popular (Gong et al. 2008) or for being rigid in their opinion (Maity & Mukherjee 2016).

Now, what is the relevance of this doctoral dissertation given the reported literature? Besides the fact that the aforementioned contributions are not very densely connected (in terms of citations) and are here brought into context with one another, this study attempts to use insights from this body of literature in observational data. That is, by reviewing the literature on such global phenomena as linguistic evolution, linguistic change, or population networks, predictions were obtained for the local level of human interaction in a real-world language, namely Spanish. This adds to the ecological validity of experimental and simulation data because theoretically predicted behaviour can be observed in real-life interactions in the Spanish language. The concrete effects were reported and interpreted in the foregoing discussion. But the importance of a detailed study on individual phenomena, even if they are only exemplary as in this case, lies in showing that the analysis of networks is not only useful in large-scale communities but yields similar results on a small scale. The study does subscribe to the position that language is a CAS (Beckner et al. 2009) and hence the replication of large-scale predictions on small-scale observations is a very happy circumstance for the embedding of network analysis in a CAS approach to language because network effects can be shown on different levels of systems.

Furthermore, the corpus obtained for this study is by no means analysed in its entirety. The corpus – published alongside the dissertation – is provided for further investigations in this or other directions, and stands as a research contribution on its own. The corpus is also unique under ethical considerations. One key problem of observational data is the observer's paradox (Labov 1970), namely the circumstance that observed agents behave differently from unobserved agents. Mitigating this paradox by observing agents who don't know that they are observed is under modern research standards regarded as unethical; especially when dealing with personal information that is processed automatically. It is protected under the European General Data Protection Regulation (EU-GDPR). The GDPR especially protects information on individuals with regard to their political inclinations, which is the case dealt with here. However, not only is the data gathered anonymised, but the data source is already fully anonymous, such that there is no conflict between scientific interest and the protection of personal data. Also, from a practical point of view, the use of this anonymous network mitigates the observer's paradox, because users of Hispachan are looking to engage with others, while further processing for scientific purposes is obscured from them.

It was mainly shown that the local and global levels are intricately linked, which means that the disentanglement of these levels is an important endeavour for future linguistic inquiries. It is important to recognise that large-scale network effects, while grounded in local communication strategies, cannot be reduced to theories of individual linguistic behaviour and cognition. Network effects such as the, rich-get-richer principle in node distribution, the effect of network structure on topic consensus, and the effects of enhanced engagement with content are the result of individual behaviour but are emergent global-scale phenomena in their own right. In the face of language as a CAS, this is far from a breakthrough finding, because CAS predicts this exact type of relationship and emergent properties under decentralised and distributed control. However, the current study succeeds in meeting these predictions not only on large-scale phenomena such as linguistic evolution, change and variation but on the level of local interaction, where individual strategies lead to measurable outcomes even in interactions of very small size, that is interactions of only tens to a few hundred contributions. The fact that this study is purely observational, furthermore adds to the ecological validity of previous findings.

However, a caveat on this claim is in order. It is not clear whether the findings generalise to all types of communications. It has been shown that the imageboard Hispachan is very different from other forms of communication in terms of anonymity and the technical capabilities of individuals to interact with one another. Thus, a generalisation of the effects found in all kinds of communication is a slippery slope. But this also shows that large-scale network effects have to be connected to the conditions for local communication. In any case, the findings of engagement-enhancing linguistic behaviours are relevant to the subsequent study of the phenomena of online radicalisation. While other studies have shown that expressivity in terms of emotivity (Castro-Toledo et al. 2020; Gretenkort et al. in press) is connected to perceptions of fear of crime and fear of terrorism, the study of online radicalisation in the future would benefit from adopting techniques of network analysis and the propagation of ideology through online social networks. So, where the very choice of the dataset put constraints on the generalisation of the reported findings, it is highly suggestive of the benefit of its application in this particular field. This is where one of the major contributions of this study can be identified.

Furthermore, while the generalisation of the findings themselves may not be of ground-breaking impact on linguistic theory as a whole, another particular advance has been put forth in terms of the generation of linguistic theories. The study set out to show how linguistic hypotheses can be generated by investigating commonalities and differences between communicative processes in other types of systems. From a science historic standpoint, it was argued that such methods have been in use for the past century, namely by stating that both the Chomskyan theory of grammar and Jakobson's theory of linguistic functions are based on metaphoric analogies between language and technologies, even though these analogies are only made explicit to a small extent. What this study has achieved is give an example of how analogies between language and technological advances can lead to the generation of explicit hypotheses about linguistic phenomena. When studied carefully, and with a sceptical eye for the shortcomings of such an analogy, the comparison between language and other phenomena in the world can lead to the production of hypotheses that can otherwise not be made. Having said this, graph theory has found applications in linguistics before, but it is through the lens of DLT and the *Byzantine Generals Problem* that particular predictions could be made, specifically about the consensus on conversation topics in networks that are big and decentralised at the same time. The human mind is an extraordinary tool for the detection and analysis of patterns and such patterns can replicate through various areas of research.

While the approach to this thesis might appear eclectic, it is maintained that the transfer from one area of expertise to another is beneficial for both areas, be it at least to conclude that the transfer is not feasible. If it is, as is believed to be shown in this study and for the particular case of language and technology, borrowing patterns for new types of investigation is highly productive to inform the field of linguistics. This study thus aims at encouraging future research to carefully examine the underlying framework and linguistic conception, also resorting to knowledge from other areas of investigation. Does language behave similarly to computational systems? Is language exclusively human? Can linguistic phenomena be reduced to mechanistic explanations of either a single mind or an agent network with no regard for the advanced capabilities that every single agent has? Such questions of adequacy of any given framework will provide researchers with better criteria as to the interpretation and extrapolation of their data, especially in light of the highly specialised scientific advances that are made in the past decades, which sometimes obscure the view on the bigger picture. In the spirit of the connection of the global and local level of network effects in linguistic interaction networks, this study encourages questioning the very core assumptions about the nature of language when describing, reporting, and interpreting the results of detailed scientific experiments.

Bibliography

Agarwal A, Xie B, Vovsha I, Rambow O, & Passonneau R (2011) Sentiment Analysis on Twitter Data. *Proceedings of the Workshop on Language in Social Media (LSM 2011)*, pp 30–38.

Agbo CC, Mahmoud QH, & Eklund JM (2019) Blockchain Technology in Healthcare: A systematic Review. *Healthcare 7*(2). Doi: 10.3390/healthcare 7020056.

Antonopoulos AM & Woods G (2018) *Mastering Ethereum—Building Smart Contracts and DAPPS*. Sebastopol, CA: O'Reilly.

Anwar H (2018) Consensus Algorithms: The Root of Blockchain Technology. *101Blockchains*. Retrieved from: https://101Blockchains.com/consensus-alg orithms-Blockchain/ (13.06.2023).

Araújo T & Banisch S (2016) Multidimensional Analysis of Linguistic Networks. In Mehler A, Lücking A, Banisch S, Blanchard P, & Job B (Eds.) *Towards a Theoretical Framework for Analyzing Complex Linguistic Networks. Understanding Complex Systems*. Doi: 10.1007/978-3-662-47238-5.

Arbib MA & Caplan C (1979) Neurolinguistics Must Be Computational. *The Behavioural and Brain Sciences 2,* pp 449–483.

Atkinson QD & Gray RD (2005) Curious Parallels and Curious Connections: Phylogenetic Thinking in Biology and Historical Linguistics. *Systematic Biology 54*(4), pp 513–526.

Attneave F & Arnoult MD (1956) The Quantitative Study of Shape and Pattern Perception. *Psychological Bulletin 53,* pp 452–471.

Austin JL (1962) *How to Do Things with Words: The William James Lectures Delivered at Harvard University in 1955* (Eds. Urmson JO & Sbisà M). Oxford: Clarendon Press.

Baayen RH & Milin P (2010) Analyzing Reaction Times. *International Journal of Psychological Research 3*(2), pp 12–28.

Baicchi A (2015) Complex Adaptive Systems: The Case of Language. In Baicchi A (Ed.) *Construction Learning as a Complex Adaptive System*. New York: Springer, pp 9–31.

Baird L, Harmon H, & Madsen P (2020) *Hedera: A Public Hashgraph Network & Governing Council v.2.1.* Retrieved from: https://hedera.com/hh_whitepaper _v2.1-20200815.pdf (13.06.2023)

Bakker P, Daval-Markussen A, Parkvall M, & Plag I (2011) Creoles Are Typologically Distinct from Non-creoles. *Journal of Pidgin and Creole Languages 26*(1), pp 5–42. Doi: 10.1075/jpcl.26.1.02bak.

Ball P (2013) Polynesian People Used Binary Numbers 600 Years Ago. *Nature News*. Doi: 10.1038/nature.2013.14380.

Banach R (2019) Punishment not Reward: Disincentivising Blockchain Application Misbehaviour. In *2019 IEEE International Conference on Blockchain and Cryptocurrency (ICBC)*. Doi: 10.1109/BLOC.2019.8751232.

Barbieri F & Saggion H (2014) Modelling Irony in Twitter Proceedings of the Student Research. In *Workshop at the 14th Conference of the European Chapter of the Association for Computational Linguistics*, pp 56–64.

Baroni M (2019) Linguistic Generalization and Compositionality in Modern Artificial Neural Networks. *Philosophical Transactions of the Royal Society 375*, 20190307.

Barsalou LW (1999) Perceptual Symbol Systems. *Behavioural and Brain Sciences 22*(04). Doi: 10.1017/s0140525x99002149.

Barsalou LW (2003) Situated Simulation in the Human Conceptual System. *Language and Cognitive Processes 18*(5–6), pp 513–562. Doi: 10.1080/01690960344000026.

Bartling S (2018) Blockchain for Science and Knowledge Creation. In Haring R (Ed.) *Gesundheit digital. Perspektiven zur Digitalisierung im Gesundheitswesen*, pp. 159–180. ISBN: 978-3-662-57611-3.

Bates D, Maechler M, Bolker B, Walker S, & Christensen RHB (2020) *lme4: Linear Mixed-Effects Models Using 'Eigen' and S4*. Retrieved from: https://CRAN.R-project.org/package=lme4 (13.06.2023).

Bauer DF (1972) Constructing Confidence Sets Using Rank Statistics. *Journal of the American Statistical Association 67*(339), pp 687–690. Doi: 10.2307/2284469.

Baxter GJ (2016) Social Networks and Beyond in Language Change. In Mehler A, Lücking A, Banisch S, Blanchard P, & Job B (Eds.) *Towards a Theoretical Framework for Analyzing Complex Linguistic Networks. Understanding Complex Systems*. Doi: 10.1007/978-3-662-47238-5.

Beckage NM & Colunga E (2016) Language Networks as Models of Cognition: Understanding Cognition through Language. In Mehler A, Lücking A, Banisch S, Blanchard P, & Job B (Eds.) *Towards a Theoretical Framework for Analyzing Complex Linguistic Networks. Understanding Complex Systems*. Doi: 10.1007/978-3-662-47238-5.

Beckner C, Ellis NC, Blythe R, Holland J, Bybee J, Ke J, Christiansen MH, Larsen-Freeman D, Croft W, & Schoenemann T (2009) Language Is a Complex Adaptive System: Position Paper. *Language Learning 59*(Suppl.1), pp 1–26.

Bellomi F & Bonato R (2005) Network Analysis for Wikipedia. *Proceedings of the 1st International Wikimedia Conference, Wikimania.* Retrieved from: http://people.cs.ksu.edu/~halmohri/files/wikipediaNetworkAnalysis.pdf (13.06.2023)

Bender A & Beller S (2013) Mangarevan Invention of Binary Steps for Easier Calculation. *PNAS 111*(4), pp 1322–1327. Doi: 10.1073/pnas.130916011.

Bender EA & Williamson SG (2010) *Lists, Decisions and Graphs: With an Introduction to Probability.* San Diego, CA: Edward A Bender & S Gill Williamson. Retrieved from: http://cseweb.ucsd.edu/~gill/BWLectSite/Resources/LDGbookCOV.pdf (13.06.2023)

Bengio Y, Ducharme R, Vincent P, & Jauvin C (2003) A Neural Probabilistic Language Model. *Journal of Machine Learning Research 3*, pp 1137–1155.

Bentov I, Lee C, Mizrahi A, & Rosenfeld M (2014) Proof of Activity: Extending Bitcoin's Proof of Work via Proof of Stake. *ACM SIGMETRICS Performance Evaluation Review 42*(3), pp 34–37. Doi: 10.1145/2695533.2695545. Retrieved from: https://eprint.iacr.org/2014/452.pdf (13.06.2023).

Bernstein MS, Monroy-Hernández A, Harry D, André P, Panovich K, & Vargas G (2011) 4chan and /b/: An Analysis of Anonymity and Ephemerality in a Large Online Community. *Proceedings of the Fifth International AAAI Conference on Weblogs and Social Media.* Menlo Park, CA: The Association for the Advancement of Artificial Intelligent Press.

Bird S, Klein E, & Loper E (2009) *Natural Language Processing with Python.* Sebastopol, CA: O'Reilly Media Inc.

Blei DM, Ng AY, & Jordan MII (2003) Latent Dirichlet Allocation. *Journal of Machine Learning Research 3*, pp 993–1022.

Bohn M, Call J, & Tomasello M (2016) The Role of Past Interactions in Great Apes' Communication about Absent Entities. *Journal of Comparative Psychology 130*(4), pp 351–357. Doi: 10.1037/com0000042.

Borgatti SP (2005) Centrality and Network Flow. *Social Networks 27*(1), pp 55–71. Doi: 10.1016/j.socnet.2004.11.008.

Bowern C (2009) Reassessing Karnic: A Reply to Breen 2007. *Australian Journal of Linguistics 29*, pp 337–348. Doi: 10.1080/07268600903232733.

Bowern C (2010) Historical Linguistics in Australia: Trees, Networks and Their Implications. *Philosophical Transactions of the Royal Society 365*, pp. 3845–3854.

Boyd R & Richerson PJ (1996) Why Culture Is Common, but Cultural Evolution Is Rare. *Proceedings of the British Academy 88*, pp 77–93.

Brandes U (2008) On Variants of Shortest-Path Betweenness-centrality and Their Generic Computation. *Social Networks 30*(2), pp 136–145.

Brandes U, Freeman LC, & Wagner D (2014) Social Networks. In Tamassia R (Ed.) *Handbook of Graph Drawing Visualization*. Boca Ratón, FL: CRC Press, pp 805–839.

Brandes U, Kenis P, Lerner J, & van Raaj D (2009) Network Analysis of Collaboration Structure in Wikipedia. *Proceedings of the 18th International Conference on World Wide Web – WWW '09*. New York: ACM Press, pp 731–740. Doi: 10.1145/1526709.1526808. Retrieved from: http://kops.uni-konstanz.de/bitstream/handle/123456789/3042/Brandes_opus-104056.pdf?sequence=1&isAllowed=y (13.06.2023).

Breen G (2007) Reassessing Karnic. *Australian Journal of Linguistics 27*(2), pp 175–199. Doi: 10.1080/07268600701522780.

Broca P (1861) Remarques sur le siège de la faculté du langage articulé, suivies d'une observation d'aphémie (perte de la parole). *Bulletin de la Société Anatomique de Paris 6*, pp 330–357.

Brown P & Levinson SC (1987). *Politeness: Some Universals in Language Usage*. Cambridge : University Press.

Brunot F (1922) *La pensée et la langue. Méthode, Principes et Plan d'une Théorie nouvelle du Langage appliquée au Français*. Paris: Masson et Cie.

Bryant D, Filimon F, & Gray R (2005) Untangling Our Past: Languages, Trees, Splits and Networks. In Mace R, Holden C, & Shennan S (Eds.) *The Evolution of Cultural Diversity: Phylogenetic Approaches*. London: University College London Press, pp 69–85.

Bühler K (1927) *Die Krise der Psychologie*. Jena: Gustav Fischer.

Bühler K (1934) *Sprachtheorie. Die Darstellungsfunktion der Sprache*. Jena: Gustav Fischer.

Byte (1995) Most Important Companies: Which of the 5000 Computer Companies Got Us Where We Are Today? Here Are the Top 20. *Byte Magazine (September 1995)*. Retrieved from: https://web.archive.org/web/20080618072507/http://www.byte.com/art/9509/sec7/art15.htm (13.06.2023).

Cabrerizo FJ, Alonso S, & Herrera-Viedma E (2009) A Consensus Model for Group Decision Making Problems with Unbalanced Fuzzy Linguistic Information. *International Journal of Information Technology & Decision Making 8*(1), pp 109–131. Doi: 10.1142/S0219622009003296.

Caldarelli G (2020) Understanding the Blockchain Oracle Problem: A Call for Action. *Information 11*. Doi: 10.3390/info11110509.

Cantor G (1897) Beiträge zur Begründung der transfiniten Mengenlehre. *Mathematische Annalen 49*, pp 207–246. Doi: 10.1007/BF01444205.

Castro-Toledo F, Gretenkort T, Esteve M, & Miró-Llinares F (2020) 'Fear in 280 characters': A New Approach for Evaluation of Fear Over Time in Cyberspace. In Ceccato V & Nalla MK (Eds.) *Crime and Fear in Public Places: Toward Safe, Inclusive and Sustainable Cities.* London, New York: Routledge.

Čech R, Mačutek J, & Liu HT (2016) Syntactic Complex Networks and Their Applications. In Mehler A, Lücking A, Banisch S, Blanchard P, & Job B (Eds.) *Towards a Theoretical Framework for Analyzing Complex Linguistic Networks. Understanding Complex Systems.* Doi: 10.1007/978-3-662-47238-5.

Centola D & Baronchelli A (2015) The Spontaneous Emergence of Conventions: An Experimental Study of Cultural Evolution. *PNAS 112*(7), pp 1189–1194. Doi: 10.1073/pnas.1418838112.

Chandler AD (2005) *Inventing the Electronic Century: The Epic Story of the Consumer Electronics and Computer Industries: With a New Preface.* Cambridge, MA: Harvard University Press.

Cheney DL & Seyfarth RM (1997) Why Animals Don't Have Language. *The Tanner Lectures on Human Values.* Cambridge: Cambridge University Press. Retrieved from: http://www.columbia.edu/~rmk7/HC/paper_filles/Cheney.pdf (13.06.2023).

Chetty N & Alathur S (2018) Hate Speech Review in the Context of Online Social Networks. *Aggression and Violent Behaviour 40*, pp 108–118. Doi: 10.1016/j.avb.2018.05.003.

Chomsky N (1956) Three Models for the Description of Language. *IRE Transactions on Information Theory 2*(3), pp 113–124. Doi: 10.1109/TIT.1956.1056813.

Chomsky N (1957) *Syntactic Structures.* The Hague: Mouton.

Chomsky N (1959a) A Review of B.F. Skinner's 'Verbal Behaviour'. *Language 35*, pp 26–58.

Chomsky N (1959b) On Certain Formal Properties of Grammars. *Information and Control 2*(2), pp 137–167. Doi: 10.1016/S0019-9958(59)90362-6.

Chomsky N (1965) *Aspects of the Theory of Syntax.* Cambridge, MA: MIT Press.

Chomsky N (1968) *Language and Mind.* New York: Harcourt Brace Jovanovich.

Chomsky N & Schützenberger M (1959) The Algebraic Theory of Context-Free Languages. *Studies in Logic and the Foundations of Mathematics 26*, pp 118–161. Doi: 10.1016/S0049-237X(09)70104-1.

Choudhury M & Mukherjee A (2009) The Structure and Dynamics of Linguistic Networks. In Ganguly N, Deutsch A, Mukherjee A (Eds.) *Dynamics on and of Complex Networks: Applications to Biology, Computer Science, and the Social Sciences.* Boston: Birkhäuser, pp 145–166. Doi: 10.1007/978-0-8176-4751-3.

Christensen P & Tylén K (2013) Gestural Representation of Event Structure in Dyadic Interaction. *Proceedings of the Tilburg Gesture Research Meeting (TiGeR) 2013.* Retrieved from: https://tiger.uvt.nl/pdf/papers/christensen.pdf (13.06.2023)

Clédat L (1923) Compte rendu de Brunot (1922). *Revue de Philologie Française et de Littérature 35*, pp 31–64.

Collins AM & Loftus EF (1975) A Spreading-Activation Theory of Semantic Processing. *Psychological Review 82*(6), pp 407–428.

Conoscenti M, Vetrò A, & De Martin JC (2016) Blockchain for the Internet of Things: A Systematic Literature Review. *Proceedings of IEEE/ACS 13th International Conference of Computer Systems and Applications (AICCSA)*, pp 1–6. Doi: 10.1109/AICCSA.2016.7945805.

Cornish H (2010) Investigating How Cultural Transmission Leads to the Appearance of Design without a Designer in Human Communication Systems. *Interaction Studies 11*(1), pp 112–137. Doi: 10.1075/is.11.1.02cor.

Coseriu E (1962) *Teoría del lenguaje y lingüística general.* Madrid: Gredos.

Creswell A, White T, Dumoulin V, Arulkumaran K, Sengupta B, & Bharath AA (2018) Generative Adversarial Networks: An Overview. *IEEE Signal Processing Magazine 35*(1), pp 53–65. Doi: 10.1109/MSP.2017.2765202.

Crystal D (2004) *The Language Revolution.* Cambridge, UK: Polity Press Ltd.

Culbertson J, Smolensky P, & Legendre G (2012) Learning Biases Predict a Word Order Universals. *Cognition 122*(3), pp 306–329.

Culbertson J, Smolensky P, & Wilson C (2013) Cognitive Biases, Linguistic Universals, and Constraint-Based Grammar Learning. *Topics in Cognitive Science 5*(3), pp 392–424.

Cunha E, Magno G, Comarela G, Almeida V, Gonçalves MA, & Benevenuto F (2011) Analyzing the Dynamic Evolution of Hashtags on Twitter: A Language-Based Approach. *Proceedings of the Workshop on Language in Social Media*, pp. 58–65.

Darwin C (1859) *On the Origin of Species by Means of Natural Selection, or the Preservation of Favoured Races in the Struggle for Life.* London: John Murray.

Daston L (1988) *Classical Probability in the Enlightenment.* Princeton, NJ: University Press.

Daston L (1992) The Naturalized Female Intellect. *Science in Context 5*, pp 209–235.

Davis JD, Winkielman P, & Coulson S (2017) Sensorimotor Simulation and Emotion Processing: Impairing Facial Actions Increases Semantic Retrieval Demands. *Cognitive, Affective, & Behavioural Neuroscience 17*, pp 652–664.

Davis M (1978) What Is a Computation? In Steen LA (Ed.) *Mathematics Today – Twelve Informal Essays*. New York: Springer. Doi: doi.org/10.1007/978-1-4613-9435-8.

Dawkins R (1976) *The Selfish Gene*. Oxford, UK: Oxford University Press.

Deacon T (1997) *The Symbolic Species. The Co-evolution of Language and the Human Brain*. London: Penguin Books.

Descartes R (1673) *El discurso del método*. Carrier-Vélez J (2009). Barcelona: Ediciones Brontes.

De Deyne S, Navarro DJ, & Storms G (2013) Better Explanations of Lexical and Semantic Cognition Using Networks Derived from Continued rather than Single Word Associations. *Behaviour Research Methods 45*, pp 480–498.

De Deyne S, Verheyen S, & Storms G (2016) Structure and Organisation of the Mental Lexicon: A Network Approach Derived from Syntactic Dependency Relations and Word Associations. In Mehler A, Lücking A, Banisch S, Blanchard P, & Job B (Eds.) *Towards a Theoretical Framework for Analyzing Complex Linguistic Networks. Understanding Complex Systems*. Doi: 10.1007/978-3-662-47238-5.

Diderot D (1746) *Pensées philosophiques. Addition aux pensées philosophiques*. Bourdin JC (2007). Paris: Flammarion.

Dingemanse M, Blasi DE, Lupyan G, Christiansen MH, & Monaghan P (2015) Arbitrariness, Iconicity, and Systematicity in Language. *Trends in Cognitive Sciences 19*(10), pp 603–615. Doi: 10.1016/j.tics.2015.07.013. Retrieved from: https://pure.mpg.de/rest/items/item_2176289/component/file_2213052/content (13.06.2023)

Dos Santos RP (2017) On the Philosophy of Bitcoin/Blockchain Technology: Is It a Chaotic, Complex System?. *Metaphilosophy 48*(5), pp 620–633.

DuPont Q (2017) Blockchain Identities: Notational Technologies for Control and Management of Abstracted Entities. *Metaphilosophy 48*(5), pp 634–653.

Dwork C & Naor M (1993) Pricing via Processing or Combatting Junk Mail. In Brickell EF (Ed.) *Advances in Cryptology – Crypto '92, LNCS 740*. Berlin, Heidelberg: Springer, pp 130–147. Doi: 10.1007/3-540-48071-4_10. Retrieved from: https://link.springer.com/content/pdf/10.1007/3-540-48071-4_10.pdf (13.06.2023)

Easley D & Kleinberg J (2010) *Networks, Crowds, and Markets: Reasoning about a Highly Connected World*. Cambridge, UK: Cambridge University Press.

Eckert P & Wenger E (2005) What Is the Role of Power in Sociolinguistic Variation?. *Journal of Socio-linguistics 9*(4), pp 582–589.

Eco U (1990) *Drift and Unlimited Semiosis*. Indiana: University of Indiana Press. Retrieved from: https://scholarworks.iu.edu/dspace/handle/2022/8497 (13.06.2023).

Ellison NB & Boyd DM (2013) Sociality Through Social Network Sites. In Dutton WH (Ed.) *The Oxford Handbook of Internet Studies*. Oxford: Oxford University Press. Doi: 10.1093/oxfordhb/9780199589074.013.0008.

Enard W, Przeworski M, Fisher SE, Lai CS, Wiebe V, Kitano T, et al. (2002) Molecular Evolution of FOXP2, a Gene Involved in Speech and Language. *Nature 418*, pp 869–872.

Escandell-Montiel D (2016) Greentexts: Minificciones de la Empatía y EL Engaño En los Espacios Sociales de la Red. In Álvarez-Ramos E, Martínez Deyros M, & Alejandre-Biel L (Eds.) *Actas del Primer Congreso Internacional. El Cuento hispánico: nuevas miradas críticas y aplicaciones didácticas*. Valladolid: Agilice Digital, pp 223–238.

Eschbach A (2015) Über die Tieferlegung der Fundamente. In Eschbach A (Ed.) *Karl Bühler: Sprache und Denken*. Köln: Herbert von Halem, pp 9–15.

Ethayarajh K (2019) Rotate 'King' to get 'Queen': Word Relationships as Orthogonal Transformations in Embedding Space. *Proceedings of the 2019 Conference on Empirical Methods in Natural Language Processing and the 9th International Joint Conference on Natural Language Processing*. Hong Kong: Association for Computational Linguistics, pp 3503–3508. Doi: 10.18653/v1/D19-1354.

Evans V (2014) *The Language Myth: Why Language Is Not an Instinct*. Cambridge: Cambridge University Press.

Fehr J (2003) *Ferdinand de Saussure: Linguistik und Semiologie – Notitzen aus dem Nachlass. Texte, Briefe und Dokumente*. Berlin: Suhrkamp.

Fellbaum C (Ed.) (1998) *WordNet: An Electronic Lexical Database*. Cambridge, MA: MIT Press.

Fernández-Anta A, Georgiou C, Konwar K, & Nicolaou N (2018) Formalizing and Implementing Distributed Ledger Objects. *ACM SIGACT News (Association for Computing Machinery, Special Interest Group on Algorithms & Computation Theory) 49*(2). Doi: 10.1145/3232679.3232691. Retrieved from: https://dl.acm.org/doi/abs/10.1145/3232679.3232691 (13.06.2023).

Ferrer-i-Cancho R (2005) The Structure of Syntactic Dependency Networks: Insights from Recent Advances in Network Theory. In Altmann G, Levickij V, & Perebyinis V (Eds.) *Problems of Quantitative Linguistics*. Chernivtsi: Ruta, pp 60–75.

Ferrer-i-Cancho R (2016) Non-crossing Dependencies: Least Effort, Not Grammar. In Mehler A, Lücking A, Banisch S, Blanchard P, & Job B (Eds.)

Towards a Theoretical Framework for Analyzing Complex Linguistic Networks. Understanding Complex Systems. Doi: 10.1007/978-3-662-47238-5

Ferrer-i-Cancho R & Solé RV (2004) Patterns in Syntactic Dependency Networks. *Physical Review E 69*, e051915.

Fisher SE, Vargha-Khadem F, Watkins KE, Monaco AP, & Pembrey ME (1998) Localisation of a Gene Implicated in a Severe Speech and Language Disorder. *Nature Genetics 18*, pp 168–170.

Fitzpatrick E & Sager N (1974) The Lexical Subclasses of the Linguistic String Parser. *American Journal of Computational Linguistics 11*(2). Retrieved from: https://www.aclweb.org/anthology/J74-1002/ (13.06.2023).

Fodor J & Pylyshyn Z (1988) Connectionism and Cognitive Architecture: A Critical Analysis *Cognition 28*, pp 3–71. Doi: 10.1016/0010-0277(88)90031-5.

Fox J & Weisberg S (2019) *An R Companion to Applied Regression*. Thousand Oaks, CA: Sage. Retrieved from: https://socialsciences.mcmaster.ca/jfox/Books/Companion/ (13.06.2023).

Freeman LC (1978) Centrality in Social Networks: Conceptual Clarification. *Social Networks 1*, pp 215–239.

Fridgen G, Lockl J, Radszuwill S, Rieger A, Schweizer A, & Urbach N (2018) A Solution in Search of a Problem: A Method for the Development of Blockchain Use Cases. *Twenty-fourth Americas Conference on Information Systems (AMICS),* New Orleans. Retrieved from: https://www.fim-rc.de/Paperbibliothek/Veroeffentlicht/751/wi-751.pdf (13.06.2023).

Frith CD (2008) Social Cognition. *Philosophical Transactions of the Royal Society of Britain 363,* pp 2033–2039. Doi: 10.1098/rstb.2008.0005.

FundéuRAE (2021) *Sobre la FundéuRAE.* Retrieved from: https://www.fundeu.es/Sobrefundeubbva/quienes-somos/ (13.06.2023).

Fusaroli R & Tylén K (2012) Carving Language for Social Coordination: A Dynamical Approach. *Interaction Studies 13*(1), pp 103–123.

Fusaroli R, Bahrami B, Olsen K, Roepstroff A, Rees G, Frith C, & Tylén K (2012) Coming to Terms: Quantifying the Benefits of Linguistic Coordination. *Psychological Science 23*(8) Doi: 10.1177/0956797612436816.

Fusaroli R, Raczaszek-Leonardi J, Tylén K (2014) Dialog as Interpersonal Synergy. *New Ideas in Psychology 30*, pp 1–11.

Galantucci B (2009) Experimental Semiotics: A New Approach for Studying Communication as a Form of Joint Action. *Topics in Cognitive Science 1*, pp 393–410.

Galantucci B, Garrod S, & Roberts G (2012) Experimental Semiotics. *Language and Linguistics Compass*, pp 1–17. Doi: 10.1002/lnc3.351.

García-Salido M (2017) On Causative *dar* and Its Alternatives in the History of Spanish. *Folia Linguistica Historica 38*, pp 91–124. Doi: 10.1515/flih-2017-0004.

Garrod S, Fay N, Lee J, Oberlander J, & MacLeod T (2007) Foundations of Representation: Where Might Graphical Symbol Systems Come From? *Cognitive Science 31*, pp 961–987.

Gigerenzer G & Goldstein D (1996) Mind as Computer: Birth of a Metaphor. *Creativity Research Journal 9*(2/3), pp 131–144.

Gillings MR, Hilbert M, & Kemp DJ (2016) Information in the Biosphere: Biological and Digital Worlds. *Trends in Ecology and Evolution 31*(3), Doi: 10.1016/j.tree.2015.12.013.

Gimpel K, Schneider N, O'Connor B, Das D, Mills D, Eisenstein J, Heilman M, Yogatama D, Flanigan J, & Smith NA (2010) *Part-of-Speech Tagging for Twitter: Annotation, Features, and Experiments.* Pittsburgh PA: Carnegie Mellon University. Retrieved from: https://apps.dtic.mil/sti/pdfs/ADA547371.pdf (13.06.2023).

Glaser F (2017) Pervasive Decentralisation of Digital Infrastructures: A Framework for Blockchain enabled System and Use Case Analysis. *Proceedings of the 50th Hawaii International Conference on System Sciences,* pp 1543–1552. ISBN: 978-0-9981331-0-2.

Goffman E (1955) On Face-Work: An Analysis of Ritual Elements in Social Interaction. *Psychiatry 18*(3), pp 213–231. Doi: 10.1080/00332747.1955.11023008.

Gong T (2008) *Computational Simulation in Evolutionary Linguistics: A Study on Language Emergence, Frontiers in Linguistics*. Taiwan: Academia Sinica.

Gong T, Minett JW, & Wang WSY (2008) Exploring Social Structure Effect on Language Evolution Based on a Computational Model. *Connection Science 20*(2–3), pp 135–153. Doi: 10.1080/09540090802091941.

Gong T & Shuai L (2016) Simulating the Effects of Cross-Generational Cultural Transmission on Language Change. In Mehler A, Lücking A, Banisch S, Blanchard P, & Job B (Eds.) *Towards a Theoretical Framework for Analysing Complex Linguistic Networks. Understanding Complex Systems.* Doi: 10.1007/978-3-662-47238-5.

Gong T & Wang WSY (2005) Computational Modelling on Language Emergence: A Coevolution Model of Lexicon, Syntax and Social Structure. *Language and Linguistics 6*, pp 1–42.

Greene VS (2019) 'Deplorable' Satire: Alt-Right Memes, White Genocide Tweets, and Redpilling Normies. *Studies in American Humor 5*(1) Special Issue: Satire Today, pp 31–69. Doi: 10.5325/studamerhumor.5.1.0031.

Gretenkort T, Castro-Toledo FJ, Esteve M, & Miró J (in press) Spreading Emotions in 140 Characters: A Pilot Study on Twitter Following the Barcelona Attacks. In Ströbel L (Ed.) *Emotion Concepts*.

Gretenkort T & Tylén K (2021) The Dynamics of Politeness: An Experimental Account. *Journal of Pragmatics 185*, pp 118–130. Doi: 10.1016/j.pragma. 2021.09.003.

Grevisse M (1973) *Le Français Correct*. Paris, Brussels: Duculot.

Grice HP (1975) Logic and Conversation. In Cole P & Morgan J (Eds.) *Syntax and Semantics Vol. 3, Speech Acts*. New York: Academic Press, pp 41–58.

Griffiths TL & Kalish ML (2007) Language Evolution by Iterated Learning with Bayesian Agents. *Cognitive Science 31*, pp 441–480.

Gruenenfelder T & Pisoni DB (2005) *Modeling the mental lexicon as a complex graph*. Indiana University: Bloomington.

Hagberg AA, Schult DA, & Swart PJ (2008) Exploring Network Structure, Dynamics, and Function Using NetworkX. In Varoquaux G, Vaught G, & Millman J (Eds.) *Proceedings of the 7th Python in Science Conference (SciPy2008, Pasadena, CA USA)*, pp 11–15.

Halliday MAK (1985) *An Introduction to Functional Grammar* (1st edn). London: Edward Arnold.

Halliday MAK (2013) Meaning as Choice. In Fontaine L, Bartlett T, O'Grady G (Eds.) *Systemic Functional Linguistics: Exploring Choice*, pp 15–36. Doi: 10.1017/CBO9781139583077.003.

Halliday MAK & Matthiessen C (2014) *Halliday's Introduction to Functional Grammar* (4th edn). London: Routledge.

Hardaker C & McGlashan M (2016) 'Real men don't hate women': Twitter Rape Threats and Group Identity. *Journal of Pragmatics 91*, pp 80–93.

Harris RA (1995) *The Linguistics Wars*. Oxford: University Press.

Harrison R & Thomas M (2009) Identity in Online Communities: Social Networking Sites and Language Learning. *International Journal of Emerging Technologies and Society 7*(2), pp 109–124. ISSN 1835-8780.

Hawlitschek F, Notheisen B, & Teubner T (2018) The Limits of Trust-Free Systems: A Literature Review on Blockchain Technology and Trust in the Sharing Economy. *Electronic Commerce Research and Applications 29*, pp 50–63. Doi: 10.1016/j.elerap.2018.03.005.

Hays D (1964) Dependency Theory: A Formalism and Some Observations. *Language 40*, pp 511–525.

Herrera F, Ferrera-Viedma E, & Verdegay JL (1996) A Model of Consensus in Group Decision Making under Linguistic Assessments. *Fuzzy Sets and Systems 78*, pp 73–87.

Herrera F, Herrera-Viedma E, & Verdegay JL (1997) Linguistic Measures Based on Fuzzy Coincidence for Reaching Consensus in Group Decision Making. *International Journal of Approximate Reasoning 16*, pp 309–334.

Hills TT, Maouene M, Maouene J, Sheya A, & Smith L (2009) Longitudinal Analysis of Early Semantic Networks: Preferential Attachment or Preferential Acquisition? *Psychological Science 20*(6), pp 729–739.

Hine GE, Onaolapo J, De Cristofaro E, Kourtellis N, Leontiadis I, Samaras R, Stringhini G, & Blackburn J (2017) Kek, Cucks, and God Emperor Trump: A Measurement Study of 4chan's Politically Incorrect Forum and Its Effects on the Web. *Proceedings of the 11th International AAAI Conference on Web and Social Media (ICWSM'17)*. Retrieved from: https://arxiv.org/pdf/1610.03452.pdf (13.06.2023).

Hinshelwood J (1917) *Congenital Word Blindness.* London: Lewis.

Horner V, Whiten A, Flynn EG, & de Waal FBM (2006) Faithful Replication of Foraging Techniques along Cultural Transmission Chains by Chimpanzees and Children. *Proceedings of the National Academy of Sciences of the USA 103*, pp 13878–13883.

Huckle S & White M (2016) Socialism and the Blockchain. *Future Internet 8*(49). Doi: 10.3390/fi8040049.

Huettel SA, Song AW, & McCarthy G (2004) *Functional Magnetic Resonance Imaging*. Massachusetts: Sinauer.

Hunnius K (1976) *Der Modusgebrauch nach den Verben der Gemütsbewegung im Französischen*. Heidelberg: Winter.

Huson DH & Bryant D (2006) Application of Phylogenetic Networks in Evolutionary Studies. *Molecular Biology and Evolution 23*(2), pp 254–267.

Ismaev G (2017) Blockchain Technology as an Institution of Property. *Metaphilosophy 48*(5), pp 666–686.

Jaffe S (2018) The Collective Power of #metoo. *Dissent 65*(2), pp 80–87. Doi: 10.1353/dss.2018.0031.

Jain AK, Mao J, & Mohiuddin KM (1996) Artificial Neural Networks. A Tutorial. *Computer 29*(3), pp 31–44.

Jakobson R (1960) Linguistics and Poetics. In Sebeok TA (Ed.) *Style in Language*. Cambridge, MA: MIT Press, pp 350–377.

Jakobson R (Ed.) (1961a) *Structure of Language and Its Mathematical Aspects. Proceedings of Symposia in Applied Mathematics* (Vol. 12). Rhode

Island: American Mathematical Society. ISBN: 0-8218-1312-9, Doi: 10.1090/psapm/012.

Jakobson R (1961b) Linguistics and Communication Theory. In Jakobson R (Ed.) *Structure of Language and Its Mathematical Aspects. Proceedings of Symposia in Applied Mathematics* (Vol. 12). Rhode Island: American Mathematical Society, pp 245–252.

James W (1907) *Pragmatism: A New Name for Some Old Ways of Thinking.* Cambridge, MA: Harvard University Press.

Johnson M (1987) *The Body in the Mind: The Bodily Basis of Meaning, Imagination, and Reason.* Chicago, IL: University of Chicago Press.

Judd S, Kearns M, & Vorobeychik Y (2010) Behavioural Dynamics and Influence in Network Colouring and Consensus. *PNAS 107*(34), pp 14978–14982. Doi: 10.1073/pnas.1001280107.

Kapatsinski V (2006) Sound Similarity Relations in the Mental Lexicon: Modeling the Lexicon as a Complex Network. *Speech Research Lab Progress Report 27*, pp 133-152. Indiana University.

Karlstrom H (2014) Do Libertarians Dream of Electric Coins? The Material Embeddedness of Bitcoin. *Distinktion Scandinavian Journal for Social Theory 15*, pp 23–36.

Kearns M, Judd S, Tan J, & Wortman J (2009) Behavioural Experiments on Biased Voting in Networks. *PNAS 106*(5), pp 1347–1352.

Kearns M, Suri S, & Montfort N (2006) An Experimental Study of the Colouring Problem on Human Subject Networks. *Science 313*, pp 824–827.

Kelso S (1995) *Dynamic Patterns: The Self-Organisation of Brain and Behaviour.* Cambridge, MA: MIT Press.

King S & Nadal S (2012) PPCoin: Peer-to-Peer Crypto-Currency with Proof-of-Stake. *Peercoin.* Retrieved from: https://www.peercoin.net/whitepapers/peercoin-paper.pdf (13.06.2023).

Kirby S, Cornish H, & Smith K (2008) Cumulative Cultural Evolution in the Laboratory: An Experimental Approach to the Origins of Structure in Human Language. *PNAS 105*(31), pp 10681–10686.

Kirby S, Dowman M, & Griffiths TL (2007) Innateness and Culture in the Evolution of Language. *PNAS 104*(12), pp 5241–5245.

Kirby S, Griffiths T, & Smith K (2014) Iterated Learning and the Evolution of Language. *Current Opinion in Neurobiology 28*, pp 108–114.

Kirby S & Hurford JR (2002) The Emergence of Linguistic Structure: An Overview of the Iterated Learning Model. In Cangelosi A & Parisi D (Eds.) *Simulating the Evolution of Language.* London: Springer, pp 121–147.

Klems M, Eberhardt J, Tai S, Härtlein S, Buchholz S, Tidjani A (2017) Trustless Intermediation in Blockchain-Based Decentralised Service Marketplaces. In Maximilien M, Vallecillo A, Wang J, & Oriol M (Eds.) *Service-Oriented Computing. ICSOC 2017. Lecture Notes in Computer Science* (vol. 10601). Springer. Doi: 10.1007/978-3-319-69035-3_53.

Knuth D (1998) *The Art of Computer Programming. Volume 3. Sorting and Searching. Second Edition*. Boston: Addison-Wesley.

Knuttila L (2011) User Unknown: 4chan, Anonymity and Contingency. *First Monday 16*(10). Doi: 10.5210/fm.v16i10.3665. Retrieved from: https://firstmonday.org/ojs/index.php/fm/article/view/3665 (13.06.2023).

Koomey J, Berard S, Sanchez M, & Wong H (2011) Implications of Historical Trends in the Electrical Efficiency of Computing. *IEEE Annals of the History of Computing 33*(3), pp 46–54.

Kövesces Z & Radden G (1998) Metonymy: Developing a Cognitive Linguistic View. *Cognitive Linguistics 9*(1), pp 37–77.

Kroll JF & De Groot AMB (Eds.) (2005) *Handbook of Bilingualism: Psycholinguistic Approaches*. Oxford: Oxford University Press.

Kruskal WH & Wallis WA (1952) Use of Ranks in One-Criterion Variance Analysis. *Journal of the American Statistical Association 47*(260), pp 583–621.

Kutas M & Hillyard SA (1980) Reading Senseless Sentences: Brain Potentials Reflect Semantic Incongruity. *Science 207*(4427), pp 203–208. Doi: 10.1126/science.7350657.

Kuzmičová A (2012) Presence in the Reading of Literary Narrative: A Case for Motor Enactment. *Semiotica 189*(1/4), pp 23–48. Doi: 10.1515/semi.2011.071.

Kwon S, Cha M, Jung K, Chen W, & Wang Y (2013) Prominent Features of Rumour Propagation in Online Social Media. *Proceedings of the 13th International Conference on Data Mining, EEEI*. Doi: 10.1109/ICDM.2013.61.

Labov W (1966) *The Social Stratification of English in New York City*. Cambridge: University Press.

Labov W (1969) Contraction, Deletion, and Inherent Variability of the English Copula. *Language 45*, pp 715–762.

Labov W (1970) The Study of Language in Its Social Context. *Studium Generale 23*, pp 30–87.

Labov W (2001) *Principles of Linguistic Change: Volume 2 Social Factors*. Oxford: Basil Blackwell.

Labov W (2007) Transmission and Diffusion. *Language 83*, 344–387. (doi:10.1353/lan.2007.0082)

Lafferty J, McCallum A, & Pereira F (2001) Conditional Random Fields: Probabilistic Models for Segmenting and Labelling Sequence Data. *Proceedings of the 18th International Conference on Machine Learning 2001*, pp 282–289. Retrieved from: https://repository.upenn.edu/cgi/viewcontent.cgi?referer=https://www.ecosia.org/&httpsredir=1&article=1162&context=cis_papers (13.06.2023).

Laghos A, Masoura S, & Skordi A (2012) Linguistics in Social Networks. *American International Journal of Contemporary Research 2*(1). Retrieved from: http://aijcrnet.com/journals/Vol_2_No_1_January_2012/1.pdf (13.06.2023).

Lai CS, Fisher SE, Hurst JA, Vargha-Kadem E, & Monaco AP (2001) A Forkhead-Domain Gene Is Mutated in a Severe Speech and Language Disorder. *Nature 413*, pp 519–523.

Lakens D et al. (2018) Justify Your Alpha. *Nature Human Behaviour 2*(3), pp 168–171. Doi: 10.1038/s41562-018-0311-x.

Lakoff G (2012) *Women, Fire, and Dangerous Things. What Categories Reveal about the Mind*. Chicago: University Press.

Lakoff G & Johnson M (1980a) The Metaphorical Structure of the Human Conceptual System *Cognitive Science 4*, pp 195–208.

Lakoff G & Johnson M (1980b) *Metaphors We Live By*. Chicago: University Press.

Lamport L, Shostak R, & Pease M (1982) The Byzantine Generals Problem. *ACM Transactions on Programming Languages and Systems 4*(3), pp 382–401. Retrieved from: https://www.microsoft.com/en-us/research/uploads/prod/2016/12/The-Byzantine-Generals-Problem.pdf (13.06.2023).

Lantolf J (2006) Sociocultural Theory and L2: State of the Art. *Studies in Second Language Acquisition 28*, pp 67–109.

Larrondo-Ureta A (2008) La investigación sobre hipertexto: fundamentación teórica del ciberperiodismo y caminos para la docencia. *Anàlisi 36*, pp 159–174. Retrieved from: http://www.raco.cat/index.php/analisi/article/viewFile/94529/119744 (13.06.2023).

Latour B (1996) On Actor-Network Theory: A few Clarifications. *Soziale Welt 47*(4), pp 369–381. Retrieved from: http://transnationalhistory.net/interconnected/wp-content/uploads/2015/05/Latour-Actor-Network-Clarifications.pdf (13.06.2023).

Learntek (2019) Categorizing and POS Tagging with NTKL Python (Blogpost). Retrieved from https://www.learntek.org/blog/categorizing-pos-tagging-nltk-python/ (13.06.2023).

Lecerf Y (1960) Programme des Conflits – Modèle des Conflits. *Rapport CETIS 4 Euratom*, pp 1–24.

Ledger (2021) *Cambridge Dictionary*. Cambridge: Cambridge University Press. Retrieved from: https://dictionary.cambridge.org/es-LA/dictionary/english/ledger (13.06.2023)

Lee Y, Collier TC, Stabler EP, & Taylor CE (2005) The Role of Population Structure in Language Evolution. *Language 22*(23), pp 24–25.

Leech GN (1980) *Explorations in Semantics and Pragmatics*. Amsterdam: John Benjamins Publishing.

Lehmann C (1995) *Thoughts on Grammaticalisation*. München, Newcastle: Lincom Europa.

Leible S, Schlager S, Schubotz M, Gipp B (2019) A Review on Blockchain Technology and Blockchain Projects Fostering Open Science. *Frontiers in Blockchain 2*(16). Doi: 10.3389/fbloc.2019.00016.

Lemieux VL (2016) Trusting Records. Is Blockchain Technology the Answer? *Records Management Journal 26*(2), pp 110–139.

Lemon JF (1927) A Psychological Study on the Subjunctive Mood in Spanish. *The Modern Language Journal 11*(4). Doi: 10.2307/313427.

Leumann M (1962) Lateinisch habere mit Infinitiv. *Museum Helveticum 19*(1), pp 65–71.

Lev-Ari S (2018) Social Network Size Can Influence Linguistic Malleability and the Propagation of Linguistic Change. *Cognition 176*, pp 31–39.

Levelt WJM (2012) *A History of Psycholinguistics: The pre-Chomskyan era*. Oxford: University Press.

Levy R, Fedorenko E, Breen M, & Gibson E (2012) The Processing of Extraposed Structures in English. *Cognition 122*(1), pp 12–36. Doi: 10.1016/j.cognition.2011.07.012.

Li J, Greenwood D, & Kassem M (2019) Blockchain in the Built Environment and Construction Industry: A Systematic Review, Conceptual Models and Practical Use Cases. *Automation in Construction 102*, pp 288–307. ISSN 0926-5805.

Lipski J (2011) Socio-phonological Variation in Latin American Spanish. In Díaz-Campos M (Ed.) *The Handbook of Hispanic Socio-linguistics*. New Jersey: Blackwell, pp 72–97.

Liu HT & Li WW (2010) Language Clusters Based on Linguistic Complex Networks. *Chinese Science Bulletin 55*(30), pp 3458–3465. Doi: 10.1007/s11434-010-4114-3.

Lupyan G & Dale R (2010) Language Structure Is Partly Determined by Social Structure. *PLoS ONE 5*(1), e8559. Doi: 10.1371/journal.pone.0008559.

Lupyan G & Dale R (2016) Why Are There Different Languages? The Role of Adaptation in Linguistic Diversity. *Trends in Cognitive Sciences 20*(9), pp 649–660. Doi: 10.1016/j.tics.2016.07.005.

Luria AR (1976) *Basic Problems of Neurolinguistics*. The Hague & Paris: Mouton.

Määttä, U (2000) Emergent Metathyeory in Linguistics. *Etusivu 104*(4). Retrieved from: http://ojs.tsv.fi/index.php/virittaja/article/view/40040 (13.06.2023).

Maity SK & Mukherjee A (2016) Emergence of Dominant Opinions in Presence of Rigid Individuals. In Mehler A, Lücking A, Banisch S, Blanchard P, & Job B (Eds.) *Towards a Theoretical Framework for Analyzing Complex Linguistic Networks. Understanding Complex Systems*. Doi: 10.1007/978-3-662-47238-5.

Mancera-Rueda A (2016) Usos lingüísticos alejados del español normative como seña de identidad en las redes sociales. *Hispanic Studies and Researches on Spain, Portugal and Latin America 93*(9), pp 1496–1493. Doi: 10.1080/14753820.2016.1181435.

Marquand A (1886) A New Logical Machine. *Proceedings of the American Academy of Arts and Sciences 21*, pp 303–307.

Martinet A (1949) La double articulation linguistique. *Travaux du Cercle Linguistique de Copenhague 5*, pp 30–37.

Mäthger LM, Denton EJ, Marshal NJ, & Hanlon RT (2009a) Mechanisms and Behavioural Functions of Structural Coloration in Cephalopods. *Journal of the Royal Society Interface 6*, pp 149–163. Doi: 10.1098/rsif.2008.0366.focus.

Mäthger LM, Shashar N, & Hanlon RT (2009b) Do Cephalopods Communicate Using Polarized Light Reflections from Their Skin? *Journal of Experimental Biology 212*, pp 2133–2140. Doi: 10.1242/jeb.020800.

Maulchy JW (1962) Pocket Computer May Replace Shopping List: Inventor Says Device Could Tell Grocery in Advance What Customer Need. *New York Times* (November 3rd, 1962). Retrieved from: https://www.nytimes.com/1962/11/03/archives/pocket-computer-may-replace-shopping-list-inventor-says-device.html?searchResultPosition=1 (13.06.2023).

McCloskey M (1991) Networks and Theories: The Place of Connectionism in Cognitive Science. *Psychological Science 2*, pp 387–395. Doi: 10.1111/j.1467-9280.1991.tb00173.x.

McCulloch G (2019) *Because Internet*. New York: Riverhead Books.

McWhorter JH (1998) Identifying the Creole Prototype: Vindicating a Typological Class. *Language 74*(4), pp 788–818.

Mehler A, Lücking A, Banisch S, Blanchard P, & Job B (Eds.) (2016) Towards a Theoretical Framework for Analyzing Complex Linguistic Networks. In *Understanding Complex Systems*. Doi: 10.1007/978-3-662-47238-5.

Meillet A (1912) L'évolution des formes grammaticales. *Scientia 6*(12).

Meillet A (1926) *Linguistique Historique et Linguistique Générale.* Paris: Librairie Ancienne Honoré Champion.

Meir I, Israel A, Sandler W, Padden C, & Aronoff M (2012) The Influence of Community on Language Structure. *Linguistic Variarion 12*(2), pp 247–291. Doi: 10.1075/lv.12.2.04mei.

Méndez LA (2017) The Variant [ʃ] in the Spanish of Ciudad Juárez. *Borealis: An International Journal of Hispanic Linguistics 6*, pp 243–260.

Menéndez-Pidal R (1908) *Cantar del mío Cid: Texto, Gramática y Vocabulario.* Madrid: Bailly-Baillière é hijos.

Merton RK (1938) Science and the Social Order. *Philosophy of Science 5*(3), pp 321–337.

Mesoudi A & Thornton A (2018) What Is Cumulative Cultural Evolution? *Proceedings of the Royal Society 285*, 20190712. Doi: 10.1098/rspb.2018.0712.

Mesoudi A & Whiten A (2008) The Multiple Roles of Cultural Transmission Experiments in Understanding Human Cultural Evolution. *Philosophical Transactions of the Royal Society of Britain 363*, pp 3489–3501. Doi: 10.1098/rstp.2008.0129.

De La Mettrie JO (1748) *L'Homme Machine.* Leiden: Elie Luzac.

Michnowicz J & Planchón L (2020) *Sheísmo* in Montevideo Spanish. In Sessarego S, Colomina-Almiñana JJ, & Rodríguez-Riccelli A (Eds.) *Variation and Evolution: Aspects of Language Contact and Contrast across the Spanish-speaking World.* Amsterdam: John Benjamins, pp 164–186.

Miller G (2007) Statistical Modelling of Poisson/log-normal Data. *Radiation Protection Dosimetry 124*(2), pp 155–163. Doi: 10.1093/rpd/ncl544.

Milroy L (2002) Social Networks. In Chambers JK, Trudgill P, & Schilling-Estes N (Eds.) *The Handbook of Language Variation and Change.* Oxford: Blackwell, pp 549–572.

Milroy L & Milroy J (1992) Social Network and Social Class: Toward an Integrated Sociolinguistic Model. *Language in Society 21*, pp 1–26.

Milutinovic M, He W, Wu H, & Kanwal M (2016) Proof of Luck: An Efficient Blockchain Consensus Protocol. *SysTEX '16: Proceedings of the 1st Workshop on System Software for Trusted Execution,* Article N° 2, pp 1–6. Doi: 10.1145/3007788.3007790. Retrieved from: https://dl.acm.org/doi/pdf/10.1145/3007788.3007790 (13.06.2023).

Miok K, Nguyen-Doan D, Škrlj B, Zaharie D, & Robnik-Šikonja M (2019) Prediction Uncertainty Estimation for Hate Speech Classification. *SLSP 19: Statistical Language and Speech Processing*, pp 286–298.

Miró-Llinares F (2016) Taxonomía de la comunicación violenta en el discurso del odio en Internet. *IDP Revista d'Internet, Dret I Política 22*, pp 82–108.

Montague R (1970) Universal Grammar. *Theoria 36*, pp 373–398.

Montes-Alcalá C (2009) Hispanics in the United States: More than Spanglish. *Camino Real 1*(0), pp 97–115.

Moore GE (1965) Cramming More Components onto Integrated Circuits. *Electronics 38*(8).

Moore GE (1975) Progress in Digital Integrated Electronics. In IEEE (Ed.) *Technical Digest 1975: International Electron Devices Meeting, December 1, 2, and 3, 1975, Washington, D.C.* New York: Institute of Electrical and Electronics Engineers, pp 11–13.

Morris CW (1938) Foundations of the Theory of Signs. In Neurath O, Carnap R, & Morris CW (Eds.) *International Encyclopaedia of Unified Science* 1(2). Chicago: The University of Chicago Press.

Nagle A (2017) *Kill All Normies: Online Culture Wars from 4Chan and Tumblr to Trump and the Alt-Right.* Winchester: Zero Books.

Nakamoto S (2008) *Bitcoin: A Peer-to-Peer Electronic Cash System.* Retrieved from: https://bitcoin.org/bitcoin.pdf (13.06.2023).

Nelder J & Wedderburn R (1972) Generalised Linear Models. *Journal of the Royal Statistical Society, Series A (General) 135*(3), pp 370–384. Doi: 10.2307/2344614.

Newcombe PI, Campbell C, Siakaluk PD, & Pexman PM (2012) Effects of Emotional and Sensorimotor Knowledge in Semantic Processing of Concrete and Abstract Nouns. *Frontiers in Human Neuroscience 6*, pp 1–15. Doi: 10.3389/fnhum.2012.00275.

Newman D, Lau JH, Grieser K, & Baldwin T (2010) Automatic Evaluation of Topic Coherence. *Human Language Technologies: The 2010 Annual Conference of the North American Chapter of the ACL*, pp 100–108.

Nielsen AKS & Dingemanse M (2020) Iconicity in Word Learning and Beyond: A Critical Review. *Language and Speech 64*(1), pp 52–72. Doi: 10.1177/0023830920914339.

Nielsen JM (1946) *Agnosia, Apraxia, Aphasia. Their Value in Cerebral Localization.* New York: Paul Hoeber.

Nieminen J (1974) On Centrality in a Graph. *Scandinavian Journal of Psychology 15*, pp 322–336.

Nölle J, Fusaroli R, Mills GJ, & Tylén K (2020) Language as Shaped by the Environment: Linguistic Construal in a Collaborative Spatial Task. *Palgrave Communications 6*. Doi: 10.1057/s41599-020-0404-9.

Ogawa S, Lee TM, Nayak AS, & Glynn P (1990) Oxygenation-Sensitive Contrast in Magnetic Resonance Image of Rodent Brain at High Magnetic Fields. *Magnetic Resonance in Medicine 14*(1), pp 68–78.

Ogden CK & Richards IA (1923) *The Meaning of Meaning: A Study of the Influence of Language upon Thought and of the Science of Symbolism*. London: Routledge.

Osgood CE, Sebeok TA (Eds.) Gardner JW, Carroll JB, Newmark LD, Ervin SM, Saporta S, Greenberg JH, Walker DE, Jenkins JJ, Wilson K, & Lounsbury FG (1954) Psycholinguistics: A Survey of Theory and Research Problems. *The Journal of Abnormal and Social Psychology 49*(4).

Papasavva A, Zannettou S, De Cristofaro E, Stringhini G, & Blackburn J (2020) Raiders of the Lost Kek: 3.5 Years of Augmented 4chan Posts from the Politically Incorrect Board. *Proceedings of the Fourteenth International AAAI Conference on Web and Social Media (ICWSM 2020)*, pp 885–894.

Parkvall M (2008) The Simplicity of Creoles in a Cross-Linguistic Perspective. In Miestamo M, Sinnemäki K, & Karlsson F (Eds.) *Language Complexity: Typology, Contact, Change*. Amsterdam: John Benjamins Publishing Company, pp 265–285.

Parra-Moyano J (2017) On the Continuity and Origin of Identity in Distributed Ledgers: Learning from Russell's Paradox. *Metaphilosophy 48*(5), pp 687–697.

Pater J (2019) Generative Linguistics and Neural Networks at 60: Foundation, Friction, and Fusion. *Language 95*(1), pp e41–e74.

Peirce CS (1878) How to Make Our Ideas Clear. *Popular Science Monthly 12*, pp 286–302.

Peirce CS (1903) *A Syllabus of Certain Topics of Logic*. Boston: Alfred Mudge & Son.

Pelli DG, Burns CW, Farrell B, & Moore DC (2006) Identifying Letters. *Vision Research 46*, pp 4646–4674.

Penas-Ibáñez MA (2005) Coseriu y los distintos planos de la actividad del hablar y del saber lingüístico en relación con el contenido y las categorías lógicas del juicio. *Cauce Revista Internacional del Filología y su Dicáctica 28*, pp 279–306.

Peng FC (1985) What Is Neurolinguistics? *Journal of Neurolinguistics 1*(1), pp 7–30.

Pérez-Sabater C (2012) The Linguistics of Social Networking: A Study of Writing Conventions on Facebook. *Linguistik Online 56*(6), pp 81–93. ISSN: 1615-3014.

Pickering MJ & Garrod S (2004) Toward a Mechanistic Psychology of Dialogue. *Behavioural and Brain Sciences 27*(2), pp 169–190.

Pinker S (1994) *The Language Instinct. How the Mind Creates Language*. New York, NY: William Morrow.

Pinker S & Prince A (1988) On Language and Connectionism: Analysis of a Parallel Distributed Processing Model of Language Acquisition. *Cognition 28*(1–2), pp 73–193. Doi: 10.1016/0010-0277(88)90032-7.

Popov S, Moog H, Camargo D, Capossele A, Dimitrov V, Gal A, Greve A, Kusmierz B, Mueller S, Penzkofer A, Saa O, Sanders W, Vigneri L, Welz W, & Attias V (2020) *The Coordicide*. Berlin: IOTA Foundation.

Princeton University (2010) About WordNet. *WordNet*. Retrieved from: https://wordnet.princeton.edu/ (13.06.2023).

Pugh B & Chung B (2017) Original RaiBlocks / Nano Whitepaper. *Github*. Retrieved from: https://docs.nano.org/whitepaper/english (13.06.2023).

Pujolà JT, García MA, & González V (2009) Textos generados en la Web 2.0. In Penas-Ibáñez MA & González R (Eds.) *Estudios sobre el texto. Nuevos enfoques y propuestas*. Frankfurt am Main: Peter Lang, pp 279–301.

Python Foundation (2021) *Time: Time Access and Conversions. 3.9.1.* Retrieved from: https://docs.python.org/3/library/time.html (13.06.2023).

Qi CH, Kaiser AP, Milan SE, Yzquierdo Y, & Hancock TB (2003) The Performance of Low-Income African American Children on the Preschool Language Scale-3. *Journal of Speech, Language, and Hearing Research 46*, pp 576–590.

Quillian MR (1967) Word Concepts: A Theory and Simulation of Some Basic Semantic Capabilities. *Behavioral Science 12*, pp 410–430.

Radden G (2011) Spatial Time in the West and the East. In Brdar M, Omazic M, Pavcic Takac V, Gradecak-Erdeljic T, & Buljan G (Eds.) *Space and Time in Language*. Frankfurt: Peter Lang. pp 1–40. Retrieved from: https://www.researchgate.net/publication/247931562_The_metaphor_TIME_AS_SPACE_across_languages (13.06.2023).

Raviv L, Meyer A, & Lev-Ari S (2019) Larger Communities Create More Systematic Languages. *Proceedings of the Royal Society of Britain 286*, 20191262. Doi: 10.1098/rspb.2019.1262.

Raviv L, Meyer A, & Lev-Ari S (2020) The Role of Social Network Structure in the Emergence of Linguistic Structure. *Cognitive Science 44*. Doi: 10.1111/cogs.12876.

R Core Team (2020) *R: A Language and Environment for Statistical Computing*. R Foundation for Statistical Computing, Vienna, Austria. Retrieved from: https://www.R-project.org/ (13.06.2023).

Reali F, Chater N, & Christiansen MH (2018) Simpler Grammar, Larger Vocabulary: How Population Size Affects Language. *Proceedings of the Royal Society of Britain 285*, 20172586. Doi: 10.1098/rspb.2017.2586.

Reijers W & Coeckelbergh M (2018) The Blockchain as a Narrative Technology: Investigating the Social Ontology and Normative Configurations of

Cryptocurrencies. *Philosophy & Technology 31*(1), pp 103–130. Doi: 10.1007/s13347-016-0239-x.

Reijers W, O'Brolcháin F, & Haynes P (2016) Governance in Blockchain Technologies & Social Contract Theories. *Ledger 1*, pp 134–151. Doi: 10.5915/LEDGER.2016.62.

Richardson L (2019) *Beautiful Soup Documentation: Release 4.4.0.* Retrieved from: https://beautiful-soup-4.readthedocs.io/_/downloads/en/latest/pdf/ (13.06.2023).

Rinker T, Gillespie C, & Citro C (2014) qdap Version 2.1.0 (Version qdapVersion2.1.0) *Zenodo*. Doi: 10.5281/zenodo.11124.

Rinker T & Spinu V (2016) trinker/sentimentr: version 0.4.0 (Version v0.4.0) *Zenodo*. Doi: 10.5281/zenodo.222103.

Roberts G (2017) The Linguist's Drosophila: Experiments in Language Change. *Linguistic Vanguard 3*(1). Doi: 10.1515/lingvan-2016-0086.

Robinson P & Ellis N (Eds.) (2007) *A Handbook of Cognitive Linguistics and SLA.* Mahwah, NJ: Lawrence Erlbaum.

Rosenblatt F (1958) The Perceptron: A Probabilistic Model for Information Storage and Organisation in the Brain, Cornell Aeronautical Laboratory. *Psychological Review 65*(6), pp 386–408. Doi:10.1037/h0042519.

Roser M & Ritchie H (2013) Technological Change. *OurWorldInData.org*. Retrieved from: https://ourworldindata.org/technological-change/ (13.06.2023).

Rueda AM (2016) Usos lingüísticos alejados del español normativo como seña de identidad en las redes sociales. *Bulletin of Spanish Studies*. Doi: 10.1080/14753820.2016.1181435.

Rumelhart DE & McClelland JL (1986) On Learning the Past Tenses of English Verbs. In Rumelhart DE & McClelland JL (Eds.) *Parallel Distributed Processing: Explorations in the Microstructures of Cognition.* Cambridge, MA: MIT Press, pp 216–271.

Russell B (1903) *The Principles of Mathematics.* Cambridge: Cambridge University Press.

Russell B (1905) On Denoting. *Mind 14*(56), pp 479–493. Doi:10.1093/mind/XIV.4.479. Retrieved from: http://bactra.org/Russell/denoting/ (13.06.2023).

Russell B (1918) *Logic and Knowledge*. New York: Capricorn Books.

Russell B (1940) *An Inquiry Into Meaning & Truth.* New York: WW Norton & Company.

Sales T (1997) Lull as Computer Scientist or Why Llull Was One of Us. In Bertran M & Rus T (Eds.) *Transformation-Based Reactive Systems Development. ARTS*

1997. Lecture Notes in Computer Science, vol. 1231. Berlin, Heidelberg: Springer. Doi: 10.1007/3-540-63010-4_2.

Salton G, Wong A, Yang CS (1975) A Vector Space Model for Automatic Indexing. *Communications of the ACM (18)*11, pp 613–620. Doi: 10.1145/361219.361220.

Sampson G (2007) There Is No Language Instinct. *Ilha do Desterro: A Journal of English Language, Literatures in English and Cultural Studies 52*, pp 35–63.

Sankararaman S, Patterson N, Li H, Pääbo S, & Reich D (2012) The Date of Interbreeding between Neanderthals and Modern Humans. *PLoS Genetics 8*(10), e1002947. Doi: 10.1371/journal.pgen.1002947.

De Saussure F (1879) *Mémoire sur le système primitif des voyelles dans les langues indo-européennes*. Leipzig: Teubner.

De Saussure F (1916) *Cours de linguistique générale* (Eds. Bally C & Sechehaye A). Paris: Payot.

Schmid H (1994) Part-of-Speech Tagging with Neural Networks. *Proceedings of COLING-94 Kyoto, Japan*, pp 172–176. Retrieved from: https://www.aclweb.org/anthology/C94-1027.pdf (13.06.2023).

Schmidt LB (2019) The Role of Social Networks in Cross-Dialectal Variation in the Perception of Rioplatense Assibilated Pre-Palatal [ʃ]. In Chappell W (Ed.) *Recent Advances in the Study of Spanish Sociophonetic Perception.* Amsterdam: John Benjamins, pp 187–209. Doi: 10.1075/ihll.21.07sch.

Schoenemann PT (2005) Conceptual Complexity and the Brain: Understanding Language Origins. In Minett JW & Wang WSY (Eds.) *Language Acquisition, Change and Emergence: Essays in Evolutionary Linguistics.* Hong Kong: City University of Hong Kong Press, pp 47–94.

Schon D (2011) Zur Katalyse des Sprachwandels in der Neuen Romania am Beispiel der Tempusbildung. *JournaLIPP 1*, pp 23–45.

Scott-Phillips TC & Kirby S (2010) Language Evolution in the Laboratory. *Trends in Cognitive Sciences 14*, pp 411–417.

Searle JR (1969) *Speech Acts: An Essay in the Philosophy of Language.* Cambridge: University Press.

Sedlemir J, Buhl HU, Fridgen G, & Keller R (2020) The Energy Consumption of Blockchain Technology: Beyond Myth. *Business & Information Systems Engineering 62*, pp. 599–608.

Segovia-Martín J, Walker B, Fay N, & Tamariz M (2020) Network Connectivity Dynamics, Cognitive Biases, the Evolution of Cultural Diversity in Round-Robin Interactive Micro-Societies. *Cognitive Science 44*, e12852. Doi: 10.1111/cogs.12852.

Shannon CE (1948) A Mathematical Theory of Communication. *Bell System Technical Journal 27*(3), pp 379–423. Doi: 10.1002/j.1538-7305.1948.tb01338.x.

Shannon CE & Weaver W (1949) *The Mathematical Theory of Communication*. Chicago: University of Illinois Press. ISBN: ISBN 978-0-252-72548-7.

Shapiro SS & Wilk MB (1965) An Analysis of Variance Test for Normality (Complete Samples) *Biometrika 52*(3–4), pp 591–611. Doi: 10.1093/biomet/52.3-4.591.

Shen C & Pena-Mora F (2018) Blockchain for Cities – A Systematic Literature Review. *IEEE Access 6*. Doi: 10.1109/ACCESS.2018.2880744.

Sherman AT, Javani F, Zhang H, & Golaszewski E (2019) On the Origins and Variations of Blockchain Technologies. *IEEE Security & Privacy 17*(1), pp 72–77. Doi: 10.1109/MSEC.2019.2893730.

Shrestha R & Nam SY (2019) Regional Blockchain for Vehicular Networks to Prevent 51% Attacks. *IEEE Access 7*, pp 95033–95045. Doi: 10.1109/ACCESS.2019.2928753. Retrieved from: https://ieeexplore.ieee.org/stamp/stamp.jsp?arnumber=8763943 (13.06.2023).

Sigman M & Cecchi GA (2002) Global Organisation of the Wordnet Lexicon. *Proceedings of the National Academy of Science 99*(3), pp 1742–1747.

Silvey C, Kibry S, & Smith K (2019) Communication Increases Category Structure and Alignment Only When Combined with Cultural Transmission. *Journal of Memory and Language 109*. Doi: 10.1016/j.jml.2019.104051. Retrieved from: https://discovery.ucl.ac.uk/id/eprint/10084279/1/jml_accepted_version.pdf (13.06.2023).

Simmel G (1900) *Philosophie des Geldes*. Leipzig: Duncker & Humblot.

Smith K, Brighton H, & Kirby S (2003) Complex Systems in Language Evolution: The Cultural Emergence of Compositional Structure. *Advances in Complex Systems 6*(4), pp 537–558.

Solé RV (2005) Syntax for Free? *Nature 434*, p 289.

Solé RV, Corominas-Murtra B, Valverde S, & Steels L (2010) Language Networks: Their Structure, Function, and Evolution. *Complexity 15*(6). Doi: 10.1002/cplx.20305.

Soutet O (2000) *Le subjonctif en français*. Gap: Ophrys.

Spielmann T (2004) *Die Irreduzibilität der triadischen Zeichenrelation – Eine Studie zu Charles Sanders Peirces Programm einer dreistelligen Semiotik*. München: Grin.

Sternberg RJ (1993) *Metaphors of Mind. Conceptions of the Nature of Intelligence. Reprinted*. Cambridge: University Press.

Stevens M (2015) *The Zipf Mystery*. Retrieved from: http://www.quizzaciously.com (13.06.2023).

Ströbel L (2011) Invisible, Visible, Grammaticalisation. In Callies M, Lohöfer A, Keller W (Eds.) *Bi-directionality in the Cognitive Sciences: Avenues, Challenges, and Limitations*. Amsterdam/New York: John Benjamins, pp 211–234.

Ströbel L (2014) Sensomotorische Strategien & Sprachwandel. In Pustka E & Goldschmitt S (Eds.) *Emotionen, Expressivität, Emphase*. Berlin: Erich Schmidt Verlag, pp 139–154.

Ströbel L (2018) Sensomotorische Konzepte – Simulationsstrategien im französischen Wahlkampf. In Issel-Dombert S & Wieders-Lohéac A (Eds.) *Wahlkampf ist Wortkampf – Präsidentschaftswahlen aus sprachwissenschaftlicher Sicht*. Bern: Peter Lang.

Ströbel L (2019) The Use of Sensorimotor-Based Concepts during and After Presidential Campaigns: Emmanuel Macron and Donald Trump. In Perrez J, Reuchamps M, & Thibodeau PH (Eds.) *Variation in Political Metaphor. Discourse Approaches to Policies, Society and Culture 85*. Amsterdam/Philadelphia: John Benjamins.

Ströbel L (2020) Sprache, Rede & Kognition – am Beispiel von verbos leves im Portugiesischen. In Meisnitzer B & Pustka E (Eds.) *Zwischen Sprechen und Sprache / Entre fala e língua*. Berlin: Peter Lang, pp 255–277.

Swan M (2015) *Blockchain: Blueprint for a New Economy*. Bejing: O'Reilly.

Swan M & De Filippi P (2017) Toward a Philosophy of Blockchain: A Symposium in *Metaphilosophy 48*(5), pp 603–619.

Tal S, Smith K, Culbertson J, Grossman E, Arnon I (2022) The Impact of Information Structure on the Emergence of Differential Object Marking: An Experimental Study. *Cognitive Science 46*(e13119). Doi: 10.1111/cogs.13119.

Tama BA, Kweka BJ, Park Y, & Rhee KH (2017) A Critical Review of Blockchain and Its Current Applications. *Proceedings of the International Conference on Electrical Engineering and Computer Science (ICECOS) 2017*, pp 109–113.

Tamariz M (2005) *Exploring the Adaptive Structure of the Mental Lexicon*. PhD thesis, Department of Theoretical and Applied Linguistics, Univerisity of Edinburgh.

Tamariz M, Ellison TM, Barr DJ, & Fay N (2014) Cultural Selection Drives the Evolution of Human Communication Systems. *Proceedings of the Royal Society: Biological Sciences 281*(1788), 20140488.

Tascón M (2012) Uso Cotidiano. In Tascón M & Cabrera-Méndez (Eds.) *Escribir en Internet. Guía para los nuevos medios y las redes sociales*. Barcelona: Galaxia Gutenberg / Fundéu BBVA, pp 87–95.

Tennie C, Frith U, & Frith CD (2010) Reputation Management in the Age of the World-Wide Web. *Trends in Cognitive Science 14*(11), pp 482–488.

Tesnière L (1953) *Esquisse d'une syntaxe structurale*. Paris: Klincksieck.

Theisen-White C, Kirby S, & Oberlander J (2011) Integrating the Horizontal and Vertical Cultural Transmission of Novel Communication Systems. *Proceedings of the Annual Meeting of the Cognitive Science Society 33*(33), pp 956–961.

Thomason S, & Kaufman T (1988) *Language Contact, Creolization and Genetic Linguistics*. Berkeley, CA: University of California Press.

Tomasello M (1995) Language Is Not an Instinct. *Cognitive Development 10*, pp 131–156.

Tomasello M (1999) *The Cultural Origins of Human Cognition*. Cambridge, MA: Harvard University Press.

Tomasello M (2003) *Constructing a Language: A Usage-Based Theory of Language Acquisition*. Cambridge, MA: Harvard University Press.

Tomasello M (2008) *Origins of Human Communication*. Cambridge, MA: MIT Press.

Torrego-González A (2011a) Algunas observaciones acerca del léxico en la red social Tuenti. *Tonos digital. Revista electrónica de estudios filológicos 21*. Retrieved from: http://www.um.es/tonosdigital/znum21/secciones/tritonos-3-torrego.htm (13.06.2023).

Torrego-González A (2011b) 'Eskriibo en el Tuenti komo pronunciioh'. Apuntes sobre la ortografía en una red social. *Tarbiya. Revista de Investigación e Innovación Educativa del Instituto Universitario de Ciencias de la Educación. Universidad Autónoma de Madrid 41*, pp 33–51. Retrieved from: https://revistas.uam.es/tarbiya/article/view/7132/7496 (13.06.2023).

Torres-Nabel LC (2017) Mente extendida y Redes Sociales. Intersecciones Entre Cerebro, Entorno Social y Virtualidad. *TELOS. Revista de Estudios Interdisciplinarios en Ciencias Sociales 19*(3), pp 545–556.

Trasmundi SB & Steffensen SV (2016) Meaning Emergence in the Ecology of Dialogical Systems. *Psychology of Language and Communication 20*(2), pp 154–181. Doi: 10.1515/plc-2016-0009.

Truby J (2018) Decarbonizing Bitcoin: Law and Policy Choices for Reducing the Energy Consumption of Blockchain Technologies and Digital Currencies. *Energy Research & Social Science 44*, pp 399–410.

Trudgill P (2009) Sociolinguistic Typology and Complexification. In Geoffrey S, Gil D, & Trudgill P (Eds.) *Language Complexity as an Evolving Variable*. Oxford: Oxford University, pp 98–109.

Turing A (1937) On Computable Numbers, with an Application to the Entscheidungsproblem. *Proceedings of the London Mathematical Society s2–42*(1), pp 230–265. Doi: 10.1112/plms/s2-42.1.230.

Turing A (1950) Computing Machinery and Intelligence. *Mind 49*, pp 433–460.

Turner M (2002) The Cognitive Study of Art, Language, and Literature. *Poetics Today 23*(1), pp 9–20.

Tuters M & Hagen S (2020) '(((They))) rule': Memetic Antagonism and Nebulous Othering on 4chan. *New Media & Society 22*(12), pp 2218–2237. Doi: 10.1177/1461444819888746.

Tylén K, Fusaroli R, Bundgaard PF, & Østergaard S (2013) Making Sense Together: A Dynamical Account of Linguistic Meaning-Making. *Semiotica 194*, pp 39–62. Doi: 10.1515/sem-2013-0021.

Tylén K, Fusaroli R, Rojo S, Heimann K, Fay N, Johannsen NN, Riede F, & Lombard M (2020) The Evolution of Early Symbolic Behaviour in Homo Sapiens. *PNAS 117*(9), pp 4578–4584. Doi: 10.1073/pnas.1910880117.

Von Uexküll T (1974) Signs, Symbols and Systems. In Sebeok T & Posner R (Eds.) *A Semiotic Landscape*. Den Haag, Paris, New York, pp 487–492.

Von Uexküll T (1984) Zeichen und Realität als anthroposemiotisches Problem. In Oehler K (Ed.) *Zeichen und Realität*. Tübingen: Stauffenburg-Verlag, pp 61–72. ISBN 3-923721-81-1.

Underwood S (2016) Blockchain beyond Bitcoin. *Communications of the ACM 59*(11), pp 15–17. Doi: 10.1145/2994581.

Ungeheuer G (1987) Vor-Urteile über Sprechen, Mitteilen und Verstehen. In Ungeheuer G & Juchem JG (Ed.) *Kommunikationstheoretische Schriften I: Sprechen, Mitteilen, Verstehen*. Aachen: Rader, pp 290–338.

Urrutia-Cárdenas, H (2009) El español de América en la Red. In Sarmiento R & Vilches F (Eds.) *La calidad del español en la Red. Nuevos usos de la lengua en los medios digitales*. Barcelona, Madrid: Ariel / Fundación Telefónica, pp 105–118.

Varela FJ, Thompson E, & Rosch E (1991) *The Embodied Mind: Cognitive Science and Human Experience*. Cambridge, MA: MIT Press.

Verhoef T (2012) The Origins of Duality of Patterning in Artificial Whistled Languages. *Language and Cognition 4*(4), pp 357–380. Doi: 10.1515/langcog-2012-0019.

Vico G (1710) *De Antiquissima Italorum Sapientia ex Linguae Originibus Eruenda Libri Tres* Palmer LM (Ed./Trans.) (1988). Ithaca: Cornell University Press.

Vieten U (2020) The 'New Normal' and 'Pandemic Populism': The COVID-19 Crisis and Anti-Hygienic Mobilisation of the Far-Right. *Social Sciences*

9(165). Doi: 10.3390/socsci9090165. Retrieved from: https://www.mdpi.com/2076-0760/9/9/165/pdf (13.06.2023).

Vitevitch MS (2004) *Phonological Neighbors in a Small World.* University of Kansas. https://cns.iu.edu/docs/netscitalks/vitevitch.pdf (12/06/2023)

Vitevitch MS (2008) What Can Graph Theory Tell Us about Word Learning and Lexical Retrieval? *Journal of Speech Language Hearing Research 51*, pp 408–422.

Vitevitch MS, Goldstein R, & Johnson E (2016) Path-Length and the Misperception of Speech: Insights from Network Science and Psycholinguistics. In Mehler A, Lücking A, Banisch S, Blanchard P, & Job B (Eds.) *Towards a Theoretical Framework for Analyzing Complex Linguistic Networks. Understanding Complex Systems.* Doi: 10.1007/978-3-662-47238-5.

Wall R (1972) *Introduction to Mathematical Linguistics.* Englewood Cliffs, NJ: Prentice-Hall.

Watzlawick P, Beavin JH, & Jackson DD (1967) Some Tentative Axioms of Communication. In *Pragmatics of Human Communication – A Study of Interactional Patterns, Pathologies and Paradoxes.* New York: Norton, pp 48–71. Retrieved from: http://neoscenes.net/teach/cu/2012_2/atls2000_mit/pdfs/Watzlawick-1967-Some_Tentative_Axioms_of_Communication.pdf (13.06.2023).

Wickham H (2019) *stringr: Simple, Consistent Wrappers for Common String Operations. R package version 1.4.0.* Retrieved from: https://CRAN.R-project.org/package=stringr (13.06.2023)

Witherspoon Z (2017) A Hitchhiker's Guide to Consensus Algorithms. *Hackernoon.* Retrieved from: https://hackernoon.com/a-hitchhikers-guide-to-consensus-algorithms-d81aae3eb0e3 (13.06.2023).

Wittgenstein L (1922) Logisch-philosophische Abhandlung. In Ostwald W (Ed.) *Annalen der Naturphilosophie 14*, pp 185–262.

Wright A & De Filippi P (2015) Decentralised Blockchain Technology and the Rise of Lex Cryptographia. Doi: 10.2139/ssrn.2580664. Retrieved from: https://papers.ssrn.com/sol3/Delivery.cfm/SSRN_ID2580664_code2373233.pdf?abstractid=2580664&mirid=1 (13.06.2023).

Yus F (2001) *Ciberpragmática. El uso del lenguaje en Internet.* Barcelona: Ariel.

Yus F (2008) Estrategias lingüísticas de los hablantes en la Red. *Lenguas y Culturas Hispánicas en Internet.* Madrid: Residencia de Estudiantes. Retrieved from: http://cedros.residencia.csic.es/docactos/4443/texto_original/texto_original044430010.pdf (13.06.2023).

Zappavigna M (2011) Ambient Affiliation: A Linguistic Perspective on Twitter. *New Media Society 13*(5), pp 788–806. Doi: 10.1177/1461444810385097.

Zetzsche DA, Arner DW, & Buckley RP (2020) Decentralised Finance. *Journal of Financial Regulation* 6(2), pp 172–203. Doi: 10.1093/jfr/fjaa010.

Zhang D (2017) A Coefficient of Determination for Generalised Linear Models. *The American Statistician 71*(4), pp 310–316.

Zipf GK (1929) Relative Frequency as a Determinant of Phonetic Change. *Harvard Studies in Classical Philology 40*, pp 1–59. Doi: 10.2307/310585.

Zipf GK (1949) *Human Behaviour and the Principle of Least Effort.* Cambridge, MA: Addison-Wesley.

Zweig KA (2016) Are Word-Adjacency Networks Networks?. In Mehler A, Lücking A, Banisch S, Blanchard P, & Job B (Eds.) *Towards a Theoretical Framework for Analyzing Complex Linguistic Networks. Understanding Complex Systems.* Doi: 10.1007/978-3-662-47238-5.

Appendix

1. Data

    final_dataset.csv

2. Data Generation (Python)

    01_hispachanscraperwithnetwork.py
    02_supressproblematiccontent.py
    03_converttotable.py
    04_topicanalysis_prep.py
    05_train_models.py
    06_finalize_dataset.pyhv

3. Data Analysis (R)

    07_data_description.R
    08_experiment_1.R
    09_experiment_2.R
    10_experiment3.R

All aforementioned code files generated and used for data collection and analysis are available for review under the following online repository:

https://github.com/TobiDschi/linguistic_network_structure

List of Tables

List of Figures

SPRACHE UND DIGITALKULTUR
LANGUAGE AND DIGITAL CULTURE

Herausgegeben von / Edited by
Gerd Antos, Matthias Ballod, Henning Lobin,
Pablo Pirnay-Dummer & Karola Pitsch

Band/Vol. 1 Svenja Heuser: Reading Aloud Practices: Providing Joint Accessibility to Texts within an Unfamiliar Interface-Mediated Game Activity. 2023

Band/Vol. 2 Tobias Gretenkort: The Semiotics of Consensus. Impact of Network Topology on Communication Strategies in Spanish Language Interaction Networks. 2023

www.peterlang.com

www.ingramcontent.com/pod-product-compliance
Ingram Content Group UK Ltd.
Pitfield, Milton Keynes, MK11 3LW, UK
UKHW021829100926
8556IPUK00004B/237

9 783631 902073